A Continent Moving West?

IMISCOE

International Migration, Integration and Social Cohesion in Europe

The IMISCOE Research Network unites researchers from, at present, 25 institutes specialising in studies of international migration, integration and social cohesion in Europe. What began in 2004 as a Network of Excellence sponsored by the Sixth Framework Programme of the European Commission has become, as of April 2009, an independent self-funding endeavour. From the start, IMISCOE has promoted integrated, multidisciplinary and globally comparative research led by scholars from various branches of the economic and social sciences, the humanities and law. The Network furthers existing studies and pioneers new scholarship on migration and migrant integration. Encouraging innovative lines of inquiry key to European policymaking and governance is also a priority.

The IMISCOE-Amsterdam University Press Series makes the Network's findings and results available to researchers, policymakers and practitioners, the media and other interested stakeholders. High-quality manuscripts authored by Network members and cooperating partners are evaluated by external peer reviews and the IMISCOE Editorial Committee. The Committee comprises the following members:

Christina Boswell, School of Social and Political Science, University of Edinburgh, United Kingdom

Tiziana Caponio, Department of Political Studies, University of Turin / Forum for International and European Research on Immigration (FIERI), Turin, Italy

Michael Collyer, Sussex Centre for Migration Research (SCMR), University of Sussex, United Kingdom

Rosita Fibbi, Swiss Forum for Migration and Population Studies (SFM), University of Neuchâtel, Switzerland / Institute of Social Sciences, University of Lausanne

Albert Kraler, International Centre for Migration Policy Development (ICMPD), Vienna, Austria

Leo Lucassen, Institute of History, Leiden University, The Netherlands

Jorge Malheiros, Centre of Geographical Studies (CEG), University of Lisbon, Portugal

Marco Martiniello, National Fund for Scientific Research (FNRS), Brussels / Center for Ethnic and Migration Studies (CEDEM), University of Liège, Belgium

Patrick Simon, National Demographic Institute (INED), Paris, France

Miri Song, School of Social Policy and Sociology, University of Kent, United Kingdom

IMISCOE Policy Briefs and more information can be found at www.imiscoe.org.

A Continent Moving West?

EU Enlargement and Labour Migration from
Central and Eastern Europe

*edited by Richard Black, Godfried Engbersen, Marek Okólski
and Cristina Panţîru*

IMISCOE Research

AMSTERDAM UNIVERSITY PRESS

Cover design: Studio Jan de Boer BNO, Amsterdam
Layout: The DocWorkers, Almere

ISBN   978 90 8964 156 4
e-ISBN   978 90 4851 097 9
NUR   741 / 763

Table of contents

1 Introduction
Working out a way from East to West: EU enlargement and labour migration from Central and Eastern Europe

Godfried Engbersen, Marek Okólski, Richard Black and Cristina Panţîru

After the fall of the communist regimes in Central and Eastern Europe (CEE), the expectation arose in Western Europe that differences in affluence between East and West would make enormous migration flows inevitable. This expectation was strengthened by political and ethnic tensions in Central and Eastern Europe. At the beginning of the 1990s, the *Financial Times* predicted that 7 million people may leave the former Soviet Union (see Codagnone 1998). Another British newspaper, *The Guardian*, referred to a meeting of former Russian politicians where a figure of as high as 25 million emigrants from the former Soviet Union to the West was mentioned (see Tränhardt 1996). Academic voices were more mixed. Some, such as Van de Kaa, concluded that there was indeed a huge migration potential in the former USSR and its satellites following the fall of communism, and formed the view that 'the main direction streams in Europe during the next decade or so [would] be from East to West' (Van de Kaa 1993: 91). In contrast, others predicted much lower numbers (see Fassmann & Munz 1994: 534; also Heisler 1992: 611).

Initially, it was the latter view that proved to be correct. The millions of migrants expected to arrive from the former USSR never arrived. Migration from the former Yugoslavia to the countries of the European Union was more substantial, much of it in the form of forced population movements, but these still represented only a small proportion of the many millions of people driven to flight by the conflict in their country. According to Sassen (1997: 150), the question is not why so many people came to the West from countries that were once part of the USSR or the Yugoslavian Federation. Rather, the question is why – given the poverty and the unstable political situation in much of the region – so many more people did *not* take the step of emigrating to the EU. One answer lies in the restrictive immigration policies pursued by

Western European countries since 1989. Fassmann and Munz (1994: 535) spoke of a cordon sanitaire erected to protect Western Europe from Commonwealth of Independent States (CIS) countries and the Balkans. Indeed, although some Western European countries had a relatively open asylum policy, this became more restrictive as time passed, whilst the opportunities for regular labour migration remained very limited in the 1990s. Another plausible answer is that it was less political change that was to promote migration than economic collapse, which in much of the region came later in the decade.

Nonetheless, there was considerable irregular migration in the early 1990s from countries such as Poland, Romania, Ukraine, Albania and Bulgaria to Western and Southern Europe (especially Germany, Italy and Spain). In turn, countries such as Germany, France, Britain, Belgium and Switzerland, and later also Spain, Greece, Norway and the Netherlands introduced specific programmes to facilitate temporary labour migration, often for the purposes of seasonal work (Martin 1994; Pijpers & Van der Velde 2007). A series of bilateral agreements concerning various forms of employment, including seasonal work, were also implemented in Germany, in an effort to legalise the previously illegal seasonal employment of East Europeans in the country that had grown significantly in the early 1990s (Okólski 2004a).

Another factor that contributed to stemming the migration 'flood', so fearfully predicted by many in Western Europe, was the intra-regional division of Central and Eastern Europe. Indeed, perceiving the region as homogeneous with regard to migration would be a misleading simplification (Okólski 1992), since for a long time, it has been divided between predominantly migrant-sending and predominantly migrant-receiving areas. The former included above all Poland, but also Romania, Ukraine and Bulgaria, as well as, after 1990, Albania, Moldova and a few other countries. In these countries, a strong propensity of the population to move abroad was observed from as early as the 1970s onwards. In contrast, the Czech Republic (formerly Czechoslovakia), Hungary and East Germany (formerly the German Democratic Republic) were mainly receiving areas before the lifting of the Iron Curtain in 1989. In this respect, a major change in the period of the post-communist transition was not so much the drawing of a new dividing line between CEE countries on the basis of migration status. Rather, it was the increased intensity and continuity of population movements, accompanied by increasing diversity of the form of these movements and their geographical directions, as well as a greater complexity of factors underlying migration.

In addition, the transition and activation of market forces in the region gave rise to the emergence of various regional 'growth poles' of the economy. These economic differences were amplified by diversity in the pace and course of transition strategies adopted by individual CEE countries and the accompanying political conditions. All this strongly influenced the movements of CEE populations and ultimately led to a new migration space in the region. This space played the role of a filter, which kept within the region's boundaries a substantial part of the migration that might otherwise have occurred. Instead of moving to the West, many migrants from the former USSR changed their residence by moving to another CIS country. As a result, in the 1990s, Russia came to rank as one of top migrant-receiving countries in the world. A quite different mechanism of this new migration space also brought hundreds of thousands of people from the former USSR (mainly Ukraine, Belarus, Moldova and Russia), as well as Romania and Bulgaria, to growth poles in the Czech Republic and Hungary. At the time, such migration was much less risky or costly than looking for opportunities in the West (Okólski 2004b).

Throughout the 1990s, however, migrants originating from CEE countries started to become more and more experienced in terms of finding opportunities in overseas labour markets. As their networks grew and transnational communities expanded, migrants increasingly started to take risks, undertaking trips to countries that were remote in terms of physical distance, institutions, language and culture. This development coincided with certain Western EU states' relaxing of restrictive admission rules, such as granting people from CEE countries access to travel in the Schengen Area, the introduction or extension of special employment programmes and a tacit tolerance of irregular residence or clandestine work by Eastern Europeans. Tolerance of irregular residence and clandestine work was especially relevant in the case of the four southernmost countries of the EU – Italy, Spain, Greece and Portugal.

How many migrants?

Providing an overall estimate of the volume of migration from and between CEE countries from 1989 to 2004 is not easy. Estimates based on total net population change, accounting for natural increase or decrease, suggest a net migration outflow of around 3.2 million over this period from the A8 and A2 countries,[1] with some 60 per cent of this flow accounted for by emigration from Romania and Bulgaria alone (Table 1.1), two countries where emigration pressure had built up under communism due to strict controls on exit. However, this estimate does not account for the fact that a significant proportion of migration from and within the region is in the form of circulation; this has the effect of inflating net migration figures, as those only temporarily absent from

Table 1.1   *Net migration flows from A8 and A2 countries, 1989-2004*

Country	Net migration, 1989-2004 (000s)
Romania	-1,245
Bulgaria	-688
Poland	-667
Lithuania	-235
Latvia	-199
Estonia	-153
Slovakia	-53
Slovenia	-5
Czech Republic	+19
Hungary	+26
Total, A8/A2	-3,200

Source: Mansoor and Quillin, 2004: Appendix 1

their country of origin are counted as migrants. Indeed, as Kaczmarczyk and Okólski (2005) note, there are at least seven distinct types of movement from CEE countries that are potentially counted in different kinds of censuses and surveys, which, in reality, should be dis-aggregated for a clear understanding of migration processes. In addition, figures of net outflows for each country in the region do not tell us anything about destinations, or whether these destinations were within or outside the region.

With the May 2004 accession of the new CEE member states (A8), the defensive attitude of Western European countries towards East European labour migrants changed further. As a consequence, migration from East to West also rose. Three EU countries – Ireland, Sweden and the United Kingdom – and non-EU Norway immediately opened their labour markets to migrants from the new member states, while others opted for a transition period and/or imposed conditions on labour migration. Since then, a large number of countries have opened their labour markets wholly or in part to A8 citizens.

Interestingly, whereas after 1989 the volume of potential East to West migration was first *overestimated*, this new labour migration was initially *underestimated*, particularly migration to certain countries. For example, projections of migration to the UK on the eve of EU enlargement suggested that between 5,000 and 13,000 new migrants would come from CEE countries each year (e.g. Dustmann, Casanova, Fertig, Preston & Schmidt 2003), whilst projections for the EU-15 as a whole suggested 180,000 migrants in the first year, rising to around 220,000 per year over time (Alvarez-Plata, Brücker & Siliverstovs 2003). In practice, it is estimated that as many as half a million Polish citizens had moved to the UK, alone, by 2007 (see Kaczmarczyk in this volume).

One reason why estimates were low was the assumption – not unreasonable at the time – that all EU-15 labour markets would be on the same footing (i.e. there would be no restrictions against A8 citizens), a result being that Germany would receive the most of the new migrants from accession countries. In practice, however, Germany did not open its labour market to A8 workers. As a consequence, countries such as the UK, Ireland and Norway have experienced large-scale labour immigration, mainly from Poland, but also from other countries like Lithuania, Slovakia and Latvia. As other countries opened their labour markets, they, too, have come to receive large groups of labour migrants, again especially from Poland.

Demographic analysis is also hampered by the lack of reliable figures on migration in the EU-15 member states. For example, in the UK, data from the Worker Registration Scheme provides useful, regionally disaggregated data on the registration of workers from A8 countries. But this does not tell us the whole story of migration, since they include registrations of workers who were already in the country, and do not account for circulation or return. In addition, the accession of Bulgaria and Romania on 1 January 2007 is too recent to allow for reliable figures. Still, it is clear that large groups of Romanians have moved to Spain, Italy, Greece and Portugal, even though, unlike migrants from the A8 countries, Bulgarians and Romanians have met greater obstacles to free movement.

Another aspect of these new migration patterns is that small numbers of new immigrants have started to arrive in Poland, Romania and Bulgaria, partly in order to cope with the local demand for cheap labour. Up until the late 1980s, there was almost no migration into Poland. Thereafter, and particularly after EU enlargement, the number of foreign migrants entering the country increased rapidly (Wallace 2002; Kicinger & Weinar 2007). A much more prominent example, meanwhile, is the Czech Republic where, between 1993 (when the state was established) and 2002, some 145,000 foreigners officially immigrated, and the net migration was positive at some 75,000 (Drbohlav 2004). By 2002, the number of (legal) foreign residents in the country was 232,000, representing approximately 2.3 per cent of the total resident population.

'Incomplete' or 'liquid' migration

It is in this context that our book seeks to analyse contemporary patterns of labour migration in Europe, as influenced by the accession of CEE countries to the EU. We look in particular at the impact on the labour market, both in destination and origin countries. As noted above, the lack of reliable data and the contemporary nature of existent data make it difficult to gain a clear insight into these consequences. In addition, the *nature* of migration processes further complicates matters. Many contemporary labour migration patterns are temporary, circular and seasonal. Many of these migrants are employed in secondary, informal labour markets. And many of these mobility patterns and labour practices are not registered, due to their temporary and illegal nature.

To describe these patterns, Okólski (2001a, 2001b) introduced the concept of 'incomplete migration'. By this he means temporary migration abroad, of varying degrees of legality, without any settlement that is mostly connected to work in a secondary segment of the labour market in a foreign country. The concept of incomplete migration returns, albeit differently formulated, in the work of Wallace who prefers to use the word 'mobility' rather than 'migration'. She points out that CEE countries have themselves become the targets of migratory flows and that previously dominant patterns of one-way migration are becoming less significant:

> an important aspect of this migration, both into and out of the country, has been the fact that rather than permanent one-way migration (the dominant pattern until recently) there has been a predominance of short-term, circulatory movements backwards and forwards across borders. This would be better termed mobility than migration. (Wallace 2002: 604)

Engbersen, Snel and De Boom (in this volume) use the concept of 'liquid migration' to describe the complex, transitory and temporary patterns of transnational work and settlement. However, this liquid migration is not a temporary phenomenon, nor necessarily a modern one. Thus, Grzymala-Kazlowska (2005) speaks in this respect of 'lasting temporariness', whilst even historic transatlantic migrations assumed by many to be permanent in practice included patterns of temporary stay and multiple return (Wyman 1993). The fluid nature of short-term, circulatory migration makes many forecasts of East-West migration unreliable (Kupiszewiski 2002: 628).

The aim of this book is to try to gain insight into contemporary 'liquid' migration processes following EU enlargement and their impact on national and local labour markets, and on labour migrants themselves. It also focuses on the role of immigration policies. The various chapters represent a range of approaches to the study of the impact of EU enlargement on the labour market. Different methods and data are used to clarify contemporary migration processes. Some authors base their work on official figures, others on surveys they have conducted themselves or on small-scale qualitative and ethnographic research. Some have carried out studies at a single research site, while others have performed multi-sited research. Taken together, the chapters provide a clearer picture of the 'super-diversity' of contemporary East-West migration (see Vertovec 2007).

The book is divided into four parts. Part I focuses on the economic aspects of the new labour migration to the UK, Norway and the Netherlands. These countries are illustrative of the three transitional regimes in the EU-15 before and after 1 May 2006 (see Friberg in this volume). The UK is an example of a 'free access regime', while Norway of a regime characterised by 'general access' subject to the conditions that migrants receive host country wages and are in full-time employment. The Netherlands is an example of a regime based on 'restricted access', at least up to May 2007. In Part II we turn to Poland. Because of the volume of emigration to Western Europe of both low-skilled and highly skilled emigrants, Poland occupies a key position in the debate on the economic impact of EU enlargement. In Part III the spotlight falls on the most recent countries to accede to the EU: Bulgaria and Romania. Both have become typical immigration countries, characterised by temporary and partly irregular flows. Part IV concentrates not on the consequences for the labour market, but on the question of the extent to which EU enlargement encourages 'welfare migration'. By this we mean migrants in search not so much of a job, but of an income guaranteed by national systems of social security and social assistance.

Post-accession migration to the UK, Norway and the Netherlands

Part I opens with a chapter by Friberg on the working conditions of Polish migrants in the Norwegian capital Oslo, with a particular look at male construction workers and female service workers. Norway introduced transitional restrictions designed to ensure a national wage standard for labour migrants from the new EU member states (A8). Combined with the introduction of new statutory wage regulations in the certain sectors, these regulations have been partially successful in protecting the basic rights of migrant workers in the Norwegian labour market. But difficulties in enforcing regulations governing different categories of labour and service migrants have helped create a gendered and differentiated labour market for migrants. Some are included in the regulated sector and enjoy corresponding basic social rights (mainly men), while others are working in a poorly regulated, semi-legal market for 'posted' and self-employed workers, where low wages, limited job security and few social rights are the norm (mainly women).

In the following chapter, Napierała and Trevena describe how the migration of Polish construction workers to Norway is primarily a 'sub-regionalised' phenomenon. The majority of Polish migrants in Oslo comes from only four Polish regions. Many of these migrants have previously worked in Germany. The authors show that the popularity of Oslo is the consequence of specific pull factors (such as reliable employers and relatively high wages) and push factors (mainly high regional unemployment), as well as of the existence of specific migration chains.

Turning to the UK, the chapter by Drinkwater, Eade and Garapich uses data from the government's Worker Registration Scheme (WRS), the database on National Insurance Numbers (NINo) and the Labour Force Survey (LFS) to examine flows of labour migrants from Poland and other A8 countries since 2002. They show how this migration appears to have had a highly seasonal element, with many migrants being young and well-educated, but intending to come for relatively short periods. Polish migrants, in particular, are found to have very high rates of employment, although data challenge the common view that they are primarily employed in construction, with rather larger numbers proportionally in relatively low-wage employment in the manufacturing and transport sectors.

In turn, Csedő's contribution deals with the primary labour market in the UK for the highly skilled. Her chapter focuses on highly skilled Romanian and Hungarian migrants and how they find jobs in London. She analyses the key components of their labour market incorporation practices: how professionals and graduates signal their availability and find out about job openings on the destination labour market, and how employers notify jobseekers about vacancies and requirements. The key question here is whether the so-called signalling stage of the labour market incorporation process is a network-dependent phenomenon and, if so, how. Csedő argues that the process of signalling is not dependent on, but only facilitated by, social networks. While some professional and graduate migrants do find employment on the primary labour market with virtually zero social capital conversion, if they rely on their social capital they may end up in different types of employment rather than being exclusively reliant on labour supply and demand forces. Social capital acts like a 'centrifugal force': professional ties sort the highly skilled 'upwards' while ethnic ties sort them 'downwards' on the labour market.

The final chapter in this section discusses the sharp rise in labour migration from the A8 countries to the Netherlands. Engbersen et al. argue that these migration movements are of a temporary, fluid and uncertain nature. As in the UK and Norway, most of these migrants are not expected to settle in the Netherlands. They also argue that there is little evidence of a significant drop in wages for low-skilled work in the Netherlands. There is also little evidence that CEE migrants are competing with many native Dutch workers. Engbersen et al. also discuss some of the social consequences of contemporary CEE migration, such as bad housing conditions and only partial integration into Dutch society. These problems are experienced – and expressed – particularly by policymakers and the residents of certain urban areas who have to deal with a large influx of CEE migrants into their neighbourhoods. Because of the 'liquid' nature of migration, it is very difficult to develop a sufficiently flexible infrastructure for temporary labour migration.

The Polish experience: Impact of new migration on Polish labour markets and on the composition of the Polish population

In the public debate on the consequences of Poland's accession to the EU, many assumptions have been made about the volume, duration and nature of the emigration of Polish workers. A clear picture of actual movements and their – national and international – consequences so far is, however, lacking. Due to the short time span since Poland became an EU member and the unreliability of official statistics, it is no easy task to provide adequate figures. Part II gives an overview of the characteristics and consequences of recent migration patterns from and into Poland. It shows how migration patterns have changed over time and it discusses some of the current and potential economic consequences for Poland, such as brain drain and skill shortages.

Anacka and Okólski report on the selectivity of migration from Poland after the country joined the EU. Given the fact that post-accession migration is different from earlier movements in its volume, structure and social impact, the authors wanted to learn more about the nature and effects of these current migration flows. Their main question was: who decides to leave? Using a Migration Selectivity Index, they show that factors such as region of origin, sex, age and educational level play an important role in the selectivity of movement. Migrants are generally young (of 'mobile age') and males are overrepresented, though differences exist between regions. A striking trend is the rise of the UK as a major country of destination. While Germany – as before – attracts many Polish migrants with a vocational education, highly skilled migrants have found their way to the UK since the opening up of the British labour market (see also the contribution of Csedő). Anacka and Okólski conclude that the losses of specific groups of Poland's population are remarkably high, reducing some categories by a quarter.

In line with the preceding chapter, Kaczmarczyk provides extensive data on recent migration from Poland, with particular reference to highly skilled migrants. Using different data sources, Kaczmarczyk shows the dynamics of recent processes and dispels several myths. A diversification is taking place in length of stay and major countries of destination. Another related diversification concerns differences in human capital. Kaczmarczyk challenges the frequently made claim that Poland has a brain drain problem. Although the migration of medical professionals, in particular, is a striking phenomenon, he does not see this as a threat. Besides the fact that highly skilled migration from Poland is not as massive as the myth proclaims, Kaczmarczyk argues that the benefits of these movements of knowledge should be recognised. Instead of talking about the dangers posed by the brain drain, we should see the opportunities offered by 'brain exchange'. However, the author concludes, the key problem will be the ability to create favourable conditions for return migration.

The final chapter on Poland by Grabowska-Lusinska discusses labour migration as one of the various factors influencing skill shortages in Poland. The collapse of communism brought about major changes in the Polish labour market. While employment in agriculture and industry declined, the service sector developed rapidly, especially in specific regions. These developments resulted in a mismatch of supply and demand caused by a shortfall of highly educated workers. Grabowska-Lusinska shows that this mismatch has not been solved by inter-regional population flows, as many migrants prefer temporary work abroad. The majority of employers in Poland experience problems in recruiting new employees caused by the substantial labour outflow. The author warns of further disharmony in the labour market and the negative effects of the brain drain.

Bulgarian and Romanian experiences: Migration, demography and local change

Part III of the volume is concerned with the two most recent additions to the EU: Bulgaria and Romania. Between 1989 and 2007, both countries were confronted by large-scale emigration flows, mainly of temporary workers, which are having huge economic and socio-cultural repercussions on their societies.

The chapter by Mintchev and Boshnakov shows that, between 1989 and 2004, the Bulgarian population declined by about 13 per cent, or 1.2 million in absolute figures (roughly 500,000 due to natural decrease and 700,00 due to emigration). They also show that Bulgarian return migrants have a preference for South European destinations where short-term and seasonal migration predominates. The vast majority of these migrants do not enjoy legal employment status. Furthermore, migrant transfers have played and are still playing an important role in keeping households from poverty during the EU integration process. It was also found that about 20 per cent of remittance-receiving households run their own businesses, while this proportion is only half as much in other families. The authors believe that improvements to the administrative and legal infrastructure for economic activity could facilitate additional investment and increase demand for highly skilled personnel. In addition, they argue that if local or foreign investors and multinational companies in Bulgaria were to offer adequate remuneration and career opportunities, this would encourage the return of such migrants.

Markova offers an historical overview of migration processes in Bulgaria (with emphasis on the period beginning November 1989), and shows that in recent years there has been a growing trend towards temporary and seasonal migration rather than permanent settlement, the preferred destinations being Greece, Turkey, Italy, the Netherlands, Germany and Spain. Seasonal and circular migration is becoming more ethnically and regionally specific. Markova shows that current emigration trends have substantial economic and demographic consequences, both positively (the contribution to poverty reduction and increase of small businesses through remittances) and negatively (the danger of brain drain).

The chapter by Sandu examines the causal chain in changes to demographic behaviour at family and community level in Romania, as induced by temporary emigration abroad since 1989. His paper supports Markova's argument that immigrants' experience of working abroad is one of the modernising factors in Romanian society, at community and regional level. His data show that migration abroad has stimulated enhanced and diversified consumption, which is an indicator of modernity for certain categories of people from specific communities and regions and within certain time periods. Experience abroad and remittances make an important contribution to the economy, but also to changes in views and value systems, both at individual and community level.

Finally, in line with Sandu (2006), Potot stresses that migration is a survival strategy that was adopted by Romanians between 1990 and 2007 to cope with the economic depression that followed the 1989 revolution. However, migration is not only a strategy to exit poverty; it generates new lifestyles and new attitudes towards consumption. Both Sandu and Potot also argue, using different methodologies and data, that Romanian migrants contribute in several ways to local transformations through their experiences abroad – through developing new work ethics, knowledge and skills, which are then employed in their home villages or hometowns.

Effects on welfare systems

The final part of the book discusses the effects of EU enlargement on Western European welfare states. In advanced welfare states, the paradox of solidarity and exclusion plays a key role. Maintaining national, comprehensive forms of *internal solidarity* (in the fields of health care, social security, education and public housing) for the benefit of citizens and permanent residents implies at the same time the exclusion of outsiders from the welfare state's social entitlements (i.e. *no external so-lidarity*). If too many immigrants too easily gain access to welfare enti-tlements, the continuation and legitimacy of those entitlements might become endangered should such groups become unemployed.

This is related to what is known as the 'welfare magnet' theory. However, having analysed the situation in the UK, Ireland and Sweden, Nowaczek shows that the welfare magnet theory is untenable. For immi-grants from new EU member states, it was work itself – rather than the possibility of social assistance – that motivated the decision to migrate. And in all three countries the amount of benefit received by immigrants from the new member states is relatively small. An important reason for this is the temporary nature of labour migration. EU migration has not proved to be a major challenge for the 'liberal welfare regimes' in the UK and Ireland or the 'social-democratic regime' in Sweden. It is worthy of note that intra-EU migration, too, has had no negative impact on public spending and social policy in the UK, Ireland and Sweden.

Ochel sees greater risks than Nowaczek. He points out that the EU Free Movement Directive has extended the right of free movement to non-gainfully employed (inactive) EU citizens. At the same time, this group of persons has been given access to the welfare benefits of host countries. Ochel argues that in the near future, especially in the period following the current transitional period, welfare migration may emerge between Poland and Germany. However, it will be a number of years before the practical effects of the Directive on migration into the welfare systems of individual EU member countries are fully charted. Ochel takes the view that in enacting the Directive, European legislators have taken considerable risks. Access to welfare systems has not been blocked, merely made more difficult through the imposition of certain conditions. In view of the still rudimentary nature of the financial com-pensation framework within the EU, it is entirely possible that the free-dom of movement accorded by the Directive will impose excessive de-mands on the solidarity of EU citizens in host countries.

Understanding East-West migration

Taken together, the chapters in this volume seek to contribute to a great-er understanding of the phenomenon of East-West migration from CEE countries since the accession of A8 countries in 2004, and A2 countries in 2007. They provide an overview of data where these are available, as well as a selection of case studies on what this migration has meant in practice for those involved in it, or affected by it at either origin or desti-nation. Some of the case studies are unusual in the context of the grow-ing literature on East-West migration. For example, whilst Polish migration to the UK has been the subject of numerous reports and articles, movement proportionally of a similar scale to Norway has received little attention outside Norway itself. Yet it is only by attention to this diversity of flows that we can come to a rounded understanding of a complex and multifaceted socio-economic process.

East-West migration flows are intrinsically linked with the post-communist political and economic transformations in the new member states from Eastern Europe. Once these countries embarked on a process of democratisation, economic reforms and European integration, the economic 'earthquakes' determined by declining state subsidies and inflation ultimately led to the impoverishment of large cohorts of the population. Against this background, migration was a non-violent response to sudden economic collapse and unsuccessful attempts to promote economic recovery in the 1990s. It was also often a successful response, given the substantial remittances that have resulted. In this context, even as the A8 and A2 member states experience rapid economic growth, determined mainly by their political stability and commitment to European integration, labour migration is still an important coping strategy for low skilled workers, as the growing post-accession temporary migration to some of the EU-15 member states shows.

As some of the chapters of this volume suggest, labour migration between East and West was a 'pre-accession' economic and cultural 'integration' or harmonisation of the would-be member states with the 'old' member states. The harmonisation happened on several levels, involving exchanges of experience and knowledge, the spread of consumerism and its consequences, the emergence of new markets for Western companies and sustained economic growth in both 'East' and 'West'. Thus, labour migration from Eastern to Western Europe – in spite of its impediments in various forms – proved to be part of the process of the EU's extension. For this reason, it should be explored in more depth to draw lessons for future EU enlargements and for the European Neighbourhood Policy. In addition, it would be interesting to compare and contrast the dynamics of East-West migration before and after early 2008's worsening of economic conditions in some of the EU-15 member states.

As with all edited collections, much remains beyond the scope of this book. First, it is impossible to encompass in one volume all aspects of the sheer diversity of flows from CEE countries that have occurred since 2004, which has seen migrants move not only to 'traditional' destinations in Western Europe, but also increasingly to Southern Europe, to the Atlantic 'fringes' of Ireland and Norway and further afield. Similarly, migration has been both 'legal' and 'illegal', 'documented' and 'undocumented' as well as 'skilled' and 'less skilled' or 'unskilled'. Across the various chapters of the volume, we have tried to encompass examples of these different types of flows, but many remain explored only briefly.

One critical problem here is that whilst official data on migrant flows remains limited, the empirical study of these new population movements is still very much in its infancy. Prior to the post-communist transition, there was virtually no research within CEE countries on migration, and little attention to migration from these countries in the West either, beyond analysis of 'refugee' flows. Nearly twenty years later, significant research effort in the region on the costs and benefits of migration is still largely limited to Poland, Hungary and the Czech Republic (Okólski 2006). Moreover, despite investment in ethnosurveys in Poland, Lithuania and Ukraine in the 1990s (Frejka, Okólski, Pyrozhkov & Sipaviciene 1998), and in Armenia, Belarus, Georgia, Moldova and Ukraine in 2005-2007 (Wallace & Vincent 2007), there remains no comprehensive, European-wide survey of East-West migration from which valid comparative conclusions could be derived.

What is clear, however, both from the contributions to this volume and from emerging literature elsewhere, is that conventional notions of migration as a one-way, permanent or long-term process are increasingly of the mark. Rather, East-West labour migration in Europe – similar perhaps to other flows in and from other parts of the world – is becoming increasingly diverse, fluid and sub-regionalised in nature, as well as gendered and differentiated in its consequences for individuals, labour markets and the wider society.

The chapters of this book seek to enrich the study of mobility of work and skills within the EU-27 and its economic and social impact at national and regional levels. The goal is to illuminate – and critically assess – the ongoing 'making' of the EU as an economic and social space. However, East-West labour migration is often overemphasised. To counteract this bias, academics and policymakers need to keep in mind that the average rate of mobility within the EU-27 remains at only 2 per cent – i.e. around 2 per cent of working-age citizens from one of the 27 EU member states currently live and work in another member state. Of course, in some of the A8 and A2 member states the mobility rate may be higher. However, the share of third-country citizens residing in the EU-27 is almost double that of the rate of EU-27 citizens living in another member state (European Commission 2007b).

Labour market mobility, either between jobs or between member states or regions, is an essential part of the Lisbon objectives. This has led the European Commission to stress the interdependence between promoting 'more and better jobs' within the EU and 'flexibility and security' (i.e. 'flexicurity') (European Commission 2007a). Moreover, the Commission has committed to two action plans for promoting jobs and mobility, first in 2002 (Action Plan for Skills and Mobility) and then in 2007 (Job Mobility Action Plan for 2007-2010). However, these objectives are considerably altered by the interplay between national sovereignty, labour market protectionism within the member states and the EU's ideal of freedom of movement for its citizens, as one of the determinants of economic growth. Against this background, research regarding the post-accession labour migration from EU-10 member states – as internal mobility of EU citizens – contributes to understanding the challenges raised by the Lisbon objectives in the member states.

Note

1   A8 comprises eight of the ten countries that joined the EU in 2004: the Czech Republic, Estonia, Hungary, Latvia, Lithuania, Poland, Slovakia and Slovenia. A2 comprises the two countries that joined the EU in 2007: Bulgaria and Romania.

References

Alvarez-Plata, P., H. Brücker & B. Siliverstovs (2003), *Potential migration from Central and Eastern Europe into the EU-15: An update.* Berlin: Deutsches Institut für Wirtschaftsforschung.

Codagnone, C. (1998), 'New migration and migration politics in Post-Soviet Russia', Ethnobarometer Programme Working Paper No. 2, www.cemes.org/current/ethpub/ ethnobar/wp2/wp2_ind.htm.

Drbohlav, D. (2004) *Migration trends in selected EU applicant countries, volume II: The Czech Republic.* Vienna: IOM.

Dustmann, C., M. Casanova, M. Fertig, I. Preston & C.M. Schmidt (2003), *The impact of EU enlargement on migration flows.* Home Office Online Report 25/03.

Engbersen, G. (2003), 'The wall around the welfare state in Europe: International migration and social exclusion', *The Indian Journal of Labour Economics* 46 (3): 479-495.

Engbersen, G., J. van der Leun, J. & J. de Boom (2007), 'The fragmentation of migration and crime', in M. Tonry & C. Bijleveld (eds.), *Crime and Justice. A Review of Research,* Special issue on Crime and Justice in the Netherlands: 389-452. Chicago: Chicago University Press Crime and Justice Series.

European Commission (2007a), 'More and better jobs through flexibility and security'. *COM* 359, 27 June 2007.

European Commission (2007b), 'Mobility, an instrument for more and better jobs: The European Job Mobility Action Plan (2007-2010), *COM* 773, 6 December 2007.

Fassman, H. & R. Münz (1994), 'European East-West migration, 1945-1992'. *International Migration Review* 28 (3): 520-538.

Frejka T., M. Okólski, S. Pyrozhkov & A. Sipaviciene (1998), 'Overview', in T. Frejka, M. Okólski & K. Sword, K. (eds.), *In-depth studies on migration in Central and Eastern Europe: The case of Poland,* 105-22. New York/Geneva: United Nations.

Grzymala-Kazlowska, A. (2005), 'From ethnic cooperation to in-group competition: Undocumented Polish workers in Brussels.' *Journal of Ethnic and Migration Studies* 31 (4): 675-697.

Heisler, M.O. (1992), 'Migration, international relations and the New Europe: Theoretical perspectives from institutional political sociology.' *International Migration Review,* Special issue: *The New Europe and International Migration* 26(2): 596-622.

Kaczmarczyk, P. & M. Okólski (2005), 'International migration in Central and Eastern Europe: Current and future trends', Paper presented to United Nations Expert Group

Meeting on International Migration and Development, Population Division, Department of Economic and Social Affairs, UN Secretariat, New York, July 2005.

Kicinger, A. & A. Weinar (eds.) (2007), *State of the art of the migration research in Poland.* IMISCOE Working Paper no. 19, http://imiscoe.org/publications/workingpapers/index.html.

Kupiszewiski, M. (2002), 'How trustworthy are forecasts of international migration between Poland and the European Union.' *Journal of Ethnic and Migration Studies* 28 (4): 627-645.

Martin, P. (1994), 'Germany: Reluctant land of emigration', in W.A. Cornelius, P. Martin & J. Hollifield (eds.) *Controlling immigration. A global perspective*, 189-225. Stanford: Stanford University Press.

OECD (2004) *Migration for employment. Bilateral agreements at a crossroad.* Paris: OECD.

Okólski, M. (1992), 'Migratory movements from countries of Central and Eastern Europe', in Council of Europe, *People on the Move. New Migration Flows in Europe*, 83-116; 203-230. Strasbourg: Council of Europe Press.

Okólski, M. (2001a), 'Incomplete migration. A new form of mobility in Central and Eastern Europe. The case of Polish and Ukrainian migrants', in C. Wallace & D. Stola (eds.), *Patterns of migration in Central Europe*, 105-128. Basingstoke: Palgrave Macmillan.

Okólski, M. (2001b), 'The transformation of spatial mobility and new forms of international population movements: Incomplete migration in Central and Eastern Europe', in J. Dacyl (ed.), *Challenges of cultural diversity in Europe*, 57-109. Stockholm: CEIFO.

Okólski, M. (2004a), 'Seasonal labour migration in the light of the German-Polish Bilateral Agreement', in OECD (ed.), *Migration for employment. Bilateral agreements at a crossroad*, 203-214. Paris: OECD.

Okólski, M. (2004b), 'The effects of political and economic transition on international migration in Central and Eastern Europe', in D.S. Massey & J.E. Taylor (eds.), *International migration. Prospects and policies in a global market*, 35-58. Oxford/New York: Oxford University Press.

Okólski, M. (2006), *Gaining from migration: costs and benefits of migration for Central European countries.* Warsaw: Centre of Migration Research, Faculty of Economic Sciences, Warsaw University, http://ec.europa.eu/employment_social/incentive_measures/studies/gain_from_migr_cmr_en.pdf.

Pijpers, R. & M. van der Velde (2007), 'Mobility across borders: Contextualizing local strategies to circumvent visa and work permit requirements', *International Journal of Urban and Regional Research* 31 (4): 819-835.

Sandu, D. (2006), 'Exploring Europe through work migrations: 1990-2006' in *Living abroad on a temporary basis. The economic migration of Romanians: 1990-2006.* Bucharest: Open Society Foundation Romania.

Sassen, S. (1997), *Migranten, Siedler, Flüchtlinge. Von der Massenauswanderung zur Festung Europa.* Frankfurt: Fischer.

Thränhardt, D. (1996), 'European migration from East to West: Present patterns and future directions', *New Community* 22 (2): 227-242.

Van de Kaa, D. (1993), 'European migration at the end of history', in A. Blum & J.-L. Rallu (eds.), *European population. Demographic dynamics*, 77-110. Paris: John Libbey.

Vertovec, S. (2007), 'Super-diversity and its implications'. *Ethnic and Racial Studies* 30 (6): 1024-1054.

Wallace, C. (2002), 'Opening and closing borders: Migration and mobility in East-Central Europe', *Journal of Ethnic and Migration Studies* 28 (4): 603-625.

Wallace, C. & K. Vincent (2007) Recent migration from the new European borderlands, *Review of Sociology* 13 (2): 1-15.

Wymahn, M. (1993), *Round-trip America: The immigrants return to Europe, 1880-1930.* Ithaca: Cornell University Press.

2 Working conditions for Polish construction workers and domestic cleaners in Oslo: Segmentation, inclusion and the role of policy

Jon Horgen Friberg

Introduction[1]

After the European Union enlargement in 2004, migration from new member states in Eastern and Central Europe to old member states in Western Europe became one of the most conspicuous population movements in Europe, affecting the demographic, social and economical situation in both countries of origin and destination. Poland is the dominant origin country, and the United Kingdom, Germany and Ireland are the main destinations (Kaczmarczyk & Okólski 2008). But Polish migrants have also entered the labour markets of Spain, Italy and the Nordic countries in substantial numbers. In Norway,[2] almost 134,000 original work permits have been granted to workers from the new EU member states in the first four years since the enlargement – a substantial addition to the existing work force of approximately 2.1 million people. Almost 114,000 of these permits have been renewed after the initial permits expired. On top of the registered applications, an unknown number of posted, self-employed and other unregistered workers have entered the Norwegian labour market. Concentrated in a few sectors, these labour migrants have made a significant impact in construction, shipyards, manufacturing industries, agriculture and household service provision, and Polish workers now make up the single largest group of immigrants in Norway (Statistics Norway).

With a relatively high wage level, a strong trade union movement and ambitious policies regarding welfare and social inclusion, Norway introduced a series of new policy measures aiming to protect the working conditions of labour migrants. These measures included transitional regulations of wages for migrants,[3] new statutory wage regulations in the construction sector and new measures for control and enforcement of labour standards. This chapter addresses the ways in which these new policy measures have affected processes of segmentation and inclusion among labour migrants in the capital city of Oslo, using survey data from a representative sample of Polish migrants. By comparing

Figure 2.1 *Number of valid residence permits held by A8 citizens in Norway, January 2003-May 2008 (in thousands)*

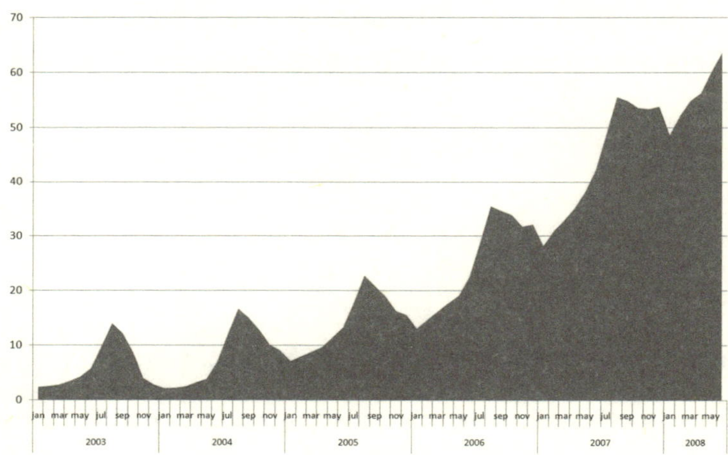

Source: Norwegian Directorate of Immigration (UDI)

legal status, wages and access to social benefits for Polish migrants working in construction and domestic cleaning in Oslo, the analysis focuses especially on whether general measures aimed at improving conditions for migrants may have unintended and biased effects for male and female migrants, as well as migrants coming through different channels (labour or mobility of services), due to gendered opportunity structures and differences in labour market functioning and institutional contexts.

Data and methodology

The analysis is based on a representative survey of 510 Polish migrants staying in the Oslo region in autumn and winter 2006, which will be referred to here as the PMO Survey.[4] The huge majority of these migrants work either as construction workers (men) or domestic cleaners (women), and these two groups form the basis of two sector-based case studies. The study employed respondent-driven sampling (RDS)[5] – a sampling and estimation technique especially designed to target hidden and hard-to-reach populations where no sampling frame exists. RDS combines elements of 'snowball sampling' (asking individuals to recruit other people they know, with these individuals being, in turn, asked to recruit people they know, and so on) with economic incentives for participation and recruiting. RDS also uses statistical software to produce estimates that adjust network effects in the sampling procedure, such as the recruitment patterns of people with different characteristics and the network size of each respondent (Heckathorn 1997). This was done in order to obtain a representative sample of all Polish migrants in the region at the time, irrespective of their registration and legal status. The survey focused on questions about migration experience, employment situation, legal status, working conditions and access to social benefits.

Migration, working conditions and labour market segmentation

The impact of migration on labour markets, wages and social standards of destination countries has become a major concern of policymakers and social partners in the old member states (Wolfson 2007). This reflects large wage differentials between new and old member states and the assumption that an increased supply of workers willing to work for low pay may lead to wage depression and eroding of collectively bargained social standards. Although often blurred in the political debate, it is useful to distinguish between concerns about the impact of migration on the working conditions of native workers and about the working conditions of the migrants themselves. Much empirical literature on the effects of labour migration on wages is concerned with the effects of migration on native wages. While conclusions on the overall effect on wages are ambiguous,[6] theory suggests that labour migration may have a negative impact on the wages of native workers who have the same kind of skills and jobs as the migrants. But if migrants have skills that are complementary to native workers, or if the labour markets in destination countries respond to immigration by increased specialisation – for example, if migrants are employed to do different jobs than those undertaken by natives – the result will be increased productivity and outcomes for native workers (Dustmann, Frattini & Preston 2007). These jobs are usually lower paid and less desirable, and studies that focus on the working conditions of migrants usually refer to this process of specialisation as *segmentation*. Theories of segmented labour markets were first developed by Doringer and Piore (1971), and later applied to the study of migrants by Piore (1979). They sought to expand the narrow economic focus on *markets*, by directing attention to institutional features of labour markets and to jobs as markers of social status as well as sources of income. According to segmented labour market theory, an intrinsic feature of modern capitalist economies is that of bifurcated labour markets divided into a core capital-intensive primary sector and a labour-intensive secondary sector in the periphery. The theory further suggests that native workers' unwillingness to take low-status jobs (due to hierarchical constraints on motivation) and employers' unwillingness to raise wages – as this may trigger claims by higher-status groups who wish to maintain wage differentials with those of perceived lower status (resulting in structural inflation) – creates demand for migrants who see work mainly as a source of income and are willing to take low-paid, low-status jobs in the periphery. As labour standards deteriorate in these sectors, those who can seek employment elsewhere do so, increasing demand for new migrants willing to work for low pay. Such processes of segmentation have been documented in a wide range of low-skilled manufacturing and service-sector jobs throughout the industrial world, where immigrant workers are concentrated in jobs and sectors with low wages, poor working conditions and few possibilities for upwards mobility (Piore 1979; Castles & Miller 2003; Massey, Arango, Hugo, Kouaouci, Pellegrino & Taylor 2005). Migrants working illegally without residential rights are often worst off, as they are cut off from legal protection and welfare entitlements.

Identifying long-term processes of labour segmentation in markets where Polish labour migrants work is beyond the scope of this chapter. However, by looking at migrants' legal status, wages, job security and access to social benefits, the chapter tries to distinguish workers who are included into the core from those who remain at the periphery of the Norwegian labour market. In addition, the chapter investigates the mechanisms by which Norwegian regulation policies have affected the situation of new migrant workers.

New labour market regulation policies in Norway

In the years after the EU enlargement in 2004, stories of exploitative working conditions for Eastern European labour migrants were routinely reported in the Norwegian media. Moreover, the issue of social dumping was placed high on the political agenda of trade unions and the government.[7] Despite initial enthusiasm about the prospect of cheap labour, a relatively broad consensus that Norwegian social and labour market standards should apply equally for migrants was established across the political spectrum. But the political tools for regulating migrant working conditions were not in place at the time of A8 accession. Unlike most Continental European countries, the Scandinavian countries do not have any tradition of statutory minimum wage regulation, leaving wages to be regulated by collective agreements negotiated between the social partners. Norway has relatively low collective agreement coverage,[8] leaving large parts of the labour market without any minimum wage regulation (Cremers, Dølvik & Bosch 2007). Being particularly vulnerable to wage dumping, Norway introduced several new statutory measures aimed at protecting basic rights and ensuring equal treatment of migrant workers from the new EU member states. The three most important of these will be considered in turn.

Transitional Restrictions

The accession treaty allowed for transitional arrangements postponing full opening of the labour markets for citizens of A8 countries for a period of two to seven years. While the majority of the old EU countries (i.e. EU-15) maintained pre-accession restrictions based on quotas or labour market demands testing, Norway – like Denmark – imposed new restrictions designed to secure proper wages and working conditions for labour migrants rather than restricting their numbers. A8 nationals are allowed to search for jobs for six months in Norway and receive residence permits if they can document full-time employment in a Norwegian-based firm, having wages in accordance with national collective agreements, regulations or customs in the same occupation or area. While several countries lifted restrictions after the first two-year period, Norway chose to prolong the transitional arrangements at least until 2009.

Generalised collective agreements in the construction sector

While mobility of individual labour migrants hired by Norwegian companies is subject to transitional restrictions, the 'mobility of services' is not. The so-called Posting of Workers Directive (Directive 96/71/EC) states that host country regulations regarding wages and working conditions should apply to posted workers on service assignments abroad. But as Norway does not have a statutory minimum wage, posted workers employed in foreign companies on service assignments in Norway could until recently be legally paid according to their home country's terms and conditions of employment. This discrepancy between regulation of individual labour migration and the mobility of services created incentives for employers to use posted or self-employed workers instead of hiring migrants directly (Dølvik & Eldring 2006). As a response to these challenges, new measures for wage regulations were introduced. The legal mechanism for generalising collective agreements in Norway was established in 1993 with the explicit purpose of preventing social dumping, but was not used until the 2004 accession. A general application of collective agreements means that they are legally binding for everyone in the affected area and sector, including non-unionised foreign companies and employees. In December 2004, collective agreements were extended to generally apply in seven petrochemical onshore sites. In September 2005, a general application of the collective agreements was imposed in the construction sector in the Oslo fiord area and, four months later, in the county of Hordaland. From January 2007, the collective agreement in the construction sector was generally applied throughout the country. In other sectors, there are no corresponding regulatory measures that apply to the wage of employees posted from abroad. Self-employed workers are not covered by either the transitional arrangements or generally applied collective agreements.

New measures of control and enforcement

Parallel with the introduction of generalised collective agreements, new regulatory measures for control and enforcement were introduced by the government's 2006 Action Plan Against Social Dumping, increasing the Labour Inspectorate's resources substantially and giving them greater authority to impose sanctions. The Norwegian Labour Inspection Authority and the Petroleum Safety Authority Norway were, amongst other things, given powers to issue orders, to make use of coercive fines and to stop operations when they make their inspection according to the Norwegian Act relating to general application of wage agreements and the Norwegian Immigration Act. In addition to these new measures, the Working Environment Act applies to all workers in Norway including migrants. Although it does not regulate wages, it does prohibit wage discrimination and ensures rights to sick leave with pay, overtime payment, holiday pay and pension rights.

Comparing different categories of Polish migrants

The rules regulating residence and wages in Norway do not apply equally to all migrants from new EU member states. Rules differ, depending on whether individuals come as regular labour migrants or through channels that permit the mobility of services, and depending on their sector of employment. Also, migrants may be working and staying in Norway on legal or illegal terms with regard to taxes and residence. Before turning to the actual situation of migrants, the following section identifies these different categories of workers in our sample.

Mobility of labour vs. mobility of services

Different EU regulations concerning the mobility of labour and the mobility of services, in conjunction with national responses to labour market challenges in the wake of increased mobility overall, have given rise to different legal categories of migrant workers. Depending on what kind of affiliation the workers have to their employers and clients, the categories are subject to different rules concerning entry and residence, wages and taxation (Table 2.1).

According to the transitional restrictions, *individual labour migrants who are employed in Norwegian firms* must have a residence permit before they can start work in Norway. In order to get a residence permit, they need a contract for full-time work with a Norwegian company offering the same wages as stated in collective agreement, or whatever is normal pay in this occupation and sector. Individual labour migrants must pay taxes in Norway. After the transitional restrictions are lifted, no wage requirements will be needed to obtain a work permit. In contrast, *posted workers employed in Polish companies subcontracting in Norway* do not need a residence permit until they have worked in Norway for three months. No wage regulations apply unless there is a

Table 2.1 *Regulation of residence, tax and wages for different categories of migrant workers from A8 countries*

Channel of migration	Residence	Taxes	Wages
Individual labour migrants employed in Norwegian firm	Residence permit required before starting work (no restrictions after end of transitional arrangements)	Paid in Norway	Transitional period: based on minimum Norwegian wage level in all sectors After the transitional period: based on minimum Norwegian wage level where generalised collective agreement exists
Posted workers employed in Polish firms subcontracting in Norway	Residence permit required after 3 months of work	Paid in Poland for first 6-12 months Paid in Norway after first year	Based on minimum Norwegian wage level where generalised collective agreement exists
Self-employed workers	No residence permit required Must join government register of enterprises	Paid in country where enterprise established	Market price

Source: Dølvik and Eldring 2008

generalised collective agreement in the sector and area where they work. So far, collective agreements have only been generalised in the construction sector. Posted workers pay taxes in their country of origin for the first six to twelve months. Meanwhile, *self-employed workers selling their services to clients in Norway* can establish their company and pay taxes in Norway. Self-employed workers with a company established in Poland must register their firm with a government register of enterprises in Norway, but pay taxes in their home country. Self-employed workers are not subject to any wage regulations, irrespective of transitional restrictions or generalised collective agreements.

Different kinds of migration vs. alternative channels of migration

Approximately half of the workers in the sample for this study were employed by Norwegian companies, either directly or through a Norwegian manpower firm. The rest were either self-employed or posted workers on service assignments in Norway. The different rules regarding labour migration and the mobility of services rest on a perception that there is a clear distinction based on duration of stay. Whilst mobility of services, according to the Posting of Workers Directive, involves limited short-term assignments, and posted workers should have their main employment in their home countries, individual labour migrants are expected to form a more integral part of the labour markets of destination countries for a longer period of time. However, data from the survey suggest that there is no such clear distinction between individual labour migrants and posted workers in Oslo regarding their own plans for their stay in Norway (Table 2.2).

These results show two things. First, it appears that the migrants' intended duration of stay is not as limited as previously expected. Only one in four plan to return home within a year, and the huge majority of these migrants expect to come back to work in Norway on a later occasion.[9] Seven per cent expected to return within five years. The majority expected to move back home one day, but did not know when. One out of five said that they most likely, or certainly will never, move back to Poland and that they planned to settle permanently. Also, 40 per cent of the male migrants who had partners living in Poland said they expected their spouses to join them in Norway in the near future. Registered applications for family reunification suggest that an increasing number of Polish migrants will settle with their families in Norway, with Polish citizens now the largest group applying for family reunification in the country. A recent survey among registered settled Polish migrants in Norway confirms this impression, as almost 80 per cent responded that they definitely or most likely will be living in Norway five years from now (IMDI 2008).

Table 2.2 *Intention to return to Poland (%)*

Polish respondents in Oslo who said they 'will most likely...'	Individual labour migrants (n=217)	Posted workers (n=84)	Self-employed workers (n=100)	Total (n=401)
Return within one year	18	35	34	25
Return within five years	10	5	5	7
Return some day, but don't know when	50	47	36	53
Not return	23	14	25	21
Total	101	100	100	100

Source: PMO Survey

Second, the survey data shows that there is no clear distinction between mobility of labour and that of services when it comes to migrants' own plans for the duration of their stay. The share of migrants who plan to go back to Poland within a year is a little higher among posted workers, but the majority even among this group said they did not know when they will return, and some plan to settle permanently. Intention to stay in Norway is even greater among the self-employed. That only 15 per cent of posted workers worked for the same company in Poland before coming to Norway and that the majority was hired after arrival in Norway both suggest that much of the observed mobility of service workers from Poland in the Oslo area is an alternative channel for migration rather than a distinct form of mobility different from ordinary labour migration.

A gendered labour market

The labour market for Polish migrants in Oslo is extremely gendered. Women make up 26 per cent of the Polish migrants staying in the Oslo area, and almost three-quarters of these women work as cleaners. In contrast, some 92 per cent of Polish men interviewed work in the construction sector (Table 2.3). The survey data can thus be used as a basis for two separate case studies that serve as examples of specific local labour markets for Polish migrants in Norway, as well as reflect differences in opportunity structures and working conditions for male and female migrants. Amongst the small number of women who do not work as cleaners, there is some employment in the state health service and in children's day care centres; men not working in construction are employed in various service occupations (transport, mechanics, etc.).[10]

Although in a sample based on RDS, it is important to account for a slightly larger error than in an ordinary random sample, it is assumed that the sample of construction workers is large enough to give reliable data on the distribution of wages and working conditions among

Table 2.3   *Sector of employment by gender (%)*

Sector	Men (n=306)	Women (n=144)
Cleaning	1	72
Construction	92	3
Other	7	24
Total	100	100

Source: PMO Survey

different groups of workers with different affiliations to their employers and different legal status. Because of the relatively small sample size – as well as the fact that the women display much less variation in employer affiliation and legal status – only single variable estimates of working conditions are presented for this group. Caution is required in claiming that these estimates are accurate and representative for all female Polish domestic cleaners in Oslo, but they do give a general picture of their labour market situation and working conditions.

Migrants in the illegal and semi-legal labour market

Data on illegal migrants in Norway have so far been scarce or non-existent. Yet it has traditionally been assumed that the market for illegal migrant workers has been relatively limited in the Nordic countries compared with Continental Europe and the United States. This has in part been attributed to the Nordic social model with a relatively high level of organisation in the labour market and a certain degree of internal discipline and self-regulation by trade unions and employers' associations (Hjarnø 2003). However, this study suggests that there is a substantial illegal market for migrant labour from Poland. Illegality may be related to illegal residence or it may be related to illegal work (Brochmann & Hammar 1999). For labour migrants these two are closely related, as having a legal taxpaying job is the entrance ticket to a residence permit and associated rights. It may, however, be difficult to determine who is in compliance and who is not. As noted earlier, individual labour migrants, posted workers and self-employed workers are subject to different rules concerning residence and taxation – the two main indicators of illegality. In order to determine the legal status of respondents, it was therefore necessary to use slightly different indicators depending on the type of affiliation individuals have to their employers in Norway.

While paying tax – either to Norwegian or Polish authorities – is a central indicator of legality for all categories of migrant workers, the rules regarding residence permits are not the same for everyone. As noted above, while individual labour migrants need a residency permit before they can start working, posted workers only need a residence permit after three months. Self-employed workers do not need a residence permit at all, but must be entered on a government register of enterprises. To supplement information about who pays tax and has legal residence, respondents were asked about other aspects that can be used as indicators for legal employment, such as whether they were paid in cash and if they had an employment contract with their employer or – if they were self-employed – whether they had a company that was registered in Norway or Poland. Based on six indicators,[11] jobs were classified as being legal, illegal or within a 'grey area' (Table 2.4).

Within the sample, 57 per cent were classified as having a legal job, 25 per cent as having an illegal job and 19 per cent as working within the 'grey area'. Working in the 'grey area' may entail having a job that has some features of a legal job and others that are illegal, or in some cases it may mean that the respondent gave contradictory information. For the sake of simplicity, the following sections do not distinguish between illegal work and work in the 'grey' area.

Male migrants in the construction sector

The construction sector has attracted the largest share of A8 migrant workers. This is also the sector where issues of social dumping and exploitative working conditions for migrants have received the most political attention. The Norwegian government, in close cooperation with the trade union movement, has developed a wide range of policies to combat exploitation and social dumping, especially designed to fit the construction sector. So far, this sector is the only one where collective agreements have been extended to cover unorganised and posted workers, and a recent government action plan against social dumping has focused most of its recourses here, in close cooperation with the social

Table 2.4 *Legal status by sector (%)*

	Sector			Migration channel			
	Cleaning *(n=94)*	*Construction* *(n=260)*	*Other* *(n=41)*	*Individual migrants* *(n=226)*	*Posted workers* *(n=90)*	*Self-Employed* *(n=105)*	*Total* *(n=421)*
Legal	17	66	65	83	33	12	57
Grey area	14	19	20	12	29	13	19
Illegal	69	15	15	5	38	74	25
Total	100	100	100	100	100	100	100

Source: PMO Survey

partners. Local trade unions in Oslo have also made substantial efforts to recruit and organise labour migrants; 14 per cent of the Polish construction workers in Oslo in autumn 2006 reported that they were members of a Norwegian trade union.

Employment relations, illegality and working conditions

Polish migrants in the Oslo construction sector have a multitude of different relations to their employers. A little more than half of them are employed directly by Norwegian companies. Some are employed directly by Norwegian production companies, but most by Norwegian temp agencies that send them to work for different clients. Nevertheless, being employees in a Norwegian company, they are subject to transitional regulations on residency and wages. But there is also a considerable share who serve as posted workers employed by Polish companies or as self-employed workers subcontracted to Norwegian clients. These workers are not necessarily covered by the transitional regulations since their work is regulatied as mobility of services rather than mobility of labour.

There is a substantial illegal and semi-illegal segment, and there is a strong connection between migration channel and legal status. Illegal work is especially widespread among those working as posted and self-employed workers. Neither subcontracting nor illegality is a new phenomenon in Norwegian construction (Dølvik, Eldring & Ødegård

Figure 2.2   *Employer affiliation and legal status (%, n=289)*

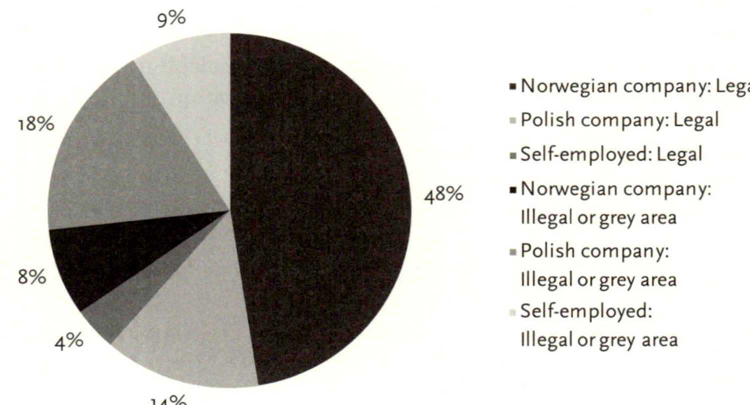

Source: PMO Survey

2005), but there is much to indicate that both – and especially in combination – have received a boost after EU enlargement.

The terms of employment vary significantly between the different categories of workers. More than half of those who were legally employed in a Norwegian company had permanent employment contracts. The rest had time-limited contracts for a few months or one to two years. The majority of legally posted workers had shorter time-limited contracts, while illegally posted workers typically had only a limited verbal agreement, rather than a written contract. In 2006, the average hourly wage for all workers in the construction sector was NOK 174 (€ 21.80).[12] Yet almost all of the Polish construction workers interviewed were paid far less (Table 2.5).

The most comprehensive breaches of the minimum wage provisions in this sector were found among posted workers, and especially among those who were working illegally or in the grey area. Minimum wages in the construction sector are NOK 132 (€ 16.50) for skilled employees; NOK 123 (€ 15.40) for unskilled workers with one year's experience; and NOK 118 (€ 14.80) for unskilled workers without experience. With the recent generalisation of collective agreements, this is legally binding for all workers employed in the construction sector except those who are self-employed. Those legally employed by Norwegian companies receive an average of NOK 97 per hour in net wages. When taxes are added we can assume that a majority receive pay close to the legal minimum requirements. Wages are lower among posted workers, despite not paying taxes; those who are working illegally or in the grey market

Table 2.5 *Employment conditions, by employer affiliation and legal status (%, n=289)*

Legal status and affiliation to employer	Average hourly wage (NOK)	Permanent employment contract (%)	Think they can get sick leave with pay (%)	Think they will lose job if sick (%)
Legally employed by Norwegian company	97	53	86	1
Legally employed by Polish company	84	37	52	0
Legally self-employed	-	-	-	-
Illegally employed by Norwegian company	100	-	67	0
Illegally employed by Polish company	68	24	41	36
Illegally self-employed	109	-	52	48
Total	92	37	71	8

Source: PMO Survey

receive, by far, the lowest net wages. The average net wage for those who are working illegally or in the grey market as posted workers is only NOK 68 (€ 8.53) – just over half the minimum wage and less than 40 per cent of the industry average. Self-employed workers receive higher hourly wages but, for them, the employer does not cover social costs, which usually add up to 30 per cent of wages. Self-employed workers are also more vulnerable to being cheated than individual labour migrants and posted workers. While three out of ten workers employed by Norwegian companies and two out of ten posted workers reported having been cheated out of pay by employers or clients, this applied to seven out of ten self-employed construction workers.

The requirement regarding pay in the construction sector is the same for individual labour migrants as it is for posted workers employed in foreign companies, but differences in wages may be explained by the way in which the regulations are controlled and enforced. While those who are employed in Norwegian companies must submit an employment contract specifying their Norwegian pay level in order to obtain a work permit, there is no such 'gatekeeper function' for posted workers. These employees do not need residence permits for the first three months and need not document their pay level to Norwegian authorities. For them, the labour inspection authorities' sporadic checks at building sites represent the only form of government control and enforcement.

Posted and illegal workers are also in a weaker position when it comes to job security and social benefits. Social insurance against losing your job and/or income when you fall ill is one of the basic features of the Norwegian model for work and social welfare. The right to absence with pay when ill is regulated by the Working Environment Act, and is designed to make sure workers do not lose their job or income if they become temporarily ill. The employer must pay for the first sixteen days of absence. After the first sixteen days, the National Insurance grants sickness benefits. The Working Environment Act includes foreign workers in Norway. However, not everyone is able to claim their rights vis-à-vis their employers, Moreover, without being registered as working legally in Norway, they cannot claim benefits from the National Insurance. While 86 per cent of those who are legally employed by Norwegian companies expect to be given sick leave with pay if they become ill, only 41 per cent of those who are working illegally or in the grey market as posted workers say the same. Thirty-six per cent of them say that they most likely will lose their jobs if they become ill, while none of those who are working legally say this.

Balancing regulation of labour and mobility of services

The transitional restrictions were introduced with the explicit, albeit not sole, purpose of protecting migrant workers against exploitation and poor working conditions in the Norwegian labour market.[13] According to the findings of this study, they seem to have worked relatively well for those Polish construction workers who are covered by them. That is not to say that these workers receive equal treatment with their Norwegian colleagues: there is no doubt that the huge majority of Polish construction workers are paid less than the sector average. And with average working weeks of more than 50 hours, many also have far longer working hours than the Norwegian standard of 37.5 hours per week. Nonetheless, examples of extremely poor working conditions are few among those who are employed by Norwegian companies and have a registered residency permit. Most of them receive wages according to the minimum requirements in the collective agreements and most have access to basic social rights while working in Norway. On the other hand, workers coming to Norway through the service channel are in a much weaker position on the labour market, and their risk of ending up in an illegal and semi-illegal market is much greater than those who come as individual labour migrants. Jobs in this market are usually characterised by low pay, insecure employment, limited access to health and welfare services and little protection against exploitation from their clients and employers.

Though some Polish construction workers reported being given fake contracts stating higher pay than they actually received, the Transitional Restrictions' obligation to register and submit working contracts with national pay level for individual labour migrants has had a disciplining effect for Norwegian employers. Moreover, they have set a general standard of working conditions for Polish workers hired by Norwegian companies. But despite the fact that generalising collective agreements have levelled the legal playing field regarding wage requirements for individual labour migrants and posted workers, the asymmetric regulation of tax, residence and employer responsibilities still incentivises employers to use foreign subcontractors. This, in turn, boosts low wage competition and illegal working conditions among Polish subcontractors and service providers. As such, the asymmetric regulation regime for labour and the mobility of services has given rise to a differentiated labour market for Polish construction workers. So far, the extended collective agreements and associated control measures have not been effective in securing decent working conditions for posted workers to the same extent as the transitional restrictions have been in regulating working conditions for individual labour migrants in the construction sector. However, several new control and enforcement measures have been implemented since this study was conducted, and recent reports from the directorate of labour inspections may suggest a decrease in illegal working conditions for labour migrants in the construction sector since 2006.[14]

Although effective in securing minimum standards, there is much to indicate that the transitional restrictions contribute to channelling mobility into other, less controllable forms: instead of migrant workers being employed in Norwegian companies, we see an increase in the use of posting, self-employment and/or illegal work. The mobility of service workers among Poles in the Oslo area is not substantially different from ordinary labour immigration with regard to duration of stay and time perspective. From a migrants' perspective, it seems to be an alternative channel for migration, and whether they get a job in a Norwegian or Polish company operating in Norway may be accidental. However, for Norwegian clients and employers, this is a way of organising work that makes it easier to avoid employer liability, with low wage competition among service providers, widespread 'bogus posting' and illegal employment conditions as a result. The incentive to employ sub-contractors instead of direct employment is not just related to differences in wages and labour costs – increasing flexibility and reducing social charges for foreign employees may also be a powerful motivator.

In 2009, Norway lifted the transitional restrictions on A8 countries, opening up the labour market for free movement of labour without the previous possibility of ensuring proper wages through immigration control measures. It remains to be seen whether the situation of migrants coming as service providers was a preview of deteriorating working conditions and more widespread wage-dumping for individual labour migrants in the construction sector after 2009. Or, perhaps the ongoing development of new labour market policy instruments, including generalised collective agreements and associated control measures, will be able to create a more symmetric and effective regime ensuring equal treatment.

Female migrants working as domestic cleaners

It has been assumed that changes in economy, family and labour market structure and gender roles led to the virtual disappearance of domestic household service providers in Norway in the early and mid-twentieth century, as both supply of workers and demand for services dried up (Hagemann & Roll-Hansen 2005). In the early twenty-first century, this category of workers is returning to the Norwegian labour market. Higher demand due to increased private purchasing power, women's participation in the labour market and a more gender-equal

Figure 2.3 *Employer affiliation and legal status among Polish cleaners in Oslo (%, n=91)*

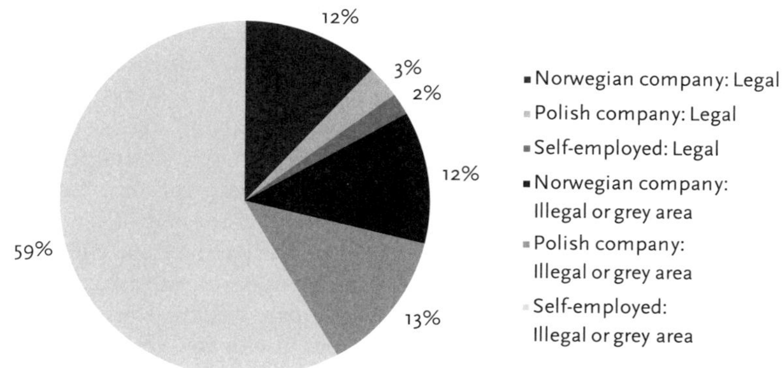

Source: PMO Survey

family life of Norwegian households are now combined with the increased supply of potentially cheap labour in the wake of the EU enlargement. This has given rise to a 'new' market for household service provision. Among Polish migrants, cleaning private homes is a strictly female job segment and one of the few labour market options for Polish women in Norway who do not speak Norwegian. About two out of three Polish women in Oslo are employed as cleaners, most of them working exclusively for private households. Some of them have come together with, or to join, husbands or boyfriends working in Norway, but the majority have come on their own. Six out of ten are *not* living with a partner in Norway, and only 12 per cent say that they came to Norway for other reasons than work. Female Polish migrants working as domestic service providers should therefore not be viewed as just an appendage to migration in the construction sector, but as a separate form of labour migration in its own right.

Privatised employment relations and illegality

Although we find a small legal segment – mostly women hired by Norwegian cleaning agencies – the huge majority, 84 per cent, are working in an illegal or semi-illegal labour market. Some of them have some kind of employment relation to a Polish or Norwegian company, but it is difficult to assess if these are regular firms or informal middlemen and recruiters. The majority are self-employed, selling their services to different private clients. Traditionally, cleaning work in Norway, both in the regular and irregular labour market, has been organised as part-time work (Skilbrei 2003). Unlike the male construction workers who usually have long working hours, Polish women in the cleaning sector are often under-employed. More than 60 per cent of the Polish cleaners work less than 35 hours a week. Many reported that they want to work more, but job competition is fierce. Few managed to obtain enough assignments to fill a whole working week. Their average hourly wages are similar to the construction workers (NOK 97, or around € 12.16).[15] Considering, however, that they work fewer hours per week and often have to travel between clients during their workday, their real wages are much lower than those of the men. Three out of ten report that they have experienced being cheated out of pay by their clients. As illegal workers, the majority are in a weak position to claim basic rights from either their employers or the Norwegian welfare state, and few have any access to social benefits as workers in Norway. Only 6 per cent reported having access to sick pay, 29 per cent expected having access to Norwegian public health care services, 8 per cent reported having pension benefits and 6 per cent reported receiving holiday pay in their present job. While there is some mobility from illegal to legal employment for Polish construction workers, Polish women working as cleaners have very few options on the legal labour market as long as they do not speak Norwegian, despite the fact that approximately one third of them have higher education from Poland. Political attention regarding migrant workers in Norway has largely focused on male migrants. As female migrants are excluded from the legal labour market, they also become invisible in official statistics, strengthening gender bias in political focus.[16]

Barriers to legalisation

In the debate on the connection between domestic work and exploitation of migrant women, there are two opposing positions. While some have argued that domestic work in itself is a site of exploitation, others have argued that domestic work can be an ordinary job if it is adequately compensated and thereby upgraded to a professional occupation (Lutz 2008:43). Studies from Sweden and other European countries have indicated that demand for cheap services among clients combined with attitudes towards paid household work as belonging to the private sphere – and being essentially different from ordinary work – contribute to disqualifying household service providers from ordinary working conditions and social rights (Anderson 2004). In Norway, work in private households has proved difficult to regulate. Usually this kind of work falls outside both the range of negotiated requirements in collective agreements and the general norms for wage standards that these agreements often create in unorganised parts of the labour market.

While the Norwegian transitional restrictions imposed a legal minimum wage standard that also includes Polish domestic cleaners, the transitional restrictions' requirement of full-time work may have become a contributing factor as to why the huge majority of female Polish cleaners are working illegally.[17] Travelling between several different clients and with difficulties in getting enough assignments, few can document full-time work in Norway, which is a requirement for obtaining a legal residence permit. Without a legal residence permit, they do not have access to any of the social benefits to which workers in the formal labour market are entitled. So far, we do not know to what extent Polish women's illegal status on the Norwegian labour market is an unintended consequence of the transitional restrictions' requirement of full-time work and national pay level or a result of more intrinsic features of the labour market for household services. However, a relatively strong correlation between having full-time work and having a legal residency permit supports the claim that the transitional restrictions make a difference; those who work more than 35 hours a week have twice as high a probability of having a residency permit than those who work less than that.

Conclusions

In a context of increasing European competition to attract labour, the discourse on labour migrants' positions on the labour markets in Norway has turned from fears of social tourism and mounting pressure on welfare state services to the question of how to include migrants in the regulated labour market with high standards of working conditions and social rights. As both registered applications and survey results show that increasing numbers of Polish migrants stay for longer periods of time or settle permanently in Norway, the challenge for Norwegian policymakers have been to accommodate the free movement of both labour and services and, at the same time, avoid the emergence of a low-paid migrant service class that is excluded from the benefits and protection of the welfare state and a regulated working life. The introduction to this chapter asked if, and in what way, the transitional restrictions, generalised collective agreements and associated control measures have affected the labour market situation, wages and access to social benefits for Polish construction workers and domestic cleaners in Oslo. On the one hand, the survey of working conditions among Polish migrants in Oslo show that these policies do matter – to a certain extent they have secured decent working conditions for many labour migrants. On the other, it shows that these policies may have differentiated and unintended consequences for different groups of migrants.

The Transitional Restrictions, in combination with the generalisation of collective agreements and associated control measures in the government Action Plan Against Social Dumping, seem to have been relatively successful in securing decent minimum standards and corresponding basic social rights for a majority of Polish migrants in the construction sector. However, the differentiated regulation policies for labour and services have facilitated the development of a dual labour market for migrant construction workers. On the one hand, there is a primary sector consisting of workers with permanent or long-term employment in Norwegian companies and residency permits according to the transitional restrictions. The majority of these workers receive wages according to collectively bargained minimum standards and have access to the same social benefits as other workers in Norway. This does not necessarily mean that they receive equal treatment as native workers. Poles working legally for Norwegian firms have lower wages than the industry average, they usually do not get compensated for their skills or education, and there is much to indicate that they are expected to work longer hours than their native colleagues. But examples of exploitation and bad working conditions are few in this group. On the other hand, there is a secondary sector in the periphery of the Norwegian labour market consisting of temporary posted and self-employed workers not covered by the transitional restrictions and often working illegally without residency permits and without paying tax. Jobs in this segment are characterised by low wages, short-term employment with little protection against dismissals and limited access to welfare benefits and services. For Polish migrant women the signs of segmentation are even more evident. The majority work as domestic cleaners in an unregulated illegal and semi-legal market for self-employed service providers in the periphery of the labour market where low wages, no job security, limited access to social benefits and few social rights are the norm. And unlike their male counterparts, Polish women in Norway have few options in the legal labour market as long as they do not speak Norwegian. For them, the transitional restrictions are just one of several barriers excluding them from regularising their employment situation and accessing social rights as members of the Norwegian workforce.

While studies of the European and Nordic social models have stressed the role of politics and labour market regimes in shaping wage structures and social standards in national labour markets (Jørgensen & Madsen 2007; Dølvik et al. 2007), theories of segmented labour markets as well as neoclassical economic theory often downplay the role of government policies and organisational structure when it comes to migrant working conditions, focusing instead on economic mechanisms within labour markets (Massey 2005; Flanagan 2006). Our study suggests that regulation policies may at least interact with the internal dynamics of different labour markets, affecting processes of segmentation. For Polish migrants in Oslo, which set of regulation policy you are subject to determines, to a large extent, whether they are included into the core labour force with corresponding rights, or if they are in the periphery – excluded from these rights.

Attempts to prevent social dumping and regime competition in different European countries have exposed two main strategies based on historical traditions of industrial relations in different countries (Cremers, Dølvik & Bosch 2007). Government imposed *legal minimum wage* legislation have been widely practiced in countries with low collective agreements coverage, while strategies based on established traditions of industrial relations and *collective bargaining* have been preferred in countries with high coverage.

After 2004, Norway has moved from a pure collective bargaining model towards a middle option, as generalising collective agreements allows for sector specific legal minimum wages based on collectively bargained standards, enforced by cooperation between social partners and government bodies. However, despite some success in the construction sector, the question is whether generalising collective agreements is an effective measure in sectors with weak trade unions and low organisational rates, such as agriculture and service provision. Domestic services is an extreme case in this vein, as no organisations exist among employers or employees, and any attempts to regulate employment conditions would rest almost entirely on legal requirements and government enforcement. Representing two very different sectors, the challenge to protect basic rights of migrant workers in construction and domestic cleaning illustrates the need to develop regulation strategies that are adapted to the specific institutional context in each sector.

Appendix: Data and methodology

Challenges in studying unsettled migrant population

Labour migrants from the new EU member states in Central and Eastern Europe have proven an elusive population for quantitative research. Quantitative studies usually require a list from which to draw a sample, but no lists of such labour migrants exist or can easily be compiled. Some migrants may only be in the country of destination for a short period of time, some may not live in registered housing and most are usually not registered as settled residents.[18] Many do not even have registered work permits because they are posted workers employed in foreign companies or self-employed workers. Finally, an unknown number of people are working illegally, without being registered or paying tax to either their country of origin or destination. Due to this lack of data on the individual level, research on migration after EU expansion has so far mostly focused on companies' labour strategies and institutional changes in the regulatory regimes in the wake of increasing mobility.

Working and living conditions of immigrant workers, their experiences and the assessments they themselves have made in connection with their stay in Norway have thus been scarcely addressed. This is why, in autumn and winter 2006, Fafo, in collaboration with researchers from the Centre for Migration Research in Warsaw, tested respondent-driven sampling (RDS) as a new method for collecting representative data in a migrant population where no sample frames exist.

Respondent-driven sampling

RDS was developed by Douglas Heckathorn (1997) to study hidden and hard-to-reach populations.[19] RDS combines elements of 'snowball sampling' (getting individuals to recruit people they know who, in turn, recruit individuals they know, and so on) with economic incentives for participation and recruiting. It also uses statistical software to produce estimates that adjust network effects in the sampling procedure, such as the recruitment patterns of people with different characteristics and the network size of each respondent. The statistical software produces variable-specific weights based on these characteristics, and makes it possible to produce statistically unbiased estimates for such hard-to-reach groups.

In his own research, Heckathorn has used the method in surveys of injection drug users (2006) and jazz musicians (2003) in the US. Others have applied it to sex workers in Eastern Europe (Simic, Johnston, Platt, Baros, Andjelkovic, Novotny & Rhodes 2006) and Vietnam (Johnston, Sabin, Hien & Huong 2006). As of yet, the method had not been used on unsettled migrant populations. Based on our experience and comparisons with available public register data, we suggest that RDS is highly applicable for research on such populations, if used in the right way and certain criteria are met. For example, in our study women make up 26 per cent of the Poles in Oslo in the autumn months of 2006, but among registered permits, they only make up 12 per cent. This discrepancy results from the fact that a much larger proportion of the women work illegally without residency permits. When we single out only those in our sample who state that they have a legal residency permit, women make up 12 per cent. However, the methodology is only useful in estimating the distribution of characteristics within a population, not for estimating the size of a population. Although able to produce statistically unbiased estimates, one must account for a larger standard error than in ordinary random sampling. Estimates based on a RDS sample will usually have larger confidence intervals than simple random samples of the same size.

Fieldwork and sample

Our sample consists of 510 Polish migrants staying in the Oslo area. The fieldwork was coordinated by Joanna Napierała and Paulina Trevena from the Centre For Migration Research at the University of Warsaw, and supervised by Guri Tyldum and Jon Horgen Friberg. The interviews were carried out face-to-face by a team of ten Polish-speaking interviewers, most of them students recruited from the University of Oslo. In the last stages of the study, two of the interviewers, Paulina Slabon and Alexandra Pytko, took over coordinating the fieldwork. Most interviews were conducted at Fafo's premises on evenings and weekends, since the majority of the respondents work very long hours. Respondents were given NOK 150 for an approximately one-hour interview and an additional NOK 200 if they recruited two more respondents. They were given the same offer and so on. Recruitment procedures were based on a system of vouchers with information about the survey and contact information. New recruits were given these vouchers by respondents who had already been interviewed, and would send a text message to our coordinators, who called back and made appointments for the interview. Seventy-one per cent of the respondents recruited new ones. When the main part of the fieldwork was completed, women only comprised 100 of the 419 respondents. It was therefore decided to extend the fieldwork with an extra female sample of 91 persons. In the analysis, women have been weighted down to their original share of 26 per cent. Therefore, the female sample size is larger than their relative small share of the population estimate would suggest, making the estimates for this group more robust. Our estimates are representative for all Polish migrants who stayed in the Oslo area in autumn 2006.

Analysis and estimates

When calculating estimates based on RDS data, one takes account of: 1) the probability of cross-recruitment between people with different characteristics (e.g. the probability of a man to recruit a woman and a woman recruiting a man) and 2) the personal network size of each respondent, meaning the number of people the respondent knows who fit the criteria for participation in the study. Together this information is used to produce weighted estimates for each variable. For example, with a two-category variable in the groups a and b, we can produce an estimate for the share of a respondents in the population using the formula, where Pa is the population estimate, S_{ba} is the share of a-members recruited by b members and N_b is the average network size of b members:

$$P_a = \frac{S_{ba}N_b}{S_{ba}N_b + S_{ab}N_a}$$

Source: Salganik and Heckathorn (2004)

Variable-specific estimates can be produced using especially designed software for RDS data (RDS-STAT). However, since it is difficult to produce multivariate estimates in RDS-STAT, we have used estimates of central characteristics of the population to produce general sample weights. The dataset was then exported to SPSS for analysis. The general weights were based on the three variables that proved to be the most important ones for the probability of cross-recruitment: 1) gender – man or woman, 2) employer affiliation – whether a posted worker or not and 3) employer – whether working for a company or for private clients. This means that our estimates are not variable-specific and may diverge slightly from the estimates produced in RDS-STAT. However, by cross-checking all variables, we found the differences to be insignificant.

Acknowledgements

The author is grateful to several colleagues at Fafo who gave valuable comments on an earlier draft of this chapter. Extra special thanks goes to Jon Erik Dølvik and Grete Brochmann, for fruitful supervision, comments and advice along the way. The analysis in this chapter is in part based on the report *Polonia i Oslo* written in collaboration with Guri Tyldum (Friberg & Tyldum 2007). Guri Tyldum also had the main responsibility for sampling and methodology during the fieldwork. The author is greatly indebted to her efforts.

Notes

1   The analysis in this chapter is based on a study conducted in the autumn of 2006, and was written in 2007 and 2008. It does not take into account events that happened after June 2008, such as the financial crisis later that year or the revoking of the Norwegian transitional restrictions in May 2009. A follow-up study was conducted in early 2010. The results from this study will be published in 2010/2011.
2   Although not an EU member, Norway is part of the single market through the European Economic Area (EEA) agreement.
3   While transitional restrictions in most old member states prolonged pre-accession restrictions based on quotas or labour market demands testing, Norway and Denmark introduced new transitional wage requirements for individual labour migrants from A8 countries.
4   A more thorough presentation of the data and methodology is given in the Appendix.
5   See www.respondentdrivensampling.org.
6   While Brücker, Epstein, McCormick, Saint-Paul, Venturini & Zimmerman (2002) and Hanson & Slaughter (2002) conclude that migration has a negligible effect on native wages, recent studies have found a much stronger negative impact (Borjas 2003; Aydemir & Borjas 2007).
7   The notion of social dumping is problematic in research, as it is a highly politicised and contested one. Most parties in the Norwegian debate agree that it is a problem, but opinions differ considerably as to how it should be defined.
8   Collective agreement coverage in the private sector in Norway is 53 per cent, being lower than both Denmark (77 per cent) and Sweden (90 per cent) (Dølvik & Eldring 2006).
9   It is likely that some respondents may have only been talking about going home for Christmas. Interviews were conducted in late autumn and 16 per cent said that they would return 'within a few weeks'. Almost every one of them said they would come back to work in Norway on a later occasion.
10   Many Polish migrants in Norway also work in agriculture, fisheries and industrial manufacturing, though these sectors are mainly located in other parts of the country.
11   The index was created by Guri Tyldum at Fafo (Friberg & Tyldum 2007). It is based on six indicators, concerning: 1) payment of taxes; 2) filing of a tax return; 3) possession of a 'd-number'; 4) possession of a work contract; 5) possession of an EEA residence permit; and 6) payment of wages into a bank account (as opposed to cash payment). Those who answered 'yes' to five or six of these indicators were classified as working legally; those who answered 'yes' to less than two of these indicators were classified as working illegally; whilst the remainder were classified as working in the 'grey area'. For posted workers who had stayed in Norway less than three months, only three indicators (1, 4, 6) were used. Here the score was 3=legal, 1 or 2=grey area and 0=illegal. Posted workers who had stayed for more than three months were assessed on four indicators (1, 4, 5, 6), and needed to answer 'no' to all four to be classified as illegal. For self-employed workers, the index was the same as for posted workers (less than three months), except that the work contract was substituted by having a registered firm.

12   Teknisk Beregningsutvalg (2007).
13   Protecting the wage level for native workers and safeguarding against so-called 'social tourism' were also important arguments.
14   At the annual national control conducted by the Labour Inspectorate in February 2008, one out of ten inspections resulted in a decision that work must stop due to severe breaches of regulations regarding wages and health and safety. In the 2007 national control, 30 per cent of inspections resulted in such a decision.
15   There are no figures for the national average pay level in the cleaning sector – nor are there any statutory regulatory measures – but the standard pay according to collective agreements in the formal cleaning sector ranges from NOK 122 (€ 15.30) to NOK 130 (€ 16.30), depending on seniority.
16   While women made up 12 per cent of registered polish migrants in Oslo in 2006, our survey, which includes undocumented migrants, reported a female share of 26 per cent.
17   Such a possible effect of the transitional restrictions was suggested by Dølvik et al. 2006.
18   According to Transitional Regulations after the EU enlargement, migrants from new accession countries needed a residency permit to work in Norway. To get a residency permit, migrants needed a work contract for full-time work with a wage-level similar to Norwegian local standards. To be registered as a settled migrant with an address in Norway, they needed a residency permit and had to stay in Norway for more than six months.
19   See www.respondentdrivensampling.org.

References

Anderson, B (2004), 'Undocumented domestic workers in private households: An overview of demand and state response', in M. LeVoy, N. Verbruggen & J. Weds (eds.), *Undocumented migrant workers in Europe*. Brussels: PICUM.

Aydemir A. & G. Borjas (2007), 'Cross-country variation in the impact of international migration: Canada, Mexico, and the United States', *Journal of the European Economic Association* 5: 663-708.

Borjas, G. (2003), 'The labor demand curve is downward sloping', *The Quarterly Journal of Economics* 118: 1335-1374.

Brochmann, Grete & Tomas Hammar (eds.) (1999), *Mechanisms of immigration control: A comparative analysis of European regulation policies*. New York: Berg Publishers.

Brücker H., G.S. Epstein, B. McCormick, G. Saint-Paul, A.Venturini & K. Zimmermann (2002), 'Managing migration in the European welfare state', in T. Boeri, G. Hanson & B. McCormick (eds.), *Immigration policy and the welfare system*. Oxford/New York: Oxford University Press: 1-150

Castles, Stephen & Mark J. Miller (2003), *The age of migration: International population movements in the modern world*, third edition. New York: Palgrave Macmillan.

Cremers, Jan (2006), 'Free movement of services and equal treatment of workers: The case of construction' *Transfer* 12 (2): 167-183.

Cremers, Jan, Jon Erik Dølvik & Gerhard Bosch (2007), 'Posting of workers in the single market: Attempts to prevent social dumping and regime competition in the EU', *Industrial Relations Journal* 38 (6): 524-541.

Doringer, P., & Michael Piore (1971), *Internal labor markets and manpower analysis*. Lexington, VA: Heath

Dustmann, C., T. Frattini & I. Preston (2007), 'A study of migrant workers and the national minimum wage and enforcement issues that arise', CReAM/Target Discussion Paper.

Dølvik, Jon Erik & Line Eldring (2008), 'Mobility of labour from new EU states to the Nordic Region – Development trends and consequences', *TemaNord* 2008:537. Copenhagen: Nordisk Ministerråd. http://norden.org/pub/velfaerd/arbetsmarknad/uk/TN2008537.pdf.

Dølvik, Jon Erik & Line Eldring (2006), 'Industrial relation responses to migration and posting of workers after EU enlargement: Nordic trends and differences', *Transfer* 12 (2): 213-231. ETUI-REHS.

Dølvik, J. E. & L. Eldring (2006), 'EU enlargement two years after: Mobility, effects and challenges to the Nordic labour market regimes', *CLR-News* 3.

Dølvik, Jon Erik, Line Eldring, Jon Horgen Friberg, Torunn Kvinge, Sigmund Aslesen & Anne Mette Ødegård (2006), *Grenseløst arbeidsliv? Endringer i norske bedrifters arbeidskraftstrategier etter EU-utvidelsen.* Fafo-rapport 548. Oslo: Fafo.

Dølvik, J.E., L. Eldring & A.M. Ødegård (2005), *Lavlønnskonkurranse og sosial dumping. Utfordringer for det seriøse arbeidslivet.* Fafo-rapport 485. Oslo: Fafo.

Dølvik, Jon Erik, Tone Fløtten, Gudmund Hernes & Jon Hippe (eds.) (2007), *Hamskifte. Den norske modellen i endring.* Oslo: Gyldendal.

Flanagan, Robert J. (2006), *Globalization and Labor Conditions. Working Conditions and Worker Rights in a Global Economy.* Oxford: Oxford University Press.

Friberg, Jon Horgen & Guri Tyldum (2007), *Polonia i Oslo – En studie av arbeids- og levekår blant polakker i hovedstadsområdet.* Fafo-rapport 2007:27. Oslo: Fafo.

Hanson, G.H. & M.J. Slaugther (2002), 'Labor-market adjustments in open economies: Evidence from U.S. States', *Journal of International Economics* 57 (1): 3-29.

Hagemann, G. & H. Roll-Hansen (2005), 'Introduction' in I.G. Hagemann & H. Roll-Hansen (eds.), *Twentieth-century housewives: Meanings and implications of unpaid work.* Oslo: Unipub: 1-12

Hjarnø, J. (2003), *Illegal immigrants and developments in employment in the labour markets of the EU. Research in migration and ethnic relations.* Aldershot/Burlington: Ashgate.

Heckathorn, D.D. (1997), 'Respondent-driven sampling: A new approach to the study of hidden populations', *Social Problems* 44: 174-199.

Heckathorn, D.D. & Joan Jeffri (2006), 'Social networks of jazz musicians', in *Changing the beat: A study of the worklife of jazz musicians,* Volume III: *Respondent-driven sampling: Survey results,* National Endowment for the Arts Research Division Report 43: 48-61. Washington, D.C.: Research Center for Arts and Culture.

Jørgensen, Henning & Per Kongshøj Madsen (eds.) (2007), *Flexicurity and beyond: Finding a new agenda for the European social model.* Copenhagen: DJØF Publishing.

Johnston, Lisa, K. Sabin, M. Hien & P. Huong (2006), 'Assessment of respondent driven sampling for recruiting female sex workers in two Vietnamese cities: Reaching the unseen sex worker', *Journal of Urban Health* 83 (Supp 1): 16-28.

Kaczmarczyk, Pawel & Marek Okólski (2008), *Economic impacts of migration on Poland and the Baltic states.* Fafo-paper 2008:01. Oslo: Fafo.

Kjeldstadli, K.(ed.) (2003), *Norsk innvandrings historie – Bind 3 I globaliseringens tid 1940-2000.* Oslo: Pax Forlag.

Kofman, E., A. Phizacklea, P. Raghuram & R. Sales (2000), *Gender and international migration in Europe. Employment, welfare and politics.* London/New York: Routledge.

Lutz, Helma (2008), *Migration and domestic work: A European perspective on a global theme.* Aldershot/Burlington: Ashgate.

Magnani, Robert, Keith Sabin, Tobi Saidel, & Douglas Heckathorn (2005), 'Review of sampling hard-to-reach and hidden populations for HIV surveillance', *AIDS,* 19 (Supp 2): 67-72

Massey, Douglas S., Joaquin Arango, Graeme Hugo, Ali Kouaouci, Adela Pellegrino & J. Edward Taylor (2005), *Worlds in motion: Understanding international migration at the end of the millennium*. Oxford: Clarendon Press.

Piore, M.J. (1979), *Birds of passage: Migrant labour and industrial societies*. Cambridge: Cambridge University Press.

Simic, M, Johnston, L., Platt, L., Baros, S., Andjelkovic, V., Novotny, T. and Rhodes, T. (2006), 'Exploring barriers to "Respondent Driven Sampling" in sex worker and drug-injecting sex worker populations in Eastern Europe', *Journal of Urban Health* 83 (Supp 1): 6-15

Skilbrei, M. (2003), 'Dette er jo bare en husmorjobb', *Ufaglærte kvinner i arbeidslivet*, NOVA-rapport 17 (3).

Wolfson, Charles (2007), 'Labour standards and migration in the new Europe: Post-communist legacies and perspectives', *European Journal of Industrial Relations* 13: 199.

Ødegård, Anne Mette, Sigmund Aslesen, Mona Bråten & Line Eldring (2007), *Fra øst uten sikring? EU-utvidelsen og HMS-konsekvenser på norske bygge- og anleggsplasser*. Fafo-rapport 2007:03. Oslo: Fafo.

3 Patterns and determinants of sub-regional migration: A case study of Polish construction workers in Norway

Joanna Napierała and Paulina Trevena

Introduction

Accession to the European Union in 2004 has had a profound impact on patterns of Polish labour migration. Norway is a very new country to experience inflows from Poland, with little migration taking place prior to 2004. However, it has seen a sharp increase in the level of migration from Poland, with a pilot study entitled 'Polish migrants to Oslo' (PMO, see Friberg in this volume) demonstrating that in the case of the Oslo area, labour migration is strictly based on demand, and driven primarily by the construction sector.

This chapter argues that migration of workers to the construction sector in Norway is a sub-regionalised phenomenon, with the majority of migrants in Oslo originating from four regions in Poland: Zachodniopomorskie, Pomorskie, Małopolskie and Śląskie. The chapter analyses the reasons behind this trend and provides an insight into the mechanisms that have shaped and channelled these flows. The first part of the chapter provides a brief overview of the current conditions in the Polish and Norwegian construction sector. An analysis of the role of migration networks in directing the current migration flow of Polish construction workers to the Oslo area follows. The final part of the chapter is devoted to an examination of the conditions on the workers' regional labour markets in Poland, and how these shape sub-regional patterns of migration.

Push and pull factors at macro level

As noted in chapter 2, an overwhelming figure of 92 per cent of the males interviewed in the PMO study was working in the construction sector in the Oslo area. Significantly, only 45 per cent of these migrants had completed formal training in construction or a related area in Poland, and could thus be considered as skilled workers upon arrival.[1]

It is therefore clearly visible that the current migration wave of Poles to Norway is indeed demand-driven, as the need for workers in the Norwegian construction sector is so strong that, besides a qualified workforce, it attracts considerable numbers of workers with no appropriate vocational background and/or work experience. Nevertheless, in our analysis we would like to concentrate on the group of skilled construction workers exclusively, i.e. those who had acquired appropriate qualifications through training in the home country and, though moving abroad, remain in the same sector of employment.

Interestingly, construction has recently been in a state of boom in both Poland and Norway. Hence, the question arises: why do Polish construction workers decide to move to Norway if their skills are equally in demand in Poland? Can this phenomenon be solely attributed to the wage level difference? In order to gain an understanding of this phenomenon, we shall analyse the issue of push and pull factors at the macro level by comparing conditions in the two countries' construction sectors.

Push factors: Conditions in the Polish construction sector[2]

Conditions in the Polish construction sector have changed considerably since the turn of the new millennium. The period of 2000-2003 was marked by a heavy recession in construction, but was followed by a period of boom since the end of 2004. Its scale is truly remarkable. For example, while the average growth in construction output for EU countries from the year 2005 to 2006 was 4 per cent, for Poland, it was as high as 19.4 per cent (Eurostat 2007). Employment in the sector has also been increasing visibly: in the first half of 2006, 11.7 per cent of all workplaces in the Polish economy were created in construction (KPM 2007). The first three quarters of 2006 also saw an increase of 2.6 per cent in the average employment rate for the sector, compared to 2005 (GUS 2006). As a consequence, the Polish construction sector started to face the problem of serious labour shortages (Bolkowska 2006).

However, these highly favourable conditions in Polish construction are not too strongly reflected in the labour market situation of construction workers. From their point of view, the sector is characterised by instability and illegality of employment, bad working conditions, many barriers to employment, and relatively low wages. Employment conditions in construction have undergone a radical change since the beginning of the transition period in Poland. Under the former system, builders were typically employed by large, state-owned companies on the basis of regular work contracts (permanent employment for an indefinite time), and thus secured employment all year-round, regardless of the work volume. After the introduction of the free market economy, the structure of the sector changed, as it became dominated by small private companies (often family businesses). As a result, employment conditions also changed greatly, with permanent employment contracts being abandoned for flexible forms of employment (Bolkowska 2006). Currently, employees in Polish construction are one of the labour groups most prone to job insecurity, as they simultaneously fall victim of the flexible employment system (flexible employment forms and short-term employment) and apparent seasonality of the Polish construction business.

However, another employment-related problem specific to the national construction sector is the widespread phenomenon of illegal employment. Since labour costs in Poland are particularly high, with employment-related taxes alone reaching as high as 43.6 per cent (Kaczmarczyk & Napierała 2007), illegal employment often appears as a beneficial solution to both employers and employees. This is especially true for construction, within which illegal employment has become a standard mode of managing market fluctuations. During the slump period (2000-2003), it had become almost standard practice for small companies to formally de-register from economic activity but to continue operating on the black market, thus falling back on illegal work (Bolkowska 2006). This fact is borne out by Central Statistical Office data (see Table 3.1), which show a radical decrease in the number of construction companies and of employment in the sector in the period 1998-2004. Between 1998 (a very good year for construction) and 2004 (a recession year), the number of construction companies decreased by 59,400. Out of this number, 57,700 were companies employing less than twenty persons (Bolkowska 2006).

Therefore, the earlier tendency towards undocumented employment in the sector was reinforced and became widespread in the period of recession. According to GUS estimates, in 2004, 372,000 people were working illegally in various branches of construction: building and installation services and renovation and home repairs, including 'neighbourhood services' (GUS 2005). Presently, the scale of this phenomenon is such that the construction sector takes second or third place in all branches of economy as far as the ratio of undeclared labour is concerned (Kus 2006).

Table 3.1   *Number of companies in the construction sector*

Period	1998	2004	1998-2004
Total number of construction companies	221.4	162.0	- 59.4
Companies employing less than 20 people	216.1	158.3	- 57.8

Source: Central Statistical Office of Poland (GUS)

This tendency towards undocumented work is additionally strength-ened by a number of other factors connected with the generally disad-vantageous employment conditions in the sector, such as seasonality. In Poland, as in some other European countries, construction acknowl-edges a 'high' season (roughly from spring to autumn) and a 'low' sea-son (typically winter, when there are below-freezing temperatures). While in Germany, for example, construction workers are employed for the full year – working longer hours in the warm periods and shorter in winter – in Poland, this problem is not legally regulated in any way. Hence, given the employers' general tendency towards choosing flexible forms of employment, Polish builders are, in practice, often employed seasonally. That is, they are employed when the work volume is higher, only to be unemployed when it is lower. Obviously, this is a highly dis-advantageous situation for employees, not only in terms of lacking work continuity and regular earnings, but also when it comes to social secur-ity fees, future pensions and health insurance entitlement.

Furthermore, bad working conditions are reported as characteristic of the national construction sector. It is frequent that employers do not provide the basics, such as working clothes and/or tools, for instance. Poor quality of equipment and malfunctioning equipment are also often reported by workers. Generally, health and safety regulations are notor-iously breached on Polish sites, thus making them particularly danger-ous workplaces (MPiPS 2007).

A number of factors posing barriers to employment in construction in Poland should also be mentioned, since these result in a paradoxical situation where, despite labour shortages, considerable unemployment among Polish construction workers (in particular professions especially) is still observable. Firstly, there is the question of skills. Polish employ-ers' requirements are generally high, and fresh building school gradu-ates or those who have been unemployed in the longer-term are typi-cally unable to fulfil them. For example, hands-on practice and knowl-edge of new technologies are standard requirements, but prospective employees often lack such traits. Moreover, as already mentioned, the construction business is dominated by small- and medium-size compa-nies in Poland, which typically seek to employ all-rounders, i.e. builders with versatile skills. Hence, workers who have one particular specialisa-tion and do not have the ability to carry out multiple tasks are in a dis-advantaged position.

Significantly, age is a barrier on the Polish labour market, particularly in construction. Workers over 45 are basically considered unemployable by a large group of employers in the sector. Internal spatial mobility is also a matter worth mentioning here. The Polish population is generally characterised by low spatial mobility, and a strong preference towards their hometowns, which is strengthened by the simultaneous shortage of housing in the areas where work is offered (Bolkowska 2006). Thus, moving to other areas within the country is problematic. This situation is particularly relevant to construction workers; due to the nature of their profession, they usually must travel to work, often long distances. Meanwhile, considering local conditions (lack of private means of transport, costs of public transport or its lack thereof in less urbanised areas), this is simply not possible for many. Paradoxically, therefore, it is in some cases easier to travel abroad for work than to commute within their home country, especially as Polish employers in construction rarely provide accommodation or transport.[3]

To round up the analysis of push factors appearing in the Polish construction sector, the issue of earnings should be mentioned. Though wages in construction have been rising steadily since 2005, the increase in real wages has not, in fact, been conspicuous. The national average gross salary in construction in the first three quarters of 2006 amounted to PLN 2,483 (equivalent to € 646), and was 8.4 per cent higher than in the same period in 2005.[4] However, construction is a perfect example of the great differences in regional economies: it should be underscored that disparities between *voivodships* of highest and lowest pay in construction were still as high as 65.3 per cent in 2006. Significantly, in a clear majority of Polish *voivodships*, salaries are in fact lower than the national average,[5] and this includes all of the regions analysed in this chapter, apart from Pomorskie where the average salary was marginally higher (by 0.6 per cent).

To summarise, we may state that, although there is currently a boom in the sector resulting in slow yet gradual improvement in working conditions and wage levels, the overall situation of Polish construction workers on the home market is far from favourable. Although the requirements of employers in construction are generally high, the sectoral labour market is a largely seasonal one. It is characterised by flexible rather than permanent employment and overly high labour costs, resulting in relatively low wages and a high rate of undocumented work, as well as being additionally characterised by bad working conditions. Finally, low labour mobility within the country, limited work experience and older age are all factors that pose a problem, becoming serious barriers to finding employment in Poland's construction sector.

Pull factors: The Norwegian construction industry boom

The Norwegian construction sector has been in a state of constant growth over the last decade, and, similar to Poland, began booming in 2004. Norway's growth in construction output is reflected by a considerable increase in employment levels, with the number of employees in the sector increasing by 26,000 over the last ten years

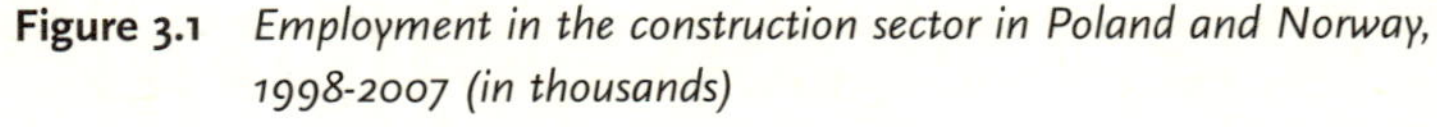

Figure 3.1 *Employment in the construction sector in Poland and Norway, 1998-2007 (in thousands)*

Source: EUROSTAT 2007

(Figure 3.1). At the same time, while gradual growth in employment levels in the Norwegian construction sector can be observed as of the late 1990s, employment in this sector in Poland has been greatly affected by recession, only now reaching the level it was at a decade ago.

The very dynamic growth in the Norwegian construction sector has, as in the Polish case, resulted in severe labour shortages: the number of unfilled vacancies in construction increased by 10 per cent in 2006. It should be noted that such a considerable shortage appeared despite the fact that there has been a significant upwards adjustment in the use of foreign labour in recent years (NHO 2006). Hence, the demand for labour in the Norwegian construction industry is indeed great. Moreover, it covers both skilled and unskilled positions, constituting a powerful pull factor for workers from abroad.

Unlike in the case of Poland, the Norwegian labour market currently offers advantageous conditions for construction workers, both in terms of wages and working conditions. The most important pull factor for Polish construction workers is no doubt the real wage level difference between the home and destination country. Generally, earnings in the Norwegian construction sector, recalculated into purchasing power parity (PPP), have for many years been as much as three times higher than earnings in the sector in Poland.[6]

An equally important factor is the lack of seasonality of employment in the Norwegian building industry. Construction work is carried out all year-round, regardless of the weather conditions. Hence, workers can count on long-term, not only seasonal, employment.

Importantly, again in contrast to the Polish case, those over age 45 are not treated as inferior on the Norwegian labour market – and the construction sector is no exception to this rule. If we consider the over-all activity rate for the 55-64 age group in the two countries, it becomes visible just how great the discrepancy is: in the year 2006, the rate for Norway was as high as 74 per cent, while for Poland it was less than 43 per cent. A comparison of the employment rate for this age group for the two countries is even more telling: 67 per cent for Norway and only 28 per cent for Poland (Eurostat 2007). It follows that the Norwegian labour market offers many more (legal) employment opportunities to older workers. Moreover, health and safety regulations are followed strictly on Norwegian building sites: regular safety checks are carried out on machinery and building equipment, and workers are not forced to undertake tasks in hazardous conditions. Polish construction workers therefore enjoy a greater feeling of safety in Norway than in their home country. Moreover, Norwegian employers provide all necessary equipment, including working clothes and tools.

Last but not least, the possibility to undertake legal work and come under the Norwegian welfare system is a strong pull factor for Polish construction workers, especially those having young children or nearing retirement age. Working in Norway legally provides Polish migrants the comfort of being insured should they have health problems. Provided appropriate requirements are met, it simultaneously gives them the chance to claim certain social benefits, such as child benefit or a Norwegian pension.

Certain pull factors beyond sector conditions should also be mentioned here, such as geographical proximity and relative ease of travel between the two countries. The appearance of cheap airlines offering flights to Norway from five big Polish cities (Warsaw, Szczecin, Wroclaw, Krakow and Gdansk) has facilitated migration decisions. The journey from Poland to Norway lasts about two and a half hours, which is often shorter than commuting to another city within Poland.

Summing up, the boom in the Norwegian construction industry has resulted in highly advantageous conditions for Polish workers. Not only is there a great demand for workers (who are paid much higher wages than in their home country), but the general working conditions are also better: all-year employment is guaranteed, older age is not a barrier to employment, and health and safety regulations are followed rigorously. Finally, working in the Norwegian construction sector provides an opportunity for legal employment and for use of the welfare system upon fulfilling appropriate requirements. Additionally, the geographical proximity of the two countries – and ease of travel between them – should also be mentioned as important pull factors.

Determinants of sub-regional migration

Based on the results of the PMO Survey, it can be stated that migration of construction workers to the Oslo area has taken a sub-regional pattern (Figure 3.2), with four regions dominating as sources of this particular wave of labour migration. They are the Zachodniopomorskie *voivodship* (34 per cent), Pomorskie (16 per cent), Małopolskie (10 per cent) and Śląskie (less than 7 per cent).

When looking at the map of Poland, the bipolar location of the four

Figure 3.2   *Regions of origin of the interviewed construction workers (in %)*

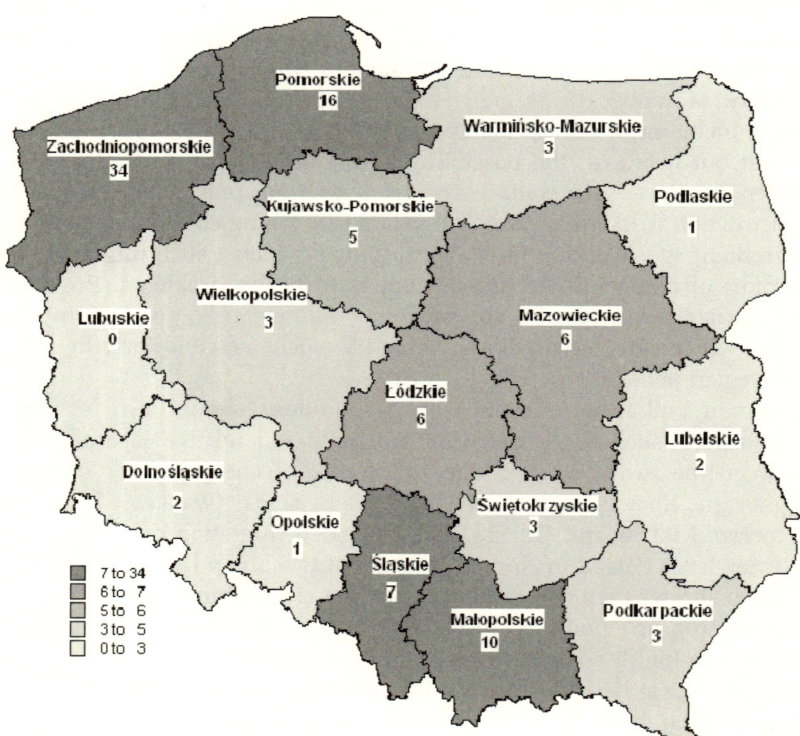

Source: Authors' own elaborations based on PMO Survey data

regions becomes conspicuous: Zachodniopomorskie and Pomorskie are neighbouring *voivodships* located on the coastline of the Baltic Sea in the north of Poland (with Zachodniopomorskie directly on the Polish-German border), while Śląskie and Małopolskie are both located in the south, on the Czech and Slovakian borders. While greater migration from the coastal *voivodships* appears to be more understandable – purely in terms of geographical location – the popularity of Norway among builders from the South is a more surprising phenomenon.

The following section attempts to pinpoint reasons for increased migration of construction workers from these four regions to Norway. We put forward the hypothesis that it is migration networks that have primarily channelled these flows of skilled labour.

The role of migration networks in shaping flows

Before we move to the role of migration networks in channelling the migration of Polish construction workers today, let us consider the issue of their earlier mobility patterns.

Migration histories

For Polish construction workers from the four regions, international mobility has been a much more popular strategy than internal mobility, i.e. within the home country.[7] All of the construction workers interviewed in Oslo who came from Małopolskie and Śląskie had previously worked abroad, as had the overwhelming majority of construction workers from Pomorskie (23 out of 25), and most from Zachodniopomorskie (42 out of 54). Thus, at 87 per cent, the vast majority of the sample group of Polish builders working in Oslo had already worked abroad.

Germany had previously been the most dominant destination country by far, with 70 per cent of the builders from the four regions having worked there previously (74 persons altogether, or roughly two thirds of workers from Zachodniopomorskie and Pomorskie, and roughly four in five workers from Małopolskie and Śląskie). The popularity of Germany partially stems from the fact that all the regions in question have established historical connections with the country (they were under German rule for certain periods), with many inhabitants having networks there (i.e. relatives, friends). Notably, a considerable number of the builders arriving in Oslo had worked in a number of other countries, mainly within Europe, but also in the Far East and the US. In this light, it appears that Norway is not only a new destination country for Polish construction workers, but also one that seems to have changed its traditional regional migration patterns.

Migration networks in Oslo

Undoubtedly, migration networks play a significant role in migration at every stage: from the moment of decision-making until returning to the home country (Guilmoto & Sandron 2001). Firstly, migration networks facilitate the decision-making process because they provide information to the prospective migrant that would be difficult to obtain otherwise. Moreover, the person deciding to migrate often leaves accompanied by somebody who had previously been to the country of migration. As such, migration networks not only facilitate access to the migrant labour market, but also intermediate in finding accommodation and accumulating social capital.

Generally, Polish migration to Norway would probably not have gained such momentum if it were not for existing migration networks. Asylum seekers who came to Norway during the political crisis of the 1980s in Poland played an important role in their formation. Owing to support on the part of Norwegian trade unions, persecuted members of the Polish Solidarity Movement and their families received asylum in Norway. However, not all families had the opportunity to emigrate at the time. In a number of cases, this was possible only after family reunion policies were introduced in 1989. While throughout the 1980s the number of Poles resident in Norway was still marginal, the early 1990s brought about a more substantial growth of the Polish community. It was only during that decade that Norway's Polish Diaspora, known as the Polonia, constituted itself. The Polonia would then help compatriots to come to Norway, particularly for seasonal jobs – namely, fruit-picking. Such seasonal migrations to the country, though not occurring on a large scale, resulted in a growing number of Poles having access to information on working and living conditions in Norway.

Migration networks indeed seem to play a significant role in channelling migration between the two countries. Data from the Polish 2002 census suggests that the existence of established networks may be the main factor determining flows from Poland to Norway, as the migratory movement to this country could predominantly be observed from given regions (Figure 3.3). In the case of the PMO construction workers, a high ratio from Pomorskie (almost three quarters: eighteen out of 25) and Zachodniopomorskie (34 out of 54) had fairly strong networks, as they knew both someone who had been to Norway before and somebody who was there at the time of their first arrival. In the case of the southern regions, however, this was not so common: as few as five out of the sixteen workers from Małopolskie and only one out of ten workers from Śląskie had such strong migration networks. A further number of migrants had weaker ties in Norway, again chiefly from the coastal regions: four persons from Pomorskie and eight from Zachodniopomorskie

Figure 3.3   *Intensity of migration to Norway per 1,000 citizens in the years 1990-2002 (by poviats)*

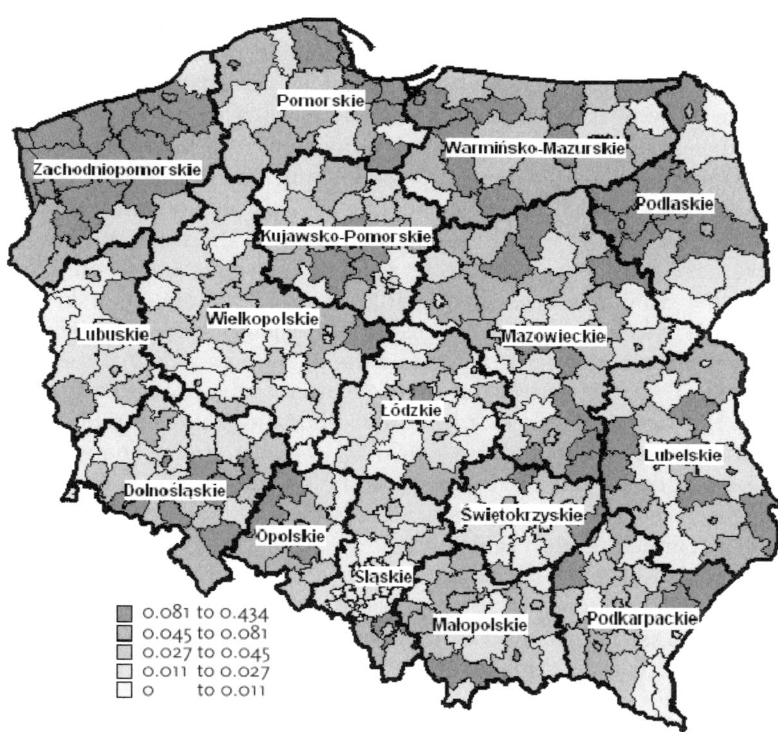

Source: Authors' own elaborations based on PMO Survey data

either knew somebody who had been to the country before or somebody who was in Norway at the time of their first arrival. The respective figures for Małopolskie and Śląskie were one and two.

While we can see that, in the case of the coastal regions, migration networks in the Oslo area are indeed strong and play an important role in shaping flows, the same cannot be said about the southern regions. In their case, the current migration wave of construction workers results chiefly from the dynamic operation of recruitment agencies: in both Małopolskie and Śląskie all migrants without migration networks were brought to Norway through recruitment agencies (nine persons from Małopolskie, and eight from Śląskie, respectively). This fact confirms the growing importance of agencies in channelling labour migration flows. It seems that recruitment agencies may effectively substitute migration networks not only in terms of providing information and facilitating the migration decision, but also by helping in the adaptation process, at least in its initial stages. Professional agencies typically offer language courses prior to migration and arrange for accommodation in the destination country.

As such, workers from Zachodniopomorskie present an interesting case. Out of the relatively high number of 36 persons who knew somebody in Norway at the time of their first arrival, as many as twenty had nevertheless decided to use a recruitment agency for intermediation. In comparison, out of the twenty persons from Pomorskie having such ties, only two decided to opt for an agency. This phenomenon could be explained by their respective network structures. The migrant networks of workers from Pomorskie were relatively stronger, based on family ties, whereas in the case of migrants from Zachodniopomorskie, the ties were weaker – primarily based on friends and/or colleagues. Another plausible explanation behind the phenomenon is that the headquarters of Adecco, one of the most dynamic agencies recruiting workers to Norway, is located in Zachodniopomorskie. This fact probably influenced those workers whose networks were not strong enough to arrange for employment in the country of migration. Under such circumstances, choosing an agency that assists with all necessary procedures is a much more reliable option.

As follows from the above analysis, in the case of the four Polish regions of higher outflow of construction workers to the Oslo area, migration networks play an important role in directing flows from two of them – the coastal regions of Zachodniopomorskie and Pomorskie. However, this does not hold true for the southern regions of Małopolskie and Śląskie. In their case, it was recruitment agencies that played a dominant role.

However, the existence of networks, on the one hand, or the operation of recruitment agencies, on the other, does not fully explain the reasons why construction workers from the four regions have decided to migrate. Let us now analyse the motives behind their decision and the push and pull factors connected with their local labour markets.

Regional labour markets and sub-regional migration patterns

Motives for migration

Respondents of the PMO Survey were asked to indicate two main reasons for their choice of Norway as a destination country in order of importance. A variety of responses were given by construction workers (Table 3.2).

Undoubtedly, the Norwegian wage level was the most significant factor in the decision-making process, and this holds true for workers from all four regions. In line with the argument above, in the case of the coastal regions, having migration networks also surfaced as a crucial motive. Workers from Zachodniopomorskie also emphasised the ease of finding work as highly important in the decision-making process.

The last two categories in Table 3.2 – not having a choice and other reasons than enumerated – present the most puzzling cases. Interestingly, in both Małopolskie and Śląskie, a considerable proportion of the builders interviewed (over one fifth and two fifths, respectively) stated that they had no other choice than to come to work in Norway. At the same time, however, the decision to go was their own. Other motives for migrating to Norway than those provided in the questionnaire were also pointed to relatively often, especially by workers from Małopolskie. Unfortunately, what is hidden behind the last two categories in Table 3.2 cannot be explained on the basis of the data received. However, because all the other reasons provided in the questionnaire were related to pull factors, we might presume that these two categories relate to push factors. Let us therefore turn to an analysis of possible push factors, i.e. the situation of the construction workers on the Polish labour market.

Structure of unemployment/employment on the regional labour markets

Unemployment is usually treated as the basic phenomenon underlying the situation on the labour market, and the unemployment rate is the principle measure of this situation (Grotkowska & Sztandar-Sztanderska 2005). We shall first take a closer look at Poland's employment conditions in general, and next at the selected regional markets.

Considering the general unemployment levels (December 2006), Zachodniopomorskie is in the worst situation out of the four major re-

Table 3.2 *Main reasons for coming to work in Norway in order of choice*

Choice	Zachodniopomorskie (N=54)		Pomorskie (N=25)		Małopolskie (N=16)		Ślaskie (N=10)	
	1st	2nd	1st	2nd	1st	2nd	1st	2nd
Norwegian wage level	28	15	21	1	10	4	9	1
Easy to get a job	3	19	-	4	-	-	-	1
Social welfare benefits	-	1	-	1	-	-	-	-
Knew someone who had been to Norway before	11	10	1	12	-	3	-	1
Friends/relatives already in Norway	2	-	-	-	1	-	1	-
Didn't have a choice	6	2	1	3	-	6	-	4
Other	4	7	2	4	5	3	0	3

Source: Authors' own elaborations based on PMO Survey data

gions of migration to Oslo, having the second highest unemployment rate in Poland at 21.2 per cent (Figure 3.4). In the other *voivodships*, unemployment levels are considerably lower: 15.5 per cent in Pomorskie, 12.9 per cent in Śląskie, and 11.3 per cent in Małopolskie, which is currently the lowest in Poland. As can be seen from the above figures alone, regional economies in Poland differ quite considerably.

As far as registered unemployment among the category of construction workers is concerned, it is fairly similar to the general unemployment rate in the regions concerned. Interestingly though, it is a few points higher in the south, at 15.3 per cent for Małopolskie, and 14.5 per cent for Śląskie. In Zachodniopomorskie, it is also slightly higher, at 22.1 per cent. In Pomorskie, in turn, at 14.1 per cent it is slightly lower than the general rate. Upon analysing the situation of the construction workers on the national labour market, it is important to underline that in Poland the structure of employment and rates of unemployment are also subject to regional variation, with reasons for unemployment differing considerably between the *voivodships* (Grotkowska & Sztandar-Sztanderska 2006).

An aspect of great significance in this respect is the age structure of the labour force. In Poland, the dominant group on the labour market

Figure 3.4 *Rate of registered unemployment in Polish voivodships in December 2006*

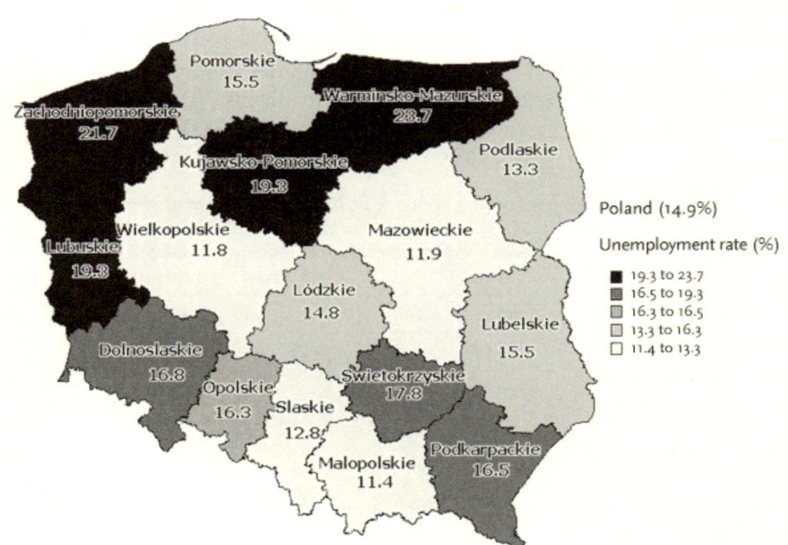

(ages 25-44) constitutes 54.4 per cent of the overall labour supply, and unemployment rates for this group generally show little regional variation. However, considerable differences are observable in the unemployment rate of the oldest labourers, i.e. the 45-54 age group. Moreover, in those *voivodships* where a high rate of short-term unemployment among those 45 and over was observed, a high rate of long-term unemployment for this group would also occur. Such is the situation particularly in Zachodniopomorskie. Małopolskie presents an exceptional case as far as durability of unemployment of those 45 and over is concerned: while the overall unemployment is relatively low in comparison to other regions, there is an unexpected overrepresentation of long-term unemployment for this group (the ratio of long- and short-term unemployed is 3.3, while the national average is 1.5).

Age is important for our analysis, too. Looking at the age structure of the migrant construction workers reveals that a relatively high proportion are 45 and over, especially in the cases of Śląskie and Zachodniopomorskie (Table 3.3). Considering this – along with the fact that older age is a barrier to employment in Poland's construction sector (though not in Norway) – we may consider this as an important push factor for the group under analysis.

The employment situation of the construction workers in Poland

As we have already noted, a considerable number of the construction workers arriving in Norway from the four regions of concern were 45 and over, an age group that is highly prone to unemployment on the Polish labour market. The question thus arises whether it was unemployment that had motivated them to migrate. As can be seen from Table 3.4, the majority of the construction workers were employed fulltime in the home country prior to coming to Norway. However, workers from Małopolskie and Zachodniopomorskie seemed to be in the least advantageous position, with a fairly high proportion of unemployed persons looking for work within the regional labour market before migration.

Employment stability on the local labour markets appears generally rather low, based on the type of labour contracts that many respondents

Table 3.3 *Numbers of construction workers aged 45 and over in selected voivodships*

	Zachodniopomorskie (n=54)	Pomorskie (n=25)	Małopolskie (n=16)	Śląskie (n=10)
Workers aged 45 and over	27	11	3	8
Workers aged 50 and over	8	10	1	4

Source: Authors' own elaborations based on PMO Survey data

Table 3.4 *Responses to the question 'What were you doing a few weeks before your first arrival in Norway?'**

	Zachodniopomorskie (n=54)	Pomorskie (n=25)	Małopolskie (n=16)	Śląskie (n=10)
Full-time employed in Poland	28	22	9	9
Part-time employed in Poland	2	-	1	-
Worked abroad	5	1	-	-
Unemployed, looking for work	15	1	5	-
Unemployed, not looking for work	1	-	-	-
Pupil/student	-	1	-	1
Other	3	-	1	-

Source: Authors' own elaborations based on PMO Survey data
* At the time of the survey, this was 70 per cent of the construction workers' first stay in Norway. As for workers from Małopolskie, it was the first stay for almost all of them (fifteen out of sixteen persons).

reported to have had (Table 3.5). Migrants from Śląskie are an exception here, as the majority were employed full-time for an indefinite period in the home country. Builders from Zachodniopomorskie also enjoyed fairly stable employment, with almost two thirds of respondents employed on a full-time basis. However, time-limited contracts appeared considerably more often in their case and, moreover, working on the basis of casual work contracts was fairly frequent. Workers from Pomorskie and Małopolskie, in turn, were more often subject to flexible employment forms, with a much lower proportion having full-time contracts. This is especially true for Pomorskie, where almost a third of the builders interviewed were self-employed. What is characteristic for all regions apart from Śląskie, is the high propensity towards illegal

Table 3.5 *Responses to the question 'On the basis of what type of contract did you work at your last job in Poland?'*

	Zachodniopomorskie (N=54)	Pomorskie (N=25)	Małopolskie (N=16)	Śląskie (N=10)
Permanent employment for an indefinite period	24	6	8	8
Time-limited: two years or more	6	3	-	1
Time-limited: 1-2 years	3	-	-	1
Contract for a specific task/ casual work contract	8	1	1	-
Verbal agreement	9	5	6	-
Irregular	-	2	-	-
Self-employed	4	8	1	-

Source: Authors' own elaborations based on PMO Survey data

employment. Over a third of workers from Małopolskie had been carrying out undocumented work in Poland, and the same is true of almost one third of those from Zachodniopomorskie and over one fifth from Pomorskie. It seems therefore that, for construction workers, the feeling of work stability was not high in their home country.

Still, if we consider the perceived possibility to remain in one's job as an indicator of the feeling of job security (Table 3.6), it seems that the type of employment contract was not so important. Surprisingly, workers from Śląskie – who enjoyed the 'safest' employment conditions, as the majority had permanent contracts for an indefinite period – felt relatively least confident about continuing work for their Polish employer. This would suggest that their companies faced some kind of problems or, simply, that the work had come to an end, thus influencing their future employment prospects. Almost one fifth of the workers from Zachodniopomorskie and one fifth from Pomorskie also felt insecure about their employment in Poland. Interestingly, however, builders from Pomorskie – most of whom were working either illegally or were self-employed – had a strong feeling of work stability, despite seemingly being most prone to frequent disruptions in employment.

Summing up, while unemployment was a push factor in the case of a minority of construction workers from the four regions (most acute in the case of Zachodniopomorskie), their overall employment situation could still have encouraged the decision to migrate. While a considerable proportion of builders from Zachodniopomorskie, Pomorskie and Małopolskie, in particular, were working illegally or on the basis of highly flexible arrangements, workers from Śląskie, despite having secure contracts, felt most apprehensive about their employment prospects.

Table 3.6   *Responses to the question 'Do you agree with the statement I could have stayed at my job in Poland if I wanted?'*

	Zachodniopomorskie (N=54)	Pomorskie (N=25)	Małopolskie (N=16)	Śląskie (N=10)
Agree (partly agree)	37	19	15	5
Neither agree nor disagree	5	1	-	-
Disagree (partly disagree)	11	5	1	4
DK/NA	1	-	-	1

Source: Authors' own elaborations based on PMO Survey data

Financial standing

Finally, we come to the economic situation of the PMO construction workers. As has been mentioned, the wage level difference between Poland and Norway was the main pull factor behind their decision to migrate. Let us thus see whether the workers were escaping hardship or simply seeking better remuneration for their work.

As data presented in Table 3.7 shows, the overall financial situation of the construction workers interviewed was fairly comfortable; most were able to support their families from the salaries received in the home country. Nevertheless, Śląskie represents an exception here, with the majority of respondents stating they were not able to live on their wages. Also, in the case of Zachodniopomorskie, a rather high ratio of one third of the workers was suffering hardship. This fact exemplifies the low wage level on certain regional markets, even in the case of professions that are very much in demand.

The answers to a series of questions relating to everyday expenses demonstrate the intensity of the problem, especially in the case of workers from Śląskie. As can be seen from Table 3.8, they suffered rather extreme hardship, having to limit expenses on food and clothes and being forced to borrow money for food or bills.

We may thus conclude that although the workers' financial situation was fairly comfortable overall, it was nonetheless a significant push factor for the majority of builders from Śląskie, one third from Zachodniopomorskie and the more than one fifth from Pomorskie who were actually living in poverty in their home country.

Conclusion

As may be concluded from the case studies drawn from the PMO Survey results, the migration of Polish construction workers to the Oslo area has taken on a sub-regional pattern. It is dominated by workers

Table 3.7   *Responses to the question 'Do you agree with the statement 'I was able to support myself and my family from my job in Poland?'*

	Zachodniopomorskie (N=54)	Pomorskie (N=25)	Małopolskie (N=16)	Śląskie (N=10)
Agree (partly agree)	34	16	14	2
Neither agree, nor disagree	1	3	-	-
Disagree (partly disagree)	18	6	2	8
NA	1	-	-	-

Source: Authors' own elaborations based on PMO Survey data

Table 3.8 *Respondents' financial situation prior to their first arrival to Norway*

	Zachodniopomorskie (N=54)	Pomorskie (N=25)	Małopolskie (N=16)	Śląskie (N=10)
I had to limit expenses on food				
Happened often	18	4	-	8
Happened sometimes	14	7	10	-
Never happened	21	14	5	2
NA	1	-	1	-
I had to borrow money for food				
Happened often	8	3	-	8
Happened sometimes	15	9	7	-
Never happened	30	13	8	2
NA	1	-	1	-
Couldn't afford new clothes or shoes				
Happened often	10	3	-	8
Happened sometimes	14	10	3	-
Never happened	30	12	13	2
I didn't have enough money to cover basic costs				
Happened often	11	1	-	8
Happened sometimes	16	11	7	-
Happened once	-	1	-	-
Never happened	27	12	8	2
NA	-	-	1	-

Source: Authors' own elaborations based on PMO Survey data

from four regions of Poland: Zachodniopomorskie and Pomorskie in the north, and Małopolskie and Śląskie in the south. But why do construction workers from these particular regions migrate specifically to Norway? There is a multitude of reasons behind this phenomenon. Having networks in the country of migration explains the phenomenon only partially. In the case of the coastal regions – Zachodniopomorskie and, in particular, Pomorskie – migration networks have played an important role in directing flows of construction workers to the Oslo area. As for Małopolskie and Śląskie, however, it was recruitment agencies that brought the majority of workers from the regions to Norway. The growing role of recruitment agencies is also exemplified by the case of Zachodniopomorskie, where many workers decided to opt for such intermediation despite having networks in Norway. We see thus how the role of recruitment agencies in channelling flows should not be underestimated in the case of skilled labour flows.

Considering the workers' migration histories, a tendency to choose Norway over the earlier dominant destination – Germany – is noticeable. This may be explained by the Norwegian wage level being higher as well as the altogether better work conditions in Norway. According to the migrants interviewed, Norwegian employers are highly recommendable, seen as honest, reliable and having a good attitude towards their staff. Moreover, they do not discriminate on the basis of age (as is often the case in Poland). This may be particularly significant for those 45 and over from Zachodniopomorskie (and to a lesser degree those from Pomorskie and Śląskie), where persons of this age are especially prone to (long-term) unemployment.

Push factors connected with the local labour markets also seem to play a significant role in shaping the sub-regional migration patterns of Polish construction workers to the Oslo area. In Zachodniopomorskie, unemployment, illegality of employment, older age and poor financial standing surfaced as meaningful push factors for roughly one third of the workers. For Pomorskie, the dominant feature of the local labour market was also a tendency towards illegal employment (almost one third of the respondents working on such a basis) and reliance on self-employment (also almost a third). Again, many of the workers were over 45, a factor making them especially prone to unemployment. However, in the case of builders from Pomorskie, the feeling of work stability was rather high and their financial situation fairly good, suggesting it was lack of employment contract – or its unbeneficial form – that had been the main push factor. Also, in Małopolskie a high proportion of the workers interviewed (over one third) were previously carrying out undocumented work. Furthermore, unemployment surfaced as a problem here as almost a third of the workers interviewed were unemployed and looking for work prior to migration. In the case of Śląskie, it appears that extreme poverty suffered by the majority of the construction workers, their older age and fears about their employment prospects forced them to decide to migrate, almost half stating they had no other option.

To sum up, Norway presents itself as a new 'promised land' to Polish construction workers from the four *voivodships*, for a variety of reasons. The sub-regional migration patterns of flows to the Oslo area appear to be determined by migration networks, the operation of recruitment agencies and additional region-specific conditions. Pinpointing the exact causes of these patterns requires further research.

Notes

1   The group of 'construction workers' was singled out by using the variable 'occupation by training' on the basis of construction and construction-related professions encompassing the following: steel fixer, carpenter, bricklayer, painter, plasterer, building technician, floor and wall tiler.

2   Information provided in this section is partly based on interviews conducted with experts from the Polish construction sector in three *voivodships* (Zachodniopomorskie, Pomorskie and Mazowieckie) in January 2007.

3   This state of affairs is slowly beginning to change, with a growing tendency among employers to arrange for transport.
4   It must be noted that the national average salary is based on data for all levels of employment in construction, including managerial, and thus is often considerably higher than the real salary of a skilled worker.
5   The Mazowieckie *voivodship*, where the capital city of Warsaw is located, is characterised by the highest rate of average pay in construction (39.4 per cent higher than in the national average).
6   In the third quarter of 2006, the average monthly wage in construction in Norway was NOK 29,000 gross (SSB 2007), which equals € 3,611.
7   The highest mobility within Poland was observed for construction workers from Śląskie: as many as eight out of the ten respondents had lived in other places than their place of origin. Śląskie was followed by Pomorskie (almost half: thirteen out of the 25 workers having lived in other places), Zachodniopomorskie (almost a third: seventeen out of 54) and finally Małopolskie (only a quarter had such experience).

References

Bolkowska, Z. (2006), 'Zatrudnienie, płace i koszty pracy w budownictwie' ['Employment, wages and Latour costs in construction'], paper presented at the conference 'Current employment situation in construction. Solution proposals based on the experience of the European Union', Warsaw, 4 December 2006.
Eurostat (2007), *EURO-Indicators, News Release* 20 February 2007.
Grotkowska, G. & U. Sztandar-Sztanderska (2006), *Bezrobocie w przekroju województw* ['Unemployment in *voivodships*'], report from the project 'Regional differences on the Polish labour market', www.rynekpracy.edu.pl.
Guilmoto, Z. Ch. & F. Sandron (2001), 'The internal dynamics of migration networks in developing countries', *Population* 13 (2): 135-64.
GUS/Central Statistical Office (2005), 'Praca nierejestrowana w Polsce w 2004r.' ['Unregistered work in Poland in 2004']. Warsaw: Główny Urzad Statystyczny.
GUS/Central Statistical Office (2006), *Information about the socio-economic situation of voivodships*, Report No 3/2006, Warsaw, December 2006.
Kaczmarczyk, P. & J. Napierała (2007), 'Labour market developments' in M. Kupiszewski (ed.), *Demographic development, labour markets and international migration in Poland – policy challenges*, CEFMR Working Papers 3/2007.
KPMG (2007), *Migracja pracowników: szansa czy zagrożenie?* ['Migration of workers: Opportunity or threat?']. Warsaw: KPMG.
Kus, J. (2006), *Undeclared labour in the construction industry. Country report: Poland.* European Institute for Construction Labour Research, June 2006.
MPiPS/Ministry of Labour and Social Policy (2007), *Aktualna sytuacja w zakresie budownictwa. Problem niedoboru wykwalifikowanych pracowników na polskim rynku budowlanym* [*The current situation in construction. The problem of labour shortages on the Polish construction market*]. Unpublished manuscript.
NHO/Confederation of Norwegian Enterprise (2006), *NHO's Economic Report.* Autumn 2006. 14 November 2006.

4 What's behind the figures? An investigation into recent Polish migration to the UK

Stephen Drinkwater, John Eade and Michal Garapich

Introduction

Migratory movements between the EU accession states and the United Kingdom following 2004 enlargement have been described as the largest-ever migration wave to have arrived in the UK (Salt & Rees 2006), and have already generated an increasing diverse set of scientific studies. It can be argued that this interest is not just attributable to the undisputable size of these flows. Because of their legal visibility, demographers, economists and sociologists have access to an array of datasets through which the composition of these flows can be analysed. This scientific visibility, which has been the result of a legal change, should not blind us from the fact that because of this, migration is part of a longer process and therefore pre-enlargement dynamics should also be taken into account. This relates not only to the labour market situation in both origin and destination countries, but also to the formation of transnational social networks, which perpetuate migration and remittance flows.

In this chapter we focus particularly on recent migration flows from Poland to the UK, exploring pre-enlargement statistics as well as current dynamics that are sustaining migratory flows. Although conditions in the labour market have changed recently, large numbers of Central and Eastern European migrants are still arriving in the UK (Accession Monitoring Report 2008). Following very high unemployment at the time of enlargement, with a national average of around 20 per cent, unemployment rates in Poland have dropped in some areas to UK levels. Yet, in spite of the visible decrease in the numbers of migrants from Poland, many still find employment in the UK an attractive opportunity for reasons that go beyond direct differences in earnings. This reminds us that migratory movements are not solely about levelling out wage levels, but also acquire a dynamic of their own due to the other, non-financial rewards.

Some of the other factors that impinge on such movements include the role of traditional migration strategies developed due to the under-urbanisation of communist states (Okólski 2001), transnational networks (Ryan, Sales, Tilki & Siara 2007), the role the migration industry plays in perpetuating a culture of migration in particular origin communities (Garapich 2008a) and migrants' attempts to offset the negative aspects of labour market discrimination, especially in relation to the position of women positions in the labour market (Coyle 2007). The strategic importance of communication and transport connections is also of relevance in this particular context (Vertovec 2007). The fast changing reality of contemporary economic factors in Europe reminds us that migrants – as individuals – respond and quickly adapt to changing conditions in the different settings in which they operate. Nevertheless, the passage of time since Polish accession to the EU allows us to look back, examining in more detail the migratory movements from Poland and answering questions regarding who, why and for how long such migrants have been coming to the UK.

The enlargement process and recent migration flows from Poland and other A8 countries

In 2003, the British government decided to effectively open up its labour market to migrants from new member states in Central and Eastern Europe (referred to here as A8 migrants). At that time, almost all EU member states had also agreed to do so, but the closer it came to the date of enlargement, more states decided to pull out of the agreement that established specific transitory periods. When enlargement thus took place in May 2004 only the British, Irish and Swedish governments decided to fully open their labour markets to A8 migrants – albeit with restrictions on access to public funds and some welfare provisions in the British and Irish cases. It has become common to attribute the UK's large influx of migrants to the transitional arrangements imposed by other states, but clearly one needs to take into account additional factors. First, migratory movements between Poland and the UK have been long established and, although small in number during the Cold War period, they have grown since the 1980s. This helped the formation of potentially important migration networks. For instance, ethnographic studies of Polish migrants have shown that the existence of the formal infrastructure of shops, churches and informal labour markets in certain areas has been a strong pull factor across generations of migrants (Garapich 2008b).

The UK's decision to allow more or less free entry in 2004 therefore not only opened a new chapter in these movements, but also accepted the reality that, by 2003, a large number of Poles had already come to the UK for various purposes, with many working illicitly. In fact, avenues with which Polish migrants could access the UK labour market were already manifold and the ease with which they could engage in the semi-compliant practices of migrant labour (Ruhs & Anderson 2006) proves that the labour market may have actually been open for many before 2004. The possibility of work as a self-employed person, on a student visa, as an au-pair through various exchange programmes and in particular sectors allowed strong networks to emerge and these were later tapped into by post-enlargement migrants.

The specific arrangements that the UK government imposed in 2004 also consisted of creating a formal way of registering migrants taking up employment: the Workers Registration Scheme (WRS). This was introduced partly in response to public fears about the free movement of labour from accession countries. Applicants were supposed to register on the scheme within one month of taking up employment, must register more than once if they have more than one employer and must also re-register if they change employers. The cost per registration was initially set at £50 but subsequently rose to £90.

The requirement that A8 nationals wishing to work in the UK for the first time should register on the WRS implies the existence of an administrative database providing an indication of inflows from these countries since 2004. Information from the database has been published on a quarterly basis by the Home Office (UK Borders Agency) in association with other government departments in the *Accession Monitoring Report*. This not only provides details of flows, but also reports some characteristics of the registrants. The questionnaire asks respondents to detail some basic demographic characteristics as well as information about the job they have taken or are about to take up. However, this is by no means a complete record of inflows since the self-employed are exempt from registration and it has been argued that relatively high proportions of A8 migrant workers have failed to register (CRONEM 2006; Anderson, Ruhs, Rogaly & Spencer 2006). It is possible to compare the WRS information with that from another administrative database, the Department of Work and Pensions' database on National Insurance Number (NINo) allocations to overseas nationals. Like the WRS, this database only records migrants entering the UK for the first time (for work-related reasons) and does not collect information on how long migrants stay or how frequently they move between labour markets. However, it does provide a more complete indication of A8 migration flows than the WRS because it includes the self-employed and non-registration is minimised since all legally employed migrants require a NINo. The database also provides information back to 2002, so we can examine some pre-enlargement flows. As it also records registrations from all other non-A8 countries, comparisons may be made.

We will therefore mainly analyse recent migration flows using NINo data, but supplement this with information from the WRS.

Figure 4.1 shows migration flows for three groups: Poles, other A8 migrants and a residual category consisting of migrants from all non-A8 countries. Probably the most notable feature of Figure 4.1 is the rapid growth in NINo registrations made by Poles in the two years immediately following enlargement. Registrations by this group almost quadrupled in this short period of time, from 61,000 in 2004-2005 to more than 220,000 in 2006-2007. This was followed by a relatively small drop (of around 10,000) in registrations in 2007-2008. Another observation is that, although flows of A8 migrants were small before enlargement, a not inconsiderable number of workers from these countries entered the UK prior to May 2004 – many of whom are likely to have been self-employed. For example, almost 6,000 NINo registrations were made by Poles in 2002-2003 and more than 11,000 in 2003-2004. Inflows from other A8 countries also increased rapidly, immediately after enlargement since they more than doubled between 2004-2005 and 2005-2006, to just under 100,000 in the latter year. However, in contrast to Poles, the number of NINo registrations made by nationals from other A8 countries fell by almost 10,000 between 2005-2006 and 2006-2007, with a further small fall in inflows observed in 2007-2008. In comparison, NINo registrations from non-A8 countries rose fairly steadily over the period, from 335,000 in 2002-2003 to almost 440,000 by 2007-2008.

Figure 4.1   *NINo registrations by nationality, 2002-2003 – 2007-2008*

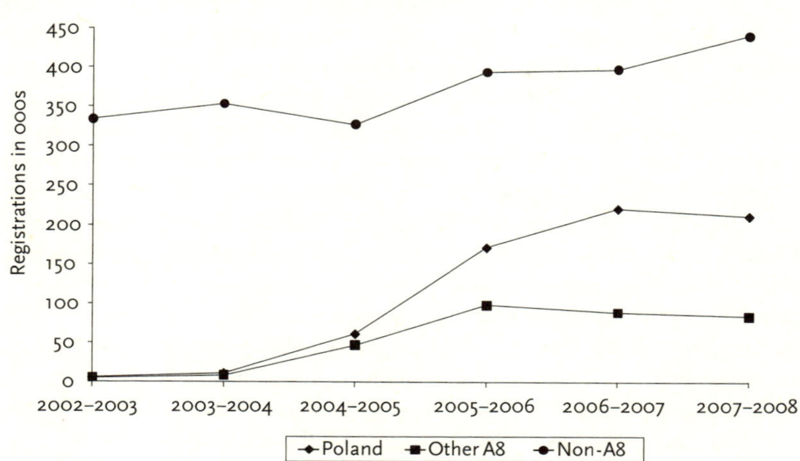

Source: Department of Work and Pensions

Thus, over the period covered by the NINo database for overseas nationals starting work in the UK for the first time, registrations by Poles were, by far, the highest of those from any single country. In total, more than 681,000 Poles were allocated a NINo from the start of 2002 until March 2008, which was almost treble the amount seen from the country with the next highest number of registrations: India (237,310). In terms of other A8 countries, nearly 100,000 registrations were made by Slovakians and Lithuanians and less than 10,000 by Estonians and Slovenians. Therefore, more than two thirds of the NINo registrations made by A8 nationals over this period were by Poles, despite Poland accounting for just over 50 per cent of the population of A8 countries at the time of enlargement. However, based on the NINo data, the country producing the highest volume of migrants as a percentage of its population was Lithuania (28.1 per million of the population), and was lowest for Slovenia (1.5 per million of the population). In comparison, the figure for Poland was 17.7 migrants per million of the population.

Further information on flows from A8 countries can be obtained from examining WRS data, as published in the *Accession Monitoring Report*. Figure 4.2 reports WRS registrations made by Poles and other A8 migrants on a quarterly basis from the time of enlargement up until the middle of 2008. It shows some of the same features indentified in Figure 4.1, including the fact that Polish migration to the UK rose rapidly until the end of 2006. Similarly, the initial rise in migration after enlargement from other A8 countries was followed by a relatively

Figure 4.2 *WRS registrations by quarter, 2004 Q2 – 2008 Q2*

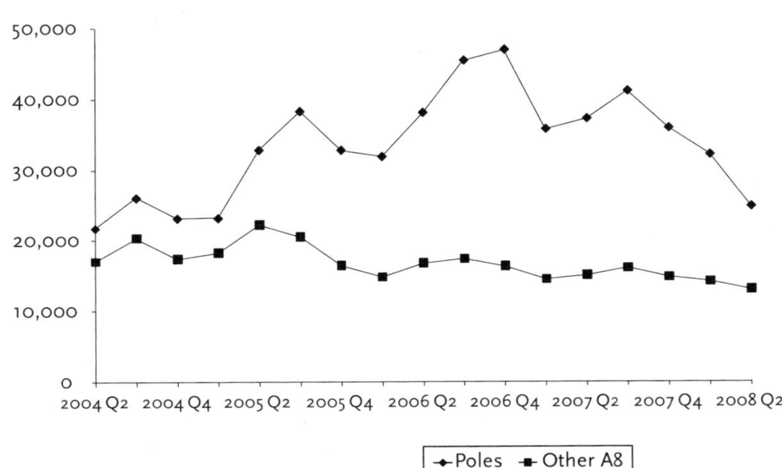

Source: Accession Monitoring Report

constant, albeit declining, stream of flows. The decline in migration from Poland in the past few years is highlighted more acutely in Figure 4.2, which shows that WRS registrations fell back to their 2004 levels in the most recent quarter. The reasons suggested for this fall include the improved Polish labour market, the depreciating value of the pound against the zloty and the movement of Poles to other destinations following the relaxation of the transitional arrangements by some other member states (Pollard, Latorre & Sriskandarajah 2008). An advantage of reporting flows on a quarterly basis is that it shows how the flows vary over the course of the year. It can be seen that registrations tend to peak in the third quarter i.e. the summer, especially for Poles, although the highest number of registrations of all for this group occurred in the fourth quarter of 2006. This would seem to indicate that there has been an important seasonal element to migration flows from A8 countries to the UK since enlargement – a point substantiated by surveys among Polish nationals in the UK (CRONEM 2006; Pollard et al. 2008) and entirely in tune with traditionally preferable patterns of migration from Poland since the collapse of communism marked by short-term, seasonal, 'incomplete' migrations (Okólski 2001, 2004).

Moreover, the nature of recent A8 migration has generally been different from the more permanent movements (especially from the New Commonwealth) that occurred to the UK during the second half of the twentieth century. In particular, a high proportion of the flows from Poland and other A8 countries has been seen on a short-term or circular basis. Evidence of this is presented in Table 4.1, which reports the responses to the question on the registrant's intended duration of stay in the UK that appears on the WRS questionnaire. The table indicates that only a small proportion of registrants, around 15 per cent, reported that they intended to stay in the UK for more than three months. This has been relatively constant since May 2004, with the remainder of registrants either responding that they intended to stay less than three months or did not know. There is, however, some variation in the

Table 4.1   *Intended duration of stay of registered workers, May 2004 – June 2008*

	May 2004– September 2006	*October 2006– September 2007*	*July 2007– June 2008*
Less than 3 months	45%	57%	61%
3-5 months	2%	2%	2%
6-11 months	3%	3%	3%
1-2 years	4%	4%	4%
More than 2 years	6%	8%	7%
Don't know/not answered	41%	26%	24%

Source: Accession Monitoring Report

breakdown of these categories over time, with a fairly even split in the immediate aftermath of enlargement, but a much higher proportion stating they intended to stay for only a short period in more recent times. Therefore, since the percentage of A8 workers stating that they intended to stay for two or more years has not exceeded 10 per cent at any point in the post-enlargement period, it appears that the vast majority of workers from these countries have moved to the UK on either a very short-term or on a circular basis.

Of course, one needs to be aware of these answers' limitations. Firstly, individuals are being asked the question at the beginning of their stay. Secondly, the WRS form is a government-backed questionnaire requesting personal details, thus potentially resulting in respondents understating their presence in the country. And finally, peoples' plans change. In addition, the question also relies on a rational actor model with an assumption that individuals do plan ahead and that the external economic conditions are constant. However, as other surveys of Polish migrants have shown (CRONEM 2006; Garapich 2008b), there is a stable percentage of individuals (around a third) who refuse to frame their migratory plans within a particular time period. This strategy of keeping options open – which has been labelled 'intentional unpredictability' – is particularly important during times of economic uncertainty. In summary, to contextualise Polish migration in terms of the temporal aspect of movements, we need to acknowledge not only the growing variety of different migratory strategies, but also the fact that these strategies have been actively updated depending on the economic situation in both countries.

There is also an obvious correspondence between the duration of a migrant's stay – either actual or intended – and the reasons why they have migrated. There is only limited information on the motivations of recent Polish migrants to the UK, although the available evidence points to a variety of motives for migration rather than just economic reasons. For example, a survey undertaken by CRONEM (2006) of more than 500 Polish migrants across seven locations in the UK found that, although financial reasons were selected most often (by 58 per cent of respondents), other factors were also important. In particular, 41 per cent of respondents said that they had moved to the UK because it was easier to live there or because it gave them more options and 31 per cent reported that it was for their personal or professional development. Lower proportions stated that they had migrated to escape from the political and economic situation in Poland or to improve the future of their children.

The information on NINo allocations and from the WRS relates to inflows essentially by those registering to work in the UK for the first time. Therefore, given the short-term nature of much of the flows from

A8 countries, these sources are not particularly useful in providing an indication of the number of Polish and other A8 migrants residing in the UK at any one time. To do so, one could use information from the Labour Force Survey (LFS) to estimate how stocks of A8 migrants in the UK have changed since enlargement. However, the LFS is likely to underestimate the number of A8 migrants because of its sampling frame, non-response and unsuitable sampling weights (Drinkwater, Eade & Garapich 2009). Nevertheless, several studies emphasise the rapid growth in the stock of A8 migrants residing in the UK. For example, Pollard et al. (2008) report that the stock of Polish-born residents in the UK rose from 84,000 in the beginning of 2004 to 458,000 less than four years later. The Polish-born population in the 2001 census was 58,000, which again points to fairly substantial flows prior to enlargement. They also estimate that over 600,000 A8 nationals were resident in the UK at the end of 2007, an increase of more than 500,000 over its pre-enlargement figure. In terms of all A8 migrant workers, Clancy (2008) estimates that there were 63,000 at the start of 2004, but this had grown to 510,000 by the beginning of 2008. However, because of the short-term nature of many of the migration episodes, Pollard et al. (2008) estimate that more than a million A8 migrant workers have arrived in the UK since the time of enlargement.

The demographic characteristics of recent Polish migrants

Not only is it interesting to examine the demographic characteristic of migrants in its own right, but we see how the composition of migration flows can have important impacts on both the source and receiving economies. For example, migrants' characteristics can have implications for brain drain and remittances for the origin country as well as influence economic growth rates and other macroeconomic variables in the destination country (Drinkwater, Levine, Lotti & Pearlman 2003). Again, because of the more comprehensive coverage of the NINo data, we will mainly use information from this source to examine the demographic characteristics of recent migrants, where they exist. However, because of the limited demographic information in the NINo database, we will also examine the characteristics of migrants from the WRS and the LFS, both of which contain a far more extensive range of socio-economic indicators, which is particularly true of the latter database. The NINo information is reported on a pooled basis from the start of 2002 up until the end of the first quarter of 2008 (i.e. up until the end of the financial year 2007-2008, which are the latest available data at the time of writing).

Table 4.2   *NINo registrations by gender, age and nationality: 2002-2008*

	Polish	Other A8	Non-A8
% male	57.18	51.96	51.80
% aged less than 18	0.31	0.68	1.39
% aged 18-24	41.32	41.04	31.45
% aged 25-34	41.12	38.90	48.24
% aged 35-44	10.12	11.81	13.59
% aged 45-54	6.21	6.43	4.11
% aged over 54	0.92	1.14	1.22
Total registrations	681,520	331,710	2,313,540

Source: Department of Work and Pensions

We begin by examining gender and age, as presented in Table 4.2. It can be seen that the percentage of males amongst recent Polish migrants is over four percentage points higher than recent migrants from other countries. In terms of age, around 80 per cent of recent migrants to the UK are 18-24. However, the age distribution of recent Polish and other A8 migrants is noticeably younger, with the 18-34 percentage being around ten percentage points higher than it is for non-A8 migrants.

The more dispersed location patterns of recent Polish migration to the UK in comparison to previous cohorts, and also to other groups of recent migrants, is displayed in Table 4.3. It shows that although London is still the most popular destination for Polish migrants, the concentration of recent migrants in the capital is far lower than it is from other parts of the world. In particular, around 44 per cent of non-A8

Table 4.3   *Regional distribution (in %) of NINo registrations by nationality: 2002-2008*

	Polish	Other A8	Non-A8
Scotland	9.2	6.4	5.1
North- East	1.6	1.2	1.8
North-West	8.9	7.4	6.3
Yorkshire and the Humber	6.8	7.2	4.7
Wales	3.0	2.3	2.0
West Midlands	7.7	6.7	6.0
East Midlands	7.8	7.6	4.1
East of England	9.0	10.2	6.7
South-East	11.7	12.2	11.5
London	22.9	26.8	43.8
South-West	7.1	5.8	4.4
Northern Ireland	3.4	4.8	2.3
Overseas Residents	1.0	1.5	1.3
Total registrations	681,520	331,710	2,313,540

Source: Department of Work and Pensions

migrants registering for a NINo since 2001 were located in London compared with only 23 per cent of Poles. The relative concentration in London by Poles is also four percentage points lower than it is from other A8 countries. Bauere, Densham, Millar & Salt. (2007) and Pollard et al. (2008) analyse the spatial dispersion of A8 migrants in further detail by examining the picture at the sub-regional level. They report that A8 migrants have located fairly large quantities in almost every local and unitary authority across the UK, including in some areas that had not seen any migration of note in the past.

Compared to other recent migrants, Poles are noticeably overrepresented in Scotland, the North-West and the South-West, whilst a relatively high proportion of recent migrants from other A8 countries have located in the East of England. The relatively low proportion of A8 migrants in London is also borne out by WRS and LFS data, although there are some differences between the data sources, which could be the result of the recording of the location of the place of work/residence as well as internal migration patterns following arrival in the UK. For example, the WRS indicates that more A8 migrants registered for work in Anglia and the Midlands than in London.

Table 4.4 reports a final set of demographic characteristics for recent immigrants to the UK using information from the LFS. The sample we use is based on pooling successive quarters of data together and is constructed by selecting only those migrants who entered the UK between 2004 and 2007, i.e. those arriving in the post-enlargement period. We also restrict the sample to those interviewed in their first wave and exclude full-time students (see Drinkwater et al. (2009) for reasons for doing this). The table indicates that just over a third of recent Polish migrants are married, which is higher than it is for other A8 migrants, but considerably lower than the observed figure for recent non-A8 migrants. Further confirmation of the fact that A8 migrants have generally migrated without families comes from the WRS, which suggests that less than 10 per cent of registered workers have brought dependants with them.

The table also reports that Poles are relatively highly educated. The measure of education is constructed using years of education and is

Table 4.4 *Other demographic indicators for post-enlargement migrants*

	Polish	Other A8	Non-A8
% married	36.1	31.3	55.8
% low education	9.1	18.8	16.3
% medium education	42.4	52.3	31.0
% high education	48.5	28.9	52.7

Source: Pooled LFS data, 2004-2007

based on the definition used by Dustmann, Frattini and Preston (2008) because of the difficulty in translating overseas qualifications into UK equivalents. In particular, almost a half of Poles were at least 21 years old when they left full-time education. This is slightly lower than the percentage of highly educated recent migrants from other countries, but less than 10 per cent of Poles left education before the age of seventeen, which is the lowest of the three groups. In comparison, recent migrants from other A8 countries have a much lower percentage of highly educated individuals as well as a higher proportion with low levels of education. However, many Poles and other A8 migrants have relatively weak English language skills. Evidence of this is provided by Clark and Drinkwater (2008), who use LFS data from the second quarter of 2006, which asked some limited questions on the English language to migrants. They report that A8 migrants were least likely to speak English at home and most likely to experience difficulties in the labour market as a result of their language capacities – or lack thereof. Further confirmation of this comes from Anderson et al. (2006), who find low levels of basic English language skills amongst A8 migrants working in low skilled sectors.

The labour market characteristics of recent Polish migrants

To analyse the position of Poles and other recent migrants in the UK labour market, we will mainly be examining data from the LFS. This information relates to non-student respondents who were interviewed in their first wave between 2004 and 2007 and who had begun arriving in the UK since 2003. We will, however, also supplement this with some information from the WRS. To begin with, Table 4.5 reports some basic employment indicators. It is noticeable that Poles have, by far, the highest employment rate of the three groups, with more than 85 per cent of recent migrants in work, which is also around ten percentage points higher than the overall employment rate in the UK labour market (Clancy 2008). The employment rate of other A8 migrants is also relatively high, whilst the much lower employment rate of other recent migrants not only reflects a higher unemployment rate, but also shows

Table 4.5 *Employment statistics for post-enlargement migrants*

	Polish	Other A8	Non-A8
Employment rate	85.2	76.5	63.6
Unemployment rate	6.2	11.2	11.8
Self-employment rate	4.7	5.9	6.4

Source: Pooled LFS data, 2004-2007

how this group displays higher levels of labour market inactivity such as individuals engaged in domestic care. Recent migrants are overwhelmingly found to be employed by others rather than running their own businesses. This is particularly the case for Poles who arrived since enlargement, a sharp contrast with the immediate pre-enlargement period when around a third of Poles entered as self-employed persons due to the prevailing immigration law at the time (Drinkwater et al. 2009). This sparked what became known as the 'Polish builder' or 'Polish plumber' phenomenon. It also explains why workers from the construction industry feature in a relatively minor way in the WRS, as many workers in this sector are self-employed. This may disguise some regional variation. For instance, among A8 migrants surveyed in one particular London borough, the rate of self-employment was around 25 per cent (Garapich 2008b).

In terms of the types of jobs that recent A8 migrants have found, the majority are in full-time employment. In particular, the WRS indicates that 86 per cent of registered workers work more than 35 hours a week. More detailed information on hours of work is available from the LFS. Drinkwater et al. (2009) report that, on average, recent Polish migrants work longer hours than other A8 migrants as well as those from other countries. Furthermore, more than a half of registered workers stated that their jobs were temporary, although the percentage of migrant workers stating they had temporary jobs was far lower in the LFS (Clark & Drinkwater 2008). Information on the industrial breakdown of those in employment is presented in Table 4.6 from the LFS and shows that the industrial distribution is very similar for recent Polish and other A8 migrants. For example, it indicates that almost 30 per cent of A8 migrants work in manufacturing. Not only is this much higher than the percentage of recent non-A8 migrants employed in this sector, but it also greatly exceeds the share of workers accounted for by manufacturing in the UK labour market, which has now declined to just 10 per cent. Although there is a higher concentration of A8 migrants in

Table 4.6   *Industrial distribution (in %) of post-enlargement migrants*

	Polish	*Other A8*	*Non-A8*
Manufacturing	29.5	29.1	13.8
Construction	8.8	8.7	3.8
Wholesale/retail	13.0	12.7	10.2
Hotels/restaurants	9.8	11.8	11.6
Transport/communications	11.2	13.9	5.1
Real estate/business activities	10.3	6.5	16.5
Health and social work	6.0	5.3	16.1
Other	11.5	12.1	23.0

Source: Pooled LFS data, 2004-2007

construction, these statistics again refute the popular view that Polish migrant workers are overwhelmingly employed in the building trade. A8 migrants are also overrepresented in transport and communications, whilst migrants from other countries are more highly concentrated in health and social work as well as real estate and business activities. The WRS also contains a breakdown of jobs by industrial sector. Since the sectors are not based on the standard industrial classification, however, it is difficult to make a comparison with the data from the LFS.

Further information on the types of jobs that recent migrants have obtained in the UK labour market can be found in Table 4.7 reporting the occupational breakdown. Again, the types of jobs, as defined on an occupational basis, is very similar for Poles and other A8 migrants. The very low percentage (less than 10 per cent) of A8 workers employed in professional and managerial positions compared to other recent migrants is particularly striking, with a correspondingly much higher proportion of A8 workers with routine and semi-routine jobs. In particular, almost 45 per cent of recent Polish and 50 per cent of other A8 migrants have routine occupations compared with only 15 per cent of other recent migrants. The WRS also collects data on the occupations of registered workers but, as with the industrial information, it is not based on standard classifications. Nevertheless, these data also indicate that the jobs in which A8 workers are employed are overwhelmingly low-skilled.

The type of jobs that A8 workers have typically found in the UK labour market, especially in terms of occupation, has resulted in relatively low earnings for this group, as reported in Table 4.8. Possible explanations for the concentration of A8 workers in low-skilled jobs include the impact of short-term migration strategies on job choices and the restrictions on the types of jobs available to workers with relatively poor English-language skills (Clark & Drinkwater 2008). This is in spite of Poles having relatively high levels of education, as shown in Table 4.4. Not only are average earnings much lower for A8 migrants than they are for those originating from outside the A8, but earnings for migrants from the new migrant states are also clustered around the bottom end of the pay distribution, as highlighted by the very low standard deviations and the relative proximity of the quartiles to the median. The

Table 4.7 *Occupational distribution (in %) of post-enlargement migrants*

	Polish	Other A8	Non-A8
Professional/managerial	7.8	7.1	45.8
Intermediate	18.4	18.3	17.8
Semi-routine	29.5	25.1	21.2
Routine	44.3	49.5	15.2

Source: Pooled LFS data, 2004-2007

Table 4.8   *Gross hourly earnings for post-enlargement migrants**

	Polish	*Other A8*	*Non-A8*
Mean	6.30	6.04	10.59
Standard deviation	2.77	2.99	8.13
1st quartile	4.94	4.65	5.51
Median	5.73	5.40	8.08
3rd quartile	7.07	6.89	12.68

Source: Pooled LFS data, 2004-2007
* Earnings are reported in May 2004 prices (£ per hour).

WRS also emphasises the compressed wage distribution of recent A8 migrants with 75 per cent of registered workers earning less than £6 an hour from the time of enlargement up until the middle of 2008 (Accession Monitoring Report 2008). Despite having slightly higher raw earnings than other A8 migrants, Poles have lower returns to their education because of their much higher levels of education (Drinkwater et al. 2009).

Conclusions

In the dynamic environment of both large flows of migrant labour and changing economic conditions in migration systems, predictions may be a risky endeavour. Nevertheless, it is clear from the size of Polish migration that fairly large numbers of nationals from the biggest of the accession countries are likely to become permanent settlers in the UK. The eventual proportion that does stay will depend on how well they progress through the British labour market, in addition to the relative conditions in the Polish labour market. Although the vast majority of recent Polish migrants initially found employment in low-skilled sectors, they are typically highly educated so many may be expected to move up the occupational hierarchy relatively quickly, especially with improving English language skills.

Furthermore, ethnographic data also shows that no matter what the proportions of long-term, short-term or seasonal migrants or those undertaking the 'intentional unpredictability' strategy are, all these behaviours are functionally connected. Settlers use the services and/or resources provided by short-term migrants who, in turn, get access to jobs, information and accommodation. Also, the operations of this large-scale 'migration industry' means that Polish migrants have created a small economy of their own which will always – more or less – generate employment and access to life in certain parts of the UK. In addition, unemployment in Poland is unevenly distributed. This means that migration will remain an attractive alternative for those from deprived areas who have benefited least from the so-far positive performance of the Polish economy following enlargement.

References

Anderson, B., M. Ruhs, B. Rogaly & S. Spencer (2006), 'Fair enough? Central and Eastern European migrants in the low-wage employment in the UK', *COMPAS Research Report*, University of Oxford.

Bauere, V., P. Densham, J. Millar & J. Salt (2007), 'Migrants from Central and Eastern Europe: Local geographies', *Population Trends* 129: 7-19.

Clancy, G. (2008), 'Employment of foreign workers in the United Kingdom: 1997 to 2008', *Economic and Labour Market Review* 2 (7): 18-30.

Clark, K. & S. Drinkwater (2008), 'The labour market performance of recent migrants', *Oxford Review of Economic Policy* 24(3): 495-516

Coyle, A. (2007), 'Resistance, regulation and rights. The changing status of Polish women's migration and work in the "New" Europe', *European Journal of Women's Studies* 14 (1): 37-50.

CRONEM (2006), 'Polish migrants survey results', *mimeo*, University of Surrey, www.surrey.ac.uk/Arts/CRONEM/CRONEM_BBC_Polish_survey%20_results.pdf.

Department of Work and Pensions (2008), *National Insurance Number Allocations to Adult Overseas Nationals Entering the UK 2007/8*.

Drinkwater, S., J. Eade & M. Garapich (2009), 'Poles apart? EU enlargement and the labour market outcomes of immigrants in the UK', *International Migration* 47 (1), 161-90.

Drinkwater, S., P. Levine, E. Lotti & J. Pearlman (2003), 'The economic impact of migration: A survey', *International Journal for Economic Development* 5 (2)

Dustmann, C., T. Frattini& I. Preston (2008), 'The effect of immigration along the distribution of wages', CReAM Discussion Paper No. 03/2008, University College London.

Garapich, M. P. (2008a), 'The migration industry and civil society: Polish immigrants in the United Kingdom before and after EU enlargement', *Journal of Ethnic and Migration Studies* 34 (5): 735-752.

Garapich, M.P. (2008b), *Between the transnational and the local. EU Accession States migrants in the London Borough of Hammersmith and Fulham*. Research Report, www.surrey.ac.uk/Arts/CRONEM.

Home Office, Department for Work and Pensions, HM Revenue & Customs and Department for Communities and Local Government (2007), *Accession Monitoring Report May 2004-June 2008*, www.ukba.homeoffice.gov.uk/sitecontent/documents/aboutus/reports/accession_monitoring_report.

Jaźwińska, E. & M. Okólski (eds.) (2001), *Ludzie na huśtawce. Migracje między peryferiami Polski i Zachodu [People on the swing. Migrations from Polish peripheries to the peripheries of the West]*. Warsaw: Scholar.

Okólski, M. (2001), 'Incomplete migration. A new form of mobility in Central and Eastern Europe. The case of Polish and Ukrainian migrants' in C. Wallace & D. Stola (eds.), *Patterns of migration in Central Europe*, 105-28. Houndmills/Basingstoke: Palgrave Macmillan.

Okólski, M. (2004), 'Migration patterns in Central and Eastern Europe on the eve of the European Union enlargement: An overview' in A. Górny & P. Ruspini (eds.), *Migration in the New Europe: East-West revisited*, 23-48. Houndmills/Basingstoke: Palgrave Macmillan.

Pollard, N., M. Latorre & D. Sriskandarajah (2008), *Floodgates or Turnstiles? PostEU enlargement migration flows to (and from) the UK*. London: Institute for Public Policy Research.

Ruhs, M. & B. Anderson (2006), 'Semi-compliance in the migrant labour market', COMPAS Working Paper No. 30.

Ryan, L., R. Sales, M. Tilki & B. Siara (2007), *Recent Polish migrants in London: Social networks, transience and settlement*. Swindon: Economic and Social Research Council End of Award Report

Salt, J. & P. Rees (2006), 'Globalisation, population mobility and impact of migration on population', ESRC Public Policy Seminar Series.

Vertovec, S. (2007), 'Circular migration: The way forward in global policy?', International Migration Institute, Working Paper No. 4, University of Oxford.

5 Markets and networks: Channels towards the employment of Eastern European professionals and graduates in London

Krisztina Csedő

Introduction[1]

Selective towards 'high skills', contemporary migration and mobility favours the well-educated, a growing share of whom move within globally integrated and expanding labour markets. Understanding this mobility is crucial because of its assumed impact on the global economy, politics and society. Attracting and retaining professionals is seen as a new tool for improving economic competitiveness and growth: young, highly educated, professional migrants add value to the economy through their supposedly high productivity rates. It is for this reason that countries are in competition for human resource skills perceived as representing national economic resources (see Salt 2005).

Yet, relatively little is known about the labour market incorporation practices of foreign professionals and graduates. Upon arrival to their destination they often become statistically, occupationally and socially 'invisible' (see Salt 1992; Findlay, Li, Jowett & Skeldon 1996; Favell 2004), making it difficult to research into the social practices of their labour market incorporation. What kinds of jobs do they actually obtain? How and why do they get those jobs? How are their credentials and work experiences recognised? Is the cross-border transfer of their human capital a seamless market process? On the one hand, the human capital approach assumes unproblematic labour market incorporation of 'highly skilled' migrants, mostly because of the assumption on which it operates: perfect transferability of human capital and its constant value on all markets (e.g. Sjaastad 1962; Becker 1964; Todaro 1976). If such an assumption is made, it is difficult to explain, for instance, why people with high human capital end up in semi-skilled or unskilled jobs at their destination. Sociologically orientated approaches to labour market incorporation, on the other hand, point out the existence of barriers to the cross-border transfer of human capital. Various host institutions such as the labour market, educational and social welfare institutions or immigration policy may limit foreign professionals' and graduates' chances of gaining employment suitable to their formal education and training (see Reitz 1998; Zulauf 2001; Reitz 2002; Waldinger & Lichter 2003; McGovern 2007). Furthermore, compared to semi-skilled and un-skilled migrants, social networks play a different role in facilitating the search for employment by the highly skilled. Meyer (2001) found that professionals tend to rely more on extensive, diverse networks of colleagues, fellows and relatives who they can mobilise for their recruitment, rather than addressing their own kinship networks.

In this chapter, I will analyse some components of foreign professionals' and graduates' labour market incorporation practices. I seek to understand how various types of professional and graduate migrants – both so-called 'cosmopolitans' and 'home-oriented' – signal their availability and find out about job openings on the destination labour market. I will also investigate whether social networks facilitate their labour market incorporation and, if so, what kind of networks and how.

Analysis in this chapter relies on data collected between January 2005 and June 2005 as part of my doctoral research on the social process of East-West mobility of professionals and graduates. The chapter is based on qualitative material, principally 54 semi-structured interviews with Hungarian and Romanian professionals and graduates in London, as well as seven interviews with London-based employers of Eastern Europeans with third level education.

Based on Jones' (1996) sociological approach to labour market processes, this chapter analyses socially constituted 'stages' to understand Eastern European professionals' and graduates' social practices of finding employment in London. The steps of socially constituted labour markets can be split into five conventionally defined stages: accreditation, signalling, screening, bargaining and secondary bargaining. Of all five stages, signalling is the most socially grounded. It denotes the way in which employers make job vacancies and requirements public and how would-be employees communicate their availability and quality to employers or agents. Signalling can occur through various channels – market or non-market – such as kinship or friendship groups (strong ties), acquaintances and professional groups (weak ties), as well as through multi-functional institutions (internal labour markets).

This chapter focuses on the social organisation of the signalling stage only: how do Eastern European professionals and graduates find out about job openings and signal their availability and productive capacities to London-based employers? Emphasising the social aspects of market exchanges encourages here a greater focus on individual agency, on dynamic exchanges between labour market participants and on the social process of ascribing value to individuals' human capital.

The chapter is organised as follows: first, I will discuss briefly the current state of literature on professionals' and graduates' possible labour market signalling channels and their network-dependence when looking for jobs abroad. Turning to my empirical evidence, I will differentiate between Eastern Europeans with high human capital who move through, respectively, markets and networks, and I will analyse their different social practices of signalling productive capacities. When discussing the role that social networks may play in facilitating the process of getting a job in London, I will address the role of professional and ethnic ties separately. Finally, I will argue that social networks may have a centrifugal role in sorting professionals and graduates into different labour market positions in London: professional ties are conducive to the achievement of higher positions; ethnic ties lead to positions that are lower than what is achievable for market movers without professional or ethnic social capital in London.

Labour markets and social networks

Most research suggests that non-market channels, especially weak ties, are more successful than market channels in flows of information between labour market participants (Granovetter 1982; Waldinger 2001). Similarly, non-market channels have long been identified as crucial to the economic behaviour of migrants (e.g. Fawcett 1987; Massey & España 1987). Scholars have repeatedly found that migrants' labour market incorporation and occupational attainment at their destination is dependent on their social capital. Hence, in migratory contexts, the channels to employment are often discussed in relation to non-market mechanisms, i.e. social networks. While semi-skilled and unskilled migrants' employment searches have often been found to be facilitated by strong ties (Massey, Alarcón, Durand & González 1987; and many others), there is little evidence for professional migrants' network-dependence when looking for jobs at their destination. If they use any networks to access the labour market, professionals are found to rely on occupational or industry ties (see Findlay & Garrick 1990; Beaverstock 1996b; Findlay & Li 1998; Meyer 2001), rather than on relatives or friends.

Amongst the respondents interviewed for this study, some did indeed signal their availability by using social networks; whilst others found out about job openings in London directly from the market. The channels to employment they used were tied in with what they expected from their mobility to London.[2] I have identified four different types of Hungarian and Romanian professionals and graduates in London, based on their motivations to work abroad (cosmopolitans vs. 'the home-oriented') and their social practices of finding out about job openings and/or signalling their availability to employees (market vs. network) (Table 5.1). Similar to Findlay and Li (1998), I have also found

Table 5.1 *Labour market practices*

Signalling through	Cosmopolitans	Home-oriented
Market/non-network channels	Individual developers	Individual diversifiers
Non-market/network channels	Elite movers	Traditional migrants

that migrants' motivations influence the kinds of networks they use in order to find employment abroad, and that these four types of movers delineate four different social practices of labour market incorporation. In the following sections I analyse market and network movers' practices in turn.

Market movers: Individual 'developers' and 'diversifiers'

Despite evidence for migration being dependent on social networks, a significant part of my interviewees used market channels to find employment in London. Similar to Poros' (2001) 'solitaries' or Favell's (2006) 'free movers' to London, many Hungarian and Romanian professionals and graduates did not rely on any occupational or industry ties to signal their availability to employers. Rather, they applied online for various openings, uploaded their CVs on jobseekers' websites or relied on an agency to find a job. The labour market, as the dominant channel for signalling availability and learning about job openings, was most frequently used by graduates and young professionals who had only a few years of work experience. Having limited access to such positions in their home labour markets or to wage levels they would expect to be suitable for individuals with their level of education, they gravitate towards labour markets perceived to be meritocratic and rewarding. Since many job advertisements are published on the internet, they are accessible from anywhere, making cross-border application for jobs easy and virtually free of charge. Moreover, some websites allow jobseekers' registration of interest even without suitable openings, thus enabling employers to search within an international skills pool whenever they look for new recruits. This particular strategy was used by one architect who, though he could imagine working in London for a while, preferred to wait for a suitable job offer instead of searching 'full-time' for employment.

> I had in the back of my mind that I would like to work once in London. So when I was fed up with my work in Budapest I looked around on the internet at half steam, sent out a couple of CVs and registered here and there with some agencies. I thought if somebody is showing interest, then I will decide whether I

really want to work in London or not. (Ferenc, Hungarian architect in London, 2004)

Young professionals such as Ferenc, looking for new challenges abroad, ultimately sought to develop their human capital at a global, cosmopolitan level within their specific profession, industry or both. They learned about open positions in employers' advertisements and they completed online forms, often while still studying or working in a different job. They lacked the social ties needed to find out about openings of their interest, so they relied exclusively on the market. The following story of this postgraduate from a British university is typical.

> I found out about job openings through email, [the website] jobs. ac.uk, newspapers or the internet. Nobody drew my attention to any jobs. [...] When I was called for an interview with my present employer, I had no more idea of how this employer is than the others. For me, it was a job application, like all the others – the 41st line of the Excel table that kept my applications in order. ... My slogan was 'Apply, apply, apply!' After a while, I lost track of deadlines, how many applications I filed and where, so I had to start a list. I knew the rule of thumb: if after three weeks I didn't hear anything, it meant I should not wait anymore. (Dan, Romanian lecturer in London, 1997)

For many graduates and young professionals, applying for jobs in London was an intensive and often lengthy process. Upon filing many applications my interviewees learned that – in Dan's words – 'if I don't apply 50 times, I won't pass the first step, which is the pain of being rejected 49 times' They also learned 'that failure is not necessarily a negative sign'. Yet, at the point of signalling availability, failing to pass even the first round of selection represented a very difficult lesson in the process of obtaining a job in London.

> I have fallen flat on my face good couple times. You submit your online application, which you have been working on for two nights and, after ten minutes, you receive an automatic email thanking you for your application and pointing out that, after careful consideration and due to the large number of applicants and their unusually high qualification levels, unfortunately your application cannot be taken forward. (Bence, Hungarian investment banker in London 2004)

Most of the individual developers I interviewed, the cosmopolitan market movers, obtained their first jobs in London by pursuing this kind of competitive, highly selective process. First they would apply – and be rejected – for many jobs, usually in finance, IT and academia, but also in consulting or architecture. They would then be interviewed a couple times, over the phone and in person. And finally, they would be offered one or two jobs.

The signalling process was less complex for individual diversifiers, the 'home-oriented' market movers, who look for jobs in London in order to learn better English, to gain new skills and experiences and perhaps to earn more. Their less advanced language skills make them hesitant to look for jobs that suit their qualifications, yet they, too, rely on the internet.

> I started to look online for possible jobs [as an au pair] in London. I found some portals which mediate between families and students wishing to work as au pairs. There are many. You can upload photos, create a website for yourself. I registered my profile on a couple of websites [...] and it was the family which I work for now that found me. First, we started to exchange emails, then spoke on the phone twice, and we found we could relate to one another, so I came. (Anikó, Hungarian au pair in London, 2004)

Inquiring about how they signalled their availability to British employers, I found that most individual movers – especially the cosmopolitans, but also the 'home-oriented' – withheld some information for the sake of preferential screening. During the process of signalling, interviewees preferred to draw employers' attention to their level of education and work experience in general. However, they chose to share the least possible information about their background, origin or reason for wishing to work in London. Taking advantage of the online application process, in the first round, they preferred to avoid mentioning their geographic location so as not to elicit any ethnic stereotypes that their prospective employers may have had. A business graduate I spoke with believed she had to withhold this information in order for employers to screen her application.

> If I send a CV to a private company, it will go straight in the bin because of the word Romania' on it. If I want a job in a public company, I cannot get it because their policy is to employ only people from the EU or the Commonwealth. [...] So I changed my strategy and reduced the occurrence of 'Romania' on my CV to the absolute minimum. (Rodica, Romanian production operator in London, 2003)

Withholding information about their background was more frequent among Romanian respondents than their Hungarian counterparts. They believed they would only be guaranteed meritocratic screening if they provided incomplete information. The reason for withholding these 'non-essential details', as one Romanian lecturer pointed out, arose from a complex about being stereotyped based on their origins.

> When applying for this job, I explained vaguely what the situation is: that I am a student at this and that [British] university. I don't think I specified that I was actually a visiting student from Romania, studying here for four months only. I tried to avoid as many details as possible since I thought that being specific would ruin my chances of getting this job. You know, how employers' stereotypes work: the more honest you are, the less you remain with. So I chose for not telling some things that I was doing; I did not lie to employers; I was concentrating on telling only the essential details. (Sergiu, Romanian lecturer in London, 1998)

My interviewees highlighted the need to direct their potential employers' attention. They preferred to have employers concentrate on advantageous characteristics of their human capital (such as credentials, knowledge or particular skills) and ignore the details perceived as non-advantageous (such as their non-British permanent domicile, their need for a work permit and/or the fact that English was not their first language). Overall, my interviewees sought to show that they are not different from their British counterparts. Dan pointed out that he did not want to be screened as 'a Romanian wanting to work in Britain'; he wanted to signal that he operates in the same mindset as everybody else within the same profession.

> I was concerned [about my Romanian citizenship]. No need to hide this. Despite all the affirmation I received that I was good, I was concerned that the system would work against me just because I am Romanian. This is part of the heavy Romanian legacy. So I never put on my CV that I need a work permit in Britain. I didn't want all my applications to end in the trash because of this. I simply wanted to be a British graduate; I was not a Romanian wanting to work in Britain. I wanted to show that I operated with the same mindset as all my colleagues from Manchester or Edinburgh who applied for the same academic jobs. I did not want to stand out as being different from the viewpoint of immigration policy; I wanted to stand out because I am good. (Dan, Romanian lecturer in London, 1997)

All my cosmopolitan-minded interviewees' accounts, including Dan's, show that when signalling availability, professional identity overwrote ethnic identity. They did not want to be screened as Romanians or Hungarians, the stereotypically 'impoverished' Eastern Europeans wishing to work in Western Europe; rather, they wanted to find jobs as well-educated bankers, academics and architects who happen to have been raised in a different country and speak a non-English mother tongue. They expected British employers to act under a universal frame of reference, within which credentials and experience make the difference rather than ethnic belonging. Yet, while expecting this, they did presume that ethnic stereotyping creates in fact a dual frame of reference, based on which employers screen natives and foreigners differently (and thus they preferred to withhold information about their ethnic belonging).

As it turns out, Waldinger and Lichter (2003) found how employers do use a dual frame of reference. Employers hiring for unskilled jobs say that immigrants are useful precisely because they *are* different from natives, which makes them ideal candidates to fill jobs others do not want. In the case of professional and graduate jobs, however, my interviewees wanted to be hired because they *are not* different. Not wanting to stand out meant they sought to apply for the same jobs as the British, and they expected British employers to rely on a single frame of reference. Therefore, unless they filled in skill shortages on the labour market, these cosmopolitan foreigners sought to compete with professionals and graduates from around the world, including the United Kingdom.

Network movers: Elite movers and traditional migrants

The market mover interviewees, especially the cosmopolitans, were proud to be able to compete on the labour market with other professionals and graduates from around the world. As Dan pointed out, Eastern Europeans' ability to compete with other professionals provides a sense of self-justification: their Eastern human capital could actually be high enough to fill Western vacancies. Being able to compete on the market showed the value of their human capital and, as many highlighted, *not* their social capital. Referring to what they perceive as a clientelistic and nepotistic 'system' at home, interviewees highlighted how getting into the labour market without having to rely on social capital was an indicator of merit. It was not their occupational or industry ties nor their kinship or friendship ties that permitted them to obtain a job in London, but rather, their credentials, work experience, language knowledge and particular skills. According to Tilly (2006), a lack of reliance on social networks leads to the democratisation of migration:

cross-border mobility also becomes possible for those who lack the relevant social capital that contributes to the decrease in costs of migration (including initial help and information flows). Yet, some interviewees acknowledged that social ties make the process of signalling more efficient.

> I have to say that social ties have opened up the doors for me, this is true. Nevertheless, they were not relevant during the recruitment process. I am convinced that social ties do not matter so much in Britain as performance and a daring attitude. This is the huge difference between Britain and Hungary: here, they would take you on board if you are good but not connected. In Hungary, they wouldn't. (Arnold, Hungarian investment banker in London, 1999)

Being embedded in social networks decreases the time and costs of job-seeking, since individuals do not, like Dan, have to file 50 applications in order to be rejected 49 times (see also Fawcett 1987; Massey et al. 1987; Findlay & Garrick 1990). Also, social ties allow circulation of more information about the job and, indeed, about the applicant than what the job description or a cover letter contains, thus making speculations about employers' single or dual frame of reference unnecessary. Favell, Feldblum and Smith (2006) suggested that individuals with high human capital would do better if they had equally high levels of social capital. This is not surprising. Social networks have long been identified as crucial to the economic behaviour of migrants. On the one hand, Massey et al. (1987) and Beaverstock (1996a) emphasised immigrants' reliance on social networks to find out about job openings or to signal availability to employers about jobs that have not yet been advertised. On the other hand, Waldinger and Lichter (2003) extensively described employers' reliance on social ties when signalling job openings and requirements. In fact, contemporary ethnographies document the tendency of employers to rely on immigrant social networks as their primary recruiting tool (Bean, González-Baker & Capps 2001). Nevertheless, the dominance of social networks has the potential of organising labour markets to partially closed, rather than open, competition for jobs (Bach 2001), thus limiting the process of democratisation of migration.

A common turn of phrase I heard during my interviews was something akin to 'an opportunity popped up and I took advantage of it'. This often referred to an idea put forward by a former colleague, an acquaintance or a friend of a friend about a possible job in London. Whether based on occupational, industry or community ties, the primary role of these links was to transfer signals of availability in two directions: from employer to future migrants and vice versa. In general, when social networks helped Hungarian and Romanian professionals and graduates find employment in London, signals reached experienced professionals through professional ties (elite movers) or ethnic ties (traditional migrants).

The professional networks of elite movers

Many of my interviewees arrived in London through intra-company transfers within major professional services providers. This was especially the trend during the 1990s when many Western companies outsourced or off-shored functional practices to Eastern Europe, usually for lower costs; these processes are well documented (see Martin 1999; Taplin & Frege 1999; Commander & Köllő 2004). At that time, internal moves within multinationals were relatively easy, especially for Hungarians (many multinational companies established their Hungarian offices shortly after the fall of the Iron Curtain; their Romanian offices followed five to ten years later). A Hungarian professional working in one of the big accountancy firms in Budapest recalled how easy the transfer was for her. The company took care of all work-related arrangements, including work permits.

> I told one of the partners that I would like to come to work in London for a while. He picked up the phone and that was it: I could come for two years. [...] Basically, I was handed over to London. My contract didn't contain a clause of return, London was paying my salary and Budapest stopped being concerned about me. (Dóra, Hungarian auditor in London, 1998)

Less experienced intra-company transferees than Dóra needed more than a phone call to obtain an assignment in London. Yet, with suitable knowledge of English, credentials and a willingness to work abroad, young professionals could obtain temporary assignments to London. These assignments were not only – but typically – within professional services firms, as a journalist I spoke with said.

> In our organisation, everybody can apply to work in a different country for a while. You just submit an application and, if you are successful, you can go; the company takes care of your replacement until you are away. [...] One of my colleagues left the London office to work somewhere else and, since I spoke good English and my employers were generally happy with what I did, I was called to London to replace her. Basically, my move to London was originally an intra-company transfer. (Árpád, Hungarian journalist in London, 2000)

The mobility of staff within multinational organisations has also been well documented (see Salt 1992; Beaverstock 1996b; Findlay et al. 1996; Beaverstock 2005). Scholars agree that intra-company transferees move along the network of offices of multinational corporations, typically towards global cities, where headquarters are often found. Multinational companies also actively encourage the global mobility of their employees. Confirming what my interviewees said, the human resources consultant of a major international financial organisation noted how mobility between headquarters and employees' home country is strongly encouraged.

> We have offices all over the world, and a lot of our [graduate] candidates may start in London, but then they may well move back to their home countries or may well move to a different region. And that is something we encourage. We actively move people geographically. (HR consultant in a major international financial organisation in London, 2002)

Similar to intra-company transfers, mobility prospects also arose for professionals when two or three firms merged and the restructuring created opportunities to change jobs, locations or functional areas. A Hungarian professional with many years of work experience whom I interviewed received a job in London as the outcome of mergers and acquisitions.

> Our company was restructured and, as always, there are opportunities around restructurings. [...] One of my options was to come internally [to London]. I was asked to build up a regional procurement business for our firm. All my life I was doing these 'building-up' things, so I thought I might even do it in London as well. (László, Hungarian director of a company in London, 2000)

In general, those Hungarian and Romanian professionals and graduates who signalled their availability or found out about job openings though occupational ties responded to labour market demand that was often connected to skill shortages in London. Some of my professional interviewees, almost all working in financial services, were head-hunted from London during the early 2000s, when the city's markets were booming and there was a shortage of individuals with experience (especially those experienced in emerging markets such as Hungary or Romania).

> My current employer head-hunted me from Hungary. I had been doing business with them, but from the other side. One day, out of the blue, a woman called me on my mobile, asking whether

> I'd be up for switching sides and do what she does now. [...] And
> even though I had a very good job at home, I didn't hesitate for a
> moment about whether I'd like to come or not. [...] It was such
> an opportunity that it was impossible to be left behind. (István,
> Hungarian investment banker in London, 2002)

Recruiting talented people from Hungary or Romania to work in more
challenging and better-paying jobs in London was a practice used by
London-based employers around the years of the dotcom boom. Many,
like István or Cristian, cited below, had been working for British companies while based in Hungary or Romania, and they all received job offers from London.

> Our company had many contracts with companies abroad and
> we had a huge client in Britain. This client offered my boss a
> job, which he accepted. Then, they offered me a job and some of
> my colleagues too. [...] Initially, I rejected the offer, but after a
> year they approached me again. (Cristian, Romanian engineer in
> London, 2001)

Cristian elaborated on how the best IT engineers were 'drained' from
Romania during the dotcom boom via international corporations.
London was struggling with skill shortages, and Romania had lots of
good engineers; by offering higher salaries and challenging jobs, talents
could be easily transferred to Britain. As another interviewee pointed
out, however, it was not only British partners who 'drained' talents from
the East. In his company, the very best employees were putting pressure
on their British partner firms to employ them, or else they would quit.
Despite contractual limitations between the collaborating Romanian
and British companies regarding cross-company recruitment, the
British firm had no choice but to breach the agreement and take on the
best specialists rather than let them move to the competitors.

> My company in Bucharest worked with a British company. The
> Romanians used to come to Britain for short assignments. After
> a couple of assignments, some of them told the British partner
> that they wanted to work for them and not for the Romanian
> company. Obviously, the main reason was financial. The problem
> was that our companies had a contract saying that partners could
> not take on the employees of the other [company]. Yet, the de-
> mand for our knowledge was so high on the British market that
> the Romanian employees had a strong case. They said that if the
> British partner didn't take them, they would go [and work] some-
> where else. Therefore, the British partner had no choice but to

breach the contract with the Romanian partner and take their IT specialists on board. At least ten came to the same UK employer that time. (Kálmán, Romanian engineer in London, 2000)

Using client-partner relations to signal job openings or productive capacities was not only specific to certain occupations, but characterised entire industries. From the end of the 1990s up until 2001, when the IT bubble burst, IT specialists were in high demand in the UK. As such, it was typical for them to experience internal or cross-company transfers during this period. In the early 2000s, the place of IT specialists was taken over by those working in financial services, especially investment bankers and financial lawyers who spoke various languages and had some experience in emerging markets.

Looking at my interviewees who used professional ties to signal their availability or to find out about job openings, I realised that the non-market, network-based signalling is a very selective social process. Only the most experienced or highly specialised Hungarians and Romanians have professional social capital that they can convert into employment benefits in London. Professional networks – by providing the right signals to the right people – select the very best of their field in Hungary and Romania. They gave relevant, detailed information for network movers in a more accessible, less costly and less time-consuming way. Much like any other social networks, professional networks lowered the social and economic costs of job-seeking. More importantly, they minimised the risk of applying for the wrong job and maximised the chance of making the 'right choice'. Through professional ties, applicants learned not only about specific openings, but also about the actual tasks that may not be included in the prospective job's advertisement. As the following interviewee pointed out, network movers do a better self-screening before applying.

> The institute I worked for earlier has some ties with the one in London. Basically, the director from here is a good friend of the director in my previous organisation. So this opening was well advertised for me. I knew exactly what I would be doing, how much experience they needed, how much time the job would take, what opportunities are available, and so on. I found out about many details of the job, and all were relevant for me. So I said, OK, I will apply since it seems to be the right choice. (Georgiana, Romanian researcher in London, 2004)

Another interviewee also described how some information about possible jobs, their content or relevance is simply not circulated openly.

> Getting a job here is tightly linked to networking, to the people
> you know and your personal initiative. [...] If you don't take the
> initiative to go, to call, to meet people, to ask for information, no-
> body cares about you. Without personal interaction you cannot
> find out anything about the system, how things work, who is
> doing what and what the planned projects are for the future.
> (Sergiu, Romanian lecturer in London, 1998)

It became increasingly clear from my interviews that professional social
capital represents a source of labour market segmentation. Eastern
Europeans in professional or higher managerial occupations in London
seemed to have much more extended professional networks than those
in lower-level service-class jobs. While it is difficult to pinpoint whether
professional social capital was the cause or the consequence of obtaining higher-level service-class jobs in London, it seems certain that they
went together. A Romanian consultant within an international financial
institution talked about the importance of building and cultivating professional and occupational networks.

> Professional networks are very important at my level. [...] It is a
> skill to generate and maintain networks. Your networks come
> firstly from your colleagues. The likelihood of their being from
> good families [with a] good background is bigger, as they ended
> up at the same place as you did. By 'good' I mean similar to
> yours. Good for you. [...] How a network gets bigger and deeper,
> that depends on you. It is a skill and it also depends on the num-
> ber of years you spend in a certain country. First, I started my
> network by getting in contact with people from here [through] re-
> lying on my relations at home. Then I had to nurture, develop
> and maintain all the new contacts: I am constantly expanding
> them. [...] Building professional networks is the only type of so-
> cial relations I put energy into. (Mircea, Romanian consultant in
> London, 1993)

Mircea's opinion is shared by a Hungarian director within a large multinational corporation. He argued that experienced professionals' friendship networks need to overlap with their professional networks.
Networking consists of learning about business opportunities, better positions, possibilities for cooperation and financial prospects rather than
about shared values or interests.

> My life has almost always been about work, and that is how it
> will be in the future. [...] At my level, the question is rather how
> much time and disposition I have to build personal relationships

outside the business... or, should I build personal relationships within the business? And I do build my relationships within the business. It simply offers more. (László, Hungarian director in London 2000)

Professional networks are generally homogenous when it comes to the occupations of their members. This was not typical for the experienced Hungarian and Romanian professionals only; expatriates were found to spend much of their time socialising with other expatriates in their host country who usually have similar occupations, rather than with host country nationals or their co-ethnics (Johnson, Kristof-Brown, Van Vianen, De Pater & Klein 2003). This suggests that foreign professionals sought relationships with like-minded people sharing professions, experiences or relevant characteristics. Such individuals not only represented business or career opportunities and provided social support in a new environment, but were also found to impact the success of international assignments overall (Black 1988).

Typically, my interviewees' professional networks, through which they signalled their availability or disposition for employment in London, were formations that while occupationally homogeneous, are also ethnically heterogeneous. Networks were formed primarily through work: current or former colleagues exchange information about job openings with former or current employers. Nurturing professional ties with former colleagues could lead to the formation of transnational professional networks since my interviewees were geographically mobile themselves, constantly between positions and countries. Some interviewees even mentioned feeling globally well connected. As Mircea, a Romanian consultant and frequent traveller noted: 'London has business with the world. [...] My job is very internationally oriented. Ninety per cent of my professional contacts are outside Britain'. The international dimension of the jobs of most professionals, the elite movers, makes them well integrated into professional labour markets.

Another type of transnational professional network was formed while studying abroad, usually in the UK or the United States, and subsequently keeping in contact with former colleagues from the university. A Romanian lecturer who completed an American postgraduate degree pointed out that, in cities such as London, it was relatively easy to stay connected with university alumni because London proves attractive for many other 'spiralists' like herself.

> Most of my contacts in London are colleagues and friends from the US: those who graduated from my university and also came to work in London. Or not only London, also Oxford or Cambridge. We managed to develop strong friendships on

> campus back in the US; now these alumni ties form a strong
> professional network, and we keep ourselves informed about the
> latest opportunities. Not having time to develop new relation-
> ships, this network is my most significant source of 'professional
> gossip'. (Irina, Romanian lecturer in London, 2002)

Besides being ethnically heterogeneous, the professional network membership was gendered. I found that women were less likely to rely on
professional networks when signalling availability or learning about job
openings than were men. While young male graduates usually signalled
their availability on the market, experienced male professionals' mobility almost exclusively relied on professional ties. This finding is not unique to my research. Some studies highlight that many moves that occur as intra-company transfers may be arranged through male networking (see Kofman & Raghuram 2005). Women's social networks'
composition, range and, often, geography differ from those of men.
Alongside their careers, women need to take care of family and friendship ties, thus limiting their time for building professional networks.
Another interviewee pointed out the disadvantages she experienced
from not seizing the opportunity to build professional networks.

> During my MBA, I did not properly understand the importance
> of building a [professional] network, and every day I had to bring
> our child to school and back. So I had to dash off after the lec-
> tures, whereas the others – mostly men – stayed on and met up
> during the evenings in the neighbouring pub. Because my hus-
> band was working and I had to take care of our family, I there-
> fore missed out on the major part of networking so important
> during an MBA. Nowadays, I could contact my former MBA col-
> leagues – and I know most of them are still in touch with each
> other – but it would come across as a bit strange: I wasn't a
> drinking buddy for them. (Mariana, Romanian consultant in
> London, 1993)

Women's professional networks were also restricted because they are often 'trailing spouses', rarely lead migrants. Frequently, their partners'
career benefited from the cross-country mobility, while the women were
expected to be adaptive followers, even if their own professional networks – should they exist – would send them to different destinations.
These women experienced a devalorisation of their productive functions
and a relegation to the domestic sphere (see also Yeoh & Khoo 1998;
Yeoh & Willis 2005). The gendered nature of professional networks,
however, has consequences. Because they are not as embedded in professional networks as men are, women's mobility between and within

firms was less likely to be prompted by arising opportunities than by a need to accommodate their partner's career moves. This is a common finding of studies on professional mobility: in many instances, the husband's career takes precedence. Moreover, there may be no appropriate employment available for well-educated women where the husband's career takes the family, especially if spouses work in different sectors (Kofman & Raghuram 2005, 2006).

While my interviewees' professional networks were typically gendered and ethnically heterogeneous, a particular form of professional network still needs to be mentioned: that of graduates and young professionals from Hungary and Romania who studied in their respective home countries yet ended up together in London. These young networks were ethnically homogeneous, though it was common profession and schooling that held these networks together rather than shared ethnicity. A young Hungarian investment banker first drew my attention to the phenomenon.

> It is very common to meet Hungarians in the City [financial district known as the City of London] who were once members of one of the colleges for advanced studies. Some are here, others were here but have already left. And through the college alumni networks you always find out who is currently in London. (Máté, Hungarian investment banker in London, 2004)

I found at least two ethnically and occupationally homogenous young professionals' networks in London. One exists for finance graduates from Budapest University of Economic Sciences who, during their undergraduate studies, were members of colleges for advanced studies and after graduation started entry-level jobs in the City of London. Bence pointed out how networks formed in their home country facilitate transnational information exchange between various cohorts of graduates. Members of the networks could learn from one another. They exchanged information about occupational and career standards in their profession, contributing thus to the formation of their reference group, as well as about the city's stance on the labour market.

> I know several Hungarians who graduated with my specialisation. Just from my year, there are four here; we were all part of the college for advanced studies. There is surely a mass attraction in the story: one graduate comes after the other. You hear what a cool job the other has and you wish the same for yourself. [...] It is difficult to say, though, who came to London first. We all applied independently, but then ended up here at the same time. [...] Thirty to 40 per cent of my main friendship circle from home is now in

London, and it also represents quite a good professional network. (Bence, Hungarian investment banker in London, 2004)

These graduates, and indeed many other Hungarian young professionals, would often meet on Wednesday evenings in a City of London pub called the 'Pubszerda'. Providing an informal institutional framework for professional network-building, the Pubszerda was considered a great place to socialise, exchange information and network for young investment bankers working locally. However, professionals not in the financial sector would find the Pubszerda less useful for widening their professional networks.

My knowledge about these Pubszerda youngsters is quite superficial. [...] It is not my main pathway, so to say. The major part of the Hungarian professional community specialises in finance, and I do not. I will gladly talk with them for a couple of hours, but I am not sure that I am interested in so many details about what happens in the City, and who made a transaction of how many billion pounds. The majority of these kids cannot stop gossiping about the City. I am simply not interested. (László, Hungarian director in London, 2000)

Although Hungarian finance graduates working in the City formed a strong ethnically and occupationally homogenous professional network in London, the same picture did not emerge for Romanian graduates of the Academy of Economic Sciences. Romanian IT graduates – namely, young engineers – were young professionals whose social networks in London were similar to Hungarian finance graduates. Their network was formed typically less on the basis of common studies than from having shared a prior employer, either in Romania or in London. Almost all IT engineers pointed out that Romanian programmers form a loose professional network in London.

In my first job in Britain I worked with colleagues from Romania. We were practically relocated from Romania to Britain. [...] It was a pleasant group of people, we were also friends, with pretty similar interests. [...] We still keep in touch, although we work for different employers now. You know, in every software company in the UK you surely find two to three Romanian programmers. (Cristian, Romanian engineer in London, 2001)

Yet, Romanians also had a semi-formal institutional framework for professional network-building. As one interviewee pointed out, the Romanian Business Club was established with the deliberate aim of increasing networking opportunities among Romanian professionals in London, mainly those working in the City.

> There were multiple elements that led to the establishment of the club. [...] It is a great networking opportunity. You not only meet similar people from different companies, so you can hear all the business gossip, but you also can find out about business opportunities, even in Romania. Additionally, you can socialise with Romanians, make friends. Nevertheless, there are always interests in the middle. Everybody is busy, generally, so there have to be some tangible outcomes of the participation. [...] To be concrete: on the one hand, networking; on the other hand, business opportunities. The social facet is of tertiary importance. [...] I was indeed keen on meeting other Romanians, as I hardly knew anybody [in London]. But of course, I was also curious: what are the others working in? Who are they? And so on. [...] I have found some great friends at the club. And, of course, we have also done some business together. (Mircea, Romanian consultant in London 1993)

The Romanian Business Club shared very similar goals to the *Pubszerda*'s initial aims. Both sought to network with co-ethnics working in the City in the hope of exchanging business information and City gossip as well as to socialise. For this reason the perceived 'problems' with the club were the same as those experienced by the *Pubszerda*. Membership of this professional network was enticing for bankers and lawyers working in the City, but non-bankers were less interested in the opportunity to obtain first-hand information about local business exchanges.

The ethnic networks of traditional migrants

Grudges held against ethnically homogeneous networks did come up during my interviews. This happened once I shifted from speaking with Hungarian and Romanian investment bankers, lawyers and IT engineers to speaking with business developers, architects, journalists, doctors and academics. This group of professionals, who did not work in the City, were not particularly interested in topics such as how many financial transactions took place in the City or detailed information about mergers and acquisitions. It was the rule rather than the exception that, at one point during the interview, my respondents noted how shared ethnicity was not enough for them to maintain social relations with other Hungarians or Romanians in London. A shared profession *and* ethnicity was a good facilitator for information exchange about the professional labour market. However, as mentioned earlier, ethnically heterogeneous professional networks were more effective when signalling availability or looking for openings. A Hungarian physician with twenty years of work experience was one of the few interviewees to touch upon the very essence of the unsuitability of ethnic networks when looking for professional jobs. As she suggested, co-ethnics generally have non-influential positions in London. Ethnic networks are therefore ineffective at placing members in higher professional or managerial jobs in London.

> The Hungarian [doctors] from London are very nice and lovely, but everywhere bosses are British. So the Hungarians from here are not in a position to be able to help [to find professional jobs]. Everybody is enthusiastic and encourages me [...], but nobody is actually helpful. (Anna, Hungarian physician in London, 2004)

In fact, when I asked interviewees about the ethnic background of three persons whose advice they would consider when looking for a job, only 10 per cent replied that all three people would be of their ethnicity. For 26 per cent, two out of three would be of their ethnicity. For 23 per cent, one out of three. The majority, 41 per cent of the survey respondents, would not turn to their co-ethnics to find a job in London. Another interviewee's response corroborated this, despite his working in an altogether separate industry and at a different level.

> When I arrived in London I didn't look for a company of Hungarians. Quickly, I realised that there is a strong positive correlation between the quality of the job you can get here and the number of your non-Hungarian acquaintances. And I needed a good job, since all this is about money. [...] Only after the summer did I start to look for Hungarians; they are nice chaps, we have great parties on the weekends, but that is it. (Sándor, Hungarian manager in London, 2004)

Poros (2001) also found that those who rely on interpersonal – that is, ethnically homogenous kinship or friendship ties – are likely to be under-employed. A lack of organisational ties fails to channel well-educated migrants into occupations consistent with their prior education or experience; community ties, however, make employment opportunities less stable. It would be wrong to argue, however, that my interviewees have not relied at all on ethnically homogeneous interpersonal ties. Sándor's observation was nevertheless true: ethnic ties, not being useful for obtaining highly skilled jobs, often perpetuated jobs within the low-skilled sector. This was verified by a Romanian geography graduate working as a plasterer whose brother encouraged him to come to London and also helped him find a semi-skilled job in the construction industry.

> I came to London because of my brother. I am staying with him now. Initially, I didn't know how the story of self-employment works, so my brother told me everything about it. First, I worked with a false name through a construction agency as a labourer. But then I quit because friends told me I should go into restaurants since [the restaurant industry] pays more. So I did. But I was sacked because I was working full-time and I didn't have the right to do so. So I had to return to construction. My brother organised a job as a plasterer for me. (Eugen, Romanian plasterer in London, 2003)

Similar to the example of Eugen, the following advertisement was posted on one of the email groups sought to recruit those who – mostly because of their poor English language skills – would have struggled to find jobs elsewhere in the labour market:

> If you would like to work for a five-star hotel or you know somebody who is looking for work, call me or drop me an email. Big chances of getting employed, even with very little English knowledge! Next round of interviews is on next Saturday. A wide variety of positions is available, depending on experience and education. (advertisement in Hungarian on the 'Magyarkocsma' email group, 20 March 2007; my translation)

While cosmopolitan-minded interviewees did not rely on ethnic ties during the signalling process for the very reasons mentioned by Anna and Sándor, the 'home-oriented' movers were more likely to take advantage of them. The reason for this was not that ethnic communities circulate more information about better-paying jobs; rather, 'home-oriented' movers' lack of English proficiency made it difficult for them to access the British labour market. This delivers yet more evidence of the strong labour market segmentational power of local language knowledge. For 'the home-oriented', ethnic communities were the most effective social institutions to channel information about job openings or productive capacities.

Overall, looking at the signalling process and employment outcomes of the Hungarian and Romanian network mover professionals and graduates, I have found that social ties 'scatter' my respondents on the labour market of London. Professional ties facilitate obtaining higher professional and managerial jobs because they connect individuals in the same industry. Moreover, they were effective channels of information about the position and its requirements. Ethnic ties, how-ever, were likely to channel my well-educated interviewees into routine and manual occupations in London. Social ties thus have a centrifugal role on the labour market, depending on the kinds that facilitate the sig-nalling process, sorting individuals into higher or lower labour market positions than what they could have obtained would they have moved exclusively on the labour market.

Conclusion

In this chapter I have showed that amongst Hungarian and Romanian professionals and graduates, the process of searching for employment in London is not always based on the mobilisation of social networks. Many of my interviewees were individual market movers who not only chose London as a destination on their own volition, but signalled their availability to potential employers exclusively on the labour market and who learned about job openings via advertisements often posted on the internet. Nevertheless, I have also argued that the process of signalling is facilitated by social networks. Some of my interviewees relied on pro-fessional or ethnic ties in order to get access to – or at least obtain em-ployment-related information about – the labour market situation in London. The cosmopolitans were more likely to signal their availability through professional ties, or on the market; the 'home-oriented' relied on signalling on the market, or through ethnic ties.

My findings confirm, as well as expand upon, the current literature. On the one hand, my research presents further evidence to support Favell's (2008) findings regarding the free, market-regulated mobility of the young and well-educated Europeans – 'Eurostars' – within the in-creasingly interconnected markets of the EU. The present research broadens the geographical coverage of the phenomenon by showing that some Eastern Europeans are a part of that segment of the intra-European mobile workforce who would not have moved, were it not for the favourable structural and institutional environment that facilitates mobility within Europe. With time, this could potentially lead to the de-mocratisation of migration within the region (see Tilly 2006). Also, si-milar to Findlay and Garrick (1990), Bagchi (2001) and Meyer (2001), I have also found that when networks facilitate professional and graduate migrants' employment search at their destination, they are overwhel-mingly formed by weak ties.

On the other hand, I also show that, despite witnessing how some signs point to the democratisation of migration within Europe, Eastern European professionals and graduates still have reservations about being accepted as integral players with full rights in Western European markets. The market movers, in particular, have a strong desire to show conformity to British professionals' and graduates' profiles, norms and standards of behaviour. They are likely to withhold information that is not directly related to their human capital (and which make them stand out as 'East Europeans' such as their country of birth, foreign education or their need for a work permit) in order to prevent employers from acting on stereotypes. Therefore they seek to *not* stand out because they are foreigners. They wish that British employers would use a single frame of reference when screening their applications (for the contrary, see evidence from the US in Waldinger & Lichter 2003).

Furthermore, I have also argued that social networks contribute to the sorting of migrants with similar levels of qualification into more polarised labour market positions in their country of origin, depending on the composition of these networks. Professional network embeddedness facilitates access to higher professional and managerial jobs in London. Professional network ties result in former colleagues or students with similar occupations working in the same industry; they are ethnically heterogeneous and gendered (i.e. predominantly male). Embeddedness in ethnic networks channels well-educated migrants into routine and manual occupations, transforming the migration patterns of the well-educated into those of unskilled or semi-skilled traditional migrants. Ethnic networks are occupationally heterogeneous and rarely comprise co-ethnics with influential positions who could channel employment signals towards professional and managerial jobs.

Overall, I found that social networks seem to be important yet invisible sources of labour market segmentation in London. Not only do Eastern European professionals and graduates self-select according to their social network membership (cosmopolitan vs. 'the home-oriented'), but network-based signalling is also highly selective among professionals. If Eastern Europeans are members of a professional network, it is easier for them to surpass various labour market processes. This is more difficult, time-consuming or both for individual movers and even more so for members of non-professional, ethnically homogenous networks. Yet, if social networks have a centrifugal force on London's labour market, the process of accreditation or employers' social practices of screening may not be as meritocratic as many foreign professionals and graduates perceive them to be.

Notes

1   This chapter is an abbreviated revision of a paper prepared for the IMISCOE Cluster A2 conference entitled EU Enlargement and Labour Migration within the EU that took place on 23 and 24 April 2007 at Warsaw University. I am thankful to Richard

Black, Godfried Engbersen and Marek Okólski for their valuable comments on the presentation in Warsaw and to the IMISCOE reviewers for their comments on earlier versions of this chapter.

2   In my PhD dissertation (Csedő 2009), on which this chapter is based, I showed how the Hungarian and Romanian interviewees have different expectations from their mobility: the so-called 'cosmopolitans' operate under global, occupational standards, seeking to obtain the maximum achievable returns to their human capital and the highest benefits in their profession; the 'home-oriented' operate from a home-country, cohort-based viewpoint, seeking to realise more than what is achievable at home for their peers of similar education.

References

Bach, R.L. (2001), 'New dilemmas of policy-making in transnational labor markets' in W. A. Cornelius, T.J. Espenshade & I. Salehyan (eds.), *The international migration of the highly skilled: Demand, supply, and development consequences in sending and receiving countries*, 113-130. San Diego: University of California, Center for Comparative Immigration Studies.

Bagchi, A.D. (2001), *Making connections: A study of networking among immigrant professionals.* New York: LFB Scholarly Publishing LLC.

Bean, F.D., S. González-Baker & R. Capps (2001), 'Immigration and labor markets in the United States in Í. Berg & A.L. Kalleberg (eds.), *Sourcebook of labor markets: Evolving structures and processes*, 669-703. New York: Kluwer Academic/Plenum Publishers.

Beaverstock, J.V. (1996a), 'Migration, knowledge and social interaction: Expatriate labour within investment banks', *Area* 28 (4): 459-470.

Beaverstock, J.V. (1996b), 'Subcontracting the accountant! Professional labour markets, migration, and organisational networks in the global accountancy industry', *Environment and Planning A* 28: 303-326.

Beaverstock, J.V. (2005), 'Transnational elites in the city: British highly-skilled inter-company transferees in New York City's financial district', *Journal of Ethnic and Migration Studies* 31 (2): 245-268.

Becker, G. (1964), *Human capital: A theoretical and empirical analysis, with special reference to education.* New York: Columbia University Press for the National Bureau of Economic Research.

Black, J.S. (1988), 'Work role transitions: A study of American expatriate managers in Japan', *Journal of International Business Studies* 19 (2): 277-294.

Commander, S. & J. Köllő (2004), 'The changing demand for skills: Evidence from the transition'. Bonn: IZA Discussion Papers No. 1073.

Csedő, K. (2009), *New Eurostars? The labour market incorporation of East European professionals in London.* PhD Dissertation. London: London School of Economics and Political Science.

Favell, A. (2004), 'London as Eurocity: French free movers in the economic capital of Europe', *GaWC Research Bulletin* 150, www.lboro.ac.uk/gawc/rb/rb150.html.

Favell, A. (2006), 'London as Eurocity: French free movers in the economic capital of Europe' in M.P. Smith & A. Favell (eds.), *The human face of global mobility*, 247-274. New Brunswick/London: Transaction.

Favell, A. (2008), *Eurostars and Eurocities: Free movement and mobility in an intergrating Europe.* Oxford: Blackwell.

Favell, A., M. Feldblum & M.P. Smith (2006), 'The human face of global mobility: A research agenda' in M.P. Smith & A. Favell (eds.), *The human face of global mobility:*

International highly skilled migration in Europe, North America and the Asia-Pacific, 1-25. New Brunswick: Transactions.

Fawcett, J.T. (1987), 'Networks, linkages, and migration systems', *International Migration Review* 23 (3): 671-680.

Findlay, A.M. & L. Garrick (1990), 'Scottish emigration in the 1980s: A migration channels approach to the study of skilled international migration', *Transactions of the Institute of British Geographers* 15 (2): 177-192.

Findlay, A.M. & F.L.N. Li (1998), 'A migration channels approach to the study of professionals moving to and from Hong Kong', *International Migration Review* 32 (3): 682-703.

Findlay, A.M., F.L.N. Li, A.J. Jowett & R. Skeldon (1996), 'Skilled international migration and the global city: A study of expatriates in Hong Kong', *Transactions of the Institute of British Geographers* 21 (1): 49-61.

Granovetter, M. (1982), 'The strength of weak ties. A network theory revised' in P.V. Marsden & N. Lin (eds.), *Social structure and network analysis*, 105-130. Beverly Hills: Sage Publications.

Johnson, E.C., A.L. Kristof-Brown, A.E.M. van Vianen, I.E. de Pater & M.R. Klein (2003), 'Expatriate social ties: Personality antecedents and consequences for adjustment', *International Journal of Selection and Assessment* 11 (4): 277-288.

Jones, B. (1996), 'The social constitution of labour markets: Why skills cannot be commodities' in R. Crompton, D. Gallie & K. Purcell (eds.), *Changing forms of employment. Organisations, skills and gender*, 109-132. London/New York: Routledge.

Kofman, E. & P. Raghuram (2005), 'Gender and skilled migrants: Into and beyond the work place', *Geoforum* 36 (2005): 149-154.

Kofman, E. & P. Raghuram (2006), 'Gender and global labour migrations: Incorporating skilled workers', *Antipode* 38 (2): 282-303.

Martin, R. (1999), *Transforming management in Central and Eastern Europe*. New York: Oxford University Press.

Massey, D.S., R. Alarcón, J. Durand & H. González (1987), *Return to Aztlán: The social process of international migration from Western Mexico*. Berkeley: University of California Press.

Massey, D.S. & F.G. España (1987), 'The social process of international migration', *Science* 237 (4816): 733-738.

McGovern, P. (2007), 'Immigration, labour markets and employment relations: Problems and prospects', *British Journal of Industrial Relations* 45 (2): 217-235.

Merton, R.K. (1957), *Patterns of Influence: Local and Cosmopolitan Influentials. Social Theory and Social Structure*. Glencoe: The Free Press.

Meyer, J.-B. (2001), 'Network approach versus brain drain: Lessons from the diaspora', *International Migration* 39 (5): 91-110.

Poros, M.V. (2001), 'The role of migrant networks in linking local labour markets: The case of Asian Indian migration to New York and London', *Global Networks* 1 (3): 243-259.

Reitz, J.G. (1998), *Warmth of welcome. The social causes of economic success for immigrants in different nations and cities*. Boulder/Oxford: Westview Press.

Reitz, J.G. (2002), 'Terms of entry: Social institutions and immigrant earnings in American, Canadian and Australian cities' in M. Cross & R. Moore (eds.), *Globalization and the new city: Migrants, minorities, and urban transformations in comparative perspective*, 50-81. Basingstoke: Palgrave.

Salt, J. (1992), 'Migration process among the highly skilled in Europe', *International Migration Review* 26 (2): 484-505.

Salt, J. (2005), *Current trends in international migration in Europe*. Strasbourg: Council of Europe, www.geog.ucl.ac.uk/research/mobility-identity-and-security/migration-research -unit/pdfs/current_trends_2004.pdf.

Sjaastad, L.A. (1962), 'The costs and returns of human migration', *Journal of Political Economy* 70 (5): 80-93.

Taplin, I. M. & C.M. Frege (1999), 'Managing transitions: The reorganisation of two clothing manufacturing firms in Hungary', *Organization Studies* 20 (5): 721-740.

Tilly, C.H. (2006), *Public lecture at IPPR on 31 May 2006*. London: Institute for Public Policy Research.

Todaro, M. (1976), *International migration in developing countries: A review of theory, evidence, methodology and research priorities*. Geneva: International Labour Office.

Waldinger, R.D. (ed.) (2001), *Strangers at the gates. New immigrants in urban America*. Berkeley/Los Angeles/London: University of California Press.

Waldinger, R.D. & M.I. Lichter (2003), *How the other half works. Immigration and the social organization of labor*. Berkeley/Los Angeles/London: University of California Press.

Yeoh, B.S.A. & L.-M. Khoo (1998), 'Home, work and community: Skilled international migration and expatriate women in Singapore', *International Migration* 36 (2): 159-186.

Yeoh, B.S.A. & K. Willis (2005), 'Singaporeans in China: Transnational women elites and the negotiations of gendered identities', *Geoforum* 36(2): 211-22

Zulauf, M. (2001), *Migrant women professionals in the European Union*. New York: Palgrave MacMillan.

6 'A van full of Poles': Liquid migration from Central and Eastern Europe

Godfried Engbersen, Erik Snel and Jan de Boom

Introduction

In May 2004, Ireland, Sweden and the United Kingdom opened up their labour markets to citizens of the new member states in Central and Eastern Europe (CEE). In the summer of 2006, Greece, Portugal and Spain also allowed workers from the new accession countries access to their labour markets. The Netherlands followed in May 2007. For Bulgaria and Romania, which joined the EU in January 2007, a transition period is in force. Workers from these two countries still need a work permit in order to work in the Netherlands. The Netherlands could be described as a 'third phase' country, in that it did not allow CEE migrants immediate access to its labour market. However, it is incorrect to imply that there was no labour migration from CEE countries to the Netherlands before May 2007. The Netherlands was the second main destination of choice for migrants from the provinces of Opele and Silesia, which formerly belonged to the Prussian empire.[1] Due to their dual Polish-German citizenship, the 'German Poles' have enjoyed free access to the Dutch labour market since the early 1990s (Pool 2004; Pijpers & Van der Velde 2007). Furthermore, under specific economic sector agreements, 'Polish Poles' and migrant workers from the new member states were already working in the Netherlands, more specifically from the early 2000s on. Polish workers dominated this labour force. Apart from this regular labour migration, from the early 1990s, there were also a significant number of irregular labour migrants from CEE who were employed in agriculture, horticulture and construction (Burgers & Engbersen 1996).

In other words, before the opening up of the Dutch labour market in May 2007, regular and irregular forms of organised labour migration could be observed in the Netherlands. Nevertheless, the European Union's enlargement has led to an accelerated growth of CEE migration to the Netherlands. The figures presented in this chapter will show that the largest category of CEE migrants arriving in the Netherlands come from Poland. The numbers of immigrants coming from the other CEE countries are still relatively small. However, we do not have complete insight into the volume of temporary and irregular immigration from the CEE countries to the Netherlands. As we shall explain later in this chapter, the Netherlands has fairly accurate figures concerning the numbers of immigrants that settle officially and for a longer period of time (at least four months during the six months following registration) in the country, but not concerning temporary and irregular migration. This implies that official immigration statistics may underestimate the volume of immigration from Poland and other CEE countries, as many immigrants stay in the Netherlands for only short periods of time.

In this chapter we will analyse the main trends of labour migration from CEE countries before and after the enlargement of the EU in May 2004 and January 2007. These countries include: Poland, Hungary, the Czech Republic, the Slovak Republic, Slovenia, the three Baltic states (Estonia, Latvia, Lithuania), Bulgaria and Romania. We will give a short overview of Dutch immigration policies vis-à-vis citizens from the new EU member states and we will briefly mention the statistical sources that provide us information about immigrants from Poland and other CEE countries. In addition, we will discuss some of the economic and social consequences of the new labour migration, with particular reference to the issues of job displacement, wage reduction and housing. In the next section, we discuss some of the new migration patterns and associated social myths that arose with the inflow of CEE migrants, and we formulate the key research questions that we will try to answer in this chapter.

'Liquid migration' and the social construction of new migration myths

Current labour migration from CEE countries to the Netherlands is interesting for several reasons. Firstly, it reveals important changes in migration flows and types of migration to the Netherlands (Engbersen, Van der Leun & De Boom 2007). The new migration of the past fifteen to twenty years differs from that experienced in the period 1950-1990. Then, migration to the Netherlands was dominated by postcolonial migration from Indonesia (after 1949) and Surinam (after 1975), and by guest worker migration (and later family migration) from Turkey and Morocco (from the 1960s up until today). In the 1970s, almost half of non-Dutch immigrants to the Netherlands came from just five countries: Turkey, Morocco, Surinam, the Netherlands Antilles and Indonesia. Now, only about 20 per cent of non-Dutch immigrants to the Netherlands come from these countries.

The new migration of the past fifteen to twenty years is characterised by new geographical patterns of migration and new types of immigrants with weak or no residence status (asylum seekers, temporary labour migrants and illegal immigrants). The new geography of migration relates to increased long-distance migration to the Netherlands from a growing number of countries. In addition, the traditional migration direction from south to north is complemented by migration flows from east to west. New categories of immigrants are increasingly being added to traditional labour immigrants, family immigrants and people from former colonies and their offspring.

First, there are asylum seekers, whose numbers – though fluctuating – increased sharply over the period 1990-2000. After a time in which the numbers of asylum applications remained high (over 40,000 a year), they began falling at the end of 2000. Second, besides the influx of asylum seekers, there was an increase in the number of temporary labour immigrants. More than two thirds of temporary labour immigrants come from Western countries (particularly the new EU member states). Furthermore, the number of temporary labour immigrants from Eastern European countries has increased sharply over the last few years. Third, there is a relatively new type of immigrant, one that has come to be known as an undocumented or irregular immigrant. The dividing lines between asylum seekers, commuting immigrants and illegal immigrants are sometimes diffuse (see Düvell 2006). Polish immigrants who work in agriculture, for instance, were commonly regarded as illegal immigrants, although they became regular immigrants after enlargement. In other words, migration to the Netherlands became much more differentiated and led to more diverse and floating populations. To paraphrase Bauman's (1999, 2005) work on 'liquid modernity', international migration has become 'liquid'. The fairly stable migration patterns that marked the period 1950-1990 have dissolved into more complex, transitory patterns in terms of transient settlement – transnational or otherwise – and shifting migration status (Engbersen, Van der Leun & De Boom 2007).

These observations are consistent with Vertovec's (2007) concept of 'super-diversity'. This notion underlines the multiple-origin, transnationally connected, socio-economically differentiated and legally stratified nature of international migration. It is therefore more difficult to pin down contemporary migration patterns now than in the decades after World War II because of their very temporary and fluid nature. There is often a discrepancy between officially documented migration and the non-registered reality of regular and irregular labour migration. Labour migrants from CEE countries, in particular, have again confronted the Netherlands with the importance of temporary labour migration, which often takes the form of 'circular migration' or 'transnational commuting'. Workers return home when a job is finished and come back another year (i.e. seasonal migration) or they travel to the Netherlands when they are required (e.g. for small-scale construction work, home improvement). This classic form of migration that has always been historically crucial for the Netherlands (Lucassen 1987) – for example in the period 1750-1800 – has gained in importance over the years, and is confusing Dutch policymakers and specialists.

In the 1970s and 1980s, policymakers embraced the myth that guest workers from Mediterranean countries would return to their countries of origin once the jobs they came for were finished. This myth of immigrants returning home dominated official Dutch thinking on immigration and immigrant integration for many years (Van Amersfoort 1982; Muus 2004). Currently, however, a new social myth seems to be emerging: that a substantial number of labour migrants will stay in the Netherlands. However, as experience in the UK and Ireland has shown, many labour migrants do return. One of the implications of this new myth is a fear that the Netherlands is not fully prepared to accommodate the large influx of temporary workers at local level. In the past, it was not equipped to effectively incorporate large groups of Turkish and Moroccan immigrants into Dutch society; at present, it is not sufficiently organised to deal with large numbers of temporary workers. Provisional arrangements have been set up, especially in the housing sector, to accommodate large groups of temporary workers. Another remarkable phenomenon is that the issue of highly skilled migrants dominates political discourse and policymaking, while fewer highly skilled temporary workers are dominant in the actual migration figures (De Boom, Weltevrede, Snel & Engbersen 2007). As a consequence, there is no comprehensive overview of current migration flows from the CEE countries to the Netherlands. In this chapter we will try to answer three basic questions: 1) From which countries do these CEE migrants come? 2) Do all have regular status or do some have irregular status? 3) Are they actually temporary workers or are some categories settling in the Netherlands?

The dominant view is that CEE migrants alleviate specific labour shortages, do not put a strain on public services or the tax system and do not compete with native workers. Nowadays, the Netherlands has a very tight labour market and most labour migrants from CEE countries work in low-skilled sectors where job vacancies have long existed, such as agriculture and horticulture, transport, construction and meat processing. Although job displacement is very difficult to measure, given the current tight labour market, it is thought to be fairly limited. A stronger argument can be made for another kind of job displacement, namely, that CEE workers are displacing irregular workers from outside the EU.

However, the issue of illegal residence is still relevant for immigrants from Bulgaria and Romania, as is the issue of illegal work. Many formerly illegal workers have become partly regularised because of EU enlargement and an opening up of the labour market, but are still partly engaged in irregular work. So the question arises as to whether current CEE migrants are still working in very specific sectors of the secondary labour market, or whether the pattern is more diverse. A related question is what the economic impact (i.e. on wage levels, job displacement) is on the labour market position of different social groups (such as native-born Dutch or irregular workers).

The inflow of CEE migrants into the Netherlands has also given rise to new concerns about their incorporation into Dutch society. Some national and local politicians are exploiting the image of a 'Polish invasion' – what they call an increase of Polish workers and the concentration of groups in specific neighbourhoods in the big cities, particularly The Hague and Rotterdam (see also Engbersen, Van San & Leerkes 2006; Leerkes, Engbersen & Van San 2007; Leerkes 2007). The presence of these groups has raised questions about the length of their stay, as well as about relevant policies to deal with temporary workers and immigrants who settle in certain neighbourhoods. More and more, the new immigrants become visible in specific neighbourhoods not only out of their sheer numbers, but also because of the institutions they create and renew, such as Polish churches, boarding houses, migrant hostels and dance halls for temporary workers (Leerkes et al. 2007). In The Hague, where many Poles live, there is an urban district known as Little Poland where one can find Polish shops, pubs, churches and a Polish newspaper providing information on Polish dentists, doctors and obstetricians. This presence has also led to serious concerns about the residents – legal or illegal – housing conditions and about quality of life in the neighbourhood. At the end of this chapter we will discuss some of the concerns formulated by Dutch municipalities.

Dutch labour migration policy on EU enlargement

When analysing immigration to the Netherlands, it is essential to distinguish different channels that each have their own policies and regulations. These include: marital migration, other family-related migration, asylum migration, labour migration and student migration. Labour migration policies and regulations are of particular relevance to migration from the CEE countries. Since the 1980s, the Dutch government has been rather hesitant about labour migration to the Netherlands.[2] Given the large numbers of jobseekers and social benefit claimants in the

Netherlands (including many with an immigrant background), it found unrestricted labour migration unacceptable (Roodenburg, Euwals & Ter Rele 2003; Engbersen 2003). Furthermore, the Dutch government would rather stimulate labour market participation by women and older employees than invite foreign workers to the Netherlands. Labour migration is only perceived as desirable for vacancies for which there are no Dutch jobseekers (or jobseekers from other EU countries) available. This is also the basic principle of the Dutch Aliens Employment Act (WAV). The purpose of this act is to selectively allow the entry of labour migrants within the more general framework of labour market policies. The WAV regulates who is eligible for a temporary work permit in the Netherlands and who is exempted from the requirements. As a general rule, all labour migrants from outside the EU are required to obtain a temporary work permit in the Netherlands, whereas labour migrants coming from other EU countries are exempted from this obligation.

Under the WAV, Dutch employers can only recruit foreign employees when there are no 'preferred-status workers' available – that is, jobseekers from within the Netherlands or other EU countries. Only when employers are unable to find a potential employee among preferred-status workers can they apply for a temporary work permit (known as a TWV) for a foreign employee. The Dutch Central Organisation for Work and Income (the public employment service known as the CWI) assesses applications made by employers for such employees. Among other things, the CWI checks whether there are no preferred-status jobseekers available for the vacancy (via a 'labour market test'). If a Dutch or European jobseeker is available or if the employer has made insufficient efforts to hire such a person, the application will be refused.

Originally, this procedure also applied in the case of labour migrants from Poland and other new EU members. However, before enlargement in 2004, several exemptions were introduced from these relatively strict labour market regulations. In the late 1990s, the Netherlands had a period of economic growth and a fairly tight labour market. In this period, there was high demand for labour, particularly seasonal labour in the Dutch agricultural and horticultural sectors. At the same time, it became clear, for instance, that in the Westland, a well-known horticultural region in the Netherlands, one in four companies employed irregular immigrants (WRR 2001; Engbersen et al. 2006). In 2002, the Dutch government tried to end this situation with its Seasonal Work Project, which made it easier for agricultural and horticultural companies to hire seasonal workers from Poland (Broeders & Engbersen 2007). In the same period, Dutch temporary employment agencies started to recruit workers from Poland and other CEE countries. Polish workers with German passports – who mainly came from the German-Polish border region – were in particular demand. Because of their

German passports, these workers did not need a temporary work permit to be employed in the Netherlands. As a result, in early 2004, at least 25,000 Polish workers were employed in the Dutch agricultural and horticultural sector. Most of them had temporary work permits, but about 10,000 Polish workers had German citizenship and therefore did not need a formal work permit (Corpeleijn 2007: 181). In other words, the years prior to EU enlargement in 2004 had already witnessed a sharp increase in the influx of workers, mainly Polish ones, to the Netherlands.

After the EU enlargement in May 2004, the number of foreign workers from Poland and other CEE countries further increased. As stated in this chapter's introduction, the Netherlands was a 'third wave' country: it kept its borders officially closed to employees from the new EU member states. In 2004, a transitional measure was announced to allow workers from the new member states access to the Dutch labour market, provided they had a temporary work permit. In May 2006, this transitional measure was prolonged for another year. However, many restrictions on foreign workers from Poland and other CEE countries were lifted as early as 2006. Although foreign workers from new member states admitted in 2004 still needed a temporary work permit, these were more easily issued and often without a labour market test. This implied that employers looking for foreign employees were no longer obligated to check whether potential personnel was available in the Netherlands and in 'the old EU'. In May 2007, all restrictions on foreign workers from Poland and other new member states were lifted. Individuals from these countries now have free access to the Dutch labour market. This does not apply to nationals of the latest arrivals to the EU, Bulgaria and Romania. Nationals of these two countries, which joined the EU in January 2007, are still confronted with a transitional period in which they need a temporary work permit in the Netherlands. Up until 2006, only limited numbers of formal immigrants from Bulgaria and Romania came to the Netherlands. In 2007, the number of regular labour migrants from Bulgaria and Romania greatly increased.

Before presenting figures on immigration from Poland and other CEE countries to the Netherlands, we should point out the statistical sources of these data. The Netherlands basically has two different statistical sources containing information about labour immigration, although both have their shortcomings. The Dutch immigration figures are based on the municipal personal records database (known as the GBA). Every person who resides for at least four months in a Dutch municipality is obliged to register in the municipality. If their former place of residence was abroad, the GBA classifies them as immigrants. The origin of an immigrant is established by place of birth. This source gives an accurate picture of registered and long-term (at least four months) immigration to (and emigration from) the Netherlands. However, many seasonal workers and other temporary workers from the CEE countries are not registered in the GBA. The second main statistical source used in this chapter concerns statistics relating to temporary work permits. These statistics show the increasing number of temporary work permits issued to residents of CEE countries. The shortcoming here, however, is that these figures refer to work permits and not to individuals (one person can and often does obtain more than one work permit per year). Furthermore, this source has no information about the number of work permits issued to residents from new EU member states after May 2007 because, after that date, they no longer required a work permit. In the following section we present data about the number of temporary work permits issued to residents from the CEE countries from the mid-1990s until May 2007.

Table 6.1 *Immigration from Poland to the Netherlands by motive of migration, 1995-2004 (number, row % in brackets)*

	Labour	Asylum	Marriage	Other family-related	Study	Other	Total
1995	87	23	540	441	47	64	1203
	(7.2)	(1.9)	(44.9)	(36.7)	(3.9)	(5.3)	(100)
1996	202	10	673	407	61	110	1462
	(13.8)	(0.7)	(46.0)	(27.8)	(4.2)	(5.3)	(100)
1997	190	24	628	286	89	220	1435
	(13.2)	(1.7)	(43.8)	(19.9)	(6.2)	(15.3)	(100)
1998	306	10	595	314	128	275	1631
	(18.8)	(0.6)	(36.5)	(19.3)	(7.8)	(16.9)	(100)
1999	248	11	335	171	161	167	1098
	(22.6)	(1.0)	(30.5)	(15.6)	(14.7)	(15.2)	(100)
2000	567	18	485	306	202	221	1800
	(31.5)	(1.0)	(26.9)	(17.0)	(11.2)	(12.3)	(100)
2001	804	1	599	266	264	186	2122
	(37.9)	(0.0)	(28.2)	(12.5)	(12.4)	(8.8)	(100)
2002	731	7	649	333	310	222	2254
	(32.4)	(0.3)	(28.8)	(14.8)	(13.8)	(9.8)	(100)
2003	771	5	651	322	240	175	2161
	(35.7)	(0.2)	(30.1)	(14.9)	(11.1)	(8.1)	(100)
2004	1896	17	825	921	464	978	5097
	(37.2)	(0.3)	(16.2)	(18.1)	(9.1)	(19.2)	(100)
Total	5802	126	5980	3767	1966	2618	20263
	(28.6)	(0.6)	(29.5)	(18.6)	(9.7)	(12.9)	(100)
Of whom							
Men	3982	73	482	1368	843	579	7477
	(53.3)	(1.0)	(6.4)	(18.3)	(11.3)	(7.7)	(100)
Women	1820	53	5498	2120	1123	2039	12786
	(14.2)	(0.4)	(43.0)	(16.6)	(8.8)	(15.9)	(100)

Source: Statistics Netherlands

CEE immigration prior to EU enlargement

In the decade before the EU enlargement in 2004, over 20,000 workers from Poland arrived in the Netherlands and almost 18,000 from the member states that acceded in 2004 and 2007 (Table 6.1 and Table 6.2). Since there is no separate information about Slovenia and the three Baltic states,[3] the figures relating to 'other new EU member states' refer only to Hungary, the Czech Republic, the Slovak Republic, Bulgaria and Romania. The figures in Table 6.1 and Table 6.2 show that the earlier waves of immigration from the CEE countries to the Netherlands were primarily family-related. Around half of all Polish immigrants came to the Netherlands for family reasons (marriage, family reunification or other family-related migration). The same goes for 45 per cent of all

Table 6.2 *Immigration from other selected A8 states* to the Netherlands by motive of migration, 1995-2004 (number, row % in brackets)*

	Labour	Asylum	Marriage	Other family-related	Study	Other	Total
1995	95	89	323	253	42	60	858
	(11.1)	(10.4)	(37.6)	(29.5)	(4.9)	(7.0)	(100)
1996	125	70	502	293	149	109	1241
	(10.1)	(5.6)	(40.5)	(23.6)	(12.0)	(8.8)	(100)
1997	182	50	500	273	219	194	1419
	(12.8)	(3.5)	(35.2)	(19.2)	(15.4)	(13.7)	(100)
1998	354	31	565	293	252	251	1751
	(20.2)	(1.8)	(32.3)	(16.7)	(14.4)	(14.3)	(100)
1999	274	79	383	271	311	179	1495
	(18.3)	(5.3)	(25.6)	(18.1)	(20.8)	(12.0)	(100)
2000	461	213	525	274	332	249	2060
	(22.4)	(10.3)	(25.5)	(13.3)	(16.1)	(12.1)	(100)
2001	698	154	692	214	341	203	2313
	(30.2)	(6.7)	(29.9)	(9.3)	(14.7)	(8.8)	(100)
2002	463	72	764	174	435	164	2078
	(22.3)	(3.5)	(36.8)	(8.4)	(20.9)	(7.9)	(100)
2003	417	60	762	186	446	148	2025
	(20.6)	(3.0)	(37.6)	(9.2)	(22.0)	(7.3)	(100)
2004	675	21	651	320	563	426	2654
	(25.4)	(0.8)	(24.5)	(12.1)	(21.2)	(16.1)	(100)
Total	3744	839	5667	2551	3090	1983	17894
	(20.9)	(4.7)	(31.7)	(14.3)	(17.3)	(11.1)	(100)
Of whom							
Men	2609	438	713	646	1376	528	6535
	(39.9)	(6.7)	(10.9)	(9.9)	(21.1)	(8.1)	(100)
Women	1135	401	4954	1354	1714	1455	11359
	(10.0)	(3.5)	(43.6)	(11.9)	(15.1)	(12.8)	(100)

Source: Statistics Netherlands
* Hungary, Czech Republic, Slovak Republic, Bulgaria, Romania

immigrants from the other CEE countries that came to the Netherlands in the period 1995-2004. The majority (over 60 per cent) of immigrants from CEE countries were women. In preceding years, the proportion of family-related immigration and of women in total immigration from these countries to the Netherlands was even larger.

Table 6.1 and Table 6.2 also show, however, that the number of labour migrants was increasing before enlargement in 2004. Since 2000, labour migrants have been the largest sub-category among immigrants coming from Poland. Another important sub-category is students. One in ten Polish immigrants settling in the Netherlands in the period 1995-2004 was a student. This figure is as high as one in six immigrants in this period from the other CEE countries. Finally, we should mention that in this period, too, the Netherlands admitted a number of asylum migrants from countries that later became EU member states. Table 6.1 and Table 6.2 only cover documented migrants who came to the Netherlands legally and who are formally registered with the local authorities.

After the EU enlargement of 2004, the number of immigrants from these countries increased significantly (Figure 6.1). Whereas the total number of immigrants from the new EU member states fluctuated around 4,000 annually in the years 2000-2003, this number almost

Figure 6.1 *Immigration from CEE countries to the Netherlands by place of birth, 1995-2007*

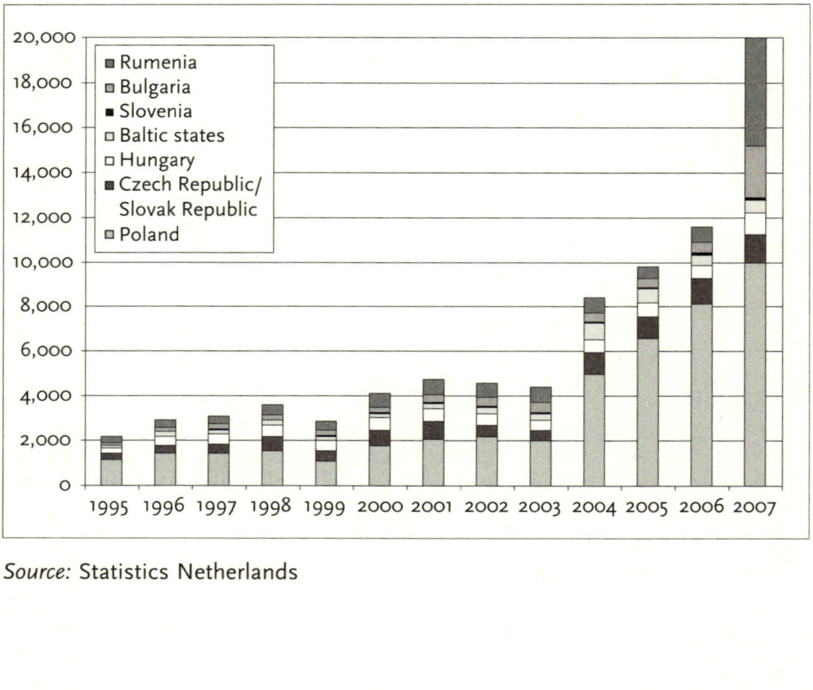

Source: Statistics Netherlands

doubled after 2004 (8,400 immigrants) and further increased in subsequent years (9,800 immigrants in 2005, over 11,000 in 2006 and almost 20,000 in 2007).[4] Immigrants from Poland are by far the largest sub-category. Total immigration from Poland and other CEE countries may be much larger, since these figures only include those immigrants that stay in the Netherlands for a longer period of time (at least four months) and who register with the municipal authorities.

This sharp increase in the number of immigrants from CEE countries also implies a change in the composition of immigrant populations. Family-related immigration is gradually making way for work-related immigration and the overrepresentation of women in immigration from the CEE countries is disappearing. Unfortunately, there is no information available about the migration motives of immigrants for the years after 2004. Figure 6.2 shows, however, a substantial increase in male immigration, particularly from CEE countries to the Netherlands following the 2004 enlargement. The immigration of women from CEE countries to the Netherlands increased less radically after enlargement.

One crucial question related to the new labour migration is whether it is a temporary or permanent phenomenon. What complicates the

Figure 6.2   *Immigration from CEE countries to the Netherlands by gender (1995-2007)*

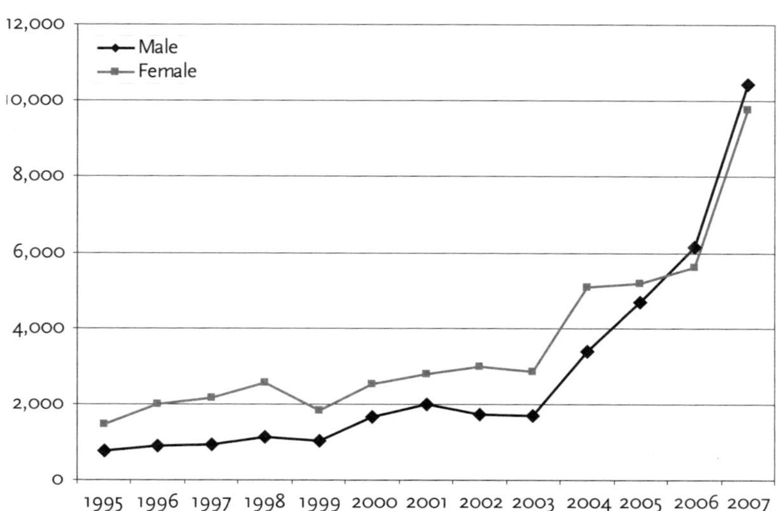

Source: Statistics Netherlands

answer to this question is that social researchers cannot decide which argument is correct. Asking immigrants whether it is their intention to stay is not a very useful method, since most of them do not know what the future will bring. Many former guest workers were also convinced their stay would be temporary, but ultimately many became permanent residents of Western European countries. The only way to obtain some indication of the prospects of CEE labour migrants is to analyse their demographic behaviour. Bringing their families over, and more specifically their children, is a clear indication they will not leave in the foreseeable future. The immigration of minor children from Poland and the other CEE countries to the Netherlands is, however, still fairly low (see Figure 6.3), and there has been only a small increase in recent years. In 2007, the immigration of minor children increased to almost 2,000, but is still relatively small.

CEE immigration after EU enlargement: A sharp increase in commuting

Whatever the future brings, most current labour migrants from Poland and the other new member states come over for temporary work. There

Figure 6.3   *Immigration from CEE countries to the Netherlands by age (1995-2007)*

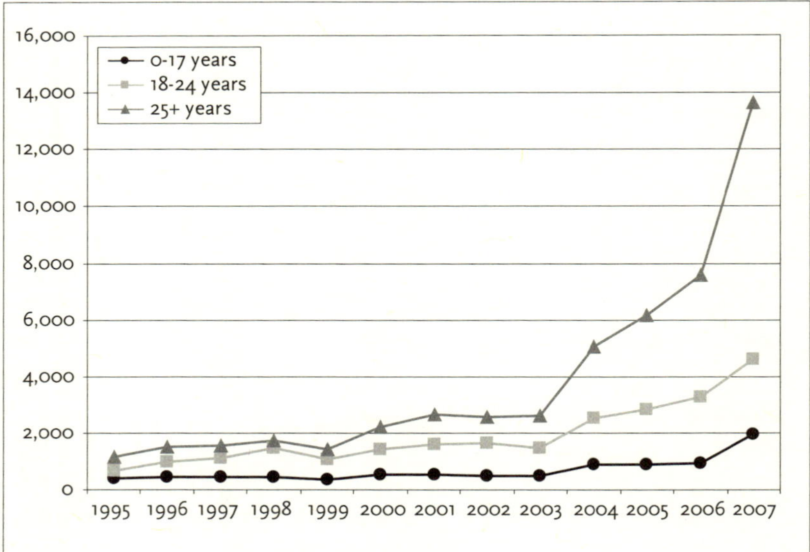

Source: Statistics Netherlands

are, in fact, numerous documented stories about buses or aeroplanes shuttling Polish workers to and from the Netherlands on a weekly basis. The fact that many temporary labour migrants fail to register with their local authorities implies that they are not included in official Dutch immigration statistics. The only way to estimate the volume of temporary labour migration is to analyse the number of TWV permits issued to CEE nationals. We then see an increase in the total number of TWVs issued in the Netherlands. This increase started in the mid-1990s, precipitated by the tight Dutch labour market at the time (Figure 6.4). But even after 2000, the number of TWVs issued further increased, despite the economic crisis and rising unemployment. After the 2004 enlargement, more specifically in 2006, the number of TWVs issued rocketed. Whereas in 1996 over 9,000 work permits were issued in the Netherlands, ten years later, in 2006, 74,000 were issued. Most of the latter TWVs were issued to CEE nationals.

In the first four months of 2007, the number of TWVs issued rose even faster. In the year's first trimester alone, no fewer than 38,261 permits were issued in the Netherlands. Again, the large majority of these work permits (34,564) were given to CEE nationals. In the next eight months of 2007, the number of TWVs fell sharply to 11,766, mainly because CEE nationals no longer needed a work permit to be employed in the Netherlands after May 2007 (see Van den Berg, Brukman & Van Rij 2007: 29). Only nationals of Bulgaria and Romania, which joined the EU in 2007, still need a TWV to work in the Netherlands.

Figure 6.4 *Number of temporary work permits (TWVs) issued in the Netherlands (1990-2006)*

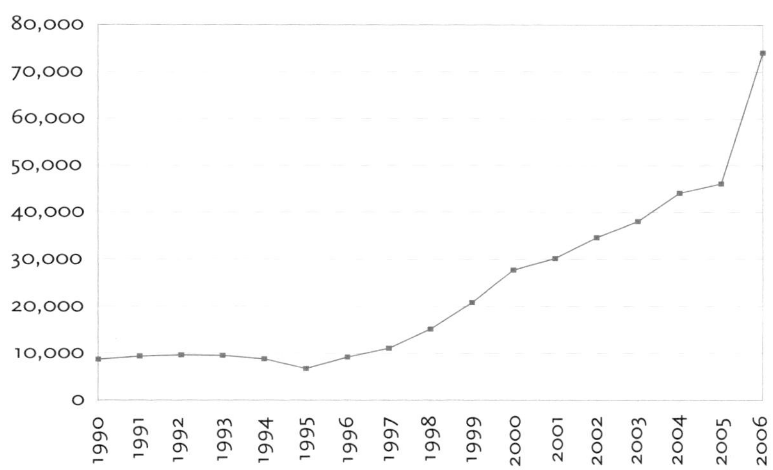

Source: Dutch Central Organisation for Work and Income (CWI)

Figure 6.5 shows the increase in the number of TWVs issued to CEE nationals in the period 1996-2006. Polish nationals are, by far, the largest sub-category among these temporary foreign workers. In 2006 alone, almost 54,000 TWVs were issued to Polish nationals (73 per cent of the total 74,000 TWVs issued in 2006). The other categories still remain limited. Table 6.3 and Table 6.4 show in which professions and economic sectors these temporary workers from the CEE countries were working in the period 2003-2006.

The figures in Table 6.3 and Table 6.4 reveal that, by far, the majority of temporary work permits are issued for agricultural and horticultural work. Moreover, this number has increased over the last few years. In 2003, 60 per cent of all work permits were issued for agricultural and horticultural work, while in 2006 this figure was almost 75 per cent. Temporary labour migrants from Poland and Romania are especially concentrated in agricultural and horticultural work. Other lower-qualified professions that attract a relatively large number of labour migrants include various industrial production jobs, chauffeurs and personnel for unskilled work. TWVs issued to nationals from Bulgaria and Romania, being EU member states that joined in 2007, increased from 1,700 in 2004 to 3,000 in 2006. In 2007, the number of TWVs issued

Figure 6.5 *Number of temporary work permits (TWVs) issued to CEE nationals (1996-2006)*

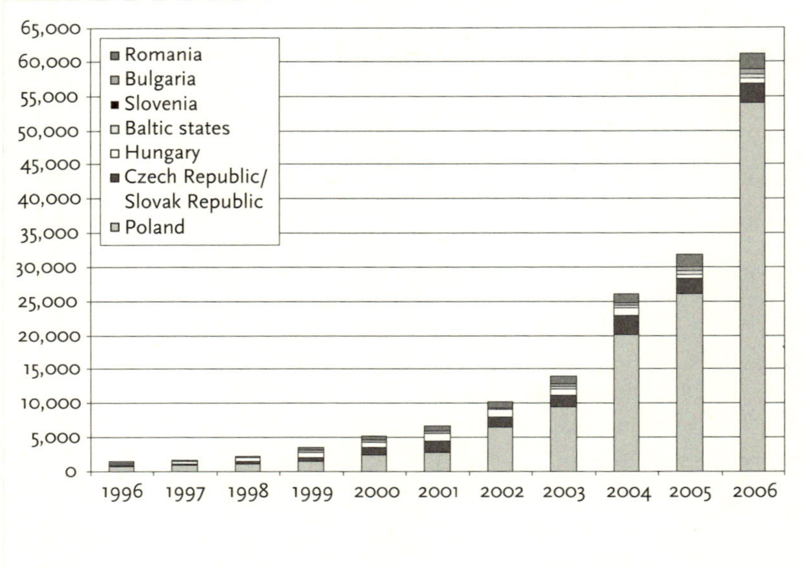

Source: Dutch Central Organisation for Work and Income (CWI)

Table 6.3 *Number of temporary work permits (TWVs) issued to foreign nationals from CEE countries by type of profession and year (2003-2006)*

	2003	2004	2005	2006
Agriculture/horticulture	60.9	68.4	76.1	74.6
Artistic professions	5.4	3.1	2.1	0.5
Production work	9.9	15.0	8.9	15.6
Science	4.7	2.6	1.5	0.8
Computer specialists	0.7	0.3	0.2	0.2
Executive professions	0.5	0.4	0.5	0.2
Advisors	0.7	0.6	0.4	0.2
Drivers	7.6	6.0	5.4	3.4
Hotel and catering	2.0	0.8	0.5	0.4
Other services	1.9	1.1	0.8	0.8
Construction	4.2	1.2	2.9	0.3
Health care	0.9	0.3	0.1	0.1
Sports	0.1	0.1	0.1	0.0
Unskilled work	0.1	0.0	0.3	3.0
Mechanics	0.0	0.0	0.0	0.1
Other professions	0.1	0.1	0.1	0.0
Total (N)	13,650	26,121	31,875	61,133

Source: Dutch Central Organisation for Work and Income (CWI)

Table 6.4 *Number of temporary work permits (TWVs) issued to foreign nationals from CEE countries by type of profession and country (2006)*

	Poland	Czech Republic/ Slovak Republic	Hungary	Baltic states	Slovenia	Bulgaria	Romania
Agriculture/horticulture	78.4	21.3	21.5	63.7	7.4	63.9	75.8
Artistic professions	0.3	1.6	1.9	1.3	3.7	7.4	1.0
Production work	15.1	24.5	51.5	18.1	48.1	9.3	6.2
Science	0.4	2.2	9.8	2.5	20.4	4.9	3.0
Computer specialists	0.0	1.7	0.6	0.9	0.0	0.9	1.2
Executive professions	0.1	0.9	2.4	0.7	0.0	0.0	0.6
Advisors	0.1	0.4	1.7	0.4	3.7	1.1	0.2
Drivers	1.6	34.8	1.4	0.9	5.6	0.5	8.9
Hotel and catering	0.1	4.1	1.1	0.7	0.0	2.3	0.4
Other services	0.6	2.6	3.6	4.5	7.4	3.7	1.2
Construction	0.1	1.2	2.7	0.0	0.0	5.4	1.2
Health care	0.1	0.3	0.6	1.4	0.0	0.3	0.1
Sports	0.0	0.2	0.5	0.4	0.0	0.3	0.1
Unskilled work	3.1	4.0	0.6	3.6	3.7	0.0	0.0
Mechanics	0.1	0.1	0.0	0.5	0.0	0.0	0.0
Other professions	0.0	0.1	0.0	0.4	0.0	0.0	0.0
Total (N)	53981	2907	633	553	54	739	2266

Source: Dutch Central Organisation for Work and Income (CWI)

to Bulgarians and Romanians further increased to over 3,600. An explanation for this is that it became much easier for Bulgarians and Romanians to enter the Netherlands once their countries joined the EU, and they no longer need residence permits (Van den Berg, Brukman & Van Rij 2007: 30).

These data on temporary work permits have their limitations. Firstly, like any official data, they do not include foreign workers who are in the Netherlands without formal residence permits or work permits. Secondly, these data only refer to foreign workers who work for Dutch employers. CEE nationals working in the Netherlands on a self-employed basis are not included. Self-employed individuals from the new EU member states had free access to the Dutch labour market as early as 2004. Thirdly, figures relating to temporary work permits refer to the number of permits issued in a certain year, but not to the number of individuals receiving a work permit. Available, however, are several estimates of the number of foreign workers in the Netherlands from Poland and other CEE countries. According to one estimate, in 2004, there were 97,000 jobs in the Netherlands taken by temporary workers coming from the CEE countries. Most of these jobs were in agriculture and horticulture and were found through temporary employment agencies. Since about one in four temporary workers from the CEE countries had more than one job, the total number of temporary labour migrants from CEE countries in 2004 is estimated at 72,000 (both employed and self-employed) (Corpeleijn 2007: 181). A more recent estimate of the number of temporary labour migrants from CEE countries in the Netherlands refers to the situation in 2008.[5] The conclusion was that a minimum of 100,000 CEE nationals were working in the Netherlands on a temporary or permanent basis in 2008. This figure is also used by the Dutch government as the official estimate of labour migration from CEE countries to the Netherlands.

Economic and social consequences

The previous sections outlined the influx of officially registered immigrants and temporary labour migrants from Poland and other CEE countries to the Netherlands after EU enlargement in 2004. This section summarises what is known about the economic and social consequences of this wave of immigration. We will focus on three issues: wage competition and the possible negative effect of CEE labour migration on wage levels for Dutch workers; labour market displacement; and the social consequences of the influx of CEE labour migrants to the Netherlands, particularly in the housing sector.

Effect on wages

Foreign workers from Poland and the other CEE countries evidently come to the Netherlands and other EU countries because of huge wage differences within the EU. Even though new labour migrants may work for lower wages than is customary in the Netherlands, they earn much more than they would in their own countries. Such practices can have a negative effect on wage levels in the receiving countries, especially on wages for low-skilled work. Earlier Dutch research based on the assumptions of Borjas (1999) concluded that:

> It is safe to assume that an increase in the number of migrant workers will lead to a fall in wages for competing workers. The greater the increase in the number of migrant workers (the expectation with the free movement of workers), the greater the wage effects will be. (Versantvoort, Vossen, Van der Ende, Zoon, Nugteren, Nauta, Azzouz, Donker van Heel, Ceglowska & Kreft 2006: 15)

Although, until now, there has been little evidence of a significant drop in wages for low-skilled work in the Netherlands, there are some indications that there is a certain wage effect.

Interviews with employers' organisations by Versantvoort et al. (2006) paint a mixed picture. According to the employers' organisations, most employers pay their foreign workers in accordance with collective wage agreements for their economic sector. However, there are also reports of employers paying less than the standard wage or even less than the minimum wage level in the Netherlands. Versantvoort et al. (2006: 85) also mention that CEE labour migrants often have no objections to working for lower wages than is customary. Employers have developed a number of strategies to avoid official wage levels. One tactic is for labour migrants to work partly for the official wage level but to work overtime for lower wages. The employers interviewed also mentioned that an increasing number of foreign labour migrants work on a self-employed basis. This construction is legal. Being self-employed allows them to ignore collective wage agreements or to pay themselves less than the statutory minimum wage. In practice, companies often pay less for work done by self-employed foreign workers than for work done by regular employees (either Dutch or foreign) (Ter Beek, Mevissen, Mur & Pool 2005). Official figures show an increase in the number of self-employed CEE nationals active in the Netherlands, from 442 in 2003, to 4,221 in 2006 (Kamer van Koophandel 2007). This sharp increase in the number of self-employed workers can partly be explained with reference to the Dutch transitional regime for labour migrants from new EU member states after 2004 (which granted only self-employed workers from those countries free access to the Dutch labour market).

The Dutch Minister of Social Affairs has initiated various policy measures to prevent unequal payment between Dutch workers and foreign workers. In principle, foreign workers should enjoy the same work conditions as their Dutch counterparts. Since May 2007, the Dutch Labour Inspection checks whether employers pay at least the legal minimum wage to temporary foreign workers. The Minister of Social Affairs also introduced a system of centres (known as *meldpunten*) where contraventions of the Minimum Wage Act can be reported. Between June and September 2007, around 50 such contraventions were reported, but they have yet to be examined (Van den Berg, Brukman & Van Rij 2007).

Job displacement

A second issue is labour market displacement. Are Dutch workers (and other immigrant workers) pushed aside by the newly arrived labour migrants from Poland and other CEE countries? The studies available come to different conclusions. Versantvoort et al. (2006: 15) expect some labour market displacement, stating that: 'It is estimated that for every one hundred labour migrants, 25 jobs of Dutch citizens will be lost.' Other studies, however, expect hardly any negative job displacement effects, particularly because of the tight Dutch labour market. The large majority of temporary workers from CEE countries work in agriculture and horticulture. These economic sectors have been unable to attract sufficient workers in the Netherlands for many years. What is more, Dutch social benefit claimants are hardly eager to take up temporary employment in these sectors. Although there may have been some displacement of Dutch seasonal workers, the general conclusion is that the temporary workers from CEE countries are a welcome and necessary supplement to the available Dutch workforce.

Van den Berg et al. (2007) argue that wage differences between the western and eastern regions of the enlarged EU are unlikely to disappear suddenly in the future. As such, CEE labour migrants will continue to come to the Netherlands. The arrival of additional workers safeguards the prolongation of production in some economic sectors and economic growth rather than displacing Dutch workers. Some agricultural companies were considering leaving the Netherlands because they could not get motivated workers willing to do open-field work and other jobs that are considered difficult, dirty and/or low-paid (see Van den Berg et al. 2007: 43; Pijpers & Van der Velde 2007: 829). But since the influx of temporary workers from CEE countries, these companies have decided to stay, the jobs they provide thereby not being lost. Nevertheless, the consequences may be different, depending on the economic sector concerned. For instance, the transportation industry may be experiencing an indirect displacement of native workers by truck drivers from CEE countries who face less strict regulations (e.g. concerning working hours) and are therefore less costly to hire than their Dutch counterparts.

The general conclusion about the economic consequences of CEE labour migration is that this has been advantageous for the Netherlands. With some exceptions, there are no clear indications of downwards wage effects or job displacement for native Dutch workers. However, these outcomes partially depend on the current economic climate. In the present positive economic climate, with its tight labour market and increasing household incomes, possible negative effects of the influx of temporary foreign workers – in terms of wage levels and labour market displacement – seem limited. It is unclear, however, how this will work out in times of economic recession.

Another impact of immigration not yet mentioned is the potential displacement of illegal workers by labour migrants from the new EU member states. It is an open secret that large numbers of irregular immigrants were informally employed in Dutch agriculture and horticulture; many of these irregular workers actually originated from the current new EU member states (WRR 2001; Leerkes, Van San, Engbersen, Cruijff & Van der Heijden 2004; 2007). One can expect that many of these irregular workers will be pushed aside by the new CEE labour migrants who have formal access to the Netherlands and the Dutch labour market. There are in fact two different mechanisms at work here. On the one hand, there may be a replacement of persons: immigrants in possession of formal residence papers would replace illegal immigrants. On the other, there may be a change in legal status: CEE immigrants who used to be in the Netherlands illegally would have obtained formal legal status because of the free movement of citizens within the EU. Whatever is true of either mechanism, the estimated number of irregular immigrants from CEE countries in the Netherlands fell significantly after EU enlargement in 2004. In the years 2002 and 2003, there were approximately 63,000 to 70,000 irregular immigrants from CEE countries in the Netherlands (Cruyff & Van der Heijden 2004). According to a new estimate made in 2005, there were approximately 41,000 irregular immigrants from both the old EU countries (Western Europe) and the new EU countries in CEE. Furthermore, there were approximately 22,000 undocumented immigrants in the Netherlands from Bulgaria and Romania, which at that time were not yet EU members (Van der Heijden, Van Gils, Cruijff & Hessen 2006). These figures show a significant decline in the number of irregular immigrants from CEE countries in the Netherlands. We take this as an indication of the displacement of former irregular immigrants who were informally active in the Dutch labour market by regular immigrants from the same countries.

Social consequences: Housing and other issues

Whereas economic studies and official reactions from the Dutch government are optimistic about new labour migration from Poland and other CEE countries, local authorities are more concerned. In December 2007, the 'Poles Summit' organised by the municipality of Rotterdam was attended by 40 Dutch municipalities that house large numbers of CEE migrants. The aim of the conference was to discuss social problems caused by the influx of such migrants into these municipalities and to bring these problems to the attention of the national government. Local policymakers argued that central government underestimates both the volume of new labour migration from CEE countries and the social issues to which it gives rise. At the conference, which was chaired by one of the authors of this chapter (Erik Snel), numerous alleged problems related to CEE migrants were raised. These included allegations such as Polish labour migrants are often insufficiently insured – if at all – to make use of Dutch medical services; that an increasing number of Polish children are entering Dutch primary schools in some neighbourhoods, but many of them hardly speak Dutch; and that Polish adults cause a nuisance in Dutch neighbourhoods, especially when alcohol is involved.

Given particular mention was the fact that many CEE migrants settle in deprived urban districts already facing serious problems with large numbers of immigrants who barely speak Dutch and are insufficiently integrated into Dutch society. Although many of these alleged problems were qualified during the discussion and the municipal authorities represented at the conference expressed their appreciation for CEE labour migration's economic contribution to society, one crucial social issue remained on the agenda: the housing problem (see also Van den Berg, Van der Lugt & De Bruin 2006).

According to the Dutch government, the employers of CEE labour migrants are responsible for providing adequate housing for their foreign employees. The employer is obliged to endeavour to house temporary foreign employees at a reasonable cost in accordance with regulations. Municipalities are responsible for monitoring the housing situation of temporary foreign workers. However, some CEE labour migrants work for unreliable temporary work agencies that make no housing arrangements for their employees. What is more, the notion of 'adequate housing' may vary among employers. As a result, there are numerous reports of inadequate housing of CEE labour migrants:

workers living in barns in farmyards, in overcrowded boarding houses, in camper-vans, in rooms with insufficient sanitation, in fire-hazardous buildings and so on. According to the municipalities that participated in this conference, these poor housing circumstances are neither in the interest of the workers involved nor in the interests of the municipality. Apart from the fire hazard, inadequate housing for foreign workers may further damage the quality of life, overall, in deprived urban districts.

In March 2007, the Dutch government set up a national bureau where unsafe or illegal housing could be reported. However, by the end of 2007, only a few formal complaints had been reported to the bureau (Van den Berg, Brukman & Van Rij 2007: 20). The municipalities responsible for monitoring the housing of foreign workers – especially in major Dutch cities such as Rotterdam and The Hague with large numbers of foreign workers from CEE countries – are nevertheless very critical of the inadequate housing of these labour migrants and the problems it causes in their areas. The municipalities are therefore demanding drastic measures to improve the housing situation of foreign workers. Above all, they want to see an offensive against the temporary employment agencies that employ foreign workers without adequate housing facilities. The municipalities also require lists with names and addresses of formally employed foreign workers from the national government, which would enable them to monitor their housing situation. The municipalities themselves are trying to find practical solutions to the problem. Some of their efforts include introducing 'agricultural campsites' in regions with many temporary foreign workers and making vacant houses due for imminent demolition available to temporary foreign workers. Central government can also be helpful in this respect, for instance, by making vacant facilities for asylum seekers – numbers of asylum seekers have declined in recent years – available for temporary foreign workers. Whether these initiatives by local and national authorities will be enough to provide adequate housing for large numbers of temporary foreign workers from CEE countries (annually 100,000 persons or more) will become clear in the future.

Local debates on Polish workers also demonstrate ambivalence on the part of Dutch citizens and policymakers. Polish workers are admired for their motivation and working skills, but they are also criticised because many of them reside in overcrowded and low-quality housing – legal or otherwise – and scarcely participate in local communities. Many labour migrants work extremely hard – six days a week and for long hours – and take Sunday to rest, watching Polish television programmes and DVDs with their compatriots. They return to Poland once their present work project is finished. Some of the observations the American sociologist W.I. Thomas made in 1921 about Poles in

New York are still resonant: 'Letters show that they frequently reply to the inquiries from home for a description of America, "I have not been yet able to see America" (Thomas 1971 [1921]: 120-121). Similar remarks are made by many Polish workers about the Netherlands. The image of Polish workers for many Dutch people can be illustrated by the lyrics of one of the most popular songs from the annual carnival celebration in the Netherlands in 2008. The content of the song also articulates the 'liquid' nature of temporary labour migration that is as difficult to grasp for the authorities as for local citizens.

> A van full of Poles[6]
> A van full of Poles
> A van, a van
> Go, go, go!
> In the morning, in the evening, late at night
> A van drives through our street, a van full of Poles
> Look at them driving, where are they coming from?
> Where are they hiding?
> On the land, in construction, they don't make such a fuss.
> They're coming together
> For a few bucks and a can of beer,
> They come to help, that's why they are here
> One spots them everywhere, they are a border case
> Yet, they are my idols
> Wherever I see them I give them a wave
> A van full of Poles
> They have hired a house in our neighbourhood
> Cosy together
> And in the evening, when the job is done
> They turn their polka music loudly on.

This song encapsulates all the current stereotypes and myths about Poles. It touches upon their geographic mobility, group cohesiveness, work ethic and limited wages, their invisibility and seclusion from Dutch society, the overcrowded, cheap housing they face, their weekend rituals involving music and drinking and their positive image as hard and reliable workers. Many Poles in the Netherlands were offended by this song and the performer Johan Vlemmix received hate mail as the local news reported (*Algemeen Dagblad* 23 January 2008). Teachers in primary schools in The Hague have had to explain the nature of the Dutch carnival to Polish children. The controversy notwithstanding, the song perfectly conveys the uncertainty of Dutch society about Polish workers. Although essential for some sectors of the Dutch economy, they are not yet fully accepted as an established immigrant group in Dutch society.

Conclusion

This chapter tried to describe and explain contemporary patterns of labour migration from CEE countries to the Netherlands. We introduced the concept of 'liquid migration' to typify current migration patterns from CEE. These migration movements are of a temporary, fluid and uncertain nature. Because of that fluidity, it is difficult to obtain a clear picture of what exactly is going on and what the future will look like. As of 2008, approximately 100,000 CEE nationals were working in the Netherlands. How many will leave and who is going to stay? There are fierce debates about these two basic questions. Critics of ongoing immigration fear that labour migrants from CEE countries, like so many of the former guest workers from the Mediterranean area, will stay permanently and eventually end up living on social benefits. Foreign workers who now appear to be an asset to the Dutch economy may eventually become a financial burden on the welfare state. However, the contemporary evidence presented in this chapter is that this 'guest worker syndrome' is not applicable to CEE migrants. The Dutch economy needs these workers now and in the foreseeable future. Furthermore, most of the CEE migrants are likely to be transnational commuters or circular migrants. They will not settle in the Netherlands. We have also argued that there is little evidence of a significant drop in wages for low-skilled work in the Netherlands. There is also little evidence that CEE migrants are competing with many native Dutch workers. The Netherlands has a very tight labour market. The number of job vacancies was 236,000 in the third trimester of 2007, and unemployment has been at its lowest point (3.2 per cent) since 2002. However, there are indications that CEE workers (including workers from Bulgaria and Romania) are displacing irregular workers from outside the EU. EU enlargement has partly regularised the irregular work force.

We have also documented some problematic aspects of contemporary CEE migration, such as poor housing conditions and their only partial integration in Dutch society. These problems are felt and expressed particularly by policymakers in urban areas who have to deal with a large influx of CEE migrants into some of their neighbourhoods. They are trying to formulate a policy that will deal more effectively with temporary labour migration, on the one hand, and help smaller groups to settle, on the other. Given the 'liquid' nature of migration, it is very difficult for them to develop a sufficiently flexible infrastructure for temporary labour migration that is also supported by the local population.

Notes

1 According to German law, these people are considered German if they are able to document their German ancestry and, as such, are eligible for a German passport. 'German Poles' have admission to various EU labour markets because they are regarded as German citizens (Pijpers & Van der Velde 2007: 827).
2 The government, however, 'tolerated' irregular migration to the Netherlands until the beginning of the 1990s. In the period 1990-2000, it was also fairly easy for irregular immigrants to work in specific sectors of the Dutch economy (Van der Leun & Kloosterman 2006).
3 In the Netherlands' statistics concerning motives for migration, these countries are treated as the former Yugoslavia or the former Soviet Union.
4 These figures include immigrants from Slovenia, Estonia, Latvia, Lithuania, Romania and Bulgaria.
5 Van den Berg, Brukman and Van Rij (2008) have examined the number of foreign workers from the new EU member states per economic sector (both employed and self-employed).
6 Nol Roos and Johan Vlemmix (2008) 'Een bussie vol met polen' (A van full of Poles). *www.youtube.com/watch?v=pg84WbfcY1E*

References

Bauman, Zygmunt (1999), *Liquid Modernity*. Oxford: Polity Press.
Bauman, Zygmunt (2005), *Liquid life*. Oxford: Polity Press.
Borjas, G.J. (1999), *Heaven's Door. Immigration Policy and the American Economy*. Princeton: Princeton University Press.
Bosniak, Linda (2006), *The citizen and the alien. Dilemmas of contemporary membership*. Princeton: Princeton University Press.
Broeders, Dennis & Godfried Engbersen (2007), 'The fight against illegal migration. Identification policies and immigrants' counter strategies', *American Behavioral Scientist* 50 (12): 1592-1609.
Burgers, Jack & Godfried Engbersen (1996), 'Globalisation, migration, and undocumented migrants', *New Community* 22 (4): 619-635.
Corpelijn, A. (2007), 'Onderzoeksnotitie: Werknemers uit de nieuwe EU-lidstaten', *Tijdschrijft voor Arbeidsvraagstukken* 23 (2): 177-182.
Cruyff, M. & P. van der Heijden (2004), 'Een raming van het aantal illegalen in Nederland' in A. Leerkes, M. van San, G. Engbersen, M. Cruijff & P. van der Heijden (eds.) (2004), *Wijken voor illegalen:Over ruimtelijke spreiding, huisvesting en leefbaarheid*, 31-41. The Hague: Sdu Uitgevers.
De Boom, J., A. Weltevrede, E. Snel & G. Engbersen (2007), *Migration, immigrants and policy in the Netherlands*. Report for the continuous Reporting System on Migration (SOPEMI) of the Organization of Economic Co-operation and Development (OECD). Rotterdam: Risbo Erasmus Universiteit.
De Boom, J., A. Weltevrede, S. Rezai & G. Engbersen (2008), *Oost-Europeanen in Nederland. Een verkenning van de maatschappelijke positie van migranten uit Oost-Europa en voormalig Joegoslavië*. Rotterdam: Risbo Erasmus Universiteit.
De Lange, T., S.R. Verbeek, R. Cholewinski & J.M.J. Doomernik (2003), *Arbeidsimmigratie naar Nederland: Regulering en demografische en economische aspecten in internationaal vergelijk*. The Hague: Adviescommissie voor Vreemdelingenzaken.

De Lange, T. & C. Pool (2004), 'Vreemde handen aan het bed. De werving van Poolse verpleegkundigen in Nederland', *Migrantenstudies*, 20 (3): 130-144.

Düvell, Franck (ed.) (2006), *Illegal migration in Europe: Beyond control?* Basingstoke: Palgrave Macmillan.

Engbersen, G. (2003), 'The wall around the welfare state: International migration and social exclusion', *Indian Journal of Labour Economics*, Special Issue on Globalisation and Exclusion, 46 (3): 479-495.

Engbersen, G., M. van San & A. Leerkes (2006), 'A room with a view. Irregular immigrants in the legal capital of the world', *Ethnography* 7 (2): 205-238.

Engbersen, G., J. van der Leun & J. de Boom (2007), 'The fragmentation of migration and crime', *Crime and Justice. A Review of Research*, Special issue on Crime and Justice in the Netherlands, eds. M. Tonry & C. Bijleveld: 389-452. Chicago: Chicago University Press.

Leerkes, A. (2007), *Illegaal verblijf en veiligheid*. Amsterdam: Amsterdam School of Social Research (doctoral thesis).

Leerkes, A., M. van San, G. Engbersen, M. Cruijff & P. van der Heijden (2004), *Wijken voor illegalen. Over ruimtelijke spreiding, huisvesting en leefbaarheid*. The Hague: SdU.

Leerkes, A., G. Engbersen & M. van San (2007), 'Shadow places. Patterns of spatial concentration and incorporation in the Netherlands', *Urban Studies* 44 (8): 1491-1516.

Lucassen, Jan (1987), *Migrant labour in Europe, 1600-1900*. Londen: Croom Helm.

Muus, P. (2004), 'The Netherlands: A pragmatic approach to economic needs and humanitarian considerations' in Wayne Cornelius, Philip Martin & James Hollifield (eds.). *Controlling immigration: A global perspective* (second edition), 262-280. Stanford: Stanford University Press.

Pool, C.(2003), 'Hedendaagse migratie van Polen naar Nederland', *Justitiële Verkenningen* 29 (4): 63-80.

Pool, C. (2004), 'Open borders: Unrestricted migration? The situation of the Poles with a German passport in the Netherlands as an example for migration after accession to the European Union', *IMIS-Beiträge*, Heft 24/2004.

Pijpers, Roos & Martin van der Velde (2007), 'Mobility across borders: Contextualizing local strategies to circumvent visa and work permit requirements', *International Journal of Urban and Regional Research* 31 (4): 819-835.

Roodenburg, Hans, Rob Euwals & Harry ter Rele (2003), *Immigration and the Dutch Economy*. The Hague: Netherlands Bureau for Economic Policy Analysis (CPB).

Ter Beek, H.M., J.W.M. Mevissen, J. Mur & C. Pool (2004), *Poolshoogte. Onderzoek naar juridische constructies en kostenvoordelen bij het inzetten van Poolse arbeidskrachten in drie sectoren*. Amsterdam: Regioplan.

Thomas, W.I. (1971 [1921]), 'The Immigrant Community' in James Short (ed.) (1971), *The social fabric of the metropolis. Contributions of the Chicago School of Urban Sociology*, 120-130. Chicago: University of Chicago Press.

Van Amersfoort, Hans (1982), *Immigration and the formation of minority groups. The Dutch experience 1945-1975*. Cambridge: Cambridge University Press.

Van den Berg, N., M. Brukman & C. van Rij (2007), *De Europese grenzen verlegd: (Eerste) evaluatie flankerend beleid vrij verkeer van werknemers MOE-landen*. Amsterdam: Regioplan.

Van den Berg, N., M. Brukman & C. van Rij (2008), *De Europese grenzen verlegd: Evaluatie flankerend beleid vrij verkeer van werknemers MOE-landen*. Eindrapport. Amsterdam: Regioplan.

Van den Berg, P., H. van der Lugt & D. de Bruin (2006), *De huisvesting van 'tijdelijke' buitenlandse werknemers afkomstig uit MOE-landen. Een globaal overzicht*. Rotterdam: Gemeente Rotterdam.

Van der Heijden, P.G.M., G. van Gils, M. Cruijff & D. Hessen (2006), *Een schatting van het aantal in Nederland verblijvende illegale vreemdelingen in 2005*. Utrecht: IOPS-Utrecht.

Van der Leun, Joanne & Robert Kloosterman (2006), 'Going underground: Immigration policy changes and shifts in modes of provision of undocumented immigrants in Rotterdam', *Tijdschrift voor Economische en Sociale Geografie* 97(1): 59-68.

Versantvoort, M.C., I. Vossen, M. van der Ende, C. Zoon, M. Nugteren, J. Nauta, K. Azzouz, P. Donker van Heel, A. Ceglowska & W. Kreft (2006). *Evaluatie werknemersverkeer MOE-landen*. Rotterdam: Ecorys.

Vertovec, Steve (2007) 'Super diversity and its implications', in *Ethnic and Racial Studies* 30 (6): 1024-1054.

Wetenschappelijke Raad voor de Regeringsbeleid (WRR) (2001), *Nederland als immigratiesamenleving*. The Hague: SdU Uitgevers.

7 Direct demographic consequences of post-accession migration for Poland

Marta Anacka and Marek Okólski

Introduction

This chapter is devoted to demographic consequences of the post-accession migration for Poland. Based on official data published by the Central Statistical Office (CSO), it is estimated that between 1 May 2004 – the day when eight Central and Eastern European (CEE) countries joined the European Union – and 31 December 2006, the stock of temporary Polish migrants increased by over one million. That probably represents the most intense outflow ever from Poland during peacetime. Drawing from the Labour Force Survey data, we examine how this enormous post-accession out-migration from Poland has been distributed across Polish regions and various categories of the resident population, and attempt to establish the direct quantitative effect of the outflow on particular regions and major population categories.

Making use of the Selectivity Index, we argue that the post-accession outflow was not only highly selective, but significantly more selective than the outflow in the immediately preceding period, especially with respect to such characteristics of the population as sex, age and education. Finally, on the basis of migrant selectivity analysis, we suggest that migration-conducive factors specific to the post-accession period, such as liberalisation of the access to labour markets in destination countries, particularly in the United Kingdom, have brought about a wider participation of various groups of the Polish population in these out-movements. This might have undermined the traditionally dominant role of social networks in migration from Poland.

Background

Poland has for a long time been a net migration loser (Frejka, Okólski & Sword 1998; Iglicka 2001). Let us focus on the last quarter of a century. According to official records, between 1 January 1980 and 1 January 2007, the number of 'permanent residents'[1] increased by 2.7

million, whereas the total natural increase was 3.7 million. Therefore, around 1 million (net) additional 'permanent residents' (27 per cent of natural increase) were lost due to emigration (Table 7.1).

In that period, however, many 'permanent residents', who as such have maintained an entry in Poland's population registers, have also become emigrants and have de facto ceased to live in Poland. In official statistical sources, however, the de facto emigrants are included in the estimates of Poland's population as long as they figure in the registers as 'permanent residents'. The only way to remove someone from a register of permanent residents is his or her voluntary act of cancellation of residence, which most Poles perceive as unnecessary even if it is not disadvantageous. For this reason, official estimates of Poland's population might be seriously biased due to not accounting for a sizeable group (and excluding that group) of the former 'permanent residents' who live in some other country.[2]

The phenomenon of mass-scale outflow to foreign countries of Poles who have retained the status of 'permanent resident' of Poland (and because of that have become excluded from the count of emigrants) has quite a long history. According to the 1988 population census, as many as 900,000 permanent residents were staying in a foreign country for longer than two months. The next (and the most recent) census of 2002 found that 789,000 Polish residents were in such a situation, 626,000 of them having stayed abroad for longer than one year. A plausible estimate based on census data suggests that, between 7 December 1988 and 21 May 2002,[3] 'invisible emigration' (not reflected in population registers) amounted to some 900,000 persons (Grabowska-Lusinska & Okólski 2009). Together with officially recorded emigration in that period (around 300,000), the outflow was 26 per cent higher than the natural increase. Before 1 May 2004, Poland, more than most other CEE countries, was renowned for a large-scale population of undocumented migrants living abroad (Okólski 2004a, 2004b).

The CSO (2007) estimate suggests that, on 1 January 2007, 1.95 million 'permanent residents' of Poland (approximately 5 per cent of the

Table 7.1   *Population of Poland and contribution of natural increase and net migration to its changes, 1980-2006 (thousands)*

Year	Population in the beginning (1 January) of a given period	Overall population increase	Overall natural increase	Overall net migration
1980-1989	35,414	2,574	2,945	-371
1990-2003	37,988	203	775	-572
2004-2006	38,191	-66	-6	-60
2007	38,125	x	x	x

Source: CSO Statistical Yearbooks

total population) lived in a foreign country. Those persons are officially termed 'temporary migrants'.[4] It follows from the CSO estimate that, on 1 January 2005, the population of Poland consisted of around one million temporary migrants (in the sense just explained). It seems plausible to assume that, between 1 May 2004, the date of Poland's accession to the EU, and 31 December 2006, the number of such temporary migrants increased by approximately 1.07 million. Bearing in mind that over the same period around 50,000 Poles emigrated (and ceased to be 'permanent residents'), the total outflow in the post-accession period might be estimated at some 1.1 million people.

It might be observed that, in the past, a large part of the flow of temporary migrants consisted in fact of long-term migrants, i.e. persons whose sojourn in foreign countries was longer than twelve months. In the Polish literature, those persons are called 'invisible emigrants' (Sakson 2002). For instance, in the period 1980-1989, the number of those invisible emigrants amounted to around 1.1 million, which stood at a little more than half of all temporary migrants (Okólski 1994). Among all temporary migrants recorded on the day of the 2002 population census, 79.6 per cent were long-term migrants (invisible emigrants). Of 626,000 long-term migrants, as many as 249,000 were out of Poland for over ten years and 63,000 had never lived in Poland; nevertheless, those persons had entries in Polish registers of 'permanent residents' (CSO 2003).

All this suggests that official statistics of migration flows in Poland are not reliable, as they substantially underestimate emigration. On top of this, the concept of 'permanent residence', which has a landmark role in the measurement of emigration and temporary outflow, hardly grasps reality and often results in a statistical fiction. The crux of the matter with recent population movements from Poland, however, is not merely in their volume but also their selectivity, the way those movements affect the composition of Polish society and the size of its particular components. Referring to past experiences, for instance, by not accounting for invisible emigration, the total population in 1988 was overestimated by 1.9 per cent, with the male population overestimated by 2.1 per cent and the female population by 1.7 per cent. The overestimation for men aged 30-39 years old was as high as 4.1 per cent, whereas for children and the elderly it was lower than 1 per cent. Furthermore, the actual population of urban areas turned out smaller by 2.6 per cent from that officially registered and the population of rural areas smaller by 0.8 per cent. Overestimation of population size was even more striking at regional level. The most highly affected region (eastern part of Upper Silesia) lost an additional 5.4 per cent due to invisible emigration, while its rural part lost 5.9 per cent, and its 25-29-year-old female segment 13.5 per cent (Sakson 2002).

Unfortunately, hardly anything is known about actual losses suffered by various groups of Poland's population due to the outflow of people, including temporary migration, after 1 May 2004. Based on the scale of total out-migration in the period quoted above and the knowledge of consequences of the outflow for various groups of population in earlier periods, we have assumed that those losses might have been substantial for some groups. Therefore, the aim of this chapter is to analyse the selectivity of the outflow from Poland in the post-accession period and to assess the impact of that selectivity on regional distribution and demographic structure of the Polish population. In pursuing that aim, we will use structural characteristics of 'post-accession migrants' derived from the Labour Force Survey (LFS) and we will juxtapose and compare respective numbers of migrants (estimated on the basis of those characteristics) and the numbers reflecting official estimates of Poland's population in 2004.

Although the LFS in Poland has been designed to address mainly economic activity and the position of households in the labour market, especially unemployment issues, its results also seem very useful for migration studies. This is true for at least three reasons. First of all, the survey provides an opportunity to obtain some basic information about those household members who had been absent (including those staying abroad) at the time when the survey was conducted. Whereas in a survey based on a simple random sample these units (individuals) would be subsumed under non-response category, in the Polish LFS they can be easily classified as migrants. This possibility allowed us to set up a special database that included information about persons who were absent in the place of their 'permanent residence' and who, at the time of the survey, lived abroad. A unit of that database is a 'temporary migrant', i.e. a person registered in Poland as 'permanent resident' who, at the time of survey, stayed in any foreign country for more than two months and whose Polish household was included in a given LFS quarterly sample.[5]

Another advantage of using LFS data in this chapter is that the so-called sample stratification has been based on regional division,[6] which makes it possible to estimate some variables at the regional level (the NTS2 level) and compare those estimates with the corresponding national data. Lastly, the scale of the survey is relatively large – the quarterly sample size amounts to 25,000 dwellings, which stands for 0.2 per cent of all households. The importance of this information ensues from the rate of emigration and, thus, the probability of having an emigrant in a sample usually is very low (close to zero), irrespective of the volume of the outflow of population in absolute terms. This means that larger sample size reduces the risk of drawing a sample with a very low number of migrants. The 'temporary migrant' database includes the

LFS data 'permanent residents' who, at the time of the survey, stayed abroad for more than two months, extending from the first quarter (Q1) of 1999 until the last quarter (Q4) of 2006. It contains more than 6,000 records with 35 variables.

Distinctiveness of the post-accession migration

Although it may appear obvious and platitudinous, we shall briefly describe basic reasons why studying the post-accession migration from Poland seems valid before resorting to proper analysis. Those reasons might be seen in three distinct characteristics of the movements: volume, structure and social role.

With regard to volume, it is sufficient to refer to the estimate dated on 1 January 2007 of the stock of temporary migrants who left Poland after 1 May 2004, which is approximately 1.07 million. That figure might be expressed in relative terms as 2.8 per cent of the (official) total of Poland's population on 1 May 2004. Assuming that 4.9 per cent of temporary migrants were persons below the age of fifteen and 1.0 per cent persons 60 years old or more,[7] we arrive at the estimate of around 1.01 million temporary migrants aged 15-59, which translates to 4.0 per cent of the respective population of Poland. Such a large outflow in such a short period of time (just 32 months) has few precedents in the recent history of labour migration.

Specificity of the structure of the outflow will be demonstrated by means of a comparison of major characteristics of migrants before 1 May 2004 and after that date.[8] Probably the most conspicuous difference is that pertaining to the distribution of migrants by destination countries. Before the date of enlargement, the role of the three countries that on 1 May 2004 fully opened their labour markets to the Polish citizens (the United Kingdom, Ireland and Sweden) was marginal, and their share barely exceeded one tenth (10.4 per cent); whereas the share of the other five major target countries (Germany, United States, Italy, Belgium and France) was overwhelmingly high (71.6 per cent). In the following period, however, nearly half of migrants (46.5 per cent) headed for the three labour markets where the access for them was free, and the proportion of the other five declined by almost one half (to 38.9 per cent). A crucial factor was the change in proportions between Germany and the UK; in the first instance from 37.8 per cent to 20.1 per cent, and in the second from 8.2 per cent to 34.5 per cent.

Another important change occurred with respect to the region of migrant residence in Poland. Pre-accession migrants originated above all from regions with a long-standing tradition of outflow and established migrant networks. For instance, the highest outflow was noted in the case of Opolskie (the eastern part of Upper Silesia) with strong ties with the diaspora in Germany and a large proportion of dual (German-Polish) citizens in the population, followed by Podlaskie (north-eastern Poland) with diasporic links to the US and Belgium; Podkarpackie (south-eastern Poland) with diasporic links to the US and Italy; Lubelskie (eastern Poland) with diasporic links to Italy and Germany; and Małopolskie (southern Poland) with diasporic links to the US, Germany and Austria. Relatively little outflow took place from the economically most highly developed regions such as Mazowieckie, Śląskie, Lodzkie and Wielkopolskie. In the post-accession period, network-rich regions generally noted a decline in the intensity of outflow, which in the cases of Opolskie, Podlaskie and Małopolskie was substantial. In most regions (ten out of sixteen), however, out-migration intensified, most strongly in those with relatively weak outflow in the pre-accession time and usually network-poor, i.e. Mazowieckie, Śląskie, Kujawsko-Pomorskie (north-central Poland) and Lodzkie. In effect, the outflow became significantly more evenly distributed across regions.

The role of networks seemed to diminish – they ceased to be a major driver of outflow – and were replaced in this role by labour demand mechanisms. In almost all the regions, Britain (the largest of all available and open receiving labour markets) came to attract, by far, the highest number of migrants. The only distinct exception among major regions of origin remained Podkarpackie, from which migrants went in almost equal proportions to three countries: the US, the UK and Italy.

It might be mentioned here that the migration pattern by type of settlement – according to which residents of villages and, especially, small- and medium-size towns tended to be overrepresented and residents of large towns underrepresented relative to the general population of Poland – changed but has not been reversed. The proportion of migrants originating from large towns (with over 100,000 inhabitants) increased (from 20.1 to 23.9 per cent), but remained lower than in the general population (29.8 per cent). Also, the share of migrants who originated from smaller towns (up to 100,000) increased (from 35.4 to 36.0 per cent), but in this case it was higher than in Poland's population (32.7 per cent) and the overrepresentation slightly increased. The proportion of inhabitants from rural areas of all migrants declined (from 44.5 to 40.1 per cent), but continued to be higher than the respective proportion in the general population (37.5 per cent).

What appears to be an additional conspicuous, accession-related change in migration structure is a strong increase in the predominance of males and a rise in their overrepresentation relative to the sex composition of the total population of Poland. While at the time of the accession, men constituted 47 per cent of the population of Poland aged over fifteen, their share in migrants was 57 per cent in the pre-accession period and 65 per cent in the post-accession period.

Finally, post-accession migrants were slightly younger and better educated than pre-accession migrants. For both characteristics, such change stemmed mainly from the reorientation of geographical distribution and directions of the outflows. For instance, a shift from Germany to Britain as a leading target country meant the declining importance of a country that systematically attracts relatively older and less highly educated Polish migrants, and the rising importance of a country that attracts migrants of a rather opposite profile. In fact, whereas the median age of all migrants decreased from 30 to 28 years, in Britain, it increased from 25 to 26 years and, in Germany, from 30.4 to 34 years. By the same token, whereas the share of all migrants with tertiary education increased from 11.8 per cent to 16.5 per cent, the respective proportion in Britain remained constant (24.4 per cent) and, in Germany, it declined from 8.1 per cent to 5.7 per cent. On the other hand, the overall share of a predominant educational category, i.e. migrants with vocational education, consistently decreased from 34.9 per cent to 31.1 per cent while, at the same time, it rose in Britain – from 18.8 per cent to 22.3 per cent – and, in Germany, from 45.1 per cent to 45.4 per cent. A supplementary factor in the shift towards generally better-educated people taking part in the outflow from Poland was an increased importance of those regions of origin where young people are relatively more highly educated and a decreased importance of regions with generally less highly educated young people.

Let us now refer to the third novel characteristic of post-accession migration from Poland, which is its newly assumed social or – in other words – modernising role. Due to space constraints, we will not elaborate on that in this chapter. It seems, however, that the outflow after 1 May 2004 decisively contributes to what might be called a necessary crowding-out of the Polish labour market. It is only then that migrant workers from Poland, being largely a part of the redundant Polish labour force, were granted equal rights in the access to – and equal career opportunities on – labour markets of highly developed economies. This enabled those workers to compete, seek regular and stable employment and pursue long-term oriented strategies in those markets. This contrasts with pre-accession migrants who were predominantly circular migrant workers engaged in various inferior and clandestine activities, and who continuously gravitated towards Poland's overcrowded labour market and Polish welfare institutions, post-accession migrants considerably relieve their home country's labour market and welfare institutions of many burdens, obligations and rigidities. With growing numbers of Polish workers who have gone away to enhance their employment prospects in some other country, the labour market in Poland is becoming more competitive, flexible and efficient. Moreover, by becoming more and more compatible with the most 'progressive' spheres of the economy, it reinforces further modernisation. Having said all this, it seems justified to take a closer look at the nature and effects of the post-accession migration from Poland. As already mentioned, we will focus in this chapter on the selectivity of that outflow and its direct demographic consequences.

Selectivity of post-accession migration

Introductory remarks

For the purpose of further analysis that exploits the LFS database that we devised,[9] it is useful to define the concept of selectivity of the outflow and to propose an empirical index to measure its value. By selectivity, we conceive a joint effect of the set of (unnamed) factors that reveals itself in a difference between the distribution of migrants who originate from a given territory and the distribution of the general population of that territory, according to a specific characteristic (variable). Selectivity will be measured by a 'Migrants' Selectivity Index' (*SI*), which can be estimated for various categories (or values) of any variable of interest. It can be presented by means of the following formula:

$$SI_{V=i} = \frac{\dfrac{M_{V=i}}{M} - \dfrac{P_{V=i}}{P}}{\dfrac{P_{V=i}}{P}},$$

where $SI_{V=i}$ represents the Migrants Selectivity Index for category i of variable V; $M_{V=i}$ represent the number of migrants in the general population falling into category (or value) i of variable V; $P_{V=i}$ represents the number of people in the general population falling into category (or value) i of variable V; and M and P respectively represent the overall number of migrants and people in the general population.

The selectivity of outflow takes place if the Migrants Selectivity Index assumes a non-zero value for any category (value) of a given variable.[10] A positive value of the *SI* denotes that migrants falling into a specific category (variable) of a given variable are relatively more numerous than people in the general population with the same characteristic, whereas a negative value (but equal to or higher than -1) means the opposite. The higher the positive value or the lower the negative value of the *SI*, the stronger the selectivity.

Subsequent sections in this chapter deal with selectivity of the outflow from Poland from the viewpoint of such variables as sex, age, education, region of residence and locality type. In the first step, the variable-specific selectivity in the pre- and post-accession period will be presented and compared at a national level (Table 7.2). This is followed by a more detailed analysis.

It is clear from *SI* values included in Table 7.2 that the selectivity of the outflow significantly differed according to various characteristics of the population. Moreover, its changes over time were far from being unidirectional or uniform. By far, the strongest selectivity was associated with age. In particular, the mobile age migrants (20-23) were greatly overrepresented relative to the general population; despite a very high pre-accession selectivity, the *SI* moved to a substantially higher level (by 25 per cent) in the post-accession period. With regard to sex and education, although selectivity was generally much lower than in the case of (mobile) age, still there was a positive selectivity of male and better-educated migrants, whilst the level of selectivity again seemed to have been influenced by the accession. Male overrepresentation increased by 75 per cent (and female underrepresentation decreased correspondingly). Overrepresentation of the migrants whose education was rather low – that is vocational (ten years of school attendance) – decreased (by 12 per cent) and remained moderate. Migrants with an academic school diploma who, before the accession, displayed a neutral propensity to migrate (*SI* close to zero) became significantly overrepresented.

Region of origin as a selective factor

The region of a migrant's origin seems a strong and rapidly changing selective factor in Poland. As shown in Table 7.3, SI_{REG} ranged from -0.63 to 1.69 in the pre-accession period and from -0.49 to 1.48 after accession. In both periods, the population of Mazowieckie was relatively the least prone to migration and the population of Podkarpackie was relatively the most highly prone. Before enlargement, as many as nine regions displayed negative values of SI_{REG} and seven showed positive values; after enlargement the proportions were the opposite. Changes in

Table 7.2 *Migrants Selectivity Index (SI) for selected variables before and after Poland's accession to the EU*

Variable	SI before EU accession	SI after EU accession
Age (mobile[*])	0.97	1.21
Vocational education	0.34	0.30
Sex (male)	0.20	0.35
Tertiary education	0.02	0.42

Mobile age here means 20-39.
Source: LFS (BAEL)/CMR database

Table 7.3 *Regional Migrants' Selectivity Index in the pre-accession and post-accession period*

Region	SI before EU accession	SI after EU accession
Dolnośląskie	-0.04	0.21
Kujawsko-Pomorskie	-0.23	0.16
Lubelskie	0.44	0.32
Lubuskie	-0.28	-0.17
Lodzkie	-0.53	-0.43
Małopolskie	0.88	0.29
Mazowieckie	-0.63	-0.49
Opolskie	1.63	0.22
Podkarpackie	1.69	1.48
Podlaskie	1.61	0.87
Pomorskie	-0.26	-0.17
Śląskie	-0.58	-0.47
Świętokrzyskie	0.27	0.53
Warmińsko-Mazurskie	-0.08	-0.06
Wielkopolskie	-0.52	-0.35
Zachodniopomorskie	-0.12	0.12

Source: LFS (BAEL)/CMR database

SI_{REG} were significant in almost all regions. However, two regions (Podkarpackie and Podlaskie) continued to send disproportionately large numbers of people abroad (SI_{REG} close to or above unity). Meanwhile, in two other regions (Małopolskie and Opolskie), a very high positive selectivity declined to a rather low (but still positive) level. Two regions (Lubelskie, Swietokrzyskie) retained a moderately positive level of selectivity and four regions (Lodzkie, Mazowieckie, Śląskie and Wielkopolskie), a moderately negative level.

Despite evident difficulty in interpreting an interregional diversity of SI_{REG}, we attempted a relevant analysis, which is included in the Appendix. A table in that appendix presents quartiles of SI_{REG} distribution, where the notations are as follows: '+' – less than first quartile inclusive; '+ +' – less than second quartile inclusive, etc.; '*' means that SI_{REG} is lower than zero.

Thanks to a specific construction of that table, it is relatively easy to extract various characteristics of the outflow from a given region and interpret their interrelations. For instance, in the pre-accession period in Opolskie the selectivity of the most highly educated migrants was negative while the selectivity of migrants with vocational education was strongly positive. This strictly copied a pattern of the outflow from Opolskie to Germany, which at that time was by far the predominant country of destination. Even though Britain appeared as a host country option in the post-accession period, a strong selectivity was preserved in the case of migrants with vocational education, who continued to head for Germany. However, sex (males), age (20-39) and especially tertiary education came to the fore in that period as many migrants moved to the UK.

Sex as a selective factor

As we have noted (Table 7.2), male migrants continue to be overrepresented in flows from Poland. This, however, differs across the country's regions. Even, in the post-accession period, the SI in some regions (e.g. Lubuskie) was close to zero. In sharp contrast, in some others (e.g. Lodzkie, Mazowieckie), it exceeded 0.6, which could be conceived as a rather high selectivity. Still, the SI in a majority of regions (ten out of sixteen) remained at a relatively low level (0.2-0.4). It might be added that, in four regions, the overrepresentation of males decreased (most strongly in Opolskie, by 0.2) whereas, in the other twelve, it increased. Are there any obvious factors behind those differences and those changes? It does not seem so. In most regions with a relatively high SI, sex-specific selectivity was rather low and its change moderate, whereas regions with a relatively low SI displayed extreme values and strong change.

Age as a selective factor

As shown below, migrants from Poland are generally very young compared to the resident population of Poland. A great majority are under age 40, and a few are younger than twenty; they are typically what is called a 'mobile age'. For this reason, the focus here will be on this category of migrants. Already in the pre-accession period, $SI_{AGE=20-39}$ at the national level was 0.97 and it typically varied across regions from 0.8 to 1.2 (with just two exceptions: 0.66 and 1.33). After EU enlargement, it went up to 1.21; the increase was observed in all but two regions (those with the highest selectivity in the past, i.e. Lodzkie and Opolskie). Symptomatically, the region of Mazowieckie, in many ways earmarked by a strong influence of its major city – Warsaw – displayed the strongest rise in $SI_{AGE=20-39}$ and its highest value in the post-accession period (1.67).

Education as a selective factor

Let us now consider selectivity of the outflow in two important categories of education: tertiary (university diploma or equivalent) and vocational.[11] Migrants with vocational education constitute the largest single category of educational attainment among all migrants aged fifteen or over,[12] whereas those with tertiary education are rightly perceived as the most 'precious' human capital, which might be subject to brain drain.

In both categories, the *SI* was positive. With regard to vocational education, the selectivity was moderate (around 0.3) either in the pre-accession or post-accession period, with $SI_{EDU=vocational}$ displaying a slight decrease. In contrast, $SI_{EDU=tertiary}$ in the pre-accession period was close to zero but, after the enlargement, it reached the level 0.42. Therefore, factors related to EU accession seemed to strongly affect migration of the most highly educated migrants and to be indifferent to migration of people with vocational education.

While for the migrants with vocational education, the *SI* was positive in all regions in both periods, its territorial dispersion was moderate and it uniformly showed relative stability over time; the selectivity in case of tertiary education was neither stable nor uniform across regions. Strikingly, $SI_{EDU=tertiary}$ was positive in ten regions in the pre-accession period and in twelve regions in the post-accession period, and it was negative in the remaining regions (six and four, respectively). In both periods, its regional values differed considerably – in the pre-accession period from -0.57 (Świętokrzyskie) to 1.50 (Lodzkie) and in the post-accession period from -0.22 (Opolskie) to 1.54 (Śląskie). Moreover, the changes in particular regions were rather diversified – from negligible (e.g. Malopolskie and Opolskie) to strong (e.g. Śląskie and Świętokorzyskie) and from negative (e.g. Lubuskie and Lodzkie) to positive (e.g. Śląskie and Świętokrzyskie). Besides, in some conspicuous cases, negative values of *SI* changed to positive (e.g. Dolnośląskie, Podkarpackie and Swietokrzyskie) or positive values changed to negative (e.g. Lubuskie). Generally, however, an increase in the selectivity was much more prevalent (twelve regions) than a decrease (four regions) and, in most cases, it was much stronger (e.g. in case of Śląskie $SI_{EDU=tertiary}$ rose by as much as 1.15 and in case of Świętokrzyskie by 0.89).[13]

The above analysis of cross-regional selectivity of the outflow of migrants with tertiary education – the conclusions' complexity notwithstanding – provides support to our hypothesis that the accession strongly influenced migratory behaviours of the most highly educated. We suggest that the different attitudes and policies of the 'old' EU countries with regard to free movements of labour from the 'new' EU countries and, in particular, the disparity between the position taken by two countries (representing two large migrant-attractive labour markets) – Germany and the UK – forms a major underlying reason for the change in migratory behaviour of the most highly educated. Under the circumstances of the restrictive German policy and the liberal British policy, a major geographical shift in the outflow from Poland took place, with the UK replacing Germany as the main destination country.

A more in-depth insight into Poland's LFS data reveals that selectivity of the outflow of the most highly educated differs not only across regions of origin, but also according to destination countries. Let us focus here solely on the UK and Germany. Due to specific institutional arrangements (e.g. bilateral agreement on labour migration) and other factors (some of them historically determined), fifteen years before Poland's accession, Germany was not only the main receiving country, but also strongly 'attracted' specific categories of migrants, such as seasonal workers. Those migrants were mainly unskilled or semi-skilled workers. The German labour market seemed 'repulsive' to the most highly skilled. In the case of Germany, $SI_{EDU=tertiary}$ in the pre-accession period took a negative value (-0.29), and the negative selection was observed in almost all regions of Poland. This tendency became even stronger in the post accession period ($SI_{EDU=tertiary}$ =-0.52). In striking contrast, the UK seemed to continuously attract better-educated migrants from Poland. Before and after 1 May 2004, the selectivity was strongly positive, with $SI_{EDU=tertiary}$ as high as 1.09 and 1.13, respectively. Thus. it might be argued that the opening up of the British labour market to Polish workers on 1 May 2004, combined with a highly selective admission policy followed by Germany, contributed to a significant structural change in the outflow from Poland. With the UK taking an upper hand over Germany, the selectivity of migration of the best-educated people became clearly positive.

The geographical shift in labour migration from Poland also had a bearing on selectivity of the less highly educated, namely those who completed vocational school. Considering $SI_{EDU=vocational}$ for Germany, we observe that, in the pre-accession period, it was not only positive, but also rather high (0.51) and, after the enlargement date, it even increased (to 0.57). However, for the UK it remained very low (0.07 and 0.11, respectively). All this explains, at least partly, why, after the accession, the selectivity of migrants with vocational education decreased and, in particular, why it became lower than the selectivity of those best educated.

Finally, we were able to throw still more light on the mechanism of selectivity of the migrants by their educational attainment by adding another potential underlying factor, namely the type of settlement. In order to do so we examined a tendency in SI_{EDU} specific to three major types of migrant settlement in Poland[14] (city, small- or medium-size town and village[15]). What follows is a sharp decline in SI_{EDU} for both categories (tertiary and vocational), with growing size of settlement/locality. For instance, in the post-accession period, $SI_{EDU=tertiary}$ in the city was 0.27 (two thirds of the national average), in small- or medium-size towns 0.52 and in villages, 1.1 (two and a half times the national average). In the case of $SI_{EDU=vocational}$, its values for both types of urban settlements were equal and rather low (0.18), and it was much higher for rural settlements (0.46). These results may suggest that post-enlargement migration from Poland presents a case of crowding out various Polish labour markets. The more backwards the area, the more crowded the labour market, and the stronger the propensity to emigrate, especially among those who are better educated. This is particularly significant given that Poland is sharply divided economically between modern growth poles in cities, and backward rural areas.

Searching for the patterns and causes of migrant selectivity, it might also be assumed that migration driven by crowding out is more visible and prominent in 'overcrowded' regions – that is, those with a high proportion of their population in rural areas. Pearson's *r*, measuring the statistical correlation between region-specific SI_{REG} and rates of urbanisation (percentage of urban population in a region), proved negative and relatively high (-0.69). It follows from Figure 7.1 that in the post-accession period regions with a low share of urban population, such as Podkarpackie, Podlaskie, Swietokrzyskie, Lubelskie and Malopolskie, generated the largest outflow of migrants relative to their population size. Of course, this does not mean that the level of urbanisation can be

Figure 7.1 *Migrants' Selectivity Index in the post-accession period and the percentage of population living in urban areas*

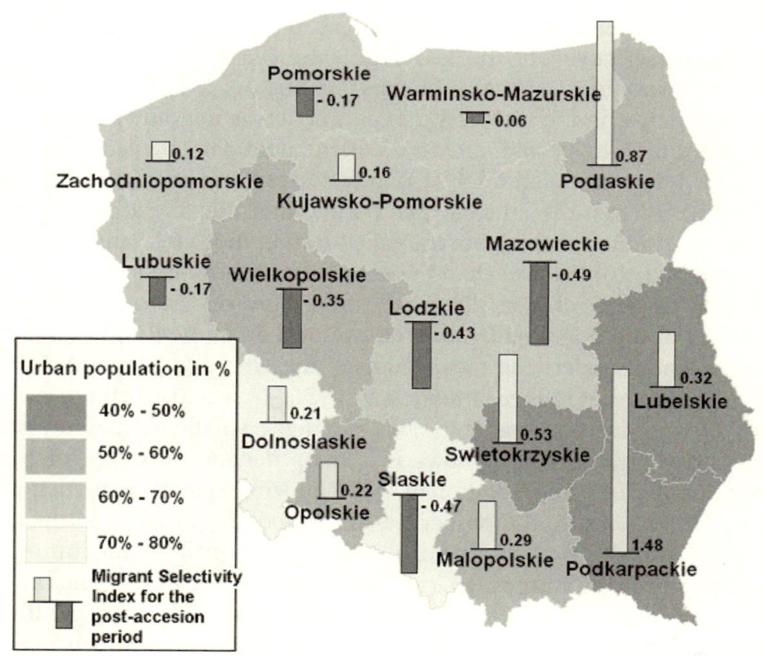

Source: LFS (BAEL)/CMR database

treated as an independent or autonomous factor of selectivity of the outflow.

An example of another underlying or intervening factor could be the region-specific unemployment rate, which, among other things, is symptomatic for labour market opportunities. However, a comparison of unemployment rates and SI_{REG} did not show any consistent relationship. For instance, whereas the lowest unemployment rates in 2004 were reported in Mazowieckie, Podlaskie and Podkarpackie (15 per cent, 16 per cent and 17 per cent, respectively), in the post-accession period in Podkarpackie, the labour market pushing-out effect was the strongest of all Poland's regions (the share of Podkarpackie in total outflow was almost 1.5 times higher than its share in the overall population). At the same time Mazowieckie was the most underrepresented region in the total outflow. Hence, there is no simple rule that could describe the pattern of post-accession migration structure and dynamics. However, considering all the facts so far mentioned, it seems that the most important factor that affected mobility of Polish migrants after 1 May 2004 was the opening of their labour markets by three of the 'old' EU countries, particularly the UK.

Direct demographic consequences of the post-accession outflow

As evidenced, the post-accession outflow proved highly selective according to such important characteristics of the population as sex, age, education, type of settlement and region of usual residence. This finding makes it legitimate and valid to hypothesise that the losses suffered by particular population groups in Poland were not only diversified, but in some important cases might also have been strikingly high. We will now present a series of estimated losses by selected characteristics of the population aged fifteen years or over (15+) as well as losses in a cross-regional perspective. Each estimate referred to below is expressed in relative terms and denotes the proportion of the population of a given group as of 1 May 2004, which it is estimated had left between the date of EU accession and 1 January 2007.

Regarding the already quoted overall outflow that accounts for 3.3 per cent of Poland's population aged 15+, the loss of males was twice as high as that of females – 4.4 per cent vis-à-vis 2.2 per cent. From the viewpoint of age, the largest loser was the group of 25-29 with 9.3 per cent, followed by the group 20-24 with 8.8 per cent and the group 30-44 with 3.8 per cent. The size of the youngest (below age twenty) and the oldest (45 or more) was hardly affected by the outflow, with 0.8 per cent and 1.1 per cent loss, respectively. That nearly one in ten people in their late twenties left Poland is probably the most conspicuous fact.

As revealed by the estimates presented in Table 7.4, the largest relative loss according to education was observed in two groups: in those with secondary education and with vocational education where it was 4.3 per cent, followed by the most highly educated group (4.0 per cent) and least highly educated group (1.0 per cent). Bearing in mind that at present people aged 15+ very rarely finish their education below vocational school level and very few migrants are recruited from among those persons, the relative outflow in the case of all three major educational categories seemed rather even. Taking those three groups into consideration, in males, the persons with secondary education suffered the largest loss (5.8 per cent) whereas in females, those with tertiary education (3.3 per cent).

Regions that lost the largest part of their population age 15+ were: Podkarpackie (7.2 per cent) and Świętokrzyskie (6.0 per cent), which strongly contrasted with Mazowieckie (1.8 per cent) and Śląskie (2.1 per cent). In other words, consistent with what has been found earlier, the least urbanised regions (40.4 and 45.4 per cent urban population in mid-2004, respectively) sent abroad relatively more migrants than the most urbanised regions (64.7 and 78.6 per cent, respectively). The two greatest losers – Podkarpackie and Świętokrzyskie – held that position in every respect, as they suffered the relatively largest losses in males (8.8 and 8.4 per cent) and females (5.7 and 3.8 per cent), and in urban (6.9 and 6.2 per cent) and rural (7.4 and 5.8 per cent) sub-populations. The third position (occupied on average by Lubelskie and Podlaskie with 4.8 per cent loss) was in contrast held by a range of regions, depending on the group: for males, it fell to Podlaskie (6.8 per cent), for females, to Lubuskie (3.8), in urban areas, to Podlaskie (5.5 per cent) and in rural areas, to Lubelskie (5.2 per cent). Mazowieckie occupied the bottom position in all respects and the losses in that region were very small; for instance, in the female sub-population it was only 0.9 per cent. Undoubtedly, despite being the most populous region in Poland, Mazowieckie, with Warsaw its major city, remained unaffected

Table 7.4   *Percentage net loss of the population age 15+ (as estimated on 1 May 2004) due to temporary outflow in the post-accession period (until 1 January 2007) by sex and the level of education*

Level of education (completed)	Males	Females	Total
Tertiary	-5.0	-3.3	-4.0
Secondary/post-secondary	-5.8	-3.1	-4.3
Vocational	-5.4	-2.4	-4.3
Lower	-1.4	-0.6	-1.0
Total	-4.4	-2.2	-3.3

Source: LFS (BAEL)/CMR database

by Poland's accession to the EU, at least insofar as migration is concerned. The main factor behind that seems to be its central position in politics, economics and culture, both literally and metaphorically, ensuring a strong attraction to local people.

The comparative situation of the various regions is illustrated in Figure 7.2. With just one (rather unimportant) exception (Lubuskie), in all regions the losses encountered by males were higher (usually substantially higher at that) than those by females. In eight regions (Kujawsko-Pomorskie, Lubelskie, Lodzkie, Małopolskie, Opolskie, Podkarpackie Pomorskie and Warmińsko-Mazurskie), the rural areas lost proportionately more people than the urban areas, whereas in the remaining regions the opposite was true (except Dolnośląskie where the loss of rural population equalled that of urban population).

One of the findings presented above suggested a very high selectivity of outflow according to age. It might be useful to take a closer look at that phenomenon by examining the two most affected age groups: 20-

Figure 7.2   *Percentage loss of population age 15+ due to the outflow,*
1 May 2004 – 1 January 2007

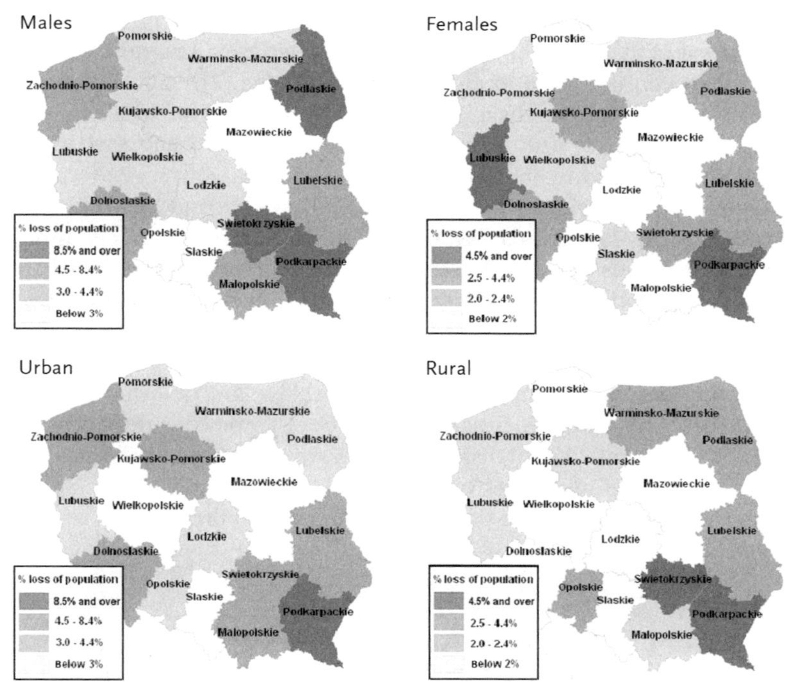

Source: LFS (BAEL)/CMR database

24 and 25-29, divided into three types of locality: city (towns with more than 100,000 inhabitants), small or medium-size town (towns with up to 100,000) and village. Table 7.5 consists of some estimates to which we will refer in the analysis to follow.

In the 20-24 age group, the largest loss occurred in the rural areas of Podkarpackie while in the 25-29 age group, in Warmińsko-Mazurskie (in fact only in two cities – Elblag and Olsztyn); the former lost more than every fifth inhabitant, whereas the latter nearly every fourth inhabitant. In striking contrast, the rural areas of Wielkopolskie lost only 2.2 per cent of their population aged 20-24 and the small and medium-size towns of Śląskie lost 3.3 per cent of the population aged 25-29. This suffices to highlight a vast interregional locality-specific differentiation of the losses caused by the post-accession outflow.

No clear tendency can be identified with respect to the most and the least affected localities across regions. In the 20-24 age group, the biggest loss was observed in rural areas and the smallest, in cities in as many as four regions. In two other regions, rural areas suffered the largest losses, but in those cases the smallest losses were noted in small- and medium-size towns. In five other regions, the maximum loss took place in small and medium-size towns; in only two of them, however, the minimum was observed in the city. In the remaining three, it was rural areas. Finally, in the five remaining regions, no significant differences between the three locality types were noted. The 25-29 age group displayed even greater dissimilarities, with a variety of locality-specific regional patterns of loss due to the outflow, and no more than two regions characterised by the same pattern.

Only in three regions (Małopolskie, Podkarpackie and Świętokrzyskie) was the locality-specific pattern of outflow the same in both age groups. All three regions lost the lowest proportion of population in villages, Małopolskie suffered the largest loss in small and medium-size towns, and the two remaining regions in cities. Most of the other regions displayed considerable differences, which, in some cases, took a striking direction. Despite our involvement in extensive and relevant empirical research, no reasonable explanation of these somewhat disorderly tendencies in the relative intensity of the loss experienced by Poland's various sub-populations comes to our minds; it might still be too early for clearer and more consistent tendencies to come to the fore.

Conclusion

The principal aim of this chapter was to describe the post-accession outflow from Poland, with an emphasis on its demographic consequences. An estimate made by the Central Statistical Office of Poland of the

Table 7.5 Top ten and bottom ten regional locality-specific units: % net loss of population age 15+ (as estimated on 1 May 2004) due to temporary outflow in the post-accession period (until 1 January 2007) in two most outflow-affected age groups[†]

| Age 20-24 (average: 8.8) | | | | Age 25-29 (average: 9.3) | | | |
| Top | | Bottom | | Top | | Bottom | |
% loss	Locality type and region	% loss	Region	% loss	Region	% loss	Region
21.1	Village, Podkarpackie	2.2	Village, Wielkopolskie	24.4	Town 100+, Warminsko-M	3.3	Town -100, Śląskie
18.1	Town -100, Lubuskie	2.7	Village, Opolskie	21.5	Town 100+, Podlaskie	3.8	Town 100+, Opolskie
17.3	Town -100, Małopolskie	2.9	Town -100, Warmińsko-Mazurskie	20.0	Village, Świętokrzyskie	3.8	Town -100, Opolskie
17.0	Town 100+, Lubuskie	3.3	Town -100, Pomorskie	18.5	Village, Podkarpackie	4.3	Town 100+, Malopolskie
14.7	Village, Podlaskie	3.4	Village, Pomorskie	16.7	Town -100, Wielkopolskie	4.4	Town 100+, Mazowieckie
14.6	Village, Świętokrzyskie	3.4	Town 100+, Wielkopolskie	16.1	Town -100, Podlaskie	5.0	Town 100+, Wielkopolskie
14.3	Village, Dolnośląskie	3.4	Town -100, Wielkopolskie	15.4	Town -100, Małopolskie	5.0	Village, Wielkopolskaie
13.8	Town -100, Dolnośląskie	3.5	Town 100+, Zachodnipomorskie	13.9	Town -100, Podkarpackie	5.1	Town -100, Lubuskie
13.8	Village, Lubelskie	3.7	Town 100+, Małopolskie	12.6	Town -100, Zachodniopomorskie	6.1	Village, Lubuskie
13.4	Town 100+, Podlaskie	4.5	Town 100+, Pomorskie	12.4	Town 100+, Zachodniopomorskie	6.1	Town -100, Lodzkie

[†] Town -100 means towns with up to 100,000 inhabitants; town 100+ means towns with more than 100,000 inhabitants

Source: LFS (BAEL)/CMR database

number of Polish residents who temporarily lived abroad served as a starting point in the analysis. That estimate led to a considerably higher figure than the official one derived from population registers and it implied, for instance, a loss of 3.3 per cent of Poland's population due to the post-accession outflow alone. To illustrate the importance of that estimate, if these populations are taken into account, Poland's GDP per capita in purchasing power parity terms stood at 55 per cent of the EU average by the end of 2006, rather than 53 per cent when the group is excluded (€ 12,900, compared to € 12,500).

By exploiting additional data that were extracted from LFS, the authors were able to present selectivity of the post-accession outflow in its various dimensions, such as region of residence, sex, age, education and type of settlement, and the change in selectivity relative to the pre-accession period. Rankings of selectivity factors and regional selectivity patterns were undertaken and interpreted. One of the important conclusions was the role of the accession-related shift in the geography of migration of the Poles on changing patterns of selectivity. In particular, the fact that Britain, rather than Germany, became the leading destination country, brought about a more even selectivity across regions and a tremendous increase in the selectivity among young males with tertiary education. Those changes signalled a growing significance of direct labour market mechanisms and a decreasing significance of migration networks in generating labour flows within the EU.

Finally, we combined the CSO estimate with LFS data and attempted a comprehensive account of population loss due to the post-accession outflow and its differentiation according to various structural characteristics. It turned out that the differences in relative losses were quite remarkable, with some categories of the population, especially those aged 20-29, reduced by a quarter (compared to the official numbers) through the effect of migration.

Our findings on migrants' selectivity and associated factors concur with intuition and predictions based on a general knowledge of migration. The time that elapsed since the date of the enlargement is probably too short to find much more. We believe, however, that our approach and the method of analysis proved to be useful and can be applied in similar research endeavours in the future. We believe that our preliminary results may be helpful in a more rigorous formulation of hypotheses in the studies to come.

Notes

1   A 'permanent resident' of Poland is someone who has been registered as such at any specific address in Poland.
2   In official Polish sources the category 'Poland's population' denotes the total number of 'persons actually living in Poland' (*ludnosc faktycznie zamieszkala*), which, at a national level, includes all 'permanent residents' irrespective of the place (i.e. foreign country) of their actual residence. In short, at the national level, all persons registered as permanent residents of Poland are treated as actual de facto residents.
3   The dates of respective population censuses.
4   To be considered as a temporary migrant one has to stay abroad for at least two months.
5   It follows from this that our 'temporary migrant' database must have incurred some bias, namely, that it omitted migrants belonging to households in which all members were staying abroad at the time of the survey. That leads to an underestimation of the volume of temporary migration.
6   Poland is divided into sixteen major administrative units called *wojewodztwo*. Those units broadly correspond to what is generally meant by regions.
7   Assumptions based on CSO records of temporary migrants (see *Rocznik Demograficzny* 2005, 2007).
8   Comparisons presented here draw on two data subsets derived from LFS – the pre-accession subset including quarterly data from Q1 1999 until Q1 2004 and the post-accession subset including data from Q3 2004 until Q4 2006. A unit of observation was an individual (a 'permanent resident') aged fifteen or over who, at the time of the survey, lived in any foreign country for longer than two months.
9   Hereafter, we will refer to the database as the LFS (BAEL)/CMR database. BAEL is a Polish acronym equivalent for LFS; CMR stands for Centre of Migration Research (University of Warsaw) to which the authors are affiliated and where the database was actually constructed.
10   If for a specific category of a given variable SI differs from zero, there must be at least one more category of that variable for which SI assumes a non-zero value.
11   Following the logic of Poland's educational system, graduates from a vocational school, which ends after ten to twelve years of schooling, are not recognised as beneficiaries of full secondary education and cannot be enrolled at any post-secondary school. Vocational schools are meant to produce manual workers in relatively narrow professions.
12   This includes six categories: tertiary, post-secondary (other than full tertiary), secondary technical, secondary comprehensive, vocational and everything lower.
13   The decrease did not exceed 0.1, with only one exception where it was 0.23 (Lodzkie).
14   Strictly speaking, that is a settlement where a migrant's household in Poland was located.
15   'City' refers to towns with more than 100,000 inhabitants and 'medium or small town' refers to those with up to 100,000 inhabitants.

References

CSO (2007), 'Informacja o rozmiarach i kierunkach emigracji z Polski w latach 2004-2006', material presented at the press conference on 23 October 2007. Warsaw: Glowny Urzad Statystyczny (CSO).

CSO (2003), *Migracje zagraniczne ludnosci 2002*. Warsaw: Glowny Urzad Statystyczny (CSO).

Frejka, T., M. Okólski & K. Sword (eds.) (1998), *In-depth studies on migration in Central and Eastern Europe: The case of Poland*. New York/Geneva: United Nations.

Grabowska-Lusinska, I. & M. Okólski (2009), *Emigracja ostatnia?*, Warsaw: Scholar.

Iglicka, K. (2001), *Poland's post-war dynamics of migration*. Aldershot: Ashgate.

Okólski, M. (1994), 'Migracje zagraniczne w Polsce w latach 1980-1989. Zarys problematyki badawczej', *Studia Demograficzne* 3 (117): 3-59.

Okólski, M. (2004a), 'New migration movements in Central and Eastern Europe' in D. Joly (ed.), *International migration in the new millennium. Global movement and settlement*, 36-56. Aldershot: Ashgate.

Okólski, M. (2004b), 'Migration patterns in Central and Eastern Europe on the eve of the European Union expansion', in A. Górny & P. Ruspini (eds.), *Migration in the New Europe. East-West revisited*, 23-48. Houndmills: Palgrave/Macmillan.

Sakson, B. (2002), *Wplyw 'niewidzialnych' migracji zagranicznych lat osiemdziesiatych na struktury demograficzne Polski*. Warsaw: Szkola Glowna Handlowa.

Appendix

Quartiles of regional SI distributions by selected factors (variables) in the pre-accession and post-accession periods

Region	Pre-accession period			Post-accession period						
	tertiary education	Vocational education		Tertiary education		Vocational education	Sex	Mobile age		
		Total outflow	Germany	Total outflow	UK			Total outflow	UK	Germany
Dolnośląskie	++*	++	+	+++	++	+	++	+	+++	+
Kujawsko-Pomorskie	++*	++	++	+*	+	+++	+++	+++	+	+++
Lubelskie	+++	+++	+++	++	++	++++	+++	++++	++	++++
Lubuskie	+++	+	+	+*	+++	++	+	++++	+++	++
Lodzkie	++++	+	++	++++	+	++	++++	+++	++++	+
Malopolskie	++	+++	++++	+*	+	+++	+	+++	+	+++
Mazowieckie	+++	+	+	+++	+++	+	++++	++++	++++	++++
Opolskie	+*	++++	++++	+*	++++	++++	+++	+	++++	++
Podkarpakie	+*	++++	++++	++	+++	++++	+	++	++++	++++
Podlaskie	+*	++++	+++	++	++	++++	++	+	++	++
Pomorskie	++++	++	+++	++++	++++	++	++++	+	+	+
Slaskie	++++	++	+	++++	++++	+	++	+++	+++	++
Swietokrzyskie	+*	++++	++++	++	+	+++	+++	++	++	+++
Warminsko-Mazurskie	+++	+++	++	++++	+++	+++	+	++	+	++++
Wielkopolskie	++++	+	++	+++	++++	+	++	++	++	+++
Zachodniopomorskie	++	+++	+++	+++	++	++	++++	++++	+++	+

Source: LFS (BAEL)/CMR database

8 Brains on the move? Recent migration of the highly skilled from Poland and its consequences

Paweł Kaczmarczyk

Introduction[1]

Poland is usually perceived and described as a typical country of emigration. International migration does in fact play a significant role in the contemporary history of Poland and in the process of its socio-economic development. However, until the late 1990s migration-related issues were almost absent in public debate with a few exceptions, such as post-1968 migration resulting from the anti-Zionist campaign, migration of 'ethnic Germans' in the 1950s and 1970s or politically driven migration in the 1980s. The debate on the causes and consequences of migration started yet again prior to Poland's accession to the European Union as part of a general discussion on the potential consequences of the accession of Central and Eastern European (CEE) countries to the EU, and then continued due to the spectacular increase in the scale of the mobility of Poles in the post-accession period. Paradoxically, in contrast to migration debates prior to EU enlargement, when numerous hazards were voiced as to what would be the impact of the expected inflow of people on EU residents, in current debate, the issue of the consequences of outflow for Polish economy and society plays the most prominent role. Commonly expressed threats include labour shortages on the Polish market and, particularly, the so-called brain drain that is understood as outflow of highly skilled persons.

The aim of this chapter is to analyse the scale and structure of mobility of the highly skilled in the broader context of recent trends in international migration from Poland. Emphasis will be put on such issues as the question to what extent migration of professionals is a statistically significant phenomenon and the real and possible consequences of recent outflows for the Polish economy and society. The structure of the chapter is as follows: section two looks at the general trends in migration behaviour in the pre- and post-accession periods. Against this background, section three analyses the phenomenon of the mobility of the highly skilled. Section four includes an attempt to assess the impact of recent migration of professionals on the Polish economy and society. Section five concludes.

Migration from Poland in the transition period[*]

Ever since the nineteenth century, Poland has been playing an ever more significant role in the global migration system as a major country of emigration. However, apart from mass movements of population caused by the redrawing of state borders and related international agreements, migration from Poland after World War II was seriously limited: a very low scale of mobility was a consequence of the restrictive migration policy imposed by the communist regime. The increase in migration was associated first with political changes in the mid-1950s. However, notwithstanding the liberalisation in cross-border movements and the normalisation of Polish-German relations in the 1970s, mass migration to the West did not really start until the 1980s (Okólski 2006).

Due to poor quality of migration data and changes in migratory behaviour, the comparison of pre-transition and transition trends is hardly plausible. Official statistical data gathered by the Central Statistical Office (based on the Central Population Register, PESEL) show a clear stabilisation in the number of departures associated with the declared change in place of residence at 20,000-25,000 annually.[2] In total, according to this data source, over 353,000 people left Poland between 1990 and 2005 with the intention to settle abroad. More recent data reveals that, in 2006, over 50,000 persons deregistered themselves from permanent residency in Poland – this number was around twice as high as the scale of migration in previous years. This extraordinary increase is to be attributed predominantly to the choices Polish migrants made as a consequence of the Polish government's tax policy.

The most reliable data concerning migrants staying abroad in the 1990s and early 2000s (i.e. in the pre-accession period) may be obtained from registries and surveys. The 1995 Microcensus showed that about 900,000 permanent residents of Poland had temporarily (i.e. for over two months) stayed abroad, which amounts to about 2 per cent of the total population. According to the 2002 national census, as many as 786,100 Polish citizens, counted as members of households in Poland, were staying abroad for longer than two months (1.8 per cent of the population) at the time of the survey. These data clearly show that

---

[*]   This chapter was written in 2007-2008 and all included data encompass the first post-accession phase (2004-2007). Thus, the analysis does not refer to the most recent migratory phenomena.

recent mobility of Poles did not start in May 2004 – during the 1990s migration was already an important socio-economic phenomenon in Poland while nearly one million permanent citizens were staying abroad.

The best source to monitor intertemporal changes in Poles' mobility is the quarterly Labour Force Survey (LFS), which, since 1994, has recorded Polish citizens staying abroad.[3] LFS data indicates that 130,000-540,000 adults were staying abroad in each year between 1994 and the second quarter of 2007 (Figure 8.1).

It is worth noting that, according to LFS data, there has been a steady increase in the number of Polish migrants observed since 1998. This trend continued after Poland's accession to the EU: in 2004, on average, 250,000 Poles stayed abroad for at least two months and this figure constituted an over 20 per cent increase in comparison to 2003. Additionally, in 2005 and 2006 in each quarter, the number of migrants was higher than in the respective quarters of the previous year.

Two important features of contemporary migration from Poland are obvious from LFS data. The first is the predominance of labour migration: according to LFS data, between 70 and 80 per cent of migrants

Figure 8.1 *Polish migrants by length of stay abroad, 1994-2007 Q2 (thousands)*

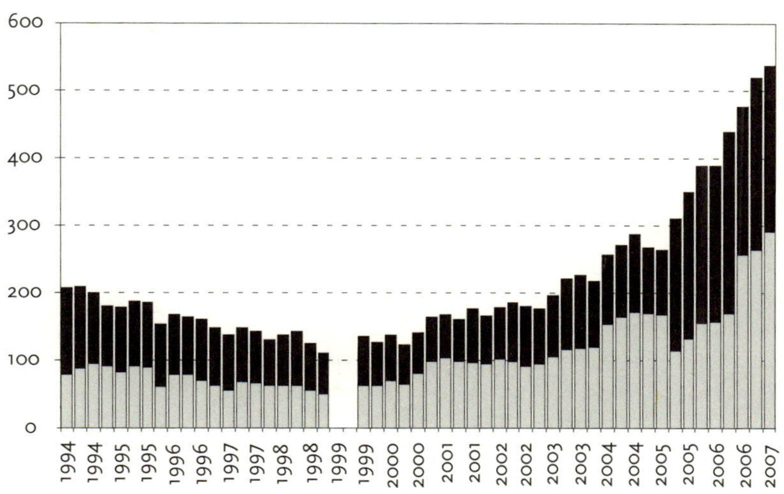

■ Persons staying abroad for longer than 12 months
□ Persons staying abroad for longer than 2 months but shorter than 12 months

Source: Author's own elaboration based on LFS data

undertake work during their stay abroad. Secondly, a significant part of all temporary migrants (60-70 per cent) tend to stay abroad for shorter than twelve months (see Figure 8.1). However, since 2006, a gradual change in migration trends can be observed: in 2006 the number of persons staying abroad for longer than twelve months more than doubled compared to 2005. This may be a clear sign that recent Polish migrants who moved in the early 2000s tend to prolong their stay abroad.

According to LFS data, the distribution of major destination countries did not change dramatically after May 2004 (Figure 8.2). However, even if we conclude that Germany remained the major receiving country of Polish migrants,[4] the most striking feature is the large increase in the number of migrants to the UK and Ireland, i.e. the countries that decided to open their labour markets for migrants from Poland and other accession countries. This tendency has led to clear domination of the UK as most important destination in 2006 and 2007.[5]

In the second quarter of 2006, the United Kingdom registered the largest increase in migration in comparison to the second quarter of 2005 (and 2004 also): 130 per cent and 380 per cent, respectively. In 2007, an increase of an additional 41 per cent (with respect to the second quarter of 2006) was noted. Consequently, in the second quarter of 2006, the share of migrants to the UK in the total number of temporary migrants from Poland reached 31 per cent and 32 per cent in 2007 (in 2000, nearly 4 per cent). In the case of Ireland, it was 7.5 per cent

Figure 8.2 *Polish migrants by country of destination (2000-2007) Q2 (thousands)*

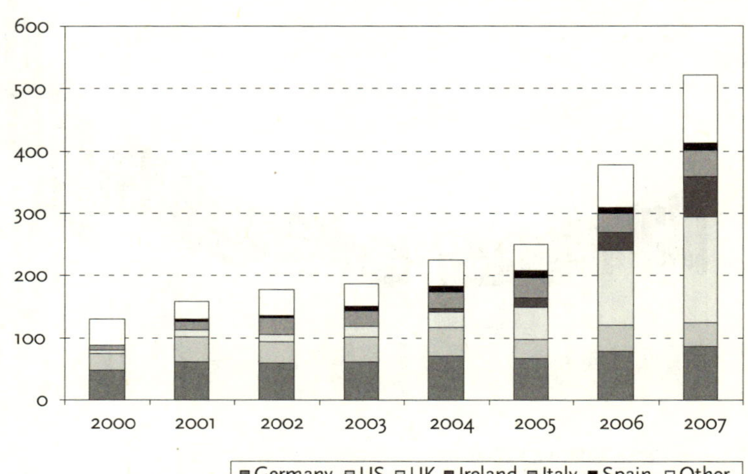

Source: Author's own elaboration based on LFS data

in 2006 and 12 per cent in 2007 (0 per cent in 2000). Figure 8.2 also clearly shows that since the early 2000s, the destinations of Polish migrants have gradually diversified, with a more and more important role played by such countries as Italy, Spain and Belgium.

Following 1 May 2004, these datasets can be supplemented by immigration-related data from those countries that decided to open their labour markets for workers from the CEE countries. The accession to the EU has, to a great extent, intensified visits to the UK by A8 citizens – that is, citizens of the eight CEE countries that joined the EU in 2004. The International Passenger Survey (IPS) records all visits to the UK and may serve as a proxy of labour mobility, though it includes all persons entering the UK, not only those arriving with an intention to undertake work. Over the years 2003-2006, the dynamics of visits to the UK by the nationals of selected A8 countries was three to five times higher than the EU-15 average. Over 1.3 million Poles visited the UK in 2006 alone, nearly five times higher than the 300,000 who visited in 2003.

In the case of the UK and Ireland, the data on labour migration are provided by specific registers applied after opening their labour markets. The Worker Registration Scheme (WRS) data – published regularly by the Home Office – shows that the total number of workers from Poland registered in the UK between May 2004 and March 2008 amounted to 540,755 approved applicants (approximately 67 per cent of all registered workers from the A8 countries). It is important to note that this data should not be used as a direct measure of the inflow of workers into the UK in the post-accession period. In fact, in May 2004, when the British labour market was opened to new EU countries, thousands of Czechs, Slovaks and Poles had already been working in the UK. Before the accession to the EU, as many as 34,000 migrants from Poland were recorded as living in Britain in the 2003 LFS, and the trend was clearly rising (Salt 2005). For most of these migrants, applying to the WRS was the only way to legitimise their employment status (Portes & French 2005).

Ireland, another EU-15 country that opened its labour market to the citizens of new accession countries in May 2004, had, since 2001, already been relatively open to inflows from these countries. The scale of immigration to Ireland is reflected by the data on Personal Public Service (PPS) numbers, required for every migrant worker. A total of 290,000 PPS numbers were issued to A8 nationals in the period 2001 to the end of October 2006, with almost 175,000 of these issued to Polish citizens.

From this data, it is hardly possible to draw a comprehensive and reliable picture of contemporary migration from Poland. This is not only due to the quality of the data, but also the very nature of the migration process – the dynamics and diversity of flows make a general assessment of recent migration from Poland an extremely difficult task. It can be argued, however, that the recent estimates provided by the Polish Central Statistical Office constitute the most reliable assessment of recent mobility of Poles (Table 8.1).

The below data shows that the stock of temporary migrants from Poland more than doubled since EU enlargement – the post-accession outflow can be estimated at around 1.1 million persons. The most important destination country became the UK (30 per cent of the total). In contrast, the most favourable destination country for Polish migrants in the pre-accession phase, Germany, received only 23 per cent of the outflow. The most notable increase was observed in Ireland, but also in the Netherlands and Sweden. All in all, Table 8.1 shows that there is not so much a tendency for concentration of Polish migrants in the UK and Ireland but, rather, a 'spilling-over' from other EU destinations. Additionally, the analysis of post-accession flows is very difficult due to the complexity of the migration process.

As suggested by studies at the regional and local level, in the post-2004 period, we observe two structurally different patterns of migration from Poland. The first stream refers to relatively young and well-educated persons, often single or in informal relationships and usually without children. A large part of this group can communicate in English, and this constitutes an important factor influencing their decision to migrate (together with an opportunity to legalise their work and stay abroad). Therefore, the UK and Ireland are the most favourable destinations for them. The second stream comprises relatively older and less educated persons, mostly with no foreign-language skills but quite often with previous migration experiences. Those migrants tend

Table 8.1   *Polish citizens staying abroad for longer than two months by major destination countries (in thousands)*

Total/destination	2002 (May)	2004	2006 (December)
Total	786	1,000	1,950
EU	451	750	1,550
Austria	11	15	34
Belgium	14	13	28
France	21	30	49
Germany	294	385	450
Ireland	2	15	120
Italy	39	59	85
The Netherlands	10	23	55
Spain	14	26	44
Sweden	6	11	25
UK	24	150	580

Source: CSO 2007

to rely on migrant networks and choose more 'traditional' destinations (Germany, Italy, Spain or the US). In many Polish regions, both forms of migration coincide though.

Highly skilled migration from Poland

Traditionally, a considerable role in Polish mobility was ascribed to the emigration of highly skilled persons. Similarly to other less developed countries, this process was described and interpreted as a form of 'brain drain'. However, upon analysis of data on international migration, this thesis seems to be rather questionable with reference to almost the whole post-War period (Kaczmarczyk & Okólski 2002). With the exception of an episode of (partially) forced migration of persons of Jewish descent (1968-1971), when over 13,000 of mostly highly educated persons left Poland, the share of persons with tertiary education among all migrants did not differ significantly from that of the total population.[6] However, the situation changed in the late 1970s and 1980s. The brain drain thesis is particularly relevant in the case of massive outflow in the 1980s. Calculations based on policy register data show that of almost 700,000 emigrants who left Poland between 1 April 1981 and 6 December 1988, 15 per cent had a higher degree and 31 per cent had secondary education. If we consider that, for the whole population, the share of university graduates was roughly 7 per cent, the data show that there was a considerable overrepresentation of emigrants of high-quality human capital in relation to the whole population of Poland (Sakson 2002). According to estimates of Okólski (1997), the scale of emigration of specialists from higher social classes in the 1980s was so large that as many as a quarter of Polish university graduates of all higher education institutions left the country each year – around 15,000.

Various data sources suggest the situation had changed significantly during the transformation. Using official data, we can conclude that, after 1990, the share of individuals with the lowest level of education who migrate increased, while the share of individuals with the highest level of educational attainment has decreased. At the threshold of the transformation in 1988, persons who had elementary or lower than elementary education constituted 37 per cent of emigrants aged fifteen and over, and people with a higher degree 9 per cent. In contrast, in 2003, there were 55 per cent in the former group, and 4 per cent in the latter. These observations were supported by the majority of studies conducted both in Poland and in the receiving countries. Research carried out by the Centre of Migration Research in the years 1994-1999 indicated that the claim about brain drain can be upheld only in relation to big urban centres. More importantly, in quantitative terms, migration from the peripheral regions was dominated by individuals with no more than secondary educational attainment and by poor human capital who took up employment almost exclusively in the secondary sectors of labour markets in the host countries. Similar results were provided by studies conducted both in Poland and in receiving countries. Each of these studies supported the observation that a greater propensity to migrate was typical for people with low cultural competencies and no knowledge of foreign languages who encountered problems with finding their feet in the new post-communist reality, particularly on the labour market. These people were almost fully dependent on the employment offer addressed to unskilled workers, willing to start work any time and for any period of time (usually on an extremely short-term basis). There were only a few exceptions observed, notably mobility to Ireland, Scandinavia and, to some extent, the US (Kaczmarczyk & Okólski 2005).

The thesis of structural change in Polish migration since 1990 was supported by a few studies on highly skilled migration from Poland, particularly in the case of scientists. The factors pushing scientists to go abroad were actually parallel to other less developed countries: low income and worse labour conditions, low prestige and social status of science and education, poorly equipped study rooms and laboratories, restricted access to the literature, lack of research funds, limited opportunities for contacting broader scientific circles. A massive migration abroad could have been expected as the education in many states of the region was of top quality.

Such a prognosis only came true, to a certain extent, as can be clearly seen from the results of an in-depth survey that covered over one thousand scientific institutions hiring roughly 45 per cent of all the scientific workers in Poland over the period 1980-1996 (Hryniewicz, Jałowiecki & Mync 1992, 1994, 1997). Between 1981-1991, the scientific centres surveyed (accounting for a total of 28,500 academics and researchers) lost over a quarter of their staff due to termination of contracts. However, emigration accounted for only 9.5 per cent of the staff complement in 1991, whilst a loss of 15.1 per cent resulted from so-called internal brain drain, i.e. taking up other posts within Poland that typically paid higher salaries or offered better career opportunities. This suggests that this migration stream originated mostly from lack of opportunities for effective application of human resources in Poland, and should be described rather in terms of brain overflow than brain drain.

Taking into account the outflow of scientists from the institutions under survey in the long-term, i.e. 1981-1996, one remarkable phenomenon is an enormous increase in the number of persons who left up until the years 1992-1993, with a radical reverse trend in 1994-1996 (Figure 8.3). The reason behind this phenomenon is easy

Figure 8.3 *Average annual number of scientists leaving the R&D sector in Poland, 1981-1996*

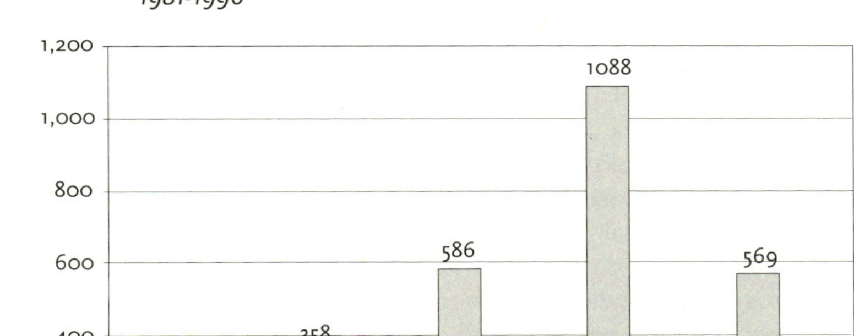

Source: Kaczmarczyk and Okólski (2005) based on Hryniewicz et al. (1997)

to pinpoint: such interdependence was determined by resignations that were not connected with emigration. Up to the early years of the transition period, an increasing number of people gave up scientific activities in order to take up positions in other industries; in the years 1981-1988, annual resignations of scientists amounted to 1 per cent, in 1989-1991, 2 per cent and in 1992-1993, as much as 4 per cent. Later, in 1994-1996, this tendency diminished; at that time the annual percentage of academic or research staff deciding to resign equalled 2 per cent.

In comparison with losses in the research and development (R&D) sector as a whole, emigration of scientists seems rather insignificant; in the long run, it has proved to be almost marginal. This is demonstrated by the share of scientists in the total outflow of scientific workers, which diminished from 52 per cent in 1981-1984 to 11 per cent in 1994-1996. Only 51 per cent of emigrants continued working in the scientific field after they had settled abroad, thus human capital should not be considered as transferred but rather as partially lost – this also applies to the case of those scientists who left for other positions within Poland. In general, the case of scientists shows that the first half on the 1990s was a period of new opportunities for well-educated Poles which significantly restrained the migratory potential.

However, in the second half of the 1990s, the trend in migration of the highly skilled reversed once again. The structure of migration changed as a consequence of the educational breakthrough, on the one hand, and economic crisis on the other, particularly the deteriorating situation in the Polish labour market. Such a picture emerges from the population census data. According to the Polish census of 2002, among the 576,000 permanent residents aged fifteen or more who had been living abroad for at least twelve months at the time of the census,[7] 0.7 per cent held a doctoral degree, 10.1 per cent a university diploma (i.e. a Master's degree) and 3.2 per cent other tertiary education diplomas (i.e. a Bachelor's degree), whereas among the general population the figures were 0.3 per cent, 7.4 per cent, and 2.7 per cent, respectively.

Table 8.2 shows that the share of highly educated migrants was the highest before the beginning of the transition (15.6 per cent), then became relatively low in the years 1989-1991 (11.8 per cent), only to rise again in the following years. The same conclusion can be drawn on the basis of LFS data, which demonstrates that, since the late 1990s, the share of migrants with tertiary education has increased significantly (particularly in the post-accession period).

Table 8.2   *Educational level of permanent citizens of Poland (aged fifteen and over) staying abroad for longer than twelve months, by year of departure (%)*

Year of departure	Tertiary	Secondary	Other
Up to 1988	15.6	34.6	49.8
1989-1991	11.8	33.4	54.9
1992-1994	13.4	36.3	50.2
1995-1997	13.4	36.4	50.2
1998-2001	15.2	35.6	49.2
Total	14.0	35.0	51.0

Source: Kaczmarczyk and Okólski (2005) based on unpublished census data

According to the CMR Migrants' Database based on the Polish LFS, the pre-accession outflow from Poland was dominated by persons with secondary vocational and vocational degrees (61 per cent of all migrants). After 2004, the share of persons with tertiary education increased significantly: from 15 to 20 per cent. The comparison of the above presented data with the share of university graduates in the overall population of Poland (in 2004, 14 per cent) leads to a conclusion that there is now a positive selection of well-educated Polish migrants. This is particularly the case of female migrants, of whom 27 per cent were highly-skilled persons (Table 8.3). This observation was strongly supported by the analysis of Migration Selectivity Rates based on the CMR databases (see Anacka & Okólski in this volume).

Table 8.3 *The education structure of Polish pre- and post-accession migrants by sex (%)*

Level of education	Pre-accession[1]			Post-accession[2]		
	Total	Men	Women	Total	Men	Women
University degree[3]	14.7	12.0	18.3	19.8	15.6	27.0
Secondary	14.0	7.1	23.1	14.2	8.8	23.8
Secondary vocational	26.1	26.0	26.3	28.1	29.8	25.1
Vocational	34.8	45.4	20.9	30.9	39.2	16.2
Primary	9.9	9.3	10.9	7.0	6.6	7.8
Unfinished	0.4	0.2	0.5	0.0	0.0	0.0
Total	100.0	100.0	100.0	100.0	100.0	100.0

Source: CMR Migrants' Database based on Polish LFS
[1]Aged fifteen and over who have been abroad for at least two months in the period 1999-2003
[2]Aged fifteen and over who have been abroad for at least two months in the period 1 May 2004 –31 December 2006
[3]Including Bachelor's, Master's and PhD degrees

Interestingly, the educational structure of Polish migration varies depending on destination. The highly educated were underrepresented among those migrating to Germany and Italy, and overrepresented among those migrating to other countries, especially to the UK (Figure 8.4). Educational structure is also closely connected to the type of migration, with seasonal migrants being relatively poorly educated.

On the other hand, the most recent migration to English-speaking countries is the domain of young and relatively well-educated persons. According to Polish LFS data, in the third quarter of 2006, migrants with tertiary education constituted over 18 per cent of all migrants. The share of persons with tertiary education was relatively higher among those staying abroad for less than twelve months (19.6 per cent compared to 16.3 per cent for those staying longer than twelve months) and for women (24 per cent compared to 15.3 per cent for men). A very similar picture is revealed by data gathered through various surveys completed in destination countries – particularly in the UK (Kaczmarczyk & Okólski 2008a, 2008b).

One of the most controversial issues in current public debate is the migration of medical professionals. This is, above all, a consequence of the permanent demand for this type of migrants in highly developed states. In the light of unfavourable demographic trends as well as fluctuations on the labour markets, the majority of Western European states are facing significant deficiencies in the number of medical staff. In addition, this field represents a typical example of intangible services: that is, the human flow cannot be easily substituted with mobility of goods and services. In effect, potential immigrants may expect highly beneficial financial and social conditions, integration support and, in at least

Figure 8.4 *Level of education of permanent citizens of Poland (aged fifteen and over) staying abroad for longer than twelve months by country of destination*

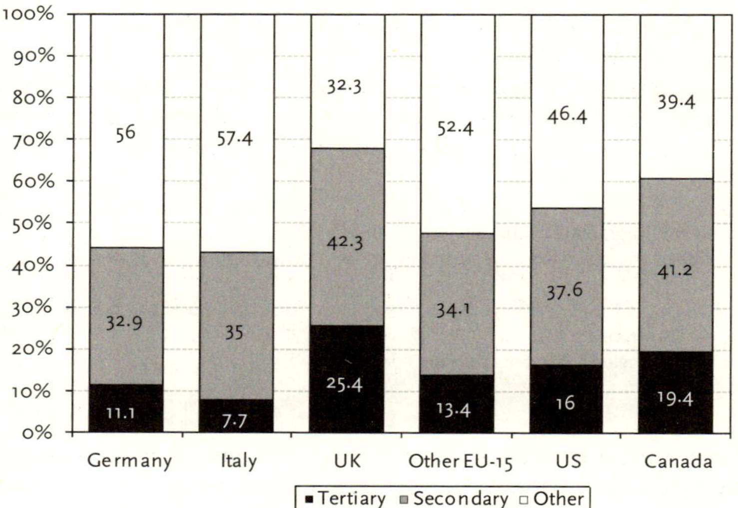

Source: Kaczmarczyk and Okólski (2005 based) on unpublished census data
Note: A similar picture can be drawn from LFS data.

several receiving countries, simplified immigration procedures. Work offers targeted at healthcare workers in CEE states are incomparably better than the opportunities created by local labour markets. As a consequence, a high migration propensity among this group should be expected.

In the case of Poland, some indication of the scale of potential migration of medical professionals is provided by the issuing of certificates that confirm the qualifications and professional experience required by employers in Western European states. The number of issued certificates – 6,724 (as of the end of December 2007) amounted to 5.7 per cent of the total number of medical doctors in Poland. In the case of dentists, certificates were issued to 1,924 persons (6.3 per cent of the total). With regard to semi-skilled medical staff, around 9,300 certificates were issued to nurses and midwives, which amounts to 0.3 per cent of the total number of registered professionals in this group. A breakdown of these figures for the period 2004-2006 by area of specialty is provided in Table 8.4.

It would be hard to consider the scale of migration estimated this way as alarming. This is the line followed in evaluations by researchers

Table 8.4 *Certificates issued to medical professionals in key specialties, May 2004 – June 2006*

Specialty	Number of economically active doctors	Number of certificates issued	Share of certificates in total number of specialists (%)
Specialties with the highest number of certificates issued			
Anaesthesiology	3,984	625	15.6
Surgery	5,395	334	6.1
Orthopaedics	2,261	168	7.4
Internal diseases*	11,792	163	1.4
Radiology	1,993	154	7.7
Specialties with the highest relation of certificates issued to the number of active specialists			
Anaesthesiology	3,984	625	15.6
Plastic surgery	142	21	14.7
Chest surgery	218	28	12.8
Radiology	1,993	154	7.7
Orthopaedics	2,261	168	7.4
Total	81,346	3.074	3.7

Source: Kaczmarczyk and Okólski (2005) based on the Ministry of Health data
* Data are until the end of June 2005.

and specialists from the Ministry of Health. Although migration of the so-called 'white personnel' is a noticeable phenomenon, its scale is not so large as to pose a threat to the healthcare system in the short term. This threat is not that significant because, in the experts' opinion, the Polish educational system 'produces' medical professionals at a rate still higher than their potential outflow to other states. In fact, to some extent, migration of medical specialists may be viewed as a brain overflow rather than brain drain, which is particularly true in the case of young professionals trapped in the Polish 'feudal' organisational structures of the medical profession with limited chances for promotion. Nonetheless, the outflow of medical doctors appears very painful in the case of certain specialisations. This is especially the case in specialties such as anaesthesiology or radiology, where incomes are relatively low in Poland, as well as specialties such as plastic surgery where there is a high demand in foreign labour markets. Moreover, a temporary or permanent imbalance on local and regional labour markets is also likely, and may already have occurred.

The data presented above may be supplemented by information on the migration of students – a group usually perceived as extremely mobile. However, the data on student mobility is very limited, whilst official data says very little about the real scale of the phenomenon. Less than 10,000 persons annually participated in exchange programmes (ERASMUS, programmes based on bilateral agreements) in the pre-accession periods. More recent data reveals a significant increase in the scale of student mobility in the last three to four years. According to data gathered in destination countries, Poland is definitely the most important country of origin of student migrants among A8 states: in the academic year 2006-2007, the number of Polish students in EU-15 countries was greater than 31,000, with the most important destinations being Germany (around 15,000), the UK (almost 7,000) and France (around 3,000). The highest increase was noted in the case of the UK – between 2005-2006 and 2006-2007 alone, the number of Polish students enrolled in the UK increased by over 55 per cent (Wolfeil 2008). Similar data can be obtained on the basis of information provided by the Polish Ministry of Education (and presented in UNESCO education statistics): in 2005, the number of Polish students studying abroad was estimated at 31,455 persons. Nevertheless, the scale of student mobility in Poland is very low and far below Western European standards: in 2005 the outbound mobility ratio equalled 1.5 per cent and was one of the lowest among the A8 countries (Wolfeil 2008). This theme is developed further in the following section.

Brain drain, brain exchange or brain waste?

The outflow of highly skilled individuals is one of the most controversial, hot topics in migration debates. However, due to the complexity of its consequences, assessment of the phenomenon seems to be very difficult. Table 8.5 summarises the variety of effects typically linked to mobility of highly skilled people and presents both costs and benefits related to this type of migration, with special reference to the situation of Poland. These effects have been grouped within three categories broken down by the level of analysis, from micro level to the macro, i.e. individual (family) level, company level and economy level, respectively. It is worth noting that, on all levels, both positive and negative aspects of highly skilled mobility can be observed, which makes the general assessment of the phenomenon hardly possible. Additionally, issues commonly appearing in the public debate are not necessarily those that are most important. In the case of Poland, effects that are typically stressed in public debates are negative points such as the loss of scarce human capital, shortages of labour and losses associated with (public) expenditure on migrants' education.

In addition, although Polish migrants are, at least to some extent, positively selected with respect to human capital, they are concentrated predominantly in the secondary sectors of receiving economies and take jobs in 'typical' migrant sectors such as construction, agriculture, cleaning and hotels. This observation is strongly supported by the WRS data.

Table 8.5   *Selected costs and benefits of highly skilled migration from Poland*

Level	Potential costs	Potential benefits
Individual/ family	Loss of insider's position Bad working/living conditions Low status of the job Depreciation of human capital Relative deprivation Racism Discrimination Separation costs Impact on family life	Better job opportunities Better working/living conditions Higher social status/higher status of the job Employment according to the skills Ability to improve the skills Higher income, no relative deprivation New experiences (social, cultural)
Company	Loss of highly skilled labour Shortages of labour leading to inflation pressure Lost expenditure on training	Skills and experience of return migrants Cooperation with migrants staying abroad Gains of the recruitment sector Gains of the migration-supporting sectors
Economy	Loss of scarce human capital Loss of young people Loss of production (potential) Negative fiscal effects (lower tax incomes) Losses associated with expenditure on migrants' education Negative impact on the R&D sector Imbalances in local and regional labour markets Growth of income inequality Socio-cultural changes – 'culture of migration'	Transfer of knowledge as a side-effect of return migration Lower demographic pressure Remittances (direct and indirect effects) Impacts on human capital formation Transfer of knowledge as an effect of cooperation with migrants staying abroad Lower unemployment Higher income equality Multicultural societies

Source: Author's own elaboration

If we assume that the number and structure of applications to the WRS may serve as a proxy of 'real' migration to the country – which does seem reasonable to some extent – the data provided by the UK Home Office allow us to build quite a precise picture of contemporary labour migration to the UK. The data reveal that migrant workers from the A8 countries tend to concentrate in such sectors as administration, business and management (39 per cent); hospitality and catering (19 per cent); agriculture (10 per cent); manufacturing (7 per cent) and agriculture-related sectors (5 per cent).

This might suggest that migrants from A8 countries are able to get into primary labour markets and achieve a relatively good position in the UK labour market. However, this picture may be misleading.

Considering the information on the occupations of applicants from accession countries, it turns out that they mainly undertake simple jobs that do not demand high skills. From this perspective, data on occupations are hardly comparable with the data on sectors in which applicants were employed (Table 8.6).[8]

The below presented data show that a vast majority (80-90 per cent) of migrants from the A8 countries are hired for occupations that need no professional qualifications. On the other hand, as noted, many sources show that, out of the total number of migrants from Poland to the UK, the share of persons holding a university degree exceeds 25 or maybe even 30 per cent. This would indicate that, certainly, positive effects related to opportunities for qualification improvement or professional development are out of range for the majority of educated migrants. Rather, 'brain waste' or deskilling, a typical phenomenon for the migration of the 1980s, should be expected. A similar conclusion is drawn from the analysis provided by Clark and Drinkwater (2008), who showed that, according to the UK LFS data, the rate of return to human capital is far lower for migrants coming from A8 countries than it is for natives or migrants from the EU-15 countries. It suggests that the

Table 8.6   *Top twenty occupations among A8 immigrants in UK, July 2004 – June 2006*

Rank	Occupation	Number of applicants	% of all occupations
1	Process operative	212,405	27.5
2	Warehouse operative	63,590	8.2
3	Packer	46,515	6.0
4	Kitchen assistant	44,810	5.8
5	Cleaner, domestic staff	42,120	5.5
6	Farm worker	32,515	4.2
7	Waitress	27,430	3.6
8	Maid/room attendant (hotel)	26,075	3.4
9	Labourer, building	26,075	3.4
10	Sales assistant	21,700	2.8
11	Care assistant	20,980	2.7
12	Crop harvester	12,860	1.7
13	Bar staff	10,025	1.3
14	Food processing operative (fruit & vegetables)	9,810	1.3
15	Food processing operative (meat)	9,135	1.2
16	Chef (other)	8,590	1.1
17	Truck driver	6,385	0.8
18	Fruit picker	6,385	0.8
19	Carpenter	6,045	0.8
20	Welder	5,490	0.7
	Total (20 occupations)	773,255	82.6

Source: Author's own elaboration based on the Home Office data

human capital of the post-accession migration in the most important destination country is not being 'employed' in an efficient way.

On the other hand, it is important to consider the changes in the structure of the Polish population. As already stated, recent migration from Poland is marked by a higher share of persons with tertiary education than for the total population. This picture may be completely misleading without assessment of the educational structure of the Polish population. In the last twenty years, Poland experienced a true educational breakthrough. Between 1970 and 2001, the share of university graduates among the Polish population increased from 2 per cent to 12 per cent. At the end of the 1990s, the number of students was 2.6 times higher than in 1990. Nowadays in Poland, there are over 1.8 million students, and the data from the Central Statistical Office shows that, in the early 2000s, the gross enrolment ratio (the ratio of those studying to the whole population) in the age group 19-24 was close to 50 per cent. This means that, as for the universality of higher education, Poland has almost reached the standards of the developed countries. If we take into consideration that a higher propensity to migrate is typically a feature of relatively young persons (aged eighteen to 35), the recent increase in highly skilled migration may be a statistical artefact only. In this context, the increase in the share of relatively well-educated migrants should be perceived as a natural consequence of educational developments in Poland. Additionally, as proven by the migration selectivity analysis, well-educated migrants tend to originate from relatively backwards regions of Poland, quite often from small towns or rural areas, i.e. from such places where labour markets cannot offer them suitable professional opportunities.

In this context, the outflow of persons with tertiary education, who often face serious problems on the Polish labour market, can thus be described as brain overflow and not brain drain. This process does not necessarily have to be negative for the Polish economy – those who leave stand a better chance to find work and will accumulate money they may use in the origin country afterwards, if they return. Additional benefits may result from gaining professional and cultural experience.[9]

Interestingly, in the early 2000s, the share of migrants with tertiary education among all expatriates in Poland was higher than in the case of the total population but, at the same time, significantly lower than for well-developed countries. In many cases the percentage of university graduates among migrants was higher than 40 per cent, as it was in case of the US (49.9 per cent), Japan (49.7 per cent), Australia (45.9 per cent) and the UK (41.2 per cent). Against this background, the relative scale of highly skilled migration from Poland seems moderate (26.6 per cent according to OECD data), and is higher only than in such countries as Turkey (6.4 per cent), Italy (13.0 per cent) and Spain (18.7 per cent).

In this context, the increasing scale of highly skilled migration from Poland is to be perceived as a rather typical – not exceptional – process, proving that the structure of migration predominantly reflects the composition of the origin society (Kaczmarczyk & Okólski 2005).

Similarly, Figure 8.5 shows that the scale of student mobility from and in Poland is far from well-developed countries' standards. In contemporary societies, student migration has become a common and inevitable phenomenon – an integral part of an academic or professional career. Looking at trends in the development of the educational systems in Poland and other CEE countries, it would also be reasonable to expect a gradual increase in the mobility of students (as indeed has happened since 1 May 2004).

Figure 8.5 *Foreign students in selected OECD countries, 1998*

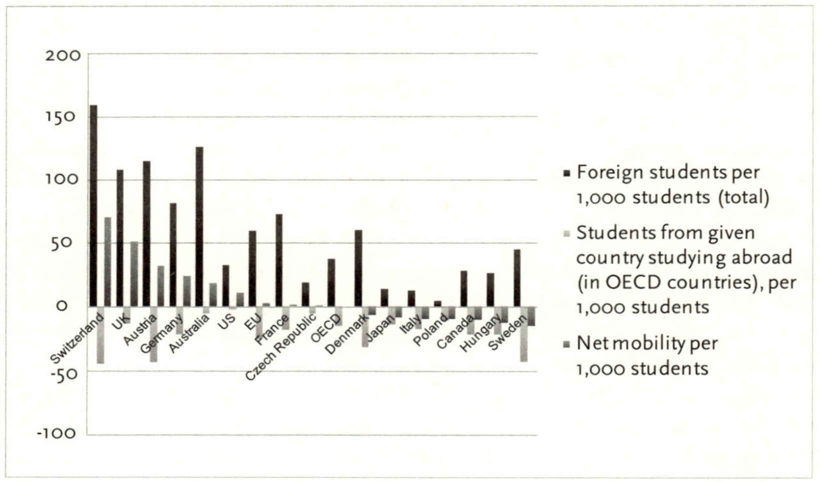

Source: Kaczmarczyk and Okólski (2005)

The mobility of the highly skilled does not necessarily lead to negative consequences as described in public debates. Recent developments do not entitle us to draw dramatic pictures of brain drain. Interestingly, the authors of a series of reports on the mobility of Polish scientists, while using the alarming title *Brain exodus* for the first report in the series, concluded their research with a relatively humble statement on the 'mobility of scientists' in the third report, spanning the period 1994-1996 (Hryniewicz et al. 1997). They argue that the outflow of scientists from Poland has not lead to a brain drain, but it also has not succeeded in terms of brain exchange, i.e. exchange of thoughts, ideas and experiences relevant for the development of scientific research in Poland.

Conclusions

The outflow of highly skilled specialists is a very complex matter that gives rise to many controversies. On the one hand, the outflow of specialists (i.e. loss of human capital) can be treated as one of the reasons of the relative technological backwardness of the states from the region. On the other hand, in the era of globalisation, migrations are becoming an inevitable phenomenon. This particularly concerns specialists or, more generally, persons with tertiary education. The global economy in its current shape generates a considerable demand for such migrants related to the recent global division of labour, entailed by the dynamic growth of new technologies in the services (including intangible services) and increasingly better opportunities in communications. Migration of highly skilled persons is becoming a natural element of economic and social processes, and human resources as well (e.g. scholarships; scientific internships; mobility within multinational companies). Therefore, the pejorative notion of 'brain drain' has been abandoned in favour of such terms as 'brain circulation' or 'brain exchange'.

The crucial issue is that a significant share of highly skilled persons among emigrants is a feature of highly developed states; the higher the level of socio-economic development the more transparent this interdependence. Therefore, the increasing contribution of immigrants from Poland and other CEE countries holding university degrees should not be a surprise. On the contrary, it is to be expected that social and economic progress will result in the relative growth in the migration of specialists from a given country or region. However, the brain drain may be a real issue for countries of origin. This may occur if a negative balance in the migration of highly skilled personnel is observed, and would be particularly painful in the case of intangible services (i.e. medical services). Such a phenomenon may be particularly true in the case of Poland – a country with no tradition of immigration, where the inflow of highly skilled persons is relatively low.

Since accession into the EU, an increase in the scale of migration has been observed. The most drastic changes concern migration to the UK and Ireland, two of the three countries that opened their labour markets in May 2004. Yet, changes in the scale of mobility observed since May 2004 concern highly skilled persons or specialists to a small degree. The most significant increase was revealed in the case of students and medical professionals. The first case should not be perceived in negative terms; to the contrary, the mobility of students in the contemporary world is an important aspect of education and may increase future productivity and stock of human capital. The case of medical professionals is the most controversial issue in recent public debates on migration. So far, this process is still far from being a mass phenomenon.

However, even today, the outflow of nurses and doctors results in serious problems in local and regional markets (particularly in the case of certain specialties). Additionally, in the face of the dramatic situation in the Polish health services sector, the scale of medical professionals' mobility may increase dramatically. The only way to stop the outflow or decrease its level would be a deep reform of the public health care system, including such spheres as education and training, working conditions and earnings.

Up until the early 1990s, the EU countries were not attractive for highly skilled migrants, who almost exclusively targeted traditional immigration countries such as the US, Canada and Australia. This situation has changed as a consequence of introducing selective pro-migratory measures in migration policies and applying recruitment programmes. This, in turn, increases the risk of outflow from Poland. The most recent migration to the UK and Ireland may serve as a perfect exemplification of this thesis.

Mobility of top specialists could be and, in many cases, is a crucial factor spurring the development of scientific disciplines, fostering research and the exchange of thoughts and experiences. For example, scientists, even when residing abroad can exert a huge influence upon scientific activities in the country of origin and contribute to the transfer of knowledge and technologies. The key obstacle is a lack of mechanisms of return migration. Thus, one of the most important tasks for migration policymakers in Poland and other CEE countries would be to create favourable conditions for those highly skilled migrants who would like to return to their home countries.

Notes

1   This chapter relies heavily on Kaczmarczyk (2006).

2   Due to the adopted definition, the population of emigrants includes only those permanent residents of Poland who left Poland in order to settle abroad, having registered their departure with an administrative unit. Therefore, the official data on migration portrays only a small fraction of the phenomenon, i.e. departures recorded as a permanent change of residence, and are useful to limited extent only.

3   These data relate only to adult persons who, at the time of the survey, had been abroad for longer than two months and, at the same time, who had at least one household member still living in Poland.

4   This is true if data on Polish seasonal workers is considered.

5   Note that LFS data encompass only those migrants who are staying abroad for longer than two months. An additional 300,000-350,000 Poles find legal employment abroad each year on the basis of bilateral international agreements. An overwhelming majority of them are seasonal workers, more than half of whom are employed in Germany (according to the 1990 bilateral agreement on labour migration between the Polish and German governments).

6   In the case of emigrating Poles of Jewish descent, this share was over eight times higher than the total population (Stola 2001).
7   That was 1.8 per cent of the total number of permanent residents of Poland aged fifteen and over.
8   This is particularly true in the case of administration, business and management, where the problem is that workers in the sector work predominantly for recruitment agencies and could thus be employed in a variety of occupations.
9   Additional benefits may arise due to the positive impact on human capital formation, i.e. through the demonstration effect as proposed by Stark (2005). However, in the case of Poland and other CEE countries – whose citizens, regardless of their skill level, are employed predominantly in secondary sectors of receiving economies – this effect seems to be rather doubtful.

References

Bijak, J., M. Kupiszewski & A. Kicinger (2004), 'International migration scenarios for 27 European countries, 2002-2052', CEFMR Working Paper 4/2004.

Clark, K. & S. Drinkwater (2008), 'The labour market performance of recent migrants', *Oxford Review of Economic Policy* 24(3): 495-516.

CSO (2007). *Informacja o rozmiarach i kierunkach emigracji z Polski w latach 2004-2006*. Warsaw: Central Statistical Office.

Fihel, A., P. Kaczmarczyk & M. Okólski (2006), 'Labour mobility in the enlarged European Union. International Migration from the A8 countries', CMR Working Paper 14 (72).

Hryniewicz, J., B. Jałowiecki & A. Mync (1992), *Ucieczka mózgów ze szkolnictwa wyższego i nauki. Raport z badań*. Warsaw: Europejski Instytut Rozwoju Regionalnego i Lokalnego.

Hryniewicz, J., B. Jałowiecki & A. Mync (1994), *Ucieczka mózgów z nauki i szkolnictwa wyższego w Polsce w latach 1992-1993. Warsaw: Europejski Instytut Rozwoju Regionalnego i Lokalnego.*

Hryniewicz, J., B. Jałowiecki & A. Mync (1997), *Ruchliwość pracowników naukowych w latach 1994-1997.* Warsaw: Europejski Instytut Rozwoju Regionalnego i Lokalnego.

Jaźwińska, E. & M. Okólski (eds.) (2001), *Ludzie na huśtawce. Migracje między peryferiami Polski i Zachodu. Warsaw: Scholar.*

Kaczmarczyk, P. (2004), 'Future westward outflow from candidate countries: The case of Poland' in A. Górny & P. Ruspini (eds.), *East-West revisited: Migration in the New Europe*. London: Palgrave.

Kaczmarczyk, P. (2005), *Migracje zarobkowe Polaków w dobie przemian*. Warsaw: WUW.

Kaczmarczyk, P. (2006), 'Highly skilled migration from Poland and other CEE countries: Myths and reality' in K. Gmaj & K. Iglicka (eds.), *Brain drain or brain gain: A global dilemma*, 33-64. Warsaw: CSM.

Kaczmarczyk, P. & W. Łukowski (eds.) (2004), *Polscy pracownicy na rynku Unii Europejskiej*. Warsaw: Scholar.

Kaczmarczyk, P. & M. Okólski (2002), 'From net emigration to net immigration. Socio-economic aspects of international population movements in Poland' in R. Rotte & P. Stein (eds.), *Migration policy and the economy: International experiences*, 319-348. Munich: ars et unitas.

Kaczmarczyk, P. & M. Okólski (2005), *Migracje specjalistów wysokiej klasy w kontekście członkostwa Unii Europejskiej. Warsaw: UKiE.*

Kaczmarczyk, P. & M. Okólski (2008a), *Economic impact of migration on Poland and Baltic states*. Oslo: FAFO.

Kaczmarczyk, P. & M. Okólski (eds.) (2008b), *Polityka migracyjna jako instrument promocji zatrudnienia i ograniczania bezrobocia*. Warsaw: WNE UW.

Kępińska, E. (2006), 'Recent trends in International migration. The 2005 SOPEMI report for Poland', *CMR Working Papers* 60.

OECD (2005), *Trends in international migration: Annual Sopemi report*. Paris: OECD.

Okólski, M. (1997), 'Statystyka imigracji w Polsce. Warunki poprawności. ocena stanu obecnego. propozycje nowych rozwiązań', *ISS Working Papers – Seria: Prace Migracyjne (currently CMR Working Papers)* 2.

Okólski, M. (2006), 'Costs and benefits of migration for Central European countries', CMR Working Paper 7 (65).

Portes, J. & S. French (2005), 'The impact of free movement of workers from Central and Eastern Europe on the UK labour market: Early evidence', Working Paper 18. Leeds: Department for Work and Pensions.

Rushton, J. (2004), 'EU enlargement and the UK labour market', *Consequences of the EU enlargement on selected EU labour markets: Evaluation of the first year*. Warsaw: Centre of International Studies.

Sakson, B. (2002), *Wpływ 'niewidzialnych' migracji zagranicznych lat osiemdziesiątych na struktury demograficzne Polski. Warsaw: Szkoła Główna Handlowa*.

Salt, J. (2005), *Sopemi report for the United Kingdom*. Paris: OECD.

Stark, O. (2005), 'The new economics of the brain drain', *World Economics* 2.

Stola. D. (2001), 'Międzynarodowa mobilność zarobkowa w PRL' in E. Jaźwińska & M. Okólski (eds.), *Ludzie na hu□tawce. Migracje między peryferiami Polski i Zachodu. Warsaw: Scholar*.

Traser, J. (2005), *Report on the free movement of workers in the EU. Who is afraid of EU enlargement?* Brussels: ECAS.

Wolfeil, N. (2008), *Student mobility from new to old member states in the European Union: Changing patterns after 1st of May 2004?*, unpublished manuscript.

9 Skills shortage, emigration and unemployment in Poland: Causes and implications of disequilibrium in the Polish labour market

Izabela Grabowska-Lusinska

Introduction[1]

The aim of this chapter is to scrutinise the apparently overlapping research problems of skill shortage, emigration and unemployment in Poland, focusing both on the causes and implications of disequilibrium in the Polish labour market. The chapter shows that there is no straightforward relationship (or correlation) between skill shortages and the outflow of people. Rather, the outflow of people (including seasonal, pendulum migration) is one among a set of factors that impacts skill shortages in Poland and cannot be analysed separately from these other factors.

The first section of the chapter provides an overview of labour market adjustments and associated challenges in Poland by tracking the process of transition in Poland. The second section sets out the concepts of structural mismatches, shortages and gaps as grounded in theory by approaching four main interpretations connected to: 1) turbulence in the economy; 2) the lack of equilibrium in micro markets; 3) the mismatch of ineffective allocations of labour and 4) the Non-Accelerating Inflation Rate of Unemployment (NAIRU) as connected to labour resources. This section also examines regional variations and divergences of the labour market in Poland. The third section refers to internal migration within, and emigration from, Poland after 1 May 2004. Section four takes into account economic gaps as a characteristic of changes and challenges in the Polish labour market, including analysis of the barriers to growth of companies as reported by employers. Finally, section five synthesises the set of factors identified across the analysis that cause skill shortages, highlighting both their short- and long-term implications for the Polish labour market.

A synopsis of labour market adjustments and challenges in Poland

The transition from a centrally planned economy to a market economy has been accompanied by far-reaching changes in the labour market. According to Dorenbos (1999: 1):

> Excess demand for labour and shortage of labour were replaced by a surplus of labour and shortage of jobs. Consequently, unemployment emerged and grew rapidly: former centrally planned economy converted from 'job rights' economy to 'job search' economy.

The next stage of this transformation seems to be a move to a 'skill search' economy. It is apparent that the role of labour structure is crucial in the process of transition to a market economy and economic growth both in qualitative and quantitative terms. Optimal allocation of labour, namely putting the right person with the right skills in the right place is an enormous and complicated process. The quality of labour is crucial to match the needs of transformed economic structures. Selection of workers on the basis of labour market characteristics, which reflect their labour productivity, is a key feature of the new structure of the economy. Moreover, job competition and crowding-out effects may lead to the segmentation of the labour market (Piore 1979).

The employment structure seems to be a barometer of adjustments to the new conditions and challenges in the economy. This is because, as a rule, changes in the division of labour across agriculture, industry and services are seen as reflecting the process of economic

Table 9.1   *Key economic indicators for Poland 2000-2007*

Indicator	2000	2001	2002	2003	2004	2005	2006	2007*
GDP growth (%)	4.2	1.1	1.4	3.8	5.3	3.4	6.1	6.6
Inflation rate (%)	10.1	5.5	1.9	0.8	3.6	2.1	1.1	2.2
Economically active population (m)	17.3	17.4	17.2	17.0	17.0	17.0	17.0	17.0
Employed population (m)	14.5	14.2	13.8	13.6	13.8	13.9	14.6	15.2
Unemployment rate (%)	16.1	18.2	19.9	19.6	19.0	18.2	13.8	10.7
Net migration	-19,670	-16,740	-14,950	-44,000	-51,790	-48,440	-47,600	-47,790
Population mid-year (m)	38.6	38.6	38.6	38.6	38.6	38.5	38.1	38.1

Source: Euromonitor International – Global Market Information Database 2007
* Forecast

development. The employment structure also relates to the stock of labour and the rationale of its utilisation at different stages of economic growth.[2]

With the modernisation of the structure of production in Poland, the sectoral composition of firms and the occupational structure of the labour force have undergone radical changes. Changes in internal and external demand from 1995-2005 caused shifts between sectors of the employment structure. The percentage share employed in agriculture declined from 25.1 per cent to 21.3 per cent during this period, whilst industry saw a decrease of about one million workers. The new employment structure, where the service sector has predominated since 1993 (increasing by 15 per cent), generated new demands for qualifications. The retrenchment of employment in agriculture and industry, which are less qualification-saturated, and the development of the service sector have increased opportunities for employment of the highly educated. Yet, this increasing share of services in the economy has resulted not in an increase in demand in this sector, but merely a lower decrease in the number of work places. This may explain why, throughout the last decade, services have failed to mitigate the process of restructuring of agriculture and industry by absorbing human resources in these sectors. Net outflow from employment to unemployment and the share that is 'non-active' has therefore been of an unprecedented scale. Throughout these changes in the structure of employment, the only group who has recorded increases in employment levels are the highly educated (UNDP 2007: 106-107).

Labour mismatches, shortages, unemployment and mobility

Disequilibrium of supply and demand creates a basis for labour market shortages.[3] However, the concept of 'structural shortage' itself covers many definitions, measures and interpretations. Schioppa (1991) presents four key interpretations of skill mismatch developed in economics. The first relates to turbulence in the economy. This approach was developed by Lilien (1982), Abraham and Katz (1986), Loungani (1986), Loungani, Rush and Tave (1990) and Davies and Haltiwanger (1992). The collapse of certain industries and growth of new forms of entrepreneurship may generate economic shocks. This process is connected to certain technological innovations, changes in foreign competition and changes in the relative prices of resources. These factors affect the structure of employment. Unemployment rates grow in declining sectors (or regions) and, at the same time, the number of vacancies grows in developing sectors (or regions). This implies deeper mismatches of demand and supply of labour across sectors and/or regions. In order to eliminate these mismatches, high flexibility in the labour market is necessary. This means flexibility of wages and prices, high mobility of labour and free access to information on the labour market (Brunello 1991: 57).

A second interpretation concerning structural mismatches relates to lack of equilibrium in micro markets, namely regional and sectoral markets; the third approach connects mismatch with ineffective allocations of labour; whilst the fourth interpretation comes from the Non-Accelerating Inflation Rate of Unemployment (NAIRU) model, which strictly relates to labour resources. However, in order to explain the situation in the Polish labour market, the approach that focuses on turbulence in an economy seems to be the most suitable and adequate.

A process of labour market restructuring such as that experienced by the Polish economy may also create regional diversification. This means that the process may cause regional mismatches of supply and demand resulting in skill shortages in some places, even though there are surpluses elsewhere. This is well grounded in the economic geography of Poland, where some branches of the economy, such as the shipping industry, heavy industry, and agriculture, are very much associated with certain regions. Indeed, many Polish regions have been defined in the past by their association with particular productive activities. One may assume that the resulting regional variations in labour markets may also cause structural mismatches (Gawronska-Nowak & Kaczorowski 2000). There are also differences in the level of real wages across different regions and, generally, low mobility of labour in Poland – both of which have a negative impact on the flexibility of the labour market and may enhance and petrify regional divergences in supply and demand (Gawronska-Nowak & Kaczorowski 2000).

Regional variations and divergence of labour market

Full employment was a major policy goal in all former centrally planned economies. Every person over school age and under retirement age was entitled to work (Dorenbos 1999).[4] Nowadays, the situation is totally different. Excess demand and a shortage of labour have been replaced by a surplus of labour and shortage of jobs, but also by a shortage of skills. The change is well depicted in Figure 9.1, which shows regional labour activity rates in Poland in the 1988 population census (towards the end of the communist era) and the 2002 census (already in the advanced transition period).

Despite the already long transition, the labour market participation rate has not changed much in Poland across this period of time. Moreover, Poland has one of the lowest – if not the lowest – employment activity rate in the EU-27: 7.6 points lower than the average of

Figure 9.1 *Regional employment activity rate in Poland in population censuses 1988 and 2002*

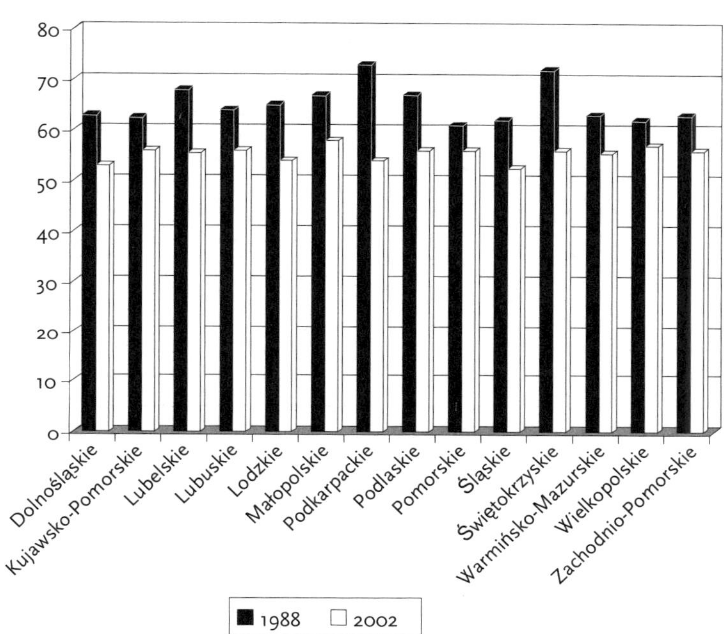

Source: Extracted from Central Statistical Office

EU-27 and nearly ten points lower than the average of EU-15 (Figure 9.2).

Why is it the case in Poland that there are low levels of labour force participation? There are at least two explanations for this phenomenon. One relates to various government schemes that put people outside the labour market, such as an early retirement scheme (covered people born before 1 January 1949); an 'unable to work' scheme (connected to health) and a scheme favouring those with a minimum number of years of employment, namely five or ten years shorter than the usual retirement age, called the 'bridging retirement scheme' at one point. The list of professions eligible to join the latter scheme covered more than one hundred professions. Another explanation relates to the ability – or rather inability – of people to become active in the labour market. The proportion of those who are unable to become active in the labour force (at least in the official registers) is one of the largest of any European

Figure 9.2 *Employment activity rate in Poland and in the EU (average): 1997-2007*

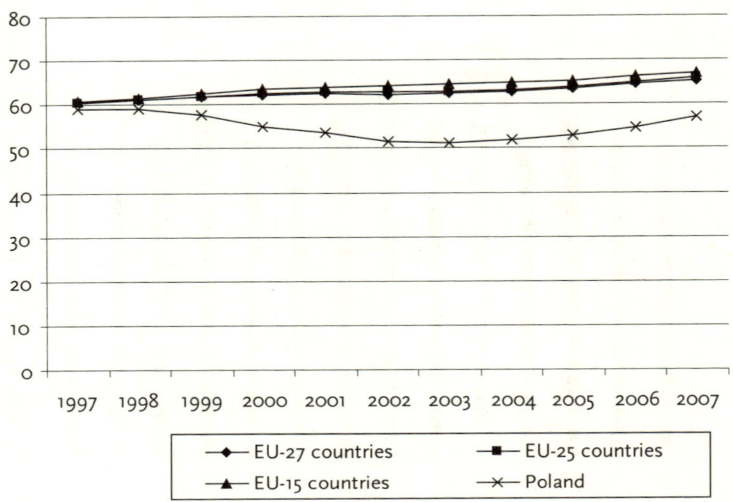

Source: Author's own elaboration based on Eurostat

country, reflecting high rates of long-term unemployment or long-term employment in the grey economy.

Changes in the labour market are also well reflected in the economic geography of Poland. Poland's regions differ considerably regarding their economies. The variation refers mainly to their economic structures, levels of development, living standards and their regional and local labour markets. This is mainly manifested in the three-sector structure of the economy (agriculture, industry and services), which can be described and defined from the perspective of sectoral split of total employment and added value by regions (see Figure 9.3). The situation in Poland is distinct for its relatively large share of the employed population concentrated in the agricultural sector but – at the same time – for the small share of this sector in terms of added value both nationally and regionally (Kwiatkowski, Kucharski & Tokarski 2004). It is worth noting that the dynamics of changes in the employment structure are significant. Although labour productivity in agriculture (measured by added value per employee) is well below average in certain regions, labour productivity in the service sector is well above average (Kwiatkowski et al. 2004).

The regions of Świętokrzyskie, Podlaskie, Podkarpackie and Lubelskie can be regarded as typically agricultural ones. They are characterised by a dispersed agrarian structure (small farms) with a predominance of

Figure 9.3 *Structure of employment in Polish regions 1995-2001 (period average, in %)*

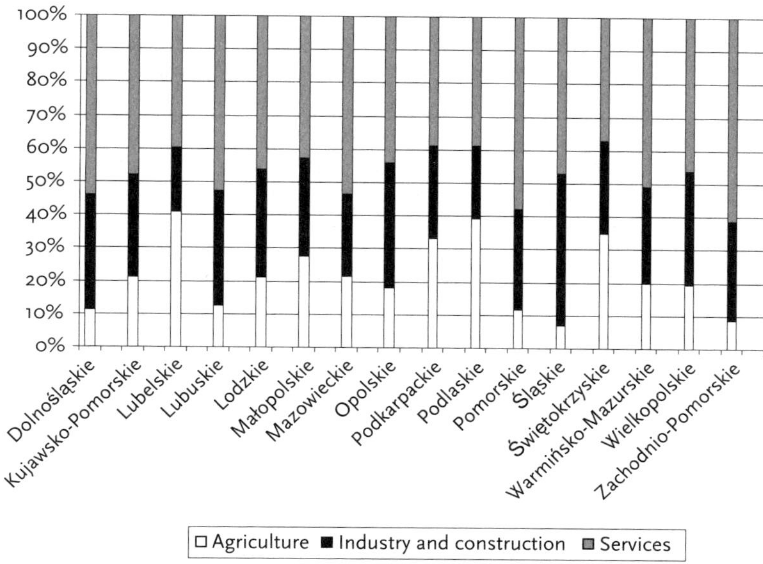

Source: Author's own elaboration based on Kwiatkowski et al. (2004)

private farms. During the transition period these farms acted as containers absorbing excess labour, accelerating social tensions in the labour market (Kwiatkowski et al. 2004). But at the end of the twentieth century, these containers had blown up, uncovering and diffusing unadjusted labour resources.

As mentioned, the transition period was accompanied by the weakening and even collapse of some branches of industry (such as the textile, coal-mining and metal industries). However, the relative share of employment of certain declining branches of industry is still large in some regions: above all in Śląskie and Dolnośląskie, but also Opolskie, Lubuskie, Wielkopolskie and Kujawsko-Pomorskie. The high level of industrialisation of the Śląskie region reflects the dominance of the mining and metal industries, which have been facing advanced restructuring at the final phase of transition, namely in the second half of the 1990s. In contrast, a substantial share of services, which reflect a modern economic structure, can be found in the Mazowieckie region and in northern Poland (Zachodniopomorskie, Pomorskie, Warmińsko-Mazurskie) where they are mostly associated with the hospitality sector.

Regions differ also with respect to their GDP per capita. The highest GDP per capita is in the Mazowieckie region, with the capital city of Warsaw, whilst second is Śląskie, the most highly urbanised and industrialised part of Poland. The lowest values are found in eastern Poland (Lubelskie, Podkarpackie, Podlaskie) and also in Warmińsko-Mazurskie, Swietokrzyskie, Opolskie, Małopolskie and Lodzkie. Interestingly, the sets of regions with the highest and lowest GDP per capita have not changed over the period of transition, with inequality even deepening in this respect. In 1995, GDP per capita in the Mazowieckie region was 64 per cent higher than the lowest regional GDP, while in 2002 the difference rose to 98 per cent (Kwiatkowski et al. 2004).

Regional differences in GDP per capita are closely linked to regional variations in labour productivity (GDP per employee). The Mazowieckie and Śląskie regions have the highest level of labour productivity, followed by regions in the west of the country. The lowest are observed in eastern, predominantly agricultural regions, namely Lubuskie, Podkarpackie and Podlaskie. Regional differentiation of wages is considerably lower than that of labour productivity: the Mazowieckie region has the highest wages, followed by the Śląskie region, whilst eastern regions have the lowest wages.

The map of unemployment in Poland is also interesting. The regional pattern that characterises employment structure, GDP per capita and productivity levels also seems useful for understanding unemployment rates. The transformation shock made regions differently vulnerable to its effects (Figures 9.4 and 9.4). A first group of regions is defined by the process of restructuring of agriculture. Among them are those regions most strongly affected by the remnants of the pre-transition system: Warmińsko-Mazurskie, Zachodniopomorskie, Lubuskie, Pomorskie and Kujawsko-Pomorskie. They all experienced a sharp decrease in labour demand. A second group of regions, those dominated by traditional industries,[5] also experienced a strong decline in labour demand, including Lodzkie, Dolnośląskie and Lubuskie. The smallest decreases in labour demand were noted in three regions with modern economic structures, characterised by a relatively high share of services in the employment structure, namely Mazowieckie, Małopolskie and Wielkopolskie. The economies of these regions managed to adapt quite flexibly to the requirements of a market-driven economy. The process of their adaptation was mainly enhanced by agglomeration effects in the cities of Warsaw, Krakow and Poznan (Kwiatkowski et al. 2004).

Unemployment and its export: A nexus?

The total unemployment rate in Poland mirrors the dynamics of the transition process. Unemployment started rising rapidly in mid-1992

Figure 9.4 *Unemployment rate by region in 2005 (end September)*

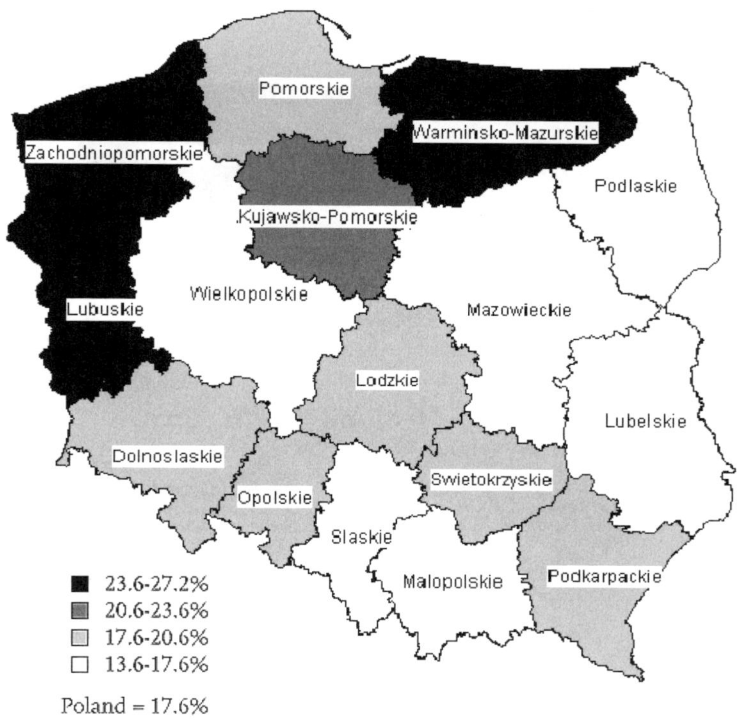

Source: Author's own elaboration based on Central Statistical Office

(12 per cent on average) up to 1995 (16.2 per cent on average), then started falling due to stabilisation of the restructuring process, reaching 10 per cent on average in 1998. The unemployment rate started rising again from 1999-2002 and remained high up to the end of 2005 (Figure 9.6). Since then, perhaps linked to the enlargement of the European Union in 2004, rates have fallen again.

Falling unemployment in the last two to three years may be a result of different factors: an economic growth effect with the end of the 'jobless economic growth' of the transition period, increased seasonal demand for workers in agriculture, construction and services (due to mild winters) and the systematic and dynamic outflow of labour and systematic inflow of remittances. In June 2007, a decline in the number of unemployed was observed in all regions (Figure 9.7), although the structure of registered unemployment is still territorially deeply differentiated.

Figure 9.5 *Unemployment rate by region in 2007 (end September)*

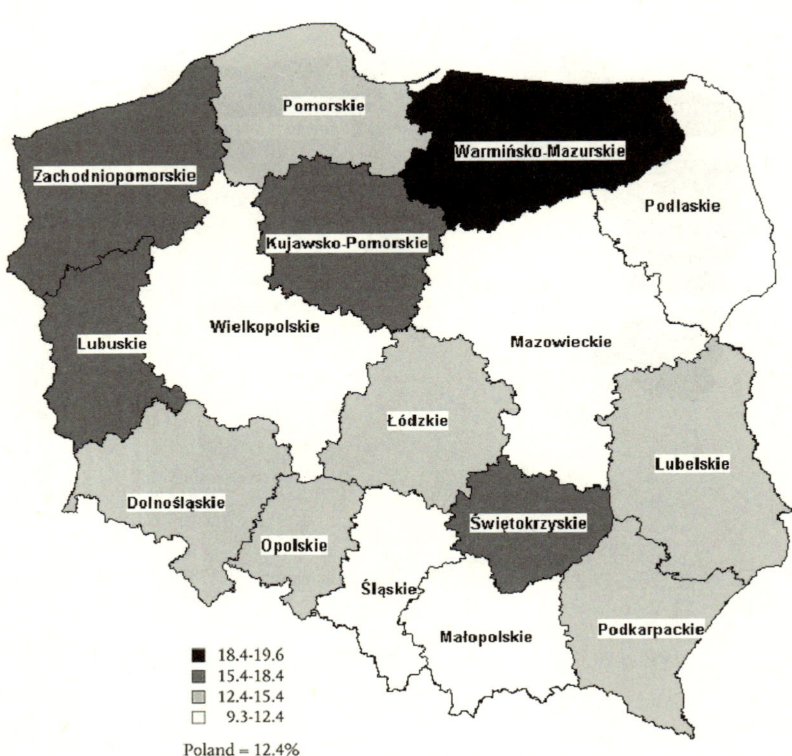

Source: Author's own elaboration based on Central Statistical Office

The share of women in the total number of the unemployed in Poland is high, at 58.5 per cent in 2007. In addition, relatively young people have been more affected by unemployment, with the largest group of unemployed people consisting of persons aged 25-34 years (Figure 9.9).

The highest percentage share of unemployed people aged between 25 and 34 in the total number of the unemployed was observed in the regions of Lubelskie (31.5 per cent), Podkarpackie (30.5 per cent), Świętokrzyskie (29.2 per cent) and Kujawsko-Pomorskie (28.6 per cent), while the lowest was in the regions of Dolnośląskie and Opolskie (25.6 per cent), and Podlaskie (25.7 per cent) (GUS 2007).

A high percentage of the unemployed registered in the labour offices consisted of persons with relatively low levels of education. The two largest groups among the unemployed were those with basic vocational

Figure 9.6 *Unemployment rate in third quarter of each year 2000-2007*

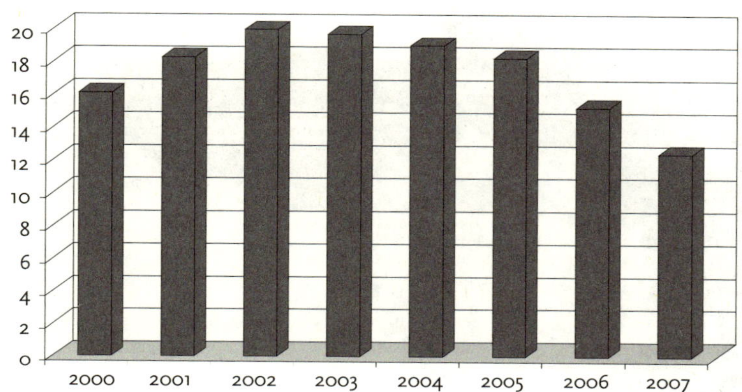

Source: Author's own elaboration based on data extracted from Central Statistical Office

education and lower secondary, primary and incomplete primary education (amounting, respectively, to 30.1 per cent and 32.5 per cent of the total number of the unemployed registered at the end of June 2007). These groups jointly amounted to 62.6 per cent of the total unemployed. In contrast, those with post-secondary certificate and vocational secondary education made up 22.3 per cent of the total number of the unemployed, those who had completed secondary school made up 9 per cent, while those who had completed tertiary education represented 6.1 per cent (GUS 2007).

Poland also experiences the problem of hidden unemployment – those who do not appear in unemployment statistics because they are considered 'not active'. This may relate to work in the grey economy and/or seasonal work abroad, which means they are recorded locally as being not economically active. This structure may also petrify mismatches of labour supply and demand in Poland, contributing skill shortages.

Is it fair to say that Poland has exported its unemployment through the outflow of people? Figure 9.9 shows the relationship between changes in unemployment and outflows of people. There appears to be a strong relationship between the two for much of the twentieth century, but not for the post-accession period, where the relationship appears to have reversed. Kaczmarczyk and Okólski (2008: 49) argue that this is because over 50 per cent of people moving abroad have permanent jobs in Poland and, whilst this should create job opportunities for

Figure 9.7   *Unemployment rate in regions: Change between 2006 and 2007*

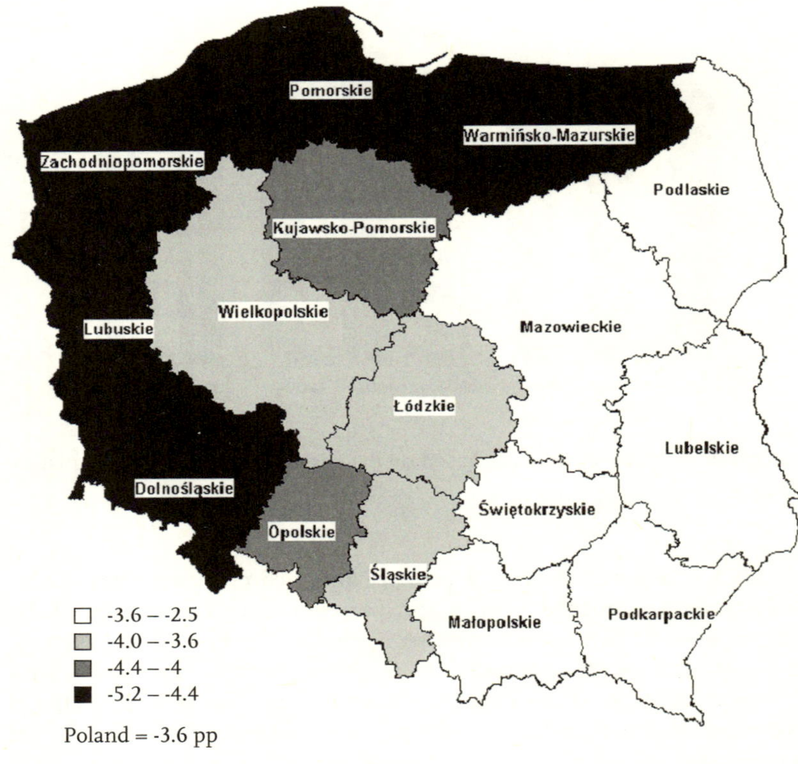

Source: Extracted from Central Statistical Office

those who are left behind, this does not happen because of internal immobility and structural disequilibria in the labour market.

Polish migration since 1 May 2004

Internal migration

This section analyses the factors that influence the performance of regional labour markets in Poland. The circumstances of the economic
transition in Poland might suggest a strong propensity for the country's
inhabitants to migrate inter-regionally. In fact, Poland has experienced a
decline in inter- and intra-provincial and regional population flows since
the beginning of the transition period. The decline in rural-urban

Figure 9.8 *Structure of registered unemployed persons by age and sex, second quarter of 2007*

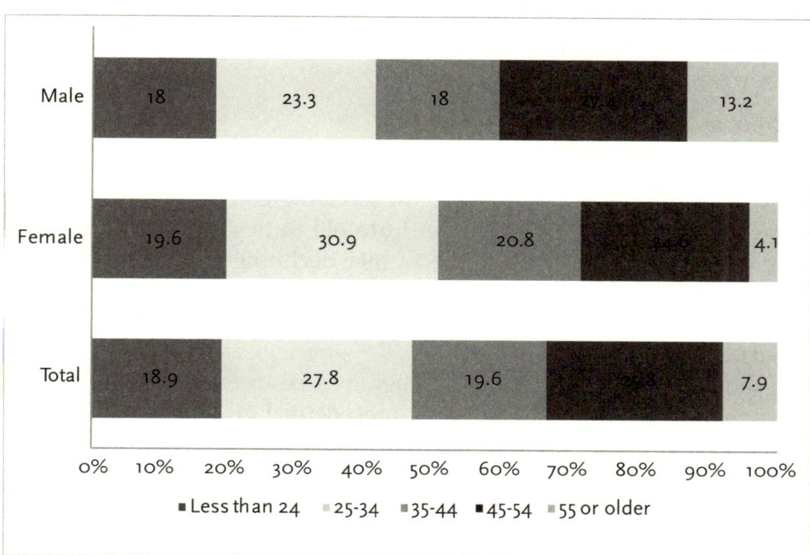

Source: Extracted from Central Statistical Office

migration and a very slight increase in flows in the opposite direction are of particular interest.

There are several significant and complex factors that tend to limit the process of internal migration in Poland: the propensity to migrate internationally because of its greater attractiveness, low wage differences between regions, an underdeveloped road and railway infrastructure and the housing market, namely shortages in housing. All these factors may imply a low level of reallocation of skills in relation to demand by a concentrated cluster of similar industries. Some scholars even argue that Poland's regional concentration of services, namely gravitation to agglomeration economies, may diminish intra-regional mobility and imply deeper inter-regional divergence (Deichamnn & Henderson 2000).[6] Moreover, working abroad seasonally or periodically may be a viable alternative, bearing in mind the effort required to move abroad and net gains of such effort. As a result, the inter-regional mobility is very low in Poland, with inter-regional flows amounting to 0.2-0.3 per cent of the population in 2005.

Inter-regional flows depend on regional variations in GDP per capita as well as on regional variations in unemployment rates. Econometric analysis by Kwiatkowski et al. (2004) shows that the regional variation in GDP affected migration outflows more strongly that the regional variations of unemployment rates. However, as mentioned above, the low number of internal migrants cannot be due to a lack of propensity and willingness to move, bearing in mind the recent dynamics of international migration from Poland.

International migration

Migration out of Poland since May 2004 is characterised by increasingly diversified flows with respect to receiving countries. In particular, there is a visible shift of migration from old to new immigration countries (Table 9.2), with flows to the former declining (e.g. Germany) and flows to the latter increasing (i.e. United Kingdom, Ireland, Spain, Italy, the Netherlands). These trends are also corroborated in the administrative data of receiving countries.

Although the growth in Polish migration is an experience of almost every 'new' receiving country, the unprecedented growth in flows of migrants was particularly marked in the UK and Ireland, where movement has also been quite seasonal with increases in summer and decreases around Christmas (Grabowska-Lusinska 2008).

Post-accession change is also occurring through the substitution of legal migration for illegal migration, with the young and the better-educated more involved in the migration stream, including those who

Figure 9.9 *Migrants from Poland and the unemployment rate according to LFS, 1994-2007*

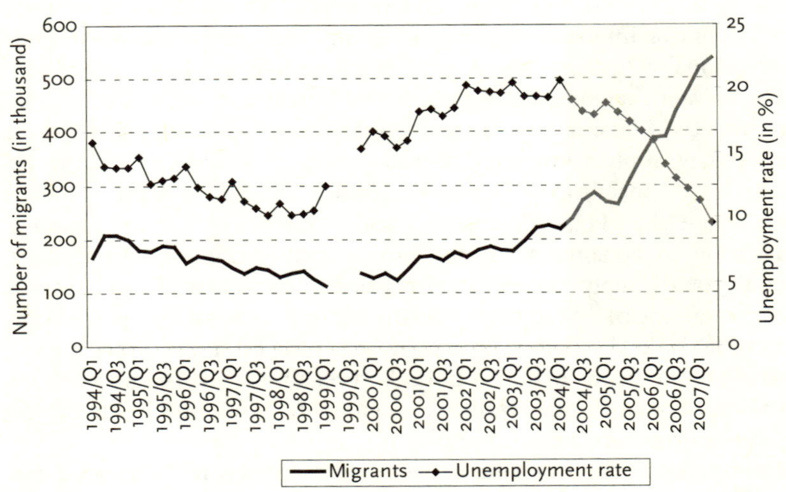

Source: CMR files (Kepinska 2007) based on Central Statistical Office

Table. 9.2   *Distribution of major countries of destination for migrants from Poland, second quarter of 2000-2007 (%)*

	2000	2001	2002	2003	2004	2005	2006	2007
UK	4	7	7	9	11	20	31	32
Germany	35	37	34	31	29	25	20	16
Ireland	0	0	0	0	3	6	7	12
Italy	6	8	14	13	11	12	8	8
US	19	23	19	20	19	11	11	7
The Netherlands	2	4	5	4	3	2	3	6
Spain	0	2	3	4	4	5	3	3
Total	100	100	100	100	100	100	100	100

Source: Kepinska (2006, 2007) based on Labour Force Survey (BAEL)

migrate in order to study. In addition, there was a growth in shuttle mobility during the transition period, as people were pushed out of their homes in order to earn money at a destination outside the country, but quickly returned in order to spend this money. This new form of migration, also referred to as 'incomplete migration', is often connected to work in a secondary segment of a labour market in a foreign country and a strategy of 'work there, live here' (Jazwinska & Okólski 2001).

Trends in migration – both internal and international – confirm findings on the co-existence of skill shortages and unemployment. Internal migration has decreased significantly since the beginning of the transition period and internal migration does not seem to have helped alleviate large unemployment differentials between small geographic areas. There is a group of factors explaining the situation of low internal and high external migration dynamics pinpointed above. It is important to realise that when these factors operate singularly they do not threaten the situation in local labour markets; but when they operate in combination may imply deeper discrepancies between Polish regions and finally put them into crisis.

Educational changes

The process of systemic transition in Poland has also influenced the education system. Up until 1989, the education system in communist Poland was autonomous in practice and was very loosely attached to the labour market. During the first years of the transformation, the effects of centrally planned education were keenly felt. They mostly resulted in a low correlation between educational programmes and education levels with demand in the labour market. The lack of a match between occupational education and the labour market generated a high rate of unemployment of graduates from vocational schools. The system of occupational education was mainly blamed for generating this unemployment (Kwiatkowski 2000). Too narrow an educational perspective made it difficult for graduates to change occupation as they were too specialised. The closure of vocational schools – predominately attached to huge communist factories – meant an effective suspension of most occupational education in the country and a reduction in the perceived value of such education. Very few substitution measures have been implemented in order to narrow future skill gaps. A net effect is that there are nowadays very few vocational schools and their graduates are almost all directly recruited by foreign companies. With expanding skill shortages and limited access to state programmes helping to alleviate these gaps (e.g. occupational training and courses), employers have taken vocational education into their own hands by sponsoring classes and training workers onsite (mostly in construction and the car industry). This often implies a very quick, unsystematic, ungrounded and narrow training, which may be associated with exploitation. This is particularly the case in the construction and services sectors, where skill shortages make these sectors unable to face up to the economic boom. Thus, skill shortages as revealed by official data reflect the inadequacy of education in Poland.

There is another side to the coin when it comes to education gaps. This relates to the emergence of new occupations in areas such as telecommunications, internet and information technology; biotechnology and its applications; environmental protection; sea and seabed exploitation; servicing of the regional integration process; modern financial operations and e-banking; e-trade; health care, health promotion, home assistance for elderly people; the popular culture and entertainment industry; education and e-learning (Borkowska & Karpinski 2001). Specialists in some of these areas already exist in the Polish labour market, but some need to be educated or properly trained in order to fill this gap, whilst some may need to be imported.

What do available data reveal in terms of skill shortages in Poland? Poland has a shortage of both specialists and qualified workers, including welders, ironworkers, upholsterers, bricklayers, drivers, crane operators and workers in routine jobs.[7] Fourteen per cent of employers report a shortage of workers and have problems in finding those with appropriate skills. The lack of such workers may also limit the productivity of affected industries. The problem has been increasing, as shown by the fact that at the beginning of 2004, 8.2 per cent of employers reported a shortage of skills, whereas in 2005, after enlargement of the EU in 2004, the number had increased up to 14 per cent. Skills gaps are differentiated across different regions and branches of the economy. For example, one in four furniture producers in Poland currently report not being able to find workers with appropriate skills, while two years ago only one in ten had this problem. In the forestry industry the situation is critical. One in three employers report having problems in finding people with appropriate skills, while before enlargement only one in five had this problem. In the construction sector, which has recently boomed in Poland (and is likely to do so in the run up to the Euro 2012 soccer tournament), every fifth company cannot find workers, whereas before enlargement only 3.7 per cent of construction companies suffered from shortages. In electronics in 2005, 22.7 per cent of companies were facing a shortage of workers, while before 1 May 2004, only 2.2 per cent reported problems. In the car industry in 2005, 20.8 per cent of companies suffered from shortages of workers, whereas before enlargement the figure was 7.4 per cent (CSO 2004-2006).

In research conducted by the National Bank of Poland in the fourth quarter of 2006 (Figure 9.10), a majority of employers reported problems with recruitment of new employees mainly due to the availability of skills in specific areas of the labour market, saying this was caused by the strong labour outflow or people leaving jobs in anticipation of migration. This means that many jobs are vacant in the long term, making employers unable to meet the needs of the booming economy (especially in certain sectors, e.g. the construction and road sector).

Figure 9.10 *Difficulties with recruiting and keeping employees in Poland in the fourth quarter of 2006 (% of replies)*

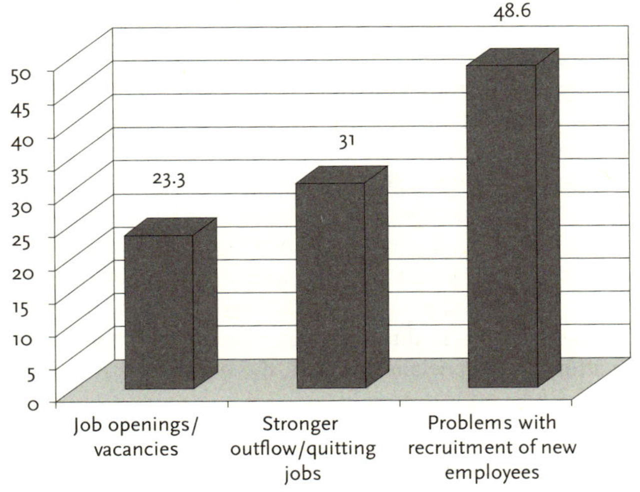

Source: National Bank of Poland (2007)

According to a range of research studies, problems with recruitment and retention of employees, as reported by employers, have a variety of causes. These include a systematic increase in employers' demands for specific skills, the creation of new workplaces, the extension of the period during which people remain in education, a rapid movement of people of productive age into non-productive activity, declining economic activity of women with small children, avoidance by employers of engagement in fixed-term contracts and the low level of interregional mobility and dynamic outflow of skills abroad, both seasonally and periodically.

Conclusions

The co-existence of skill shortages, outflows of labour and unemployment results from a constellation of factors that operate in combination. This combination of factors have different implications for the labour market. First, an increase in mismatches of supply and demand across sectors, regions and occupations may lead to disharmony and divergence and may deepen disequilibrium in the labour market. Second, a high share of agriculture in the employment structure and low share of services may lead to slow adaptation to global markets, resulting in high long-term, structural unemployment and a declining employment activity rate. Third, low inter-regional mobility of labour caused by shortages in housing, underdeveloped road and railway infrastructure, small wage differences, low level of re-specialisation of regions and high concentration of services may lead to a sustaining of the status quo of skill shortages and skill surpluses, resulting in a large waste of human resources and the perpetuation of under-utilised labour pools. At the end of the day, this may deepen systemic transition gaps between regions.

In addition, segmentation of the Polish labour market with an enlarging secondary sector may lead to an excess of labour along with increasing shortages, which may unevenly lead to an increasing demand for foreign labour. Gaps between the nature of the education system and actual demand for labour may also progressively complicate the labour market situation, given the development of new technologies on the one hand, and the narrowing and specialisation of the economy on the other. These gaps should create an urgent need for recognition of new occupations and specialisations in the education system as well as changes in the way education addresses the demands of existing occupations, in order to meet labour market requirements. Otherwise, skill shortages will be an indigenous defect of the transition process, which can be cured only by exogenous labour, recruited from outside the Polish labour market.

Finally, in the short term, periodic emigration may be a solution for high unemployment (constituting the export of unemployment), but may in the long term contribute to a 'brain drain', both nationally and regionally. 'Incomplete migration', both in the short term and the long term, may also lead to a disharmony of employment activity of indigenous labour resources because people working abroad seasonally prefer not to be economically active in the local labour market when they are back in Poland.

Notes

1   A part of this text was originally published under the theme 'Political economy of migration and mobility in the EU' at www.migrationonline.cz. The initial conclusions presented in this chapter are part of an analysis conducted for the project 'Migration policy as a measure of promoting and combating unemployment in Poland' (module 2 'Demand for foreign labour in Poland') co-financed by the European Social Fund, Sectoral Operational Programme Human Resources (activity 1.1).

2   Sadowska-Snarska (2000) demonstrated a correlation between changes of employment structure and economic growth in Poland.

3   Beveridge curves provide a useful perspective on potential skilled labour shortages as well as on structural changes in the labour market. High and increasing levels of unfilled job vacancies, especially at low levels of unemployment, may denote skilled worker shortages and labour market tightening. If combined with sustained levels of high unemployment, they may indicate a mismatch in the labour market between skills available and skills required. In addition, an outward (or inward) shift of the curve over time may denote a decrease (or increase) in the efficiency of labour market matching. However, any analysis of the Beveridge curve must bear in mind the deficiencies of currently available job vacancies data as indicators of unsatisfied labour demand (OECD 2001, Employment Outlook).

4   Except the indigent, students, the clergy and homemakers, those temporarily in work deliberately avoided statutory retirement.

5   The fall in demand in heavy industries was fairly mild, and dispersed over time. 'Soft' rather than shock measures were implemented during the process of restructuring the heavy industries. This was achieved thanks to strong pressure from trade unions who managed to win special treatment from the state, including protective and preventive programmes.

6   The recent recovery of the construction sector might enhance internal migration, particularly if international migration loses its attraction.

7   Data extracted from Central Statistical Office.

References

Abraham, K. & L. Katz (1986), 'Cyclical unemployment: Sectoral shift or aggregate disturbances', *Journal of Monetary Economics* 94: 507-22

Brunello, G. (1991), 'Mismatch in Japan' in F.P. Schioppa (ed.), *Mismatch and labour mobility.* 57. Cambridge: Cambridge University Press..

Borkowska, S. & A. Karpinski (2001), *Emergence of new occupations and labour demand forecasting (synthesis)*. Warsaw: Government Centre for Strategic Studies, Inter-Departmental Group for Labour Demand Forecasting.

Davis, S. & J. Haltiwanger (1992), 'Gross job creation, gross job destruction and employment reallocation', *Quarterly Journal of Economics* 107 (3): 819-63.

Deichmann, U. & V. Henderson (2000), 'Urban and regional dynamics in Poland', *World Bank Research Working Papers* 2457.

Dorenbos, R. (1999), *Labour market adjustments in Hungary and Poland*. Groningen: Graduate School in Systems, Organization and Management.

Gawronska-Nowak, B. & P. Kaczorowski (2000), 'Regionalne niedopasowania na rynku pracy, a zmiany poziomu zatrudnienia w Polsce', *Ekonomista* 2: 223-241.

Gawronska-Nowak, B., E. Kwiatkowski & P. Kubiak (1998), 'On some determinants of regional unemployment in Poland in transition', *Discussion Paper* 2. University of Padua.

Grabowska-Lusinska I. (2008), 'Migrations from Poland after 1 May 2004 with special focus on British Isles: Post-accession migration strategies as hidden behind statistics', *Espace Population Sociétés* 2008/2: 247-60.

Jazwinska, E. & M. Okólski (eds.) (2001), *Ludzie na huśtawce. Migracje między peryferiami Polski i Zachodu*, 17-22. Warsaw: Wydawnictwo Naukowe Scholar.

Kaczmarczyk, P. & W. Lukowski (eds.) (2004), *Polscy pracownicy na rynku Unii Europejskiej*. Warsaw: Wydawnictwo Naukowe Scholar.

Kaczmarczyk P. & M. Okólski (2008), 'Economic impacts of migration on Poland and Baltic states', *Fafo-paper* 1.

Kępińska, E. (2005), 'Recent trends in international migration. The 2005 SOPEMI Report for Poland', *Seria: Prace Migracyjne* 60. Warsaw: Instytut Studiów Społecznych.

Kwiatkowski, E., L. Kucharski & T. Tokarski (2004), 'Regional economic and labour market performance and inter-regional labour market balance: The case of Poland', *Journal for Labour Market Research* 37(4): 409-24.

Kwiatkowski, S.M. (2000), *Kształcenie zawodowe i prozawodowe w reformowanym systemie edukacji a potrzeby rynku pracy i oczekiwania pracodawców*. Rzadowe Centrum Studiow Strategicznych, Międzyresortowy Zespol do Prognozowania Popytu na Prace (unpublished manuscript).

Lilien, D.M. (1982), 'Sectoral shift and cyclical unemployment', *Journal of Political Economy* 90.

Loungani, P.,M. Rush & W. Tave (1990), 'Stock market dispersion and unemployment', *Journal of Monetary Economics* 25(3): 367-88.

Piore, M. (1979), *Birds of passage*. Cambridge: Cambridge University Press.

Schioppa, F.P. (ed.) (1991), *Mismatch and labour mobility*. Cambridge: Cambridge University Press.

Sadowska-Snarska C. (2000), *Zmiany strukturalne w zatrudnieniu jako czynnik rozwoju regionalnego (na przykładzie regionu północno-wschodniej Polski)*. Bialystok: Wydawnictwo Wyższej Szkoły Ekonomicznej w Białymstoku.

UNDP (2007), *Edukacja dla pracy. Raport o Rozwoju Spolecznym. Polska 2007*. Warsaw: Program Narodów Zjednoczonych ds. Rozwoju.

10 Optimising migration effects: A perspective from Bulgaria

Eugenia Markova

Introduction

Research on Bulgarian migration has been rather sketchy, often being based either on small purposive samples in selected host countries or on macro data of unreliable quality from Bulgaria itself. More recently, some analyses have focused on certain socio-economic impacts of the emigration phenomenon on Bulgaria. These analyses mainly refer to the effects of remittances and of a 'brain drain' on labour supply and on family structures, particularly on the children of migrant parents.

A better and more thorough understanding of the positive and negative consequences of migration for Bulgaria is needed as this would heighten the possibility for policymaking, both in receiving and origin countries, to help optimise the benefits of migration. This chapter aims to enhance this understanding by identifying the size and nature as well as the dynamics of emigration, providing empirical evidence on the economic and social costs and benefits of emigration for Bulgaria and discussing the most recent government measures to maximise the benefits of migration. The chapter concludes by summarising the major challenges for policymakers in Bulgaria.

The discussion is supported by data from the 2001 population census in Bulgaria, the Bulgarian National Bank, the National Statistical Institute, the Institute for Market Economics, the OECD and the Council of Europe, the Agency for Bulgarians Abroad, in-depth interviews with local authority officials and returned seasonal migrants (Guentcheva, Kabakchieva & Kolarski 2003) and quantitative evidence from household survey data (Mintchev & Boshnakov 2006), together with micro survey data collected by the author (Markova 2001; Markova & Sarris 2002; Markova 2006; Markova & Reilly 2007). The last section of the chapter draws on policy documents produced by the Bulgarian government.

The dynamics of migration from Bulgaria: An overview

The period: September 1944 – November 1989

The end of World War II marked a fundamental change in the migratory processes and policies in Bulgaria and a new era for Bulgarian ethnic minorities as well. A ban on the free movement of Bulgarian citizens was introduced through sophisticated border policing systems and a very restrictive and highly complicated system for issuing passports. Bulgarian emigration in this period was predominantly motivated by political reasons or was related to ethnicity. Labour emigration was entirely controlled by the state. Labour supply was regulated by bilateral agreements either with other countries from the Warsaw Pact or with countries in the Arab world, such as Syria, Libya, Tunisia, Iraq and others that followed policies that were sympathetic with communist principles.

Ethnic emigration

Ethnic emigration during this period occurred mainly in three massive waves. The first occurred in the period 1946-1951 when predominantly Bulgarian Turks, Jews, Armenians and Russians left Bulgaria. The emigration of Bulgarian Turks remained the most significant phenomenon in the history of post-World War II Bulgaria. Facilitated by a bilateral agreement signed with Turkey, some 154,000 Bulgarian Turks migrated to Turkey in the period 1950-1951. They settled primarily in the Marmara and the Aegean Sea regions. The collectivisation of land in Bulgaria was also considered a strong 'push' factor for the first mass outflow of ethnic Turks since the majority of them were farmers and the expropriation of the land in 1949 was felt as a severe shock. In subsequent years, several agreements were signed with Turkey to reunite divided Turkish families, and another 130,000 people left for Turkey between 1968-1978 (Zhelyaskova 1998; Petkova 2002). After the Turks, Jews were the second-largest group involved in the post-World War II ethnic emigration flows from Bulgaria.[1] Between 1948-1949, some 32,106 Jews emigrated from Bulgaria to Israel. Earlier, another 4,000 Jews, mainly youth and children, had migrated to Israel to join the Zionist struggle (Guentcheva et al. 2003: 12). In the period 1946-1951, there was a mass emigration of Armenians as well. Actively facilitated by the Soviet government, about 8,000 left, mainly to Armenia (Mintchev 1999). Several dozen Russian families from north-eastern Bulgaria also left for the Soviet Union. Around 2,000 Slovaks and Czechs returned to their home country from Bulgaria between 1949 and 1951 (Guentcheva et al. 2003: 12-13).

The second wave of mass ethnic emigration occurred during the period 1966-1980, when the total net emigration from Bulgaria reached

115,309 people. Almost all of these emigrants were ethnic Turks who moved to Turkey in accordance with bilateral agreements (Guentcheva et al. 2003: 11). This emigration was particularly intense between 1976 and 1979, with a highpoint in 1978 when net emigration from Bulgaria reached 33,000 (Gächter 2002).

In the spring of 1989, a few months before the fall of the communist government, there was a large exodus of Bulgarian Turks leaving for Turkey. This was the infamous mass exodus, ironically called 'the big excursion', which most political scientists in Bulgaria believed had a great impact upon the shattering of the communist regime (Guentcheva et al. 2003: 14). It marked a dramatic culmination of years of tensions and resilience among the Turkish community, which intensified with the Bulgarian government's assimilation campaign in the winter of 1985 that attempted to make ethnic Turks change their names to Bulgarian Slavic names. The campaign began with a ban on wearing traditional Turkish dress and speaking Turkish in public places followed by the forced name-changing campaign. This 'Bulgarisation' policy provoked resistance among the Turkish minority, expressed in the form of protests and demonstrations, many of which were violently suppressed by troops. Some Turks went on hunger strike. In May 1989, the Bulgarian authorities began to expel Turks (Poulton 1993). When the Turkish government's efforts to negotiate with Bulgaria for an orderly migration failed, Turkey opened its borders to Bulgaria on 2 June 1989. A mass influx followed. Some claimed that Turkey was given more than US$ 250 million in grants and loans by the United States government and the Council of Europe in order to open its borders to Bulgarian Turks (Bobeva 1994: 225). However, the Turkish government decided on 21 August 1989 to reintroduce immigration visa requirements for ethnic Turks, which had been temporarily lifted in June (Kirisci 1996). It was estimated that about 360,000 ethnic Turks had by then left for Turkey (Zhelyazkova 1998). More than a third would subsequently return to Bulgaria once the ban on Turkish names had been revoked in December 1989 (Guentcheva et al. 2003: 14).

Political emigration

The establishment of the communist regime determined a wave of political emigration from Bulgaria, especially after 1948 when the leftist opposition parties were dissolved. According to figures from the International Refugee Organisation (IRO), in the period 1947-1952 about 2,000 Bulgarians demanded political asylum in Yugoslavia, 850 in Australia, 590 in the US, 560 in Canada and 360 in Brazil; some 1,500 Bulgarians were granted political asylum in the German Federal Republic.[2] At that time, there were also about 900 Bulgarian refugees in Yugoslavia and 800 in Turkey (Vernant 1953). According to data from the IRO, there were 14,283 applications for asylum in Europe made by Bulgarian nationals between 1947 and 1987 (Gächter 2002).

From the end of World War II until 1949, the principal channels used by political emigrants were through Turkey and Greece. However, during the 1944-1949 civil war in Greece, access to the country became difficult and even dangerous. Moreover, the frontier was very strictly guarded by the Bulgarian authorities and entry was forbidden into a twenty-mile deep military zone to all persons lacking a special permit. These difficulties did not prevent several thousands of Bulgarians from fleeing the country and some even chose the roundabout route through Romania and Hungary on their way to the West. The deterioration of Bulgaria's relations with Yugoslavia created a third migration channel through the western border between the two countries (Vernant 1953).

The largest communities of political emigrants were concentrated in the neighbouring countries of Greece, Turkey, Yugoslavia and in Western Europe, namely Italy and France. Bulgarian political emigration was ideologically and politically divided. It was even more divided in 1950 when the communist government decreed an amnesty that allowed a one-year grace period for all political refugees to return to Bulgaria, the only exception being those found guilty of political espionage. As a result, Bulgarian political emigration never managed to consolidate itself and become a powerful opposition to the communist government (see Guentcheva et al. 2003). The number of Bulgarian political asylum seekers grew in the late 1940s and early 1950s and then decreased in the late 1950s, when only 1,063 managed to emigrate. The numbers decreased further in the 1980s to just 684 registered emigrants between 1981 and 1988 (Table 10.1). However, the accuracy of the official emigration data contained in the Statistical Yearbooks of Bulgaria, from 1952-1989, is highly debatable as it would not have captured those who had used 'illegal' ways to leave the country and requested asylum abroad. For example, the official statistics in Bulgaria point to 684 emigrants who left the country in 1981-1988. For the same period, the statistics of the host countries have registered 2,761 asylum applications lodged by Bulgarian citizens: 893 in Germany, 851 in Austria, 384 in Italy, 166 in Switzerland, 119 in Greece, 105 in Turkey, 67 in Belgium, 55 in Sweden, 41 in Spain, 24 in the Netherlands, 20 in the UK, 19 in Denmark, 13 in Norway, 3 in Portugal and 1 in Finland (calculations based on data in UNHCR 2001).

Table 10.1 *Total number of emigrants from Bulgaria, 1946-1988*

Year	Emigrants
1946-1950	100,121
1951-1955	101,454
1956-1960	1,063
1961-1965	429
1966-1970	14,280
1971-1975	27,139
1976-1980	73,890
1981-1988	684

Source: Statistical Yearbooks of Bulgaria, 1952-1989

The period after November 1989

On 10 November 1989, the Bulgarian communist regime fell after 45 years of uninterrupted rule, and Bulgarian citizens were allowed freedom of travel again. According to the National Statistical Institute (1992), some 218,000 Bulgarians left the country in this particular year and emigration flows were mainly directed towards Turkey (Table 10.2). This emigration wave is estimated to have been the highest since 1989.

The subsequent emigration wave was prompted by continuously deteriorating economic conditions and widespread disillusionment, especially amongst young people, with the first democratic elections in 1990 won by the renamed communist party. Almost 88,000 people left in 1990. Once again, most of them were Bulgarian Turks. This time, however, they were 'pushed' by economic reasons since the country's economic decline affected especially ethnically mixed regions of Bulgaria, where people's main livelihoods were tobacco growing and

Table 10.2 *Bulgarian emigration 1989-1996*

Year	Men	Women	Total
1989	106,432	111,568	218,000
	(48.8%)	(51.2%)	(100%)
1990	68,759	19,136	87,895
	(78.2%)	(21.8%)	(100%)
1991	19,112	21,152	40,264
	(47.5%)	(52.5%)	(100%)
1992	Figures for these years are not broken		65,250
1993	down by gender		69,609
1994			64,000
1995			54,000
1996			66,000

Source: National Statistical Institute

construction. The prices of tobacco were plummeting, the markets in the former socialist block countries were lost, the construction sector was collapsing whilst residents in the border regions no longer enjoyed state privileges as part of the border control system during communism. In addition, there was rising unemployment. At the end of 1990 the total official number of unemployed reached 70,000. Although this was a small proportion of a workforce of almost four million, it had a significant psychological impact. Many people were leaving the country because of fears of growing unemployment (Hutchings 1994). The most popular country of destination was Germany, chosen by 20 per cent of total emigrants. In 1991, the German Ministry of Foreign Affairs recorded about 13,000 Bulgarian asylum seekers. Seasonal migration to Greece intensified in 1990. According to unofficial data from the Bulgarian Ministry of Interior, around 33,000 Bulgarian citizens migrated to Greece in 1990 as seasonal farm workers. This emigration wave was characterised by a 'brain drain' as well because 55 per cent of the emigrants had an educational level at secondary school or higher, and 12 per cent were university graduates. Of the highly qualified workers, 10 per cent came from engineering and technical fields, followed by economics and agricultural specialisations. The main driving force for the highly qualified was their desire to work in their chosen professions while there was a growing threat of unemployment due to the closure of many Bulgarian research institutes and the redundancy of management posts in the public sector (SOPEMI 1993).

In 1991-1992, the emigration of highly qualified workers continued. Some 12 per cent of emigrants were university graduates and 18 per cent had post-secondary diplomas. In the autumn of 1992, emigration to Turkey resumed at an even greater rate. The 'push' factors were mainly related to the depressed economic conditions. The semi-mountainous regions inhabited by ethnically mixed groups, especially Bulgarians of Turkish origin, were left without state subsidies or other forms of state assistance and experienced deep recession (SOPEMI 1993). According to the 1992 census, some 344,849 Bulgarians of Turkish origin had migrated to Turkey between 1989 and 1992, which resulted in significant demographic decline in southern Bulgaria and the complete depopulation of some municipalities (SOPEMI 1995).

In 1993, Bulgaria was placed on the EU's visa 'blacklist'. Restrictive visa regimes by EU countries significantly changed the direction and character of the migration flows. Official emigration to Western Europe – excepting Austria, a traditional economic and commercial partner, and Germany – dropped dramatically. Emigration to Greece and Italy was largely undocumented in character.

After 1993, Bulgarian emigration had a predominantly economic character. In the period 1990-1994, employment levels dropped by 45 per cent and the real-wage rate by 52 per cent. The real-wage decline was affected by two price shocks in 1991 and 1994, together with an inadequate compensation policy for the population (Beleva, Dobrev, Zareva & Tsanov 1996). Therefore, higher living standards and the desire for prosperity were the most important 'pull' factors for emigration.

By 1996, Bulgaria was facing its most severe political and economic crisis. The average monthly salary plummeted to less than US\$ 70 in the second half of May 1996, following the drastic devaluation of the national currency; the rate of inflation was officially recorded at 310.8 per cent for 1996. This level of inflation was reminiscent of the figure for 1991, when, for the first time in Bulgaria, prices were liberalised and inflation hit the record level of 438.5 per cent. Survival was the most powerful reason for leaving the country. In 1997 and 1998, emigration was facilitated by the Central European Free Trade Area (CEFTA), which favoured migration between the countries in transition. Emigration was directed mainly towards the Czech Republic, Hungary and Romania (SOPEMI 1999). Spain, in addition, became an attractive destination for Bulgarian migrants in the second half of the 1990s. Anecdotal evidence attributes this migration mainly to the comparative tolerance of the Spanish authorities, employers and local people towards undocumented foreign workers. Researchers at the Gabinet d'Estudis Socials (GES) in Barcelona estimated the total number of registered Bulgarians in Spain on 1 January 2007 to be 118,182 (GES 2008). In the second half of the 1990s, the number of Bulgarians choosing the UK as a destination became more significant, when Bulgarians started making use of the ECAA visas that allowed them entry into the UK as self-employed business people.

Since 2001, Bulgaria has experienced appreciable though declining rates of emigration. According to OECD data for the period 2001-2004, an estimated 60,000 to 100,000 people left the country, which represented a considerable fall compared to an estimated 210,000 people who emigrated during the period 1998-2001. With about 88,000 Bulgarian immigrants registered in European Union countries in 2004,[3] Bulgaria ranked fourth amongst the top ten countries of origin for migrants in the EU, after Romania, Poland and Morocco (SOPEMI 2006). This was a period of intensive reconstruction and implementation of sound macroeconomic policies in an attempt to fulfil the EU accession criteria. As a result, average growth exceeded 6 per cent per year in 2004-2007. The country successfully completed EU negotiations in June 2004 and then, in April 2005, the accession treaty was signed in Luxemburg. On 1 January 2007, Bulgaria joined the European Union. Per capita income increased by an average of 6 per cent per year since 1998 (at purchasing power parity in real terms). Unemployment was reduced substantially from close to 20 per cent in 2000 to below 7 per cent in 2007. In the first half of 2007, the tendency for a real growth of GDP above 6 per cent continued to signify a stable pattern of economic development in the country.[4] However, despite an overall positive performance, Bulgaria continues to be one of the poorest countries in the EU. The country's per capita income in 2006 at purchasing power parity was just 37 per cent of the average level of the EU-27.[5] The large income differences reflect significant gaps in investment and productivity and in the functioning of product and factor markets, and still propel emigration. A recent EU audit of the management of EU funds in the country published in July 2008 revealed that Bulgaria was not able to fully benefit from the EU assistance because of critical weaknesses in administrative and judicial capacity at all levels. High levels of corruption and organised crime exacerbated these problems.[6] However, the 'push-pull' factors of emigration from the 1990s are still valid.

Following the country's EU accession in 2007, Bulgarians continue to leave the country because of low living standards, for better professional realisation and for access to education. Key amongst emigrants are young people accepted at universities abroad and seasonal workers. The growing tendency towards temporary and seasonal migration, rather than permanent settlement – with the most preferred destinations being Greece, Turkey, Italy, the Netherlands, Germany and Spain – intensified in the spring of 2001 when Bulgaria was removed from the Schengen 'blacklist'. As a result, Bulgarian citizens could travel freely within the Schengen area for three months. Many exploited this opportunity to undertake illegal employment in Europe while residing there legally. This phenomenon has further expanded with Bulgaria's EU membership. Most member states have imposed labour market restrictions for Bulgarian citizens except for self-employment; however, Bulgarian workers are exercising their right for free movement in the EU zone; while doing so they often undertake semi-legal jobs for a few months; they are a particularly mobile category of temporary semi-legal workers. The rise in temporary or circular (repeated) economic migration, predominantly undocumented or semi-documented (with a legal right to residence but not to work) in character, is attributed to increased unemployment in certain regions within Bulgaria. Pockets of extreme poverty still persist in the country, especially in ethnically mixed rural areas. Thus, seasonal and circular migration becomes more ethnically and regionally specific. In some municipalities in Bulgaria, the emigrants are entirely of Turkish origin while, in others, there are ethnic Bulgarians. In some other municipalities, Roma people are predominant. For example, of all undocumented Bulgarian migrants in the Netherlands, 80 per cent were said to be ethnic Turks, most of them coming from the south-eastern Bulgarian district of Kurdzhali (Guentcheva et al. 2003).

Last but not least, the US, via its Green Card lottery system, remains an important destination for permanent settlement, attracting annually between 5,000 and 6,000 Bulgarian immigrants (SOPEMI 2005).

Review of the empirical evidence on the effects of migration on Bulgaria

Migration impacts a home country in a variety of ways, depending upon the magnitude, composition and nature of migration flows as well as upon the specific context from which migrants are drawn. In the case of Bulgaria as a migrant origin country, six key aspects of migrations may be distinguished: the demographic effects that also include the effects of working-age labour migrants; the economic effects that encompass the contribution of remittances, the consequences of a brain drain and the potential for gain routed through an educated, economically active diaspora and the importance of return migration; and the social consequences. What does the empirical evidence on Bulgarian migration indicate with respect to each of these?

Demographic effects

In the years between the last two censuses of 1992 and 2001, the Bulgarian population fell by 6 per cent and over one third of the reduction was attributed to emigration – some 217,809 people left the country during this period (National Statistical Institute 2004: 43). This figure is inconsistent with previous official statistics for the same period. For instance, for the period 1993-1996, the National Statistical Institute (NSI) estimated that the number of emigrants was 253,609 people (Table 2). For 1998-2001, official estimates put the emigrant number at 210,000 people (SOPEMI 2006). Results from Bulgaria's 2001 census put the country's population at 7.9 million, a decrease of about half a million from the previous census in 1992. The Economist Intelligence Unit in London gave even lower population figures, estimating Bulgaria's population in 2001 at 7.7 million and forecasting a further fall to a total of 7.3 million by the year 2006.[7]

At the end of 2004, the permanent population of Bulgaria was 7,761,049, a decrease of 40,224 people compared to the population figures of 2003 (National Statistical Institute 2005: 14). The negative development in the last few years is attributed to both a negative natural population growth (a low fertility level and an extremely high mortality rate) and emigration. Bulgaria is amongst the five 'oldest' countries in

Europe together with Italy, Greece, Germany and Spain, with a share of the older-age group (65 and over) at more than 16 per cent of the total population (Council of Europe 2004). At the end of 2004, the share of young people under fifteen years of age was 1,073,000 (13.8 per cent). For the period 1998-2004, this share decreased by 268,000 and the share of people above 65 years of age increased by 26,000, and by the end of 2004 reached 1,331,000 people (17.1 per cent). In 2004, the working-age population was 4,782,000 people (61.6 per cent); as a result of mainly legislative changes, this category of people had increased by 35,000 people (0.7 per cent) compared to 2003. Nevertheless, the country's old-age dependency ratio (the number of people below fifteen and over 64 per 100 of the population between fifteen and 64) dropped to 44.9 per cent in 2004, a reduction of 4 per cent compared to 1998 (National Statistical Institute 2005: 16).

Massive emigration, especially from the ethnically mixed regions in south-east Bulgaria resulted in the depopulation of some areas.[8] Research on the home impacts of seasonal migration from Bulgaria (Guentcheva et al. 2003) pointed to some serious political consequences of the phenomenon. For example, as a result of the decline in the population in the ethnically mixed Kurdzhali region, two parliamentary seats were lost, which diminished the region's overall political power. Bulgaria is already experiencing labour shortages both of high- and low-skilled labour. Recently, the government announced the transformation of the country from a migrant origin and a transit country into a migrant receiving one (Ministry of Labour and Social Policy 2008).

Forecasts by the National Statistical Institute (NSI) of Bulgaria indicate that in the next 50 years the population of Bulgaria will shrink to 5.1 million, regardless of increasing birth rates. The annual drop in population will be 40,000 people if current rates of socio-economic development persists and policies remain unchanged. The Director of the NSI's Population Department has commented in the press that emigration was the main reason for the dramatic population decrease. His calculations estimated about 20,000 Bulgarians leave the country each year. However, the Minister of Labour and Social Policy presented a more optimistic picture of the Bulgarians' intensions for emigration – in 2007, the share of Bulgarians who were planning to work abroad decreased by 80 per cent compared to 2001. Employment agencies in the country claim that recently they have been receiving requests from qualified Bulgarians living abroad who are interested in finding a job and returning more permanently to the country.

Economic impact of migration

Remittances

Data released by the Bulgarian National Bank show that the amount of money sent by Bulgarians abroad to relatives in the country has increased consistently in absolute terms and as a percentage of GDP, from 1998 onwards (Table 10.3). For example, money transfers in 2004 comprised about 4.2 per cent of Bulgarian GDP and amounted to a greater share of national income than the educational and healthcare budget of the country. In 2006, the World Bank registered an increase in the amount of remittances, recording a total flow of US$ 1,695 million, or about 5.4 per cent of the country's GDP (World Bank 2008: 71). Given the existence of informal methods of remitting money (transfers in cash and in-kind from returning Bulgarians emigrants), this figure is likely to under-report the actual scale of such transfers. Mintchev and Boshnakov (2006) estimate that the official figures register just some 45-50 per cent of actual migrant remittances.

According to data released by the Agency for Bulgarians Abroad,[9] at least 300,000 people send amounts ranging between US$ 100 to US$ 300 to their families on a regular monthly basis. Remittances are used primarily to cover basic needs and the purchase of durable goods. Stanchev, Kostadinova, Dimitrov, Angelov, Dimitrova, Karamakalakova, Cankov and Markova (2005) argue that remittances have become very important for improving living standards and reviving local economies through increased consumption and investment. These macroeconomic effects, they claim, can also have the effect of delaying government

Table 10.3 *The size of remittances and their share of main macro-indicators*

Year	Remittances (€ million)	Exports (%)	Imports (%)	GDP (%)	FDI (%)	Healthcare budget (%)	Educational budget (%)
1998	170.2	3.18	3.20	1.48	35.61	...	...
1999	233.3	4.30	3.81	1.92	30.75	...	...
2000	305.9	4.01	3.66	2.24	27.82	...	50.0
2001	472.5	5.83	5.01	3.11	52.94	77.3	77.5
2002	531.7	6.22	5.45	3.22	55.90	72.3	76.8
2003	613.0	6.48	5.50	3.48	49.64	89.2	87.9
2004	812.3	7.15	6.08	4.18	35.66	103.2	101.5
2005 (January-September)	587.0	3.09	2.53	1.95	22.60	...	...
2006*	1,356**	...	...	5.4	...	...	...

Source: Bulgarian National Bank and National Statistical Institute (in Kostadinova 2005, available at www.ime.bg)

* World Bank (2008: 71)

** The figure is based on the average exchange rate for 2006, US$ 1 ≈ € 0.80 (www.x-rates.com/d/EUR/USD/hist2006.html).

reforms for economic restructuring and policies to tackle underlying causes of emigration. The ability of the private households to satisfy their immediate needs independently from the government can create a disincentive for the authorities to work for a better business environment and to deal with the economic and structural problems that pushed the people to leave initially.

A qualitative study on the effects of seasonal migration on Bulgaria by Guentcheva et al. (2003) confirms the use of remittances for consumption and the purchase of houses and flats. In an interview about the use of remittances, the secretary of the Momchilgrad municipality, in the Kurdzhali region, commented:

> In spite of the widespread belief that remittances in the Kurdzhali region are at least € 100 million a year, they are considered 'dead capital', immobilised into purchases of apartments, houses or luxury cars. This money does not circulate, does not serve local businesses. Money from seasonal workers abroad is not significant, because such people work primarily in low-wage sectors, do not bring much money and whatever they bring is used for consumption (often conspicuous). Our municipality is the region with the most Mercedes cars per person in the whole country. (in Guentcheva et al. 2003: 49)

Bulgarian migrants do report spending money on health during their short visits home, notably on dentistry as they cannot afford to visit a dentist in Italy or Greece, where they live.

The pattern of allocating migrants' money to houses and apartments has boosted the real estate market in the region, significantly pushing up prices. A quantitative study by Mintchev and Boshnakov (2006), which used data from a random sample of 1,000 households, found that migrant remittances were mainly used for consumption, purchasing a car and property; very few, though, expressed an interest in buying land. This was explained by reference to the underdeveloped land market. Interestingly, it was also found that every fifth household receiving transfers from abroad was involved in some kind of entrepreneurship – to establish a new business and/or to support an existing one – whilst this was true for only one in ten households not receiving remittances. Transport, services and trade were the main sectors of productive investment. These were usually small- and medium-size businesses as well as leasehold (e.g. purchase of a car and its use as a taxi).

Research regarding seasonal and undocumented migrants suggests that they remit more and remit more often. A study by the author based on questionnaire interviews with 100 undocumented Bulgarian immigrants living in Athens, Greece, in 1996, revealed that undocumented

Bulgarians remitted on a monthly basis over half of their earnings and there was no differentiation by marital status, number of family members in Bulgaria, intentions to stay in Greece or any other attributes. The only exception was the gender variable, indicating that women were sending a larger share of their income to Bulgaria compared to men. This could be explained by the fact that most of the women in the sample – divorced or married – had their children or whole families in Bulgaria. The analysis of another sample of 153 Bulgarian immigrants interviewed by the author in Athens and Crete in 1999, some ten months after the implementation of the first legalisation programme in Greece, showed considerable alteration in immigrants' remitting and saving behaviour. Almost half of the sample, having acquired legal status and access to the banking system in Greece, had started saving more money there, thus reducing the amount sent home. In contrast, undocumented migrants being uncertain about their stay in Greece remitted more often and remitted almost their entire income. The variable on the number of family members in Bulgaria had a significant explanatory power (at 1 per cent level of significance); an additional family member in Bulgaria increased the probability of remitting by 34 per cent (Markova 2001; Markova & Saris 2002). These findings are similar to those reported by Markova and Reilly (2007). These authors, utilising data from a sample of 188 Bulgarian immigrants living in Madrid in 2003-2004, found that the volume of remittances was higher, on average and ceteris paribus, for females and those married. The impact effect for the gender control suggested that, on average and keeping all other variables constant, a female remitted annually about € 588 more to Bulgaria than a male migrant. A married individual remitted over € 420 more in the reference year than those in all other marital status categories. If the number of family members in Bulgaria rose by one, the volume of annual remittances would rise by € 135. In contrast, one additional family member in Spain corresponded with a fall of € 402. The legal status of the respondents had the strongest effect. Bulgarian immigrants who were living and working legally in Spain remitted almost € 1,220 less per year than those who were undocumented.

Brain drain effects

In addition to the impacts on demography and the availability of financial capital through remittances, SOPEMI (1998) suggests that a large proportion of emigrants from Bulgaria are highly skilled, triggering worries that Bulgaria is losing development potential (Gächter 2002). According to Stojtchev, director of the Sofia branch of Gallup international polling agency, 50-60 per cent of the emigrants are highly-educated, and include well-trained specialists (Tomiuc 2002). Analysing brain drain and brain gain within Europe, Wolburg (2002) points out that some 20,000 scientists left Bulgaria in 1989 heading West, primarily to Germany, Ireland, the UK and France. In the period between 1990 and 1992, another 40,000 specialists left the country (Straubhaar 2000). For the same period, Bulgarian sources report an exodus of some 40,000 Bulgarian scientists (Sretenova 2003). Chobanova (2003: 24 cited in Gill & Guth 2005: 6) states that in the case of Bulgaria: 'The country has lost one small town of 55,000 to 60,000 of its highest educated and skilled population each year during the last decade'. Horvat (2004) argues that Bulgarian students are among the largest Southern and Eastern European student populations in many European countries and scientists from Bulgaria usually have a very high skill ratio. An increasing number of Bulgarian citizens applied for the Highly Skilled Migrant Programme (HSMP) in the UK during 2002-2005. The number of successful applicants ranged from six in 2002, when the scheme began, to 40 in 2005.[10]

It is plausible to assume that the unfavourable demographic trends – namely the dramatically declining birth rate and the emigration of young people and whole families – have strongly affected the school enrolment rate in Bulgaria in recent years, which has resulted in job losses for teachers. The number of children enrolled in primary and secondary education has dropped since the mid 1990s. In turn, the number of teachers in primary education fell from 24,601 in 1993-1994 to 16,585 in 2007-2008, a decrease of 32.6 per cent; the decrease of the number of secondary school teachers for the same period was 33.6 per cent (12,160 teachers).[11] This author's research has shown that some 6 per cent of a sample of 100 undocumented Bulgarians in Athens in 1996 were last employed in Bulgaria as primary and secondary school teachers; the figure rose to 9 per cent for Bulgarians interviewed in Athens in 1999, in a sample of 153 (Markova 2001). In a subsequent sample of 202 Bulgarian immigrants interviewed by this author in Madrid in 2003-2004, some 7 per cent were teachers (Markova 2006).

Nonetheless, brain drain had particularly severe consequences for the development of the ethnically mixed regions in the country. Guentcheva et al. (2003: 52) provide empirical evidence for this, showing that recent emigration from these areas involved the most active and qualified segment of the population, i.e. those who had lost their privileged social status during the transition years of the 1990s. Among them were former mayors, representatives of municipal councils, former policemen, technicians, students and doctors. In an earlier piece of research based on a set of Turkish statistics, Bobeva (1994: 227) showed that the community of Bulgarian Turks lost 9,000 university graduates to emigration during the early 1990s.

Other researchers, however, believe that 'there has been just a trickle of highly qualified emigrants, and even cumulatively it is not big enough to make any difference at all' (Gächter 2002). They argue that there has been no dearth of professionals and specialists in Bulgaria, at least compared to other Balkan countries. The number of scientists and researchers among Bulgaria's working-age population still remained high, especially in relation to GDP per capita at purchasing power parity (PPP). Moreover, the reduction in the number of scientists and professionals only served to bring the numbers of technicians to a more realistic and sustainable level, in line with other, wealthier, countries in the area (Gächter 2002).

Bulgarian diaspora
There are still no accurate numbers on the size of the Bulgarian communities abroad. The recently published National Strategy of the Republic of Bulgaria on Migration and Integration (2008-2015) contains some estimates both of the old political immigrants and the new immigrants who left the country after 1989: over 50,000 in Germany, about 25,000 in Austria, about 10,000 in the Czech Republic, about 50,000 in Italy, about 3,000 in the Slovak Republic, about 5,000 in Hungary, about 4,000 in Belgium, about 110,000 in Greece, over 60,000 in the UK, about 2,000 in Sweden, over 15,000 in France, around 10,000 in Portugal, over 120,000 in Spain. Another 200,000 Bulgarians are in the US, about 45,000 in Canada, some 15,000-20,000 are thought to be in South Africa, and another 15,000-20,000 in Australia (Ministry of Labour and Social Policy 2008: 5). However, Council of Europe data on the stock of registered Bulgarian citizens in selected European destinations for the period 2000-2004 suggest much lower numbers (Table 10.4).

Even without repatriation, the diaspora has the potential to play an important role in Bulgaria's economic development. In 2003, the Agency for Bulgarians Abroad conducted a unique survey on the problems faced by the Bulgarian migrant community abroad in their attempts to participate in Bulgaria's economy.[12] The survey found that a lack of sufficient and reliable information on privatisation deals, investment possibilities and other aspects of economic reform in Bulgaria, as well as corruption at all levels of governance and onerous bureaucratic procedures, were amongst the main issues pointed out by Bulgarians abroad as issues that affect the willingness of the Bulgarian migrant community to invest in Bulgaria. Based on their responses, the survey identified four main groups of Bulgarian migrants, according to their economic relations with the country.

The first group consisted of very rich expatriates (about 50-70 persons) who had made some large investments in the country. However,

Table 10.4   *Stock of Bulgarian citizens in selected European countries*

	2000	2001	2002	2003	2004
Germany					
Council of Europe, 2004	32,290	34,359	38,143	42,419	...
Federal Office for			42,420	44,300	
Migration and Refugees					
Germany (Haug 2005)					
Greece					
2001 census		35,104			
Baldwin-Edwards 2004					46,114
Denmark*	394	408	426	460	...
Iceland*	44	58	62	72	68
Spain*	3,031	...	...	44,151	63,155
2005 census					91,509
Italy*	5,637	6,758	...	...	...
Latvia*	22	24	25	23	28
Norway*	355	...	464	533	567
Portugal*	343	376	431	...	...
Romania*	92	86	92	92	67
Slovenia*	127	66	68	...	...
Hungary					
Council of Europe 2004	1,499	1,200	1,146	1,085	1,118
SOPEMI 2005	1,200	1,100	1,100		
Finland*	317	297	308	326	
The Netherlands*	713	870	1,074	1,360	...
Czech Republic					
Council of Europe 2004	5,454	4,131	3,558	3,783	3,904
SOPEMI 2005	4,000	4,100	4,200	4,100	
UK					
2001 census		5,154			
(England & Wales)			5,350		
Switzerland*	1,943	2,012	2,293	2,596	2,589
Sweden*	1,065	1,002	805	796	...

* *Source:* Council of Europe (2004: 310)

some of them have been accused of destabilising actions against the
state. Others were sceptical about investing in Bulgaria, fearing the
strong, 'hidden' influence of the former communist party. The second
group represented the 'middle class' of Bulgarian emigration (about
20,000 people). It is mainly in the US, Canada, Germany, Austria and
other Western European countries. They are considered as an already
established Bulgarian 'lobby' and a good investment potential for the
country. They are usually in professional occupations, with good managerial skills and in good social and institutional positions in the host
countries. The third group comprised a wider range of Bulgarian emigrants, from those who migrate on a seasonal or temporary basis and
who are usually undocumented migrants, to legal migrants in the lower

social strata of the host country. Some 80 per cent of these people were estimated to remit small amounts of money each month to their families and relatives in the country. Finally, the fourth group included ethnic Bulgarian who have resettled, usually close to Bulgarian borders. They strive to establish economic ties with their motherland.

In the last few years, some young Bulgarian financial brokers have set up organisations which aim to attract business interest to Bulgaria. The City Club in London and the Wall Street Club in New York were the most successful among them. It was the former prime minister, Ivan Kostov, who in 2000 first attempted to attract the interest and expertise of young Bulgarian expatriates to Bulgaria, organising an event titled 'Bulgarian Easter'. Shortly after this, a similar initiative followed in the summer of 2000, and was organised by the then president, Peter Stoyanov. Ironically, just a year later, some of those invited to the event, such as financial brokers from London, became the main reason Kostov's party suffered major losses in the election of June 2001. Ironically, just a year later, some of those invited to the event, such as financial brokers from London, became the main reason Kostov's party suffered major losses in the election of June 2001. This election presented a very interesting situation: the winner was a party formed at the last minute and led by a former king (who became prime minister following the elections). Among this party's candidates were professional Bulgarian emigrants – including prominent participants in recent Bulgarian government initiatives to attract highly skilled migrants to Bulgaria – who put on hold their careers in the West to participate in Bulgarian politics. They formed the first government comprised mainly of returned professionals.

Greek banks in Bulgaria: Another emigration effect?
At the beginning of the 1990s, increasing transactions and rising demand for financial services had motivated Greek banks to expand their services into Bulgaria. The establishment of banks in Bulgaria, as in other countries in the region, has also been prompted to a large degree by the increased level of emigration and has thus facilitated remittances. Legalised migrants are the main users of the banking system in transferring their money home. Since 1998, when the Greek government implemented its first regularisation programme to grant legal status to undocumented foreigners, the number of Bulgarian immigrants legally residing and working in Greece has substantially increased. Statistics from the database on residence permits, cited in the 2004 Hellenic Migration Policy Institute (IMEPO) report and compiled for the year 2003-2004 by the Mediterranean Migration Observatory (MMO), identify 66,787 Bulgarians in Greece (Baldwin-Edwards 2004). This increase may explain the growing number of Greek bank branches

in Bulgaria in recent years. For example, Alpha Bank has now opened branches in twenty cities in Bulgaria. Five Greek banks – National Bank of Greece (which owns 99.9 per cent of the United Bulgarian Bank), EFG-Eurobank (affiliated with Postbank), Alpha Bank, Piraeus Bank and Emporiki Bank – currently have a market share of 25-30 per cent in Bulgaria.[13] It is plausible to assume that these bank branches are increasingly turning into important employers for local people, especially for those who have worked in Greece.

In addition to the Greek banks in Bulgaria, there are 419 Greek businesses operating in the country; some 40 per cent of them were registered after the year 2000 following almost a decade of Bulgarian immigration to Greece.[14] Anecdotal evidence suggests that some of them, especially small- and medium-size companies have been established through connections with Bulgarian immigrants in Greece, and have been recruiting bilingual returnees from Greece.

Social effects

There is little empirical evidence – with the exception of a few studies – on the social effects of emigration in Bulgaria. Most of the available information is anecdotal and discussed in the press. The main social effects of emigration reported in Bulgaria consist of changes in family composition and child outcomes in terms of health and education.

Changes in family composition occur either when only one partner emigrates – which sometimes leads to a break-up – or when both partners emigrate and the children are left at home. Research on Eastern European immigrants in London and Brighton, UK, conducted in 2005, revealed that a little over one in five Bulgarians had left their partners in Bulgaria and most of their children lived there (Markova & Black 2007). Some male migrants involved in circular migration to Greece reported having families in both the home and the host country. As many have been reported as saying: 'I have a home here and there; I have a wife in Bulgaria and two children; now, I have a partner and a child in Greece as well' (Markova 2005).

Children are most affected by the emigration of their parents. A study by Guentcheva et al. (2003) warns of the high dropout school rates amongst children of migrant parents who have been left behind in Bulgaria in the care of grandparents or aunts. According to teachers, such pupils enjoy the freedoms associated with having more money than children whose parents did not migrate. They become easily spoiled and undisciplined and do not obey their elderly grandparents or other relatives serving as their guardians. They start smoking and drinking and eventually leave school altogether.

In the last few years, the Bulgarian press has often described these children as having 'Skype parents'.[15] One study on access to education in Bulgaria found that the most frequently cited reason for dropping out of school was to join family members who have left for seasonal short-term or longer-term stay abroad (Iliev & Kabakchieva 2002). However, research also reveals some positive stories of families of returned seasonal migrants who have invested their savings into securing a better education for their children (Guentcheva et al. 2003).

State management of emigration

State policy towards emigration has changed significantly since the communist era. Prior to 1989, emigration policies were directed at eliminating or reducing international travel. Bulgaria's post-communist migration policy aimed to achieve an optimal balance between the freedom of movement of people and the control of undocumented migration, whilst at the same time respecting the fundamental human rights and freedoms as guaranteed by international and European standards and conventions (Mintchev 1999). Strategic policy goals included: improvement in the management of economic migration; increasing border security in view of taking on regional responsibilities for the protection of the external borders of the EU; protecting the rights and promoting the integration of legal immigrants in Bulgaria; international cooperation and compliance with international treaties on migration (Ministry of Labour and Social Policy 2004). In an attempt to stem undocumented migration, since 1991, several bilateral agreements for employment of seasonal or temporary workers have been signed.

At present, bilateral employment agreements exist with Germany, Spain, Switzerland, France, Luxembourg, Portugal, the Czech Republic, the Flemish Union of Belgium and the region of Lombardy in Italy.[16] These agreements provide for the employment of a limited number of Bulgarian nationals, including students, for specified periods of time and in professions where there are skill shortages in the host country. Bilateral agreements on social security exist with Germany, Poland, Spain, Luxembourg, the Czech Republic, Slovakia, FYROM, Ukraine, Croatia, Serbia, Turkey, Hungary, Austria, Cyprus, Romania, Albania, Montenegro, Bosnia-Herzegovina and Libya.[17]

As a response to the dramatic depopulation of the ethnically mixed regions in Bulgaria, the government attempted to resettle ethnic Bulgarians from abroad. The 'unwritten' policy amounted to an attempt to achieve an ethnic balance in 'ethnically sensitive areas' – border areas in the south with ethnically mixed populations. Thus, returning ethnic Bulgarians from Moldova and Ukraine were resettled in the Kurdzhali region. However, the programme was not particularly successful as most of the returning ethnic Bulgarians wanted to settle in the cities, where some of the young ethnic returnees were enrolled at universities through a special government programme (Guentcheva et al. 2003: 53).

Recently, the Bulgarian government introduced its long-awaited national strategy on migration and integration for the period 2008-2015. Its main objective is to attract Bulgarians living abroad and foreign citizens of Bulgarian origin to settle more permanently in the country; it also plans to attract highly skilled third-country nationals to cover labour shortages. However, the government tends to ignore the fact that low-skilled shortages will be more acute or as acute as highly skilled labour shortages in the medium and long run, and will also need to be covered by migrant labour. The new state policy to attract Bulgarian emigrants to permanently return will be implemented by several institutions that will be established and coordinated by the Council of Bulgarians Abroad of the Council of Ministers. In the autumn of 2008, information campaigns for Bulgarians working in Spain, Germany, Greece and the UK were organised – with Bulgarian employers present – to discuss employment opportunities at home with potential returnees. These four countries were selected because of the large Bulgarian communities there and because of the presence of labour attachés in the respective embassies who are able to inform Bulgarian emigrants about current working conditions and remuneration in Bulgaria. State measures also include the establishment of websites on the labour market conditions in Bulgaria and current vacancies. Bulgarian students abroad are of special interest. The government plans to include them in a special register that will be made available to interested employers (Ministry of Labour and Social Policy 2008).

Conclusion

Emigration from Bulgaria continues, albeit at a declining rate. In recent years, a clear pattern of circular and temporary migration can be identified, especially after April 2001 when Bulgarian citizens were allowed a three-month visa-free stay in countries within the Schengen zone and more recently, after the country's EU membership in January 2007. Preferred destinations are Greece, Spain, Italy, the Netherlands, Germany, Turkey and the UK. The US remains an important destination for permanent settlement. Temporary migration has become more regionally and ethnically specific with migrants increasingly originating from poor, ethnically mixed rural areas.

Large out-migrations have considerably distorted the demographic profile of the population between 1989 and 2001. Young people and whole families have migrated abroad, thus contributing to the continuously decreasing birth rate and steadily placing Bulgaria amongst the five 'oldest' countries in Europe.

Brain drain through emigration is not a clear-cut issue for Bulgaria. However, it has had more severe consequences for the development of ethnically mixed regions in the country, where emigration involved the most active and qualified segments of the population.

An estimated four million Bulgarians live abroad. The newly adopted National Strategy of the Republic of Bulgaria on Migration and Integration for 2008-2015 targets these people for a more permanent return. The group of Bulgarians who do not plan to return but are willing to contribute to Bulgaria's economic development should not be ignored by policymakers. They need to be provided with accurate and reliable information by the relevant state institutions, such as information on privatisation deals, conditions for investment and other aspects of economic reform in the country. Trade departments and labour attachés within Bulgarian diplomatic missions abroad can play an important role in the process.

Bulgaria is already experiencing a turn from being a migrant origin and transit country into a migrant receiving country. There is the need not only for highly skilled professionals, but also for unskilled labour. This particular development has been ignored in the National Strategy on Migration. It is crucial that policymakers reconsider this issue and incorporate it in their plans. If they fail to do this, the country risks attracting unskilled undocumented migrant labour and expanding its already flourishing shadow economy.

Notes

1   With the help of prominent Bulgarians, MPs and the Bulgarian king himself, some 50,000 Jews were saved from Nazi concentration camps during World War II (Guentcheva et al. 2003: 12)
2   Some of them were already abroad when they acquired refugee status.
3   It should be noted, however, that this figure includes new residence permits as well as renewed ones for people who had left the country in previous years and then returned.
4   See www.ime.bg.
5   See www.worldbank.org.
6   See www.europe.bg/en/htmls/page.php?category=230&id=15949.
7   Radio Free Europe (RFE)/ Radio Liberty (RL), Prague, 27 August 2002 (www.rferl.org/nca/features/2002/08/27082002142636.asp).
8   At the end of 2004, 144 formerly populated areas in the country became entirely depopulated (population=0). These areas are mainly border regions in the south and west of the country. See Capital (2006), 'Peasants of urban type: Government policy is needed to put an end to the depopulation of villages', issue 28 (in Bulgarian). This is

due to increased urbanisation and external migration. According to NSI data, 67.1 per cent of the population in 1990 lived in urban areas while in 2004 this figure had risen to 70 per cent.

9   The Agency for Bulgarians Abroad (ABA) is a state institution tasked with collecting data about expatriate Bulgarians. It also coordinates and supports the activities of state institutions towards expatriate Bulgarian communities (www.aba.government.bg). It should be noted that ABA uses the term 'expatriate Bulgarian' and does not use the concept 'Bulgarian emigrant'.

10 The HSMP started on 1 February 2002, so data for 2002 are for 1 February to 31 December 2002.

11 Author's own calculations based on data made available by the NSI in Bulgaria; www.nsi.bg/SocialActivities/Education.htm (in Bulgarian).

12 See www.aba.bg.

13 www.invgr.com/se_europe.htm.

14 Data provided by the Economic and Trade Office of the Greek Embassy in Sofia, Bulgaria during the author's research visit there on 7 November 2006.

15 So-called after the Skype voice over internet programme that facilitates free video and telephone calls.

16 www.mlsp.government.bg/bg/integration/agreements/index.htm (in Bulgarian); accessed 17 August 2008.

17 ibid.

References

Amnesty International (1986), *Bulgaria: Imprisonment of ethnic Turks.* EUR 15 March 1986: 26.

Baldwin-Edwards, M. (2004), Statistical data on immigrants in Greece: An analytical study of available data and recommendations for conformity with European Union standards. Research undertaken by the Mediterranean Migration Observatory (MMO) on behalf of the Migration Policy Institute (IMEPO). Athens: MMO, Panteion University. www.mmo.gr.

Beleva, I., P. Dobrev, I. Zareva & V. Tsanov (1996), *Labor market in Bulgaria: Reflection of the contradictory economic realities.* Sofia: Gorex Press.

Bobeva, D. (1994), 'Emigration from and emigration to Bulgaria', in H. Fassmann & R. Munz (eds.), *European migration in the late twentieth century: Historical patterns, actual trends, and social implications.* Aldershot: Edward Elgar: 221-38.

Chobanova, R. (2003), 'Flows and non-EU Europe–Bulgaria'. www.merit.unimaas.nl/braindrain/Part5.Flows_non_-EU per cent20Europe-Bulgaria.pdf.

Council of Europe (2004), *Recent demographic developments in Europe.* Strasbourg: Council of Europe.

Gabinet d'Estudis Socials (2008), *Migrant statistics in Spain.* Barcelona: GES (mimeo).

Gächter, A. (2002), 'The ambiguities of emigration: Bulgaria since 1988', *International Migration Papers* 39. Geneva: ILO.

Gill, B. & J. Guth (2005), 'Deciding whether and where to move: Why Eastern European doctoral researchers go West'. Paper prepared for the conference 'New patterns of East-West migration in Europe', 18-19 November 2005, Hamburg, Hamburg Institute of International Economics (HWWA).

Guencheva, R., P. Kabakchieva & P. Kolarski (2003), *Bulgaria: The social impact of seasonal migration.* Vienna: IOM & European Commission Project.

Haug, S. (2005), 'Migration trends from Central and Eastern Europe to Germany', Paper presented at the conference 'New Patterns of East-West Migration in Europe', 18-19 November 2005, Hamburg, Migration Research Group, HWWA.

Horvat, V. (2004), 'Brain drain: Threat to successful transition in South East Europe?', *Southeast European Politics* 5(1): 76-93.

Hutchings, R. (1994), 'Bulgaria: The economy', in *Eastern Europe and the Commonwealth of Independent States*. London: Europa Publications Ltd.

Kirisci, K. (1996), 'Refugees of Turkish origin: "Coerced immigrants" to Turkey since 1945', *International Migration* 34 (3): 385-412.

Kostadinova, S. (2005), *'We need your money'*. Sofia: IME. www.ime.bg.

Markova, E. (2005), 'Circular and temporary migration: Towards an integrated regional market in South-East Europe'. Paper presented at the Second Annual IMEPO-MPI International Migration Conference 'Capturing the Benefits of Migration in Southeastern Europe', 10-11 October 2005, Athens.

Markova, E. (2006), 'The performance of Bulgarian undocumented and legalised immigrants in the Spanish labour market', *Sussex Migration Working Paper* 31.

Markova, E. & R. Black (2007), *New East European immigration and community cohesion*. York: Joseph Rowntree Foundation.

Markova, E. & B. Reilly (2007), 'Bulgarian migrant remittances and legal status: Some micro-level evidence from Madrid', *South-Eastern Europe Journal of Economics* 5 (1): 55-71.

Ministry of Labour and Social Policy (2004), *East-West migration in an enlarged Europe*, report prepared for the conference 'Migration: Trends and policies', organised by ICMPD and the Open Society Institute, 9-10 December 2004, Sofia.

Ministry of Labour and Social Policy (2008), *National strategy of the Republic of Bulgaria on migration and integration*. Sofia. www.mlsp.government.bg/bg/docs/index.htm. (in Bulgarian).

Mintchev, V. (1999), 'External migration and external migration policies in Bulgaria', *South East Europe Review for Labour and Social Affairs* 3: 123-50).

Mintchev, V. & V. Boshnakov (2006), The economics of Bulgarian migration: an empirical assessment, *Economic Thought*, 7: 134-61

Mintchev, V., V. Boshnakov, I. Kalchev & V. Goev (2006), 'The modern Bulgarian emigration' *Convergence and European Funds: Report for the President of the Republic of Bulgaria*, 135-144. Sofia: Bulgarian National Bank Publications.

National Statistical Institute (1992), *Internal and international migration of the population at the end of 1999*. Sofia: National Statistical Institute..

National Statistical Institute (2004), 'Demographic and social characteristics of the population', *Population* 1 (1). Sofia: National Statistical Institute (in Bulgarian).

National Statistical Institute (2005), *Bulgaria 2004: Socio-economic development*. Sofia: National Statistical Institute. (in Bulgarian).

Petkova, L. (2002), 'The ethnic Turks in Bulgaria: Social integration and impact on Bulgarian-Turkish Relations', *The Global Review of Ethnopolitics* 1(4): 42-59.

Poulton, H. (1993), *The Balkans: Minorities and states in conflict*. London: Minority Rights Publications.

SOPEMI (1993), Trends in international migration. Paris: OECD.

SOPEMI (1995), Trends in international migration. Paris: OECD.

SOPEMI (1999), Trends in international migration. Paris: OECD.

SOPEMI (2005), Trends in international migration. Paris: OECD.

SOPEMI (2006), International migration outlook: Annual report. Paris: OECD.

Sretenova, N. (2003), 'Scientific mobility and "brain drain" issues in the context of structural reforms of research and development and the higher education sector in Bulgaria', *CSLPE Research Report* 2. Leeds: University of Leeds.

Stanchev, K., S. Kostadinova, M. Dimitrov, G. Angelov, K. Dimitrova, G. Karamakalakova, S. Cankov & E. Markova (2005), *Bulgarian Migration: Incentives and Constellations*, Sofia: Open Society Institute.

Straubhaar, T. (2000), 'International mobility of high skilled: Brain gain, brain drain or brain exchange', *HWWA Discussion Paper* 88.

Tomiuc, E. (2002), 'Brain drain – Southern regions bear the brunt', *Radio Free Europe/Radio Liberty*, 3 December. www.rferl.org/features/2002/12/03122002191936.asp.

UNHCR (2001), *Asylum applications in industrialised countries – 1980-1999: Trends in asylum applications lodged in 37 mostly industrialised countries.* Population Data Unit, Population & Geographic Data Section. Geneva: UNHCR.

Vernant, J. (1953), *The refugee in the post-war world.* London: George Allen & Unwin Ltd.

Wolburg, M. (2000), On brain drain, brain gain and brain exchange within Europe, PhD Dissertation. Hamburg: HWWA.

World Bank (2001), *World development indicators 2000.* Washington, D.C.: The World Bank.

World Bank (2008), *Migration and remittances factbook 2008.* Washington, D.C.: The World Bank.

Zhelyazkova, A. (1998), 'The social and cultural adaptation of Bulgarian immigrants in Turkey'. www.omda.bg/imir/studies/nostalgia_1.html.

11 Return migration and development prospects after EU integration: Empirical evidence from Bulgaria

Vesselin Mintchev and Venelin Boshnakov

Introduction[1]

Substantial research interest has been directed towards the intensified out-migration from Central and Eastern Europe's (CEE) transition countries since the start of reforms in the early 1990s. This out-migration has been an important aspect of the radical socio-economic changes in post-communist countries, and a number of issues have driven the debate about the effects of migration to Western Europe on labour markets and long-term demographic trends. Although many EU countries started to reassess their migration policies upon considering the benefits of labour migration (regarding the labour shortages in some economic sectors), there is still much concern about increased trafficking of irregular migrants and the potential destabilisation of social security and asylum systems in Europe (see Straubhaar 2001; Laczko 2002; Piracha & Vickerman 2003; Martin 2003).

A range of publications reveals CEE migration's various idiosyncrasies, positioning the migration behaviour of Eastern Europeans between the extremes of 'developmentalism' and 'Dutch disease' (Taylor 1999). Some indications also support the assertion that migrants from South-Eastern European transition countries tend to favour Mediterranean countries as new EU destination countries. This migration is characterised by predominantly short- to medium-term (mainly seasonal) employment, subsequent return or circular migration and a high share of unregistered remittances with a considerable supplementary effect on sending households consumption, but also some use of remittances for household assets acquisition and small business development (Leon-Ledesma & Piracha 2004).

Bulgaria is often considered a country that has not been as severely affected by out-migration processes, as was expected in the context of unfavourable patterns of the early market transition. In fact, during the fifteen years of transition (1989-2004), the Bulgarian population decreased by about 13 per cent or 1.2 million in absolute figures – about

500,000 of which was due to natural decrease and 700,000 due to emigration (Mansoor & Quillin 2007). It could plausibly be argued that the total Bulgarian diaspora, both historical and newly generated, amounts to 2.5 to 3 million, compared to Bulgaria's current domestic population of around 7.5 million. Yet several studies of potential CEE emigration have shown that, despite intensive emigration processes during the economic transition between 1990 and 1994, Bulgarian out-migration pressure ten years later (during the European Union accession period) was felt only within a small percentage of the population (Bauer & Zimmermann 1999; Wallace 1999; Mintchev, Kaltchev, Goev & Boshnakov 2004). These findings were confirmed in a report by the European Commission on the functioning of the transitional arrangements introduced in 2004 concerning international labour mobility (European Commission 2006).

Empirical studies on return migration, remittances and their usage in Bulgarian households are challenging for several reasons. Firstly, there is a lack of trustworthy information and comprehensive studies on these issues. Secondly, there is the difficulty of obtaining a representative sample of return migrant households in order to draw reliable conclusions regarding their consumption and/or investment patterns. We attempt, therefore, to assess some facets of the impact that return migration and remittances have had on development Bulgaria during the process of EU integration. Our analysis will be based on micro-data from a representative household survey conducted at the end of 2005. The period of interest was retroactively extended five years so as to capture the intensified international mobility of Bulgarian citizens after the EU visa regime was lifted in 2001.

Remittances and economic performance during the EU accession period

During the period in focus, we notice a considerable upwards shift of current transfers from abroad. In absolute figures, the inflow of these transfers grew nearly twofold for the years 2001-2005, compared with the previous years, reaching a level of almost € 1.2 billion with a relative share in GDP of about 4-5 per cent at the end of the period (Table 11.1). A number of analysts devote special attention to this fact underlying the foreign currency influx, showing how it contributed to trade deficit compensation and thus sustained the macroeconomic stability in the country (Stanchev, Kostadinova, Dimitrov, Angelov, Dimitrova, Karamakalakova, Cankov & Markova 2005). Some caution, however, is necessary when considering the amount of remittances. According to the methodology applied by the Bulgarian National Bank (BNB), current

Table 11.1 *Inflow of current transfers and compensation of employees in Bulgaria*

	2001	2002	2003	2004	2005*	2006**
Current transfers (€ million)	674.0	676.9	762.5	1051.2	1171.8	956.8
Compensation of employees (€ million)	476.6	766.8	913.7	1004.9	902.1	960.7
as a % of GDP	3.1%	4.6%	5.2%	5.1%	4.2%	4.0%
as a % of exports	8.3%	12.6%	13.7%	12.6%	9.5%	8.1%
as a % of imports	6.4%	9.7%	10.0%	9.2%	6.5%	5.8%
as a % of the trade balance	-26.8%	-40.8%	-37.7%	-34.0%	-20.8%	-20.9%
as a % of FDI	52.8%	78.2%	49.4%	36.8%	38.8%	25.6%
per capita (€)	60.18	97.52	116.94	129.14	116.46	126.01

Sources: BNB, NSI, February 2007

* Data are preliminary for 2005.

** Authors' forecasts for 2006 are based on the preliminary data for the first three quarters of 2006.

transfers inflow are recorded as unilateral free transfers to Bulgarian residents where two main recipients are distinguished: i) public sector units (receiving grants transferred from governments or international organisations) and ii) private sector units (households and NGOs receiving private transfers, donations, etc.). A basic component of the transfers to the government sector encompasses funds received from EU pre-accession instruments – current public transfers account for about a quarter of total current transfers from abroad on average for the period. Although the transfers to individuals (i.e. household members) are of particular interest for our study, they are not currently distinguished in the official data from transfers to other entities.

The official figures for private transfers to individuals obtained through bank system records are commonly considered to underestimate their actual level. Precise recording is hampered by the widespread practice of importing foreign currency in cash (personally or with assistance from acquaintances), thus avoiding bank transfers or non-bank electronic financial services. In this respect, starting from year 2001, Bulgarian National Bank (BNB) experts apply a methodology for indirect estimation of the *compensation of employees working abroad* as an element of the income account in the balance of payments that is assumed to be remitted to the home country. The item 'compensation of employees' comprises wages, salaries and other benefits earned by individuals in economies different from those where they are residents and paid by residents of host economies; 'employees' include seasonal or other short-term workers (i.e. less than one year) having centres of economic interest in their own economies. According to this methodology, the income is estimated as a product of the number of workers and the minimum wages in the respective country. It is assumed that Bulgarians illegally employed abroad stay for three months in the country and then return to Bulgaria. Assuming that illegal workers receive the minimum wage in this country (without paying any taxes, insurance, etc.), their expenditures are estimated by the cost of living for the respective country. The number of workers is estimated on the basis of data for Bulgarian citizens leaving the country for 'tourist reasons' (provided by Border Police), surveys among Bulgarian tour operators and additional household surveys.[2]

The development impact of remittances are generally considered, in migration literature, as beneficial at both micro and macro levels, being an important source of foreign exchange and funds for domestic consumption and investment (e.g. Ammassari & Black 2001; Lucas 2005). The aggregate level of the compensation of Bulgarian employees abroad was estimated at about € 4 billion for 2001-2005, reaching over € 900 million at the end of the period. With a persistently decreasing population for the period, its *per capita* significance has doubled since 2001 (Table 11.1). The modest share of the compensation of employees working abroad in GDP (4-5 per cent), however, supports the widespread view that Bulgarian economy cannot be considered as substantially dependent on remittances.

Compared to the level of foreign direct investments, employees' compensation amounted to over 40 per cent of FDI inflow in the country during the EU accession period. The remittance level amounts to about 10 percent of exports, thus positively influencing the negative current account balance through the compensation of about one third (on average) of the foreign trade deficit. Also having in mind the stable albeit low annual GDP real growth rates (4-6 per cent) and comparatively low annual inflation rates, macroeconomic analysts agree on the important role that remittances inflow played in sustaining macroeconomic stability in the country during the period. According to the insights provided by the New Economics of Labour Migration theory, the household perspective of the analysis of migration behaviour should be explored in order to obtain a solid microbase for the economic analysis. Various

Table 11.2 *Selected Bulgarian macroeconomic indicators, 1999-2006*

	1999	2000	2001	2002	2003	2004	2005*	2006**
GDP real growth (%)	2.3	5.4	4.1	4.9	4.5	5.7	5.5	6.3
CPI (%, end of year)	6.2	11.4	4.8	3.8	5.6	4.0	6.5	6.5
Unemployment (%)	16.0	17.9	17.3	16.3	13.5	12.2	10.7	9.1
Population growth (%)	-1.4	-0.4	-3.1	-0.7	-0.6	-0.4	-0.5	-1.6
GDP per capita (€)	1482	1674	1919	2101	2258	2515	2771	3123

Sources: BNB, NSI, February 2007
* Data are preliminary for 2005.
** Authors' forecasts for 2006 based on the preliminary data for the first three quarters of 2006.

household attributes (e.g. physical and human capital attained by household members) are possibly influencing migration decisions through their effects on migration costs as well as the potential impacts of remittances on income security and the overall household well-being (Taylor 1999; Mora & Taylor 2006).

Bulgarian return migration: A 'snapshot' at the end of 2005

To date, there is no comprehensive evaluation of the development potential of return migration and remittances on the basis of micro-studies among return migrants in Bulgaria. The usual approach of studies focused on Bulgarian return migration and remittances is based on in-depth interviews with households whose members have returned after being employed abroad. Typically, surveys are conducted among households in settlements in Bulgaria with high migration rates (Guentcheva, Kabakchieva & Kolarski 2003) as well as among migrant communities in order to explore Bulgarian emigrants' performance (Markova & Sarris 1997; Markova 2004; Markova & Reilly 2006). A recent World Bank multi-country study reveals some details on the basis of quite large samples of return migrants in Bulgaria and five other countries (Mansoor & Quillin 2007).

Mintchev and Boshnakov (2006) present various empirical results concerning the profile and experience of Bulgarian return migrants interviewed at the end of 2005. This study was initially set up as an exploratory survey aimed at providing descriptive data for the profile of Bulgarian return migrants, their expenditures and savings abroad, as well as for the use of remittances and their impact on the economic status of migrant households. Data was collected through a representative sample survey[3] among Bulgarian households, with an initially planned sample size of 1,000 households using a two-stage cluster design, typically used by NSI and professional agencies in Bulgaria. Census enumeration clusters of households were used as primary sampling units. In each selected unit, twenty households in urban clusters and fifteen in rural clusters were randomly chosen and interviewed. As households with a return migrant were of particular interest for this study, 52 such households were additionally interviewed. In order to preserve the originally obtained number of return migrant households (136 out of 1,000), all observations of that type were weighted by a reduction ratio. The discrepancy of the sample structure regarding two main demographic variables, i.e. the household size and area of residence (urban-rural), was compensated by additional adjustment of the observations using weights according to the expected structure of Bulgarian households population obtained during the last population census in 2001.

One of the main goals of the survey was to estimate some indicators of the degree of penetration of migration processes among all Bulgarian households. For this purpose, a specific definition for 'return migrant' was adopted: a person who had stayed abroad at least once during the last five years (2001-2005), for a period of three months or longer, and who is currently in Bulgaria. Consequently, a 'return migrant household' is a household with at least one return migrant. The relative share of return migrant households was assessed at about 12 per cent. Additionally, if the 'current migrant' households (having at least one member who is currently abroad) are taken into account, the share of households with at least one return or current migrant was estimated at about 15 per cent at the end of 2005. Out of a total of 2.9 million Bulgarian households, it is estimated that the total number of return migrant households is approximately 345,000; moreover, roughly 440,000 Bulgarian households had participated (or were currently involved) in international migration through their member(s) who had been or were currently residing abroad. Furthermore, the average number of persons per household who have stayed abroad in 2001-2005 for a period of at least three months was estimated at 0.143 (or 143 persons per 1,000 households). This was used for the estimation of the total number of return migrants at the end of 2005 at about 415,000.

Although not directly comparable, a recent multinational IOM sample survey on human trafficking (with 1,007 respondents in Bulgaria) also provides estimates for some migration penetration ratios (IOM 2006). It estimates the share of extended families (with a median size of seven members) with persons who have been abroad for the period 2003-2005 at 8.3 per cent (past penetration) as well as current penetration (as of 2006) of about 11.4 per cent of these families (or 120,500 currently working abroad). Surprisingly, the rate of legal employment abroad (approximated by the ratio of family members who work legally to all family members that work abroad) was estimated at 72 per cent.

Socio-demographic profile and foreign experience of return migrants

This section summarises the main findings regarding the socio-demographic profile of respondents on the basis of 162 interviews with return migrants (for more details see Mintchev & Boshnakov 2006). The evidence shows that the majority of migrants were male (69 per cent). Young and middle-aged persons prevailed (43 per cent were aged under 35, and 44 per cent aged 36-55). More than half of the women interviewed were under 35 years of age. The majority (about 60 per cent) of respondents was married. The proportion of individuals with at least secondary education was over 80 per cent and the proportion of return migrants with some secondary professional (vocational) education was almost 40 per cent.

Even though the educational level of return migrants was relatively high, a large proportion of them had left the country without any knowledge of the language spoken in the host country. Almost half of respondents did not have any command at all (45 per cent) and about one third had only elementary knowledge of the respective official language. However, one fifth of migrants said they spoke the language fluently (11 per cent) or at least at an intermediary level (10 per cent) at the time of their departure. About two thirds of respondents went abroad by bus (53 per cent) or by car (14 per cent), reflecting the proximity of migrant destinations, and the availability of inexpensive transport services that have developed over the years, and which facilitate migration.

The interviews revealed several aspects of Bulgarian migrant networks. About 80 per cent of return migrants declared that they had already arranged for their accommodation in the host country prior to departure. In more than one third of cases, the housing was provided by compatriots who had already settled in the host country and, in the remaining cases, by the intermediary company/person arranging the employment, or by the employer. However, one in five individuals had left without having ascertained some accommodation in the target country in advance. At the same time, almost half of the women had arranged housing with their acquaintances, mainly members of their family that had already settled in the target country. Less than one third of male migrants had this option.

A similar situation is observed regarding the prior arrangement of a job – over 70 per cent of return migrants declared that they had arranged for a workplace before leaving Bulgaria. They relied mainly on contracts with employers (26 per cent) or assistance from acquaintances residing in the respective country (17 per cent). There are, however, significant gender differences in this respect – about one third of female migrants did not have any arrangement of a job at the time of their departure, whereas only one fourth of male respondents were in this situation.

EU member states were the leading destinations of Bulgarian return migrants in the period of interest (Table 11.3). Germany was the most attractive country for men, and Greece for women. The Mediterranean states of Greece, Italy and Spain attracted over 40 per cent of interviewees, or almost half of those who went to Southern European destinations.

The average duration of the stay in the destination countries of return migrants is slightly over one year (15.6 months), but over two thirds of them have resided there for periods of less than a year. In southern EU countries, such short-term migration prevailed (83 per cent) compared

Table 11.3 *Distribution of respondents by countries of destination (%)*

Country/region	Men	Women	Total
Germany	16.7	11.8	15.5
Greece	12.5	20.6	15.1
Spain	16.7	8.8	14.0
Italy	16.7	8.8	13.8
Other EU country	13.9	26.5	18.7
Turkey	4.2	8.8	5.6
US, Canada	5.6	8.8	5.7
Other countries (Russia, Israel, etc.)	13.7	5.9	11.6
Total	100.0	100.0	100.0

Source: Mintchev and Boshnakov (2006)

to the other European destinations where a third of respondents had stayed for more than two years. Therefore, the profile assessed by the study should be considered as valid more for short-term (i.e. temporary or circular) Bulgarian migrants than for returnees who had spent prolonged periods abroad.

A plausible explanation of the preferences for these destinations and the length of stay abroad can be found when the employment of return migrants by economic sectors is considered. Almost a quarter of respondents were employed in agriculture, one in six in the transport sector, one in seven in tourism and the same share in constructions (Table 11.4). About 43 per cent of respondents who had been in Southern European countries were employed in agriculture while about 40 per cent of respondents who had been in other EU member states had jobs in construction and tourism. More women were employed in housekeeping, social care and tourism services and, to a lesser extent in agriculture, industries or education. Male migrants have found jobs mainly

Table 11.4 *Sector of main employment of respondents (%)*

Sector of employment	Men	Women	Total
Agriculture	26.8	12.1	22.3
Construction	19.7	–	13.7
Industry, crafts	5.6	3.0	5.4
Transport	23.9	3.0	17.0
Tourism/bars, hotels, restaurants	8.5	27.3	13.8
Housekeeping, childcare, healthcare	–	21.2	7.4
Care for the elderly/ill/disabled	–	15.2	5.0
Science/education	1.4	6.1	2.4
Other	14.1	12.1	13.1
Total	100.0	100.0	100.0

Source: Mintchev and Boshnakov (2006)

in agriculture, transport, construction and, to some extent, tourism services. It is worth mentioning that most return migrants (almost 80 per cent) had no direct contacts with the local labour administration. However, this could hardly serve as a basis for conclusions regarding the scale of non-documented Bulgarian emigration, as contacts with labour administration are usually a prerogative of employers.

Determinants of satisfaction and re-migration likelihood

The self-assessment of respondents' satisfaction from their stay abroad provides valuable opportunities for identifying particular factors of successful emigration (Table 11.5). It is noteworthy that over 80 per cent of respondents reported a degree of satisfaction (complete or to some extent) with regard to their professional advancement during the work abroad. The acquisition of skills and experience abroad is perceived as a potentially useful benefit for return migrants when considering the future employment or economic activity either in the home country or abroad. The highest satisfaction related to the occupation of qualified jobs as well as to jobs under official contracts with employers.

The level of professional satisfaction was related to particular sectors of employment in the host countries. The most satisfied respondents had jobs in industries, transport and tourism. Significant shares (25-40 per cent) of unsatisfied return migrants were employed in agriculture, care for elderly and housekeeping. Clear differences in satisfaction levels were found also regarding the region of stay. For instance, almost each third respondent returned from Southern Europe was dissatisfied with their experience abroad. In contrast, almost all migrants who have been in other EU countries were more or less satisfied. A similar

Table 11.5 *Responses to the question 'Are you satisfied with your stay abroad, in terms of professional advancement?' (%)*

Characteristics of main occupation abroad	Yes, completely	Yes, to some extent	No	Total
Full-time job				
No	33.3	41.7	25.0	100.0
Yes	36.5	45.9	17.6	100.0
Qualified job				
No	19.0	47.7	33.3	100.0
Yes	51.9	44.2	3.9	100.0
Job under an official contract				
No	28.8	44.2	26.9	100.0
Yes	44.7	48.9	6.4	100.0

Source: Mintchev and Boshnakov (2006)

distribution is found for those respondents who have returned from non-European destinations.

To learn more about the determinants of a successful stay abroad, we asked respondents to rank a series of factors in response to the question: 'In your opinion, what are the most important things that provide a successful emigration?'. Table 11.6 shows the main results for both categories of respondents – those who said they had a qualified job abroad and those who said they did not. In the table, 'rank' refers to the average rank attached by the interviewees and 'response' refers to the share of respondents from each sub-group who chose each answer.

It is not surprising that 'personal skills and qualification' is the factor most frequently ranked by qualified return migrants (77 per cent). The other two important factors are the preliminary job contracting (40 per cent) and the language proficiency (43 per cent). The answers of low-skilled migrants are more dispersed and the modal factor here is the language proficiency (59 per cent), which is strongly perceived as a serious advantage. Besides qualifications, the importance of having acquaintances abroad as well as a job and accommodation already arranged were quite often emphasised. This suggests that migrants participating in this labour market segment are relying on informal migrant networks to support the success of their migration abroad.

In order to identify the determinants of re-migration likelihood, two binary logistic regression models were estimated (Table 11.7). The

Table 11.6   *Opinion on the factors of successful migration*

Determinants of a successful stay abroad	Did your job abroad require particular qualification?			
	Yes (55.2%)		No (44.8%)	
	Rank	Response	Rank	Response
Preliminary contract or arrangement (official or verbal) with an employer or agency	1.61	40.3%	1.93	27.5%
Good professional qualification	1.71	77.4%	1.96	28.8%
Availability of friendly/close citizens of the country	2.11	18.2%	2.51	17.0%
Availability of acquaintances settled in the country	2.19	19.1%	2.04	31.7%
Good foreign language proficiency	2.47	43.9%	1.96	58.8%
Availability of initial funds for financing the move abroad	2.62	19.4%	2.08	29.8%
Accommodation arranged beforehand	2.63	28.7%	2.68	27.4%
Tolerant attitude of the authorities to immigrants	2.67	10.3%	2.64	15.7%
Appropriate labour legislation	2.92	21.1%	1.94	19.8%

Source: Authors' own calculations

Table 11.7 *Binary logistic regressions for the likelihood to leave*

	1) Likely to leave again			2) Long-term preference		
	B		Exp(B)	B		Exp(B)
Gender	-0.750		0.472	0.187		1.205
Age	-0.045		0.956	-0.029		0.971
Family status	-3.115	***	0.044	-1.006	*	0.366
Education	-1.556	**	0.211	0.620		1.859
Household size	0.369		1.446	-0.257		0.774
Household income per capita	0.008	*	1.008	-0.006		0.994
Satisfaction	0.781		2.183	-0.216		0.806
No prospects in Bulgaria	1.162	*	3.197	1.504	***	4.497
Number of observations (unweighted)	144			137		
% of correct prediction	79.1			77.7		

Source: Authors' own calculations
* Significant at 0.10 level
** Significant at 0.05 level
*** Significant at 0.01 level

dependent variable of the first model uses the answers to the question 'How likely is it for you to go abroad again?', where 1 stands for 'very likely' or 'somewhat likely' and 0 for 'little likely' and 'not likely'. The second model aims at discriminating between short-term and long-term intentions on the basis of the question 'What is the desired length of the intended stay abroad?' (0 combines the answers 'just a few months' and 'up to 1 year'; 1 combines the answers 'a few years' and 'emigration for good'). The following independent variables were included in the specification:

– gender (1 for 'female'; 0 for 'male');
– age (number of years);
– family status (1 for 'married'; 0 otherwise);
– education (1 for 'higher education'; 0 for 'secondary or lower education');
– household size (number of household members);
– household income per capita (monthly average, in euro);
– satisfaction from the previous stay abroad (1 for 'completely'; 0 for 'in some extent' and 'no');
– no prospects for our future in Bulgaria (1 for those indicated this reason for their international migration).

Neither model revealed any net effects of the gender and age; only family status appeared to be a limiting factor in respect to re-migration likelihood. However, higher educated return migrants were less willing to leave again (the correlates of this attitude should be considered in some more detail). Household characteristics did not show the expected effects – migrants from larger families were not significantly more willing to leave again, and the household income per capita obtained a positive coefficient sign (although significant only at the 10 per cent level). The better position of return migrants households' wellbeing did not act as a limiting factor regarding re-migration intentions.

One of our hypotheses was that there will be a positive net impact of the degree of satisfaction – that return migrants more satisfied with their previous stay abroad will have a higher likelihood to leave again – but this was not confirmed. At the same time, the inclusion of the 'future prospects' perception shows significant stimulating impact on re-migration intentions. Apparently, those who do not see any domestic perspective for improvement in their well-being and also have experience in a foreign country are persistently oriented towards consecutive out-migration (mainly long-term) as a realistic development alternative at the micro level.

As Black and Gent (2004) note, return itself is not enough, it needs to be 'successful' and 'sustainable'. Although they focus on refugees' return, the issues raised with regard to success and sustainability of a return to the country of origin are valid for economic migrants, too. However, the doubts regarding the opportunities of returnees to reintegrate in the home countries are still considerable. Mansoor and Quillin (2007) outline various aspects of a problematic return: changes in the labour market might have taken place during their absence and these could reduce the attractiveness of job opportunities; migrants perception of inferior local conditions in comparison to the income, professional and social experience gained abroad; migrants with longer periods abroad may also experience difficulties with their adjustment to their sometimes considerably changed communities.

Development prospects of remittances use in receiving households

The migration literature suggests that return migrants gain useful professional skills and social capital during their stay abroad, except when working in a low-skill labour market segment. Moreover, it is argued that in sending households, remittances sent during migrants stay abroad or brought upon return, support not only current consumption levels, but can also induce personal and community development (Gatcher 2002; Guentcheva et al. 2003; Vladimirova 2004; Mansoor & Quillin 2007). The distribution of households by type of migrants and whether they receive remittances or not does reveal that a variety of

Table 11.8 *Distribution of households by migrant type and receipt of remittances (%)**

Households	Current migrant in the household:		Total
	No	Yes, at least 1	
Not received			
No return migrant in the household	84.0	1.3	85.3
At least 1 return migrant	2.1	0.6	2.7
Total	86.1	1.9	88.0
Received			
No return migrant in the household	0.9	2.1	3.0
At least 1 return migrant	6.9	2.1	9.0
Total	7.8	4.2	12.0

Source: Authors' own calculations
* Percentages are calculated on the basis of the sample size of 1,000 weighted cases.

cases were found in the sample (Table 11.8). There are cases with and without return or current migrants who both received and did not receive remittances during the period under study. Thus, the unit of concern with respect to the use of remittances is households that receive remittances – and, in some cases, 'return migrant households'.

It is commonly assumed that Bulgarian emigrants still rarely use official channels for transferring remittances (Gächter 2002; BNB 2007). The channels of money transfers to Bulgarian households were of particular interest for the survey. A total 56 per cent of households received funds mainly in cash on a regular basis (directly from migrants or from intermediaries), and 19 per cent received money just once when the migrant returned. In fewer cases, bank transfers (24 per cent) or other electronic transfer systems like Western Union or MoneyGram (19 per cent) were used regularly or once (Mintchev & Boshnakov 2006). Undoubtedly, such financial services are yet underexploited and there is a potential market for both bank and money transfer institutions.

The survey provided various insights on remittances use although such estimates should be considered cautiously, as has been suggested in migration literature (e.g. Taylor 1999; Rapoport & Docquier 2005). Lucas (2005) outlines two aspects of remittances' impact: 1) their effect on poverty and inequality and 2) the potential stimulus upon savings, investment and economic growth. The recent World Bank survey in selected transition countries revealed the importance of remittances as a stable source of income for many households in the region, especially in the rural areas. The estimations of remittances' macroeconomic impact suggest that there is some positive impact on long-term growth. However, the evidence on remittances' impact on the incidence of poverty is mixed (Mansoor & Quillin 2007).

Our survey reinforces these conclusions. According to our research, the use of remittances is more 'subsistence'-oriented rather than 'development'-oriented (Table 11.9). Almost 38 per cent of households receiving remittances used at least three quarters of the funds for consumption. This share was found to be higher (43 per cent) for the sub-group of households with a migrant who had returned after a short-term stay abroad, compared to those with returnees who stayed abroad longer (28 per cent). Moreover, only 36 per cent of households with short-term returnees had spent on consumption, whereas 60 per cent had done so in the other sub-group. This provides clear evidence that temporary and seasonal Bulgarian migration in the period 2001-2005 is used mainly to provide funds for covering the current subsistence needs of sending households. At the same time, however, about 26 per cent of the households with short-term returnees have saved at least a quarter of the money, as a protection against future income risks.

The second direction of remittances is the acquisition of motor vehicles – 26 per cent of all receiving households have, to some extent, used the funds for this purpose. This trend is observable mainly in the households with long-term return migrants (40 per cent compared to 23 per cent in the other group) where the absolute level of remittances is reasonably higher. The share of home buyers is relatively lower (about 14 per cent), and there is no significant divergence between short and long-term migrant households. It is interesting to compare and contrast the acquisition of particular types of properties by receiving and non-receiving households. The survey provides evidence that the shares of households that have acquired real estate property, cars, land and home appliances among those receiving remittances are quite higher in comparison to households that do not receive such funds (Table 11.10). The divergence is quite evident in regard to the purchase of cars

Table 11.9   *Use of remittances by receiving households (%)*

For what household needs did/do you use the funds from abroad?	*All of it*	*About 3/4*	*About 1/2*	*About 1/4*	*None*
Consumption	28.8	8.9	16.7	31.4	14.3
Loan repayment	1.1	0.8	3.8	18.9	75.4
Saving	3.5	1.5	4.0	12.7	78.2
Education	2.4	1.6	1.9	11.9	82.2
Health care	3.4	1.4	2.1	12.5	80.6
Private business	0.4	1.1	3.1	8.4	87.0
Motor vehicle(s)	8.6	4.8	5.2	7.9	73.6
Dwelling(s)	4.3	2.1	6.7	0.7	86.1
Other real estate	1.0	–	2.3	0.7	96.0

Source: Authors' own calculations

Table 11.10 *Shares of households that have acquired assets, by remittances receipt status (%)*

Receipt of funds from abroad in the household	Has your household acquired the following kind of property during the last 5 years?			
	Housing property	Motor vehicles	Land	Household appliances
Not received	7.7%	14.3%	1.7%	41.9%
Received	11.7%	38.3%	3.3%	75.8%
Total sample	8.2%	17.2%	1.9%	46.0%

Source: Mintchev and Boshnakov (2006)

and household appliances. Yet, it is worth noting the very weak interest, as a whole, in buying land. The latter is usually found as a consequence of the rudimentary and inadequately regulated agricultural land market as well as persistent administrative complications (e.g. problems with the cadastre, uncompleted process of farmlands restitution and ineffective legal procedures).

The World Bank survey of return migrants reveals some general improvement in household living standards in Bulgaria, Bosnia and Herzegovina and Romania, even though various difficulties were met by migrants' families during member's stay abroad. Respondents reported an increased capacity to cover the purchase of food, clothing, public utilities, household appliances as well as to buy cars or to travel abroad (Mansoor & Quillin 2007).

With regard to the use of remittances for business the study suggests that 20 per cent of the households receiving transfers from abroad engaged in entrepreneurial activities, while this was the case for only 10 per cent among households not receiving remittances. Funds were used either for start-ups or for investing in already established businesses (Table 11.11). Remittances are invested mainly in transport, services and trade and rarely used for the production of goods. These businesses are usually small or medium size, or people launch in various forms of formal or informal self-employment, e.g. the purchases of automobiles for use as taxis and the establishment of cafes and neighbourhood shops. (Guentcheva et al. 2003; similar cases are described by Nicholson 2001).

Conclusions

Our study suggests the following in regard to the possible impact of return migration and remittances on development. Firstly, remittances' inflow covers a substantial share of the trade deficit providing a positive impact on the recent economic development. Undoubtedly, remittances

Table 11.11   *Use of the funds for development of one's business*

If there are funds used for own business development, what was the main purpose?	Share of those indicating	Of which:		
		investment capital	working capital	both
Establishment of a new firm	6.8%	48.4%	26.7%	25.0%
Supporting an existing firm	7.5%	15.1%	54.3%	30.6%
Total	14.3%	30.9%	41.2%	28.0%

Sector of the main activity of the firm:				
Agriculture	2.7%	Trade	25.7%	Construction	3.5%
Manufacturing	2.1%	Transport	38.3%	Services	27.7%

Source: Mintchev and Boshnakov (2006)

transferred by Bulgarian return and current migrants play an important role in the macro-economic stability of the economy. Yet, funds are transferred mainly through unofficial channels and it is difficult to estimate their volume.

Our sample survey shows that although the bulk of Bulgarian migration is engaged in low-skilled temporary jobs in agriculture, construction, transport, housekeeping and child/elderly care, return migrants feel satisfied with their stay abroad. The vast majority of these migrants were not legally employed and the improvement of labour regulations in host countries regarding the temporary hiring of foreign workers may provide substantial progress in the formalisation of circular migration processes.

The survey estimates that roughly 15 per cent of Bulgarian households have participated in the international migration process in the period 2001-2005. Bulgarian return migrants showed a high propensity for savings. Remittances sent home had a significant impact on households' well-being mainly through supporting consumption and, to some extent, providing funds for other acquisitions (real estate and cars). Thus, migrants' transfers have played – and are still playing – an important role in keeping households away from poverty during the process of economic reforms. Moreover, 20 per cent of receiving households run their own businesses while this share is twice as low for the other families.

There is little evidence of direct impact of economic development through productive investment of remittances. Even in a worldwide perspective, it is debatable whether remittances lead to additional investments and assets accumulation (Lucas 2005). Nevertheless, even if households spend remittances on consumption, automobiles and houses, an economy-wide multiplication effect definitely takes place (see also Gächter 2002). From the perspective of this study, along with the overall positive effect on the balance of payments, this is the major development benefit of migrant remittances in Bulgaria during the process of its integration in the EU.

Notes

1   This chapter presents some of the results from a research project entitled 'Bulgarian Return Migration and Households Wellbeing', conducted by the Centre for Comparative Studies (CCS) in Sofia. It was supported by a research grant from the Global Development Network – South Eastern Europe (GDN-SEE) under the supervision of Vienna Institute for International Economic Studies (WIIW). We are grateful to our discussant Danny Sriskandarajah as well as to helpful comments from Vladimir Gligorov, Michael Landesmann, Anna Iara and other participants in the GDN-SEE workshop that took place in May 2006 in Vienna.

2   For methodological notes, see www.bnb.bg.

3   The sample survey was conducted in November 2005 by a research team consisting of experts from the CCS, the Institute of Sociology at the Bulgarian Academy of Sciences (BAS) and the National Statistical Institute (NSI). Acknowledgements are due to Emilia Chenguelova (BAS) and her team as well as to Yordan Kaltchev (NSI) for questionnaire and survey design as well as fieldwork organisation.

References

Ammassari, S. & R. Black (2001), 'Harnessing the potential of migration and return to promote development', *IOM Migration Research Series* 5.

Bauer, T. & K. Zimmerman (1999), 'Assessment of possible migration pressure and its labour market impact following EU enlargement to Central and Eastern Europe', *IZA Research Report* 3.

Black, R. & S. Gent (2004), 'Defining, measuring and influencing sustainable return: The case of the Balkans', Working Paper T7. Brighton: Development Research Centre on Migration, Globalisation and Poverty.

Bulgarian National Bank. www.bnb.bg.

BNB (2007), 'Methodology for estimation of flows due to illegal employment', First IMF Seminar on Remittance Statistics, Ljubljana, February-March 2007.

Gächter, A. (2002), 'The ambiguities of emigration: Bulgaria since 1988', *International Migration Papers* 39. Geneva: ILO.

Guentcheva, R., P. Kabakchieva & P. Kolarski (2003), 'The social impact of seasonal migration', Country Report to EC Project 'Sharing experience: Migration trends in selected applicant countries and lessons learned from the "new countries of immigration" in the EU and Austria', Volume I. Vienna: IOM.

IOM (2006), 'Human trafficking survey: Belarus, Bulgaria, Moldova, Romania, and Ukraine', Report prepared by GfK-Ukraine for the International Organisation for Migration, Mission in Ukraine, Kiev.

Laczko, F. (2002), 'Introduction' in IOM and ICMPD, *New challenges for migration policy in CEE*, The Hague: T.M.C. Asser Press.

Leon-Ledesma, M. & M. Piracha (2004), 'International migration and the role of remittances in Eastern Europe', *International Migration* 42 (4): 65-83.

Lucas, R.E.B. (2005), 'International migration and economic development: Lessons from low-income countries'. Stockholm: Expert Group on Development Issues (EGDI), Swedish Ministry for Foreign Affairs.

Mansoor, A. & B. Quillin (2007), *Migration and remittances: Eastern Europe and the former Soviet Union*. Washington, D.C.: The World Bank.

Markova, E. (2004), 'Migration processes in enlarged Europe', *Economic Policy Review* 164. Sofia: IME. www.ime-bg.org.

Markova, E. & A. Sarris (1997), 'The performance of Bulgarian illegal immigrants in the Greek labour market', *South European Society & Politics* 2: 55-77.

Markova, E. & B. Reilly (2007), 'Bulgarian migrant remittances and legal status: Some micro-level evidence from Madrid', *South-Eastern Europe Journal of Economics* 1: 5-69.

Martin, P. (2003), 'Managing international labour migration in the 21st century', *South Eastern Europe Journal of Economics* 1: 9-18.

Mintchev, V., Y. Kaltchev, V. Goev & V. Boshnakov (2004), 'External migration from Bulgaria at the beginning of the XXI century: Estimates of potential emigrants' attitudes and profile', *Economic Thought* Yearbook XIX. Sofia: Institute of Economics at Bulgarian Academy of Sciences.

Mintchev, V. & V. Boshnakov (2006), 'The profile and experience of return migrants: Empirical evidence from Bulgaria', *South-East Europe Review for Labour and Social Affairs* 2: 35-59.

Mora, J. & J. E. Taylor (2006), 'Determinants of migration, destination, and sector choice: Disentangling individual, household, and community Effects' in M. Schiff & C. Ozden (eds.), *International migration, remittances, and the brain drain*, Chapter 1. Basingstoke: Palgrave Macmillan & Washington, D.C.: The World Bank.

Nicholson, B. (2001), 'From migrant to micro-entrepreneur: Do-it-yourself development in Albania', *South-East Europe Review for Labour and Social Affairs* 3: 39-42.

Piracha, M. & R. Vickerman (2003), 'Immigration, labour mobility and EU enlargement' in C. Jenkins & J. Smith (eds.), *Through the paper curtain: The insiders and outsiders in Europe*, Chatham House Papers. London: Blackwell.

Rangelova, R. & K. Vladimirova (2004), 'Migration from Central and Eastern Europe: The case of Bulgaria', *South-East Europe Review for Labour and Social Affairs* 3: 7-30.

Rapoport, H. & F. Docquier (2005), 'The economics of migrants' remittances', *IZA Discussion Paper* 1531.

EC (2006), *Report on the functioning of the transitional arrangements set out in the 2003 Accession Treaty (1 May 2004 – 30 April 2006)*. Brussels: European Commission

Stanchev, K., S. Kostadinova, M. Dimitrov, G. Angelov, K. Dimitrova, G. Karamakalakova, S. Cankov, and E. Markova. (2005) *Bulgarian Migration: Incentives and Constellations*, Sofia: Open Society Institute.

Straubhaar, T. (2001), 'East-West migration: Will it be a problem?', *Intereconomics* July/ August.

Taylor, J.E. (1999), 'The new economics of labour migration and the role of remittances in the migration process', *International Migration* 37 (1): 63-88.

Wallace, C. (1999), *Migration potential in Central and Eastern Europe*. Vienna: IOM Technical Cooperation Centre for Europe and Central Asia.

12   Transitioning strategies of economic survival: Romanian migration during the transition process

Swanie Potot

Introduction

Whereas West European countries often treat economic migration from poorer countries with a certain degree of misgiving, in departure regions migration is often viewed as a valuable opportunity, a way of opening new horizons. This chapter deals with temporary Romanian migrations to Western Europe, focusing particularly on understanding their causes and effects in the source country.

The chapter draws on several years of qualitative fieldwork conducted with Romanian migrants both within their home regions and during their stays in France (Paris and Nice), Spain and the UK. It concentrates on two particular groups. The first is composed of relatively young adults, aged 18-30, who come from Târgoviste, a mid-sized city located near Bucharest, and were working in London, Paris or Nice at the beginning of the 2000s. The second group involves individuals who come from rural parts of the Danube Plain, from the Teleorman County, and who were working in Almeria province in Andalusia in the same period.[1]

The first group mostly migrated to Nice between 1998 and 2000 as tourists and then extended their stay by claiming asylum, or by remaining illegally. The principal occupation of these migrants was as street newspaper vendors and, although some settled in France for several years, the more common migratory pattern consisted of short stays of a few months, renewed regularly, but always interrupted by long periods (at least six months) in their home city. This practice changed at the end of 1999 when newspaper agencies, under pressure from public authorities, increasingly refused to employ foreigners without a work permit. Then some of these migrants turned to London, where unskilled work abounds and where the black market is relatively tolerated. London has become a particularly popular destination because salaries in the construction and hotel sectors are substantially higher than in Southern Europe and the authorities are perceived as less likely to expel foreigners having entered illegally.

The social profile of the second group of migrants is different, in that they are of diverse age groups, are less often qualified and are more often from small cities or villages. At the time of the fieldwork, they were working, like many other foreigners, as daily workers in agriculture in Spain for low salaries, around € 5 per hour, and in hard physical conditions. In the area of Almeria, this group was growing constantly, as recently arrived European migrants were preferred to traditional workers from Maghreb or Africa.

However, both migrant categories resemble each other in their frequent travel between Romania and Western Europe. These movements are oriented and reinforced by the increasing number of individual migration experiences, which enable migrants to raise their own standard of living as well as that of family members in their home country. Such migration is of great significance in Romania: Sandu (2000) reports that between 1990 and 2000, 35 per cent of Romanian households had at least one member abroad.

Interviews with these migrants showed that their objective was not to flee Romania in order to build a new life elsewhere but, rather, to temporarily compensate for the deficiencies of a faulty social and economic system (Morokvasic 1999). Their migration thus becomes a way of life that involves movement back and forth between a relatively comfortable home and an undefined elsewhere.

This chapter looks first at the national context from which these migrations emerged, and suggests that this transnational activity is one of a number of survival strategies used by Romanians to counter the economic hardship that has ensued since the 1989 revolution. The chapter also argues that these new economic strategies are the prolongation and modernisation of informal activities developed during communist times. The second part of the chapter argues that migration – although it emerged from a destabilising context – may work in favour of the transition process. Even though Romanian migration has long been considered a problem in terms of the process towards EU accession, Romanian migrants have contributed in many ways to the economic restructuring of their homeland. By investing remittances in Romania and developing transnational culture and networks, they have actually accelerated the transformations of the country towards European lifestyles and standards.

Post-communist Romania and survival strategies

Romania: An economy in transition

December 1989, for the Romanian people marks the end of one of the most authoritarian regimes of the communist system. The revolution is also remembered, however, as the event that marks the beginning of the socio-economic crisis engendered by the *transition* process. In the first years following 1989, recession seemed a natural phase in the course of events. Social difficulties induced by the adoption of the market economy, once surpassed, were expected to be compensated by the growth and development of a consumer society. Yet neither economic reforms, in the form of aid from international institutions such as the International Monetary Fund or the World Bank, nor political reforms, ever truly led to such growth. Only in 2004 did the EU finally characterise Romania's market economy as 'viable'. During the first ten years of the transition, recession was constant; only at the turn of the millennium did the country finally experience positive GDP growth.

By 2000, the day-to-day difficulties faced by many Romanians led some to the conclusion that, regardless of the dictatorship, 'things were better before'.[2] They thus turned their efforts towards the satisfaction of personal needs. Although the situation has noticeably improved over the last five years, the average monthly salary remained under € 295 in 2007 and many households are still unable to meet their minimum needs. For example, inflation fell from 15.3 per cent in 2003 to 5.7 per cent in 2007, but is still high enough to limit the purchasing power of the middle class. In this context, the country's dreams of rapid Westernisation have slowly given way to basic material concerns. For many Romanians, the principal objective during the last ten years has been to maintain their family's basic standard of living.

Partly as a result, the informal economy, already flourishing under the communist regime, has become more developed during the years following the revolution (Rainer 2002). Informal transactions were already commonplace at the time of Ceausescu, allowing individuals to compensate for the deficiencies of the formal economy and to maintain a minimal standard of living (Kideckel 1993; Verdery 1996). The size of the parallel economy today can be understood as an extension of these earlier practices. Under communism, the informal economy primarily took the form of selling everyday consumer products. A study conducted by Schneider (2002) shows that the shadow economy passed from an average of 27.3 per cent of Romanian GDP in the period 1990-1993 to an average of 33.4 per cent for the period 2000-2001.[3] It also shows that this trend is shared by all the Central and Eastern European countries. A decade after the fall of communism, Rainer (2002) estimated that the informal sector concerned two thirds of Romanian households.

The unemployment rate, rarely surpassing 11 per cent between 1989 and 2000 and reaching a record low of 5.9 per cent in 2007, does not explain this boom in the informal economy (Duchêne 1999). Whereas during the dictatorship, the informal economy was attributed to a lack of products on the market, today it is attributed to organisational flaws of the official system. For example, administrative complexity and disarray, corruption in the public services and the emergence of an unreliable legal structure since 1989 have encouraged people to resort to the parallel economy, since business on the black market has become easier and less costly. Meanwhile, in the context of low average salaries, the informal economy allows for people to make ends meet. Indeed, Rainer (2002) argues that the parallel economy is in no way the privilege of a corrupt or marginal few but, rather, is a common strategy throughout all of Romanian society. It not only affects smugglers or traffickers, but also many who have a formal job, who supplement their earnings with a second, undeclared activity or through the sale of produce from their gardens.

The parallel economy subsists in several domains that are outlined below in order to clarify the link between this sector and transnational migrations. Duchêne (1999: 36) offers the following definition of informal activities:

> the ensemble of legal and illegal economic activities undertaken by small-scale (family or individual) units which generate production in the sense of the National Accounts System and which operate on the margins of the regulated socio-fiscal systems enforced by the State.

To clarify what we are dealing with here, we can refer to the notion of 'small tricks' proposed by Heintz (2002: 79), contrasting with the 'big tricks' that concern a high level of corruption or traffics of national size. In what follows, an abridged typology is sketched of the principal informal activities in Romania, according to the level of involvement required.

Some sections of the informal economy develop on the margins of formal economic institutions. The agricultural sector is unique in that sales on the rural market are only rarely declared, thus situating this sector firmly within the informal economy (Duchêne, Albu & Kim 2002). Other small-scale businesses are more ambiguous, however. Professions such as mechanical repairs, tailoring, painting and decorating or private teaching can be practised partially or totally beyond state control. Such work therefore falls within the black market, which represents either the individual's principal activity (primary source of revenue) or a complementary activity to salaried work or unemployment. Recourse to this form of secondary economic activity does not involve just one specific social category but, rather, is commonplace throughout the working population; Pelinescu (2003) states that 36.1 per cent of the interviewed households had an income from a second job in 1996.

Petty trade is also a major component of the parallel economy. Although the majority of this market consists of products that are not illegal to sell, the conditions of commercialisation, however, often are illegal, with merchandise procured illegally from large businesses for resale on a small scale. This sometimes involves theft from state companies, a practice frequent under communism, which continues today, although undoubtedly in smaller proportions. Take the example of a national train company factory that makes windows in Teleorman County. Because for years, some of the factory parts were stolen by employees and then sold to local inhabitants, nowadays, many residences in the area have train panes for windows. This unexpected appearance – of small, curve-shaped windows – illustrates in the landscape just what a survival economy can be. A second form of illegal trade consists of legally purchasing merchandise from the manufacturer, but selling it clandestinely in retail or wholesale markets, avoiding state tax and control. One of the informants had, for example, legally bought the engines of a wood factory that was closing and intended to sell them to entrepreneurs he knew without paying any taxes.

On top of these black market transactions are numerous other exchanges that are outside of the monetary system, relying on reciprocity (Mingione 1991). As such, the trade of vegetable conserves from the numerous small private gardens is as frequent as the traffic of influence or 'influence peddling'. For instance, an individual can request that a civil servant help accelerate an administrative procedure, offering in exchange untaxed petrol from a relative who works at a petrol station. Present in nearly every aspect of domestic life, the parallel economy is not limited to minor transactions. The entrepreneur who built the house of one interviewee, for example, was paid entirely in bottles of *tsuica*, a highly sought-after homemade alcohol made from plums. Beyond the ability to negotiate face to face (Péraldi 2001: 6), these exchanges require social actors to place themselves within an extended network of relations where each is both debtor and creditor towards the others, daily and in the long term. Such reciprocity therefore involves a socialising that relies on and maintains close relations of confidence, placing social actors in situations of perpetual interdependence.

Another type of trade, directly tied to the mobility of individuals, took on new dimensions when European borders opened. The 'suitcase trade' entails small-scale undeclared import and export activities that, although extremely risky during the dictatorship, have become widespread since 1990 (Aktar & Ôgelman 1994). These small business ventures, orientated particularly towards Turkey, Hungary and Serbia, are composed of individuals acting either alone or in partnerships rarely of more than two or three persons who collaborate to divide the tasks. The objective is to sell products that were individually acquired on foreign markets in Romania: audio cassettes and clothing from Istanbul are well-known examples. The comings and goings are generally by bus or train and the stays abroad are for no more than a day or two. At the crossroads of transnational migration and local trade, this type of business takes advantage of the international setting to minimise the effects of unfavourable economic circumstances.

Transnational migration as an alternative survival strategy

According to Badie (1995: 16): 'reflecting on transnational networks (...) consists of analysing the construction of the social relations that bring reality and life to globalisation'. Short of aligning with Portes' (1997) concept of 'globalisation from below', it can be argued that migration is part of the process of social and economic global exchange, which increasingly exceeds the limits drawn by national borders. As Badie highlights, the power of states on an international level is tending to lose some of its hegemony in favour of greater leeway for the strategies of autonomous social actors. The social networks they establish are increasingly spreading across multiple poles, whether through multinational companies or through the 'globalisation from below'. This does not suggest, however, that borders or spatial, social and economic disparities no longer play an important role for the migrants.

On the contrary, transnational migration relies on the specific capacity of certain social actors to interrelate dissimilar localities, crossing from one to the other. The migratory networks thus create a 'transnational social field' (Glick Schiller & Levitt 2007) that links different places of passage, situated 'neither here nor there, but here and there at the same time' (Tarrius 1993). The fact of simultaneously belonging to different and dissociated localities is indeed what renders the situation of migrants advantageous. Such advantages are not drawn uniquely from differences in wealth, something highlighted by Piore (1986) and confirmed in the case of Romanian migrants whose meagre salaries earned in the West can still be spent in Romania at multiplied value. Rather, the fieldwork conducted on Romanian migrants shows that advantages are also drawn from increased social distance, which also makes the migration worth the sacrifice, in that the degraded social status endured abroad has little or no impact on experiences in the home society.

The application of the term 'transnational' not only refers to the geographic dimension, which engenders increased autonomy, but also calls attention to the spaces of socialisation, which underlie these movements. These spaces are characterised by 'a horizontality of social relations [which], scarcely institutionalised (...), are constituted within informal sphere' (Badie 1995: 22). Apart from dependency on state power, there is in fact no pre-established hierarchy. The social relations, less codified than in institutional structures, contribute to a constant evolution, and even at times to a reversal of power relations over time. Within these networks, as in the transactions that connect them to the societies they cross, negotiations and interpersonal relations have the utmost importance, much more than that of any strict regulations. Thus, when referring to transnational Romanian migrations, it is important to consider the practices of circulatory mobility, in the form of continual movements between the home city and various migratory poles in the European space, as well as the forms of organisation and structuring of social relations that underlie this mobility (Potot 2008).

In Romania, these migrations must be understood as the multiplicity of individual strategies that are developed to minimise the deterioration of socio-economic conditions. As Morokvasic (1995: 119) writes, they 'concern people who are reacting to a crisis situation by hitting the road, in order to avoid being left behind in societies engaged in a rapid and particularly unpredictable process of transformation'. Searching elsewhere for the means to live better at home is the principal guide to these practices. According to Sandu (1999), temporary business trips to richer countries are associated with an older habit of 'shuttling' between city and countryside. This 'shuttling', known in Romania as *navetism*, once enabled the inhabitants of rural zones to improve their living conditions by commuting to work in the city, without entering entirely into the urban economic circuit. The parallel with current international mobility is clear in that the objective still consists of extending one's activities to a new territory without socially or economically breaking from the former.

In this way, transnational movements do not disrupt the local equilibrium but, rather, represent a specific form of adaptation to a crisis. It is in this way that Romanians interpret their temporary migrations, more as an alternative to the local bartering system than as a way to definitively escape the Romanian condition (Diminescu 2003; Michalon 2005; Morokvasic 2004; Potot 2007; Sandu 2000). This continuity allowed the idea of 'doing a season' in the West to become very popular (Diminescu & Lagrave 1999). According to the Public Opinion Barometer, in 2007, 12 per cent of the Romanian population considered their principal preoccupation to be leaving in order to work abroad (Fundatia Soros Romania 2007: 45).

For many Romanians we met during the fieldwork, migration was an option that requires somewhat more investment than informal trade, but which, in exchange, promises greater profit. Similarly, the legal restrictions imposed upon border-crossing appear more as challenges to surmount than as actual barriers to migration. Until 1 January 2002, the EU, through the Schengen space, kept its borders closed to

Romanian citizens, who were forced to obtain sparingly delivered visas. Even with the opening of borders to circulation in 2002, and full accession to the EU in 2007, several European countries have continued to protect their labour markets, so much so that labour migration to the West is often still considered an illegal practice.

Diversified migratory practices

In order to situate the case study that follows, this section provides a brief chronological sketch of international migration from Romania since 1989.[4] At first, seasonal labour migration intensified to the neighbouring countries of Hungary, Yugoslavia and Turkey at the beginning of the 1990s, reflecting established ties with these countries and opportunities to combine such migration with business trips. Then, from 1993-1994, departures to countries that were more distant and more difficult to access became increasingly widespread. Two types of migrations were juxtaposed. On the one hand, several countries – Germany and Israel in particular – recruited Romanian labour. In the framework of the *Werkertrage* agreements, German firms signed contracts with Romanian firms that provided not only the workers, but also the materials needed for certain construction sites. Particularly popular between 1993 and 1996, these exchanges have now practically disappeared. In Israel, the authorities decided each year on a quota of guest workers by nationality. Romanians, who represented 29 per cent of legal foreign workers in Israel in 2000, constituted the most represented national group.[5] This recruitment always took place through local Romanian agencies that served as intermediaries between candidates for departure and foreign private employers (Ellman & Laacher 2003). Financed either by the recruitment agency or by the company itself, the latter generally committed to housing workers onsite. Concretely, this meant the possibility to obtain, from Romania, a temporary contract for migration in which everything was included and the migrant was taken care of. The advantage is clear for individuals with no experience of living abroad, particularly at a time when circulatory migration was just beginning, and the migratory networks that would later facilitate temporary migration were not yet in place. For example, the availability of free housing and organised travel was attractive, in a context where emigration overall appeared quite risky. In turn, this attractiveness inspired a great deal of corruption: we could witness during the fieldwork that, despite being remunerated by the foreign companies, the Romanian agencies in charge of recruitment systematically sold contracts to migrant workers. As the number of contracts was limited, the agencies were able to increase the cost of work contracts on the black market. Some contracts could thus be sold for up to US$ 2,500; whereas the monthly salary guaranteed by the contract only amounted to around US$ 1,000.

Since 1995, these temporary migrations under contract have begun to serve more independent initiatives. Some contractual workers abroad maximise their revenue by accumulating jobs. In addition to the work for which they were employed, they devote their evenings or days off to undeclared second jobs. The value of the official contracts for the Romanian public is therefore directly related to the control exerted over the labourers' free time. As a result, housing that is located at the construction site itself, for example, is now in low demand, due to the difficulties that this represents to circumvent the employers' supervision. These contracts can also serve as passports for more independent migrants. After having made the trip with the company and perhaps having worked some time for the official employer, some migrants leave for more generous positions nearby. Indeed, the salaries of 'imported workers' are always rather low, reduced all the more by the withholdings that supposedly compensate for food and/or board. Once in the country, migrants can easily find more advantageous conditions on the national labour market. As such, the initial contract presents two manifest advantages: first, the migrant can take the time to appraise his place of work and analyse other employment options while being assured work. Some migrants maintain this initial employment for several months before moving on. Furthermore, formal recruitment attributes the right to stay legally in the country until the end of the contract. However, as the Israeli Central Bureau of Statistics notes, the workers often do not immediately return to their home countries at the end of these contracts (Ellman & Laacher 2003). Familiar with the area after several months of working legally at the initial site of employment, they may consider staying on in the country illegally for some time.

This partially accounts for the fact that mainly illegal individual migrations first appeared alongside legally organised migrations (Diminescu 2003). Migrants bound by no contract followed in the footsteps of those who were, at least initially, contractual. The preferred destination of illegal movements was, as of 1993-1994, Germany. Having procured a contract there, migrants often served as relays for their independent compatriots. Even without giving any real assistance onsite, they were the initial link between the homeland and the host destination. Having conveyed information to their families and friends about their experience abroad, they implicitly encouraged journeys to these regions. Likewise, the Aussiedler[6] recently emigrated from Romania created ties between certain regions of Germany and departure regions in Transylvania (Michalon 2003), prompting the independent migrants to follow the same paths. In this way, legally framed migrations have oriented undocumented migrations since their outset.

Migration later expanded to other European countries, facilitated by the very concept of the Schengen space. The convention that binds the signatory countries stipulated the elimination of the control of people, regardless of their nationality, at interior borders, through the harmonisation of customs controls at the exterior borders and the development of homogeneous visa policies. As a result, after crossing the first border, migrants are no longer hindered in travel between one country and another. It has since been possible for them to explore different countries with the aim of identifying the particularly attractive destinations. Thus, informants explain that when Germany increased its labour controls in 1997, restricting black market labour, or when France limited the requests for asylum in 1998,[7] reducing the opportunities to remain legally in its territory, they simply left these countries for other European destinations.

The range of destinations was once again modified with the integration of Romania and Bulgaria into the EU in 2007 and the subsequent opening of their labour markets. Numerous discussions with Romanian migrants of both groups studied reveal that the choice of a migratory destination depends on several factors. The most important is undoubtedly the profitability of the migration. In other words, it is indispensable for them to have the possibility to work upon arrival. Their arrival must therefore coincide with labour potential in the host country's labour market.

In the south of Spain, for instance, a substantial 'pull factor' in the local agricultural sector has attracted a high number of migrants from Teleorman County. Undocumented immigration has been greatly utilised by the agricultural sector in this region over the last twelve years. Thanks to low salaries and the lack of legal rights offered to this workforce, the sector has been able to reduce its production costs and become a leading European region for the fresh produce. Yet, besides domestic work, which provides employment for some women, undocumented Romanians have no other employment opportunities in the province of Almeria. Their arrival in this region is thus clearly correlated with opportunities offered by the agricultural sector where the working conditions were quite hard. It is then clearly the guarantee to easily find a job that 'pulled' migrants to this region.

The case observed in the French Riviera also illustrates the factors influencing migrants' geographical and labour trajectories. For four years, migrants from Târgoviste interviewed by this author worked as street vendors for a newspaper in Nice. This activity allowed them not only to meet their needs onsite, but also to put aside savings for their return. Although black market labour in construction sometimes complemented this income, Romanians were not able to obtain full-time employment due to the lack of positions. It was thus the initial activity that assured the success of the migration. As of 1997, the popularity of street newspaper sales in France began to decline. Then in 1998, in order to restore its image, the publishing company in Nice terminated employment of undocumented migrants among its vendors, consequently ending the principal occupation of the Romanians who were the focus of my research. The outcome within the migrant network was immediate; Nice was abandoned in favour of regions such as Milan and London, which promised other opportunities. Some of them left for London where they could work principally in the construction, hotel and catering industries in positions generally taken up by foreigners. With minimal controls on illegals working in the UK, Romanian migrants appear to have no difficulty in being employed alongside legal co-workers. These observations show that the type of job does not matter for these people as they can easily pass from one sector to the other if it gives them the opportunity to improve their earnings and/or their living conditions.

A second essential factor in choosing a migratory destination concerns the collective knowledge of the location. Only the most informed migrants dare to conquer new territories. The majority take positions already tested by the network they are affiliated with, in locations where they already have friends who have provided useful information. The migrant is thus bound to the collective memory of the group, which is utilised to orient his or her actions. Each experience enriches the stock of shared knowledge, orienting new migrants in the same direction. The migrants therefore branch out into niches (Waldinger 1994) throughout the European space, inhabiting some territories and leaving others.

Another important element in the choice of destination includes the relations of local authorities with undocumented migrants. As being expelled to one's home country before having collected sufficient savings constitutes a failure, migrants seek destinations that present the least possible amount of risk. For undocumented migrants,[8] who constitute the majority of independent migrants interviewed,[9] the way that laws are applied is more important than the legislation. Some countries, including France, Germany or Austria, are particularly uncompromising towards illegal migrants, while others – where the economies make massive use of undeclared labour – are more indulgent. The study conducted in Almeria provides a good example of the informal management of undocumented migration. In this agricultural province, migrants are not stopped by the police during farming breaks, between noon and 4 p.m. However, foreigners are systematically monitored if they loiter in public spaces during working hours. In this way, the authorities 'sort' migrants who fulfil the economic role expected of them from those who attempt to leave the agricultural sector. Likewise, undocumented migrants are aware that police leniency ceases at the perimeter of the agricultural territory. Travelling in the rest of the country means leaving the zone of leniency that characterises the province of Almeria. These observations demonstrate that beyond national borders, there are *enclaves* in the European space that are willing to constitute migratory niches.

In other words, there is evidence that working migrations, even when not officially acknowledged, do not only serve the interests of individual migrants or their family; they also play a role at a more collective scale. In Western economies, the use of low paid, foreign manpower allows weak economic sectors to remain competitive despite the globalisation process (Potot 2007). Meanwhile, remittances sent by migrants in countries of origin can be a valuable income for relatively poor states. The economic impact of the migratory activities on national economies is a recurrent subject of studies, both in receiving countries (Borjas 2001; Friedberg & Hunt 1995) as in countries of origin (Domingues Dos Santos & Postel-Vinay 2003; Drinkwater, Levine, Lotti & Pearlman 2003; Ratha 2005; World Bank 2008). Contrasting, there are not many sociological surveys evaluating the social evolutions engendered by migrations in the country of departure.

The migrants during the transition process

The aim here is not to evaluate the overall economic contribution of migration but, rather, to use concrete observations to indicate the different aspects of local socio-economic life that are noticeably influenced by migratory activity. Three principal means can be observed through which the migrants, in bridging their city of origin with Western locations, transform Romanian lifestyles. To begin with, their activity generates new lifestyles for themselves and new attitudes towards consumption in Romania. Secondly, the formation of a social group identified by migration and rising social status fosters an increasingly capitalist outlook within the middle classes, which encourages the creation of small businesses in the departure regions. Thirdly, transnational skills can be put to the service of other social actors in order to facilitate trade and, above all, to support the implantation of foreign companies in Romania. Each of these phenomena is explored in more detail below.

A new consumerist model

To understand how migration has transformed modes of consumption in Romania, we must first briefly return to the economy of Romanian households and individuals. The transition from one political system to another can be summarised in the words of one of the interviewees: 'Before we had money but the stores were empty. Today the stores are full but we no longer have the means to buy the bare minimum.'[10] Indeed, although, as noted above, the average monthly salary after tax in 2007 was only around € 295, the prices of many commercial products are now only slightly lower than in the West. This situation leads the majority of Romanian households to employ strategies in order to meet their daily needs. Besides various financial solutions for buying things that they cannot afford with one salary, like credit or leasing, the informal economy, which once served to compensate for supply shortages in the official market, is today therefore a precious resource to compensate for reduced purchasing power. Thus, the role of the shadow economy is still to maintain the standard of everyday life when the official system does not offer this possibility.

According to my research, before their first departure, migrants were often already involved in informal transactions; their behaviour transforms when they return. At this point, they tend to abandon the informal market, turning towards the formal consumer economy, which they perceive as typically Western. Everyday consumer products such as food or clothing are primarily bought in retail stores, preferably in the local subsidiaries of foreign chain stores. In the city studied, the mini-mart of the Total petrol station had become the primary source of necessities for returning migrants. For them, the 50 square metres of this shop incarnated the Western European mode of consumption. Direct access to products of brightly coloured and illustrated packaging led Romanian clients to consider these purchases in a new and amusing way. Within a few years, Carrefour stores became the symbol of Western consumerist modernity. By shopping regularly in this type of store, in spite of higher prices than at the traditional market, returning migrants show their fellow citizens to what extent the migration has transformed their lives. On the one hand, it has provided the financial means to abandon the black market that is now described by the informants as the pathetic legacy of a time past; while, on the other hand, it has conditioned them to a different and more modern lifestyle that has been integrated into their daily lives.

The fact that these practices are part of a performance aimed at showing the different sides of the image of the migrant is of little importance here. What emerges is not only that part of the profit from migration that is reinvested in the formal economy, but that the latter has amplified value on a symbolic level. The migrants' behaviour associates the notion of social mobility with consumer practices in the formal economy. Now spread beyond the migrant circle, this tendency contributes to reducing the number of informal transactions and encourages behaviour that more resembles European standards. This inclination is also supported by widespread advertisements promoting a very modern Western way of life, which developed with the growing implantation of Western brand shops throughout the country. In parallel, the political elite – whose objective was, until 2007, to integrate Romania into the EU – tend to encourage such a model. Adopting this way of consumption is then seen as a testimony of modernity. Such trends increase the clientele of legitimate businesses, boosting their economic situation. From this standpoint, it appears that migratory movements contribute to transforming not only the perceptions of the middle classes, but also their economic behaviour.

Emulation of capitalism

Although these attitudes undeniably impact consumption behaviours concerning daily needs, we cannot conclude that all of the profits from migration are reinvested in the formal economy, nor that migrants have given up taking advantage of their social networks to obtain certain resources. On the contrary, migration also enriches migrants' *social capital* (Bourdieu 1985), which is highly valuable in the home regions. From the fieldwork conducted in Romania, we can learn that this shared social status of 'returnee' in Romania, along with the shared experience of 'migration' abroad, engenders a sort of social group in the departure regions. Rapid upwards mobility and the sense of belonging to an extended geographical space create ties between migrants that lead them to distinguish themselves from their fellow citizens and to rally around a common culture. The two principal markers that identify the returned migrant group in Romania thus concern a shared experience abroad and the collective construction of the migrants' image in the home region. Although some migrants may have helped each other out during the stays abroad, there is little observable sense of community belonging amongst migrants whilst they are abroad (Potot 2007). It is really only in the country of origin that the migrants publicly demonstrate a collective identity. Groups of migrants are commonly encountered in the fashionable bars and discothèques, verbosely expressing their affection for the region of their recent migration. Many symbols are employed to express this attachment, such as using certain words in French, English or Spanish, wearing clothing of Western brand names or arriving in cars with foreign plates even several months after the return to Romania.[11] Not only do these public demonstrations enable the migrants to boast about their upwards mobility, but they are also useful in the world of business.

In addition, migrants generally put aside some savings for their return and, although one part of this will be spent in ostentatious fashion, many will attempt to exploit this capital once they are back in Romania.

To do so, belonging to a defined social group of returned migrants could prove to be useful. For example, we observed that migrants may find that their peers have an investment capacity more or less equivalent to their own, are willing to take some financial risks, generally have partners abroad they can rely on and have a similar goal to maintain their new living standard. It is thus common for migrants to engage in small-scale business activities together. This often entails transitory business ventures: examples from fieldwork included buying material from a factory that was going out of business to resell it for a profit, exporting wood to Turkey or reselling telephones from Germany. Each time, an ex-migrant found such an opportunity within his own social network – connected with the transnational social capital he acquired during his migration (Rusinovic 2008) or not – and then invited one or two colleagues to take part in the business. This can be a simple financial support, but the other participants can also bring some contacts with potential clients or any administrative support for international business. The dynamics that encourage the spirit of enterprise also occasionally lead to the creation of more perennial businesses. In one example, a taxi business in Bucharest was created when a migrant's stay in France enabled him to buy a car, for which he employed a driver in order to return abroad and save enough funds to buy a second vehicle. While some of these endeavours, as in the example cited, were planned before the initial departure and represent the principal reason for migration, others were generated from opportunities arising directly from the experience abroad. A young man who had spent a few months in the agricultural sector of Andalusia, for example, returned to Romania in order to open an exporting business of window boxes, which he sold directly to his former Spanish employer through a compatriot who had remained there.

Migration not only provides the economic means to launch this type of business, it also develops the necessary skills such as the capacity to negotiate, to handle uncertain situations and to make a profit from the marginal domains that are neglected by the public authorities. Similarly, Taylor (1999) reveals an indirect effect of the migrations on entrepreneurship: because they accumulate capital, migrants can serve as financial guarantors for friends and family. In this way, even when unspent, the existence of savings to rely upon in the event of bankruptcy has encouraged risk-taking even by those not directly involved in migration. It therefore appears clear that, even if many of these business ventures have a limited life span, migratory movements support the development of small-scale enterprises through individual initiatives in a country where the majority of the private sector emanates from foreign investments and the privatisation of large state businesses.

Transnational mediators

Finally, the migrants can be considered as strategic elements in foreign investments, as their multinational culture enables them to bridge foreign businesses or investors and Romanian society. Their skills can be put to a multitude of uses. Stocchiero (2002) highlights the role of migrants in the region of Veneto, Italy, during the relocation of the Italian clothing industry to the region of Timisoara-Arad. The study argues that there is an association between the arrival of undocumented Romanian workers in this Italian province during the 1990s and the massive relocation of the clothing sector to Romania that subsequently took place.

A qualitative approach enables clarification of the part played by the migrants. Not only were they familiar with several languages but, having lived abroad, they were in a position to anticipate some of the difficulties and expectations of foreign entrepreneurs investing in Romania. They are therefore better able to assist investors in dealing with Romanian bureaucracy, as well as in negotiating with public authorities or potential partners of the budding businesses. For a small-scale foreign investor, the support of a person of confidence is often essential. Additionally, regardless of the migrants' occupation during their stay in the EU, their experiences usually involve their working in an environment that contrasts starkly with that in post-communist businesses. Even when relegated to the least respected positions, they were obliged to conform to Western styles of working, to accept company rules, to work long hours and/or to show initiative. These tendencies are often absent in state enterprises where, for several decades during communism, work was mandatory, over-employment the general rule, inactivity frequent due to the lack of raw materials and the plundering of the company a normal way to compensate for the failures of the system. Even today, it is noticeable that the behaviour of an employee of a large Romanian company, such as the Romanian National Railway Company, is a far cry from the conduit of a young dynamic employee promoted by Carrefour or McDonald's who is at the service of the customer. Foreign businesses, which not only import products but also new working codes, require that their Romanian employees adapt in a number of ways. Although this adaptation is encouraged by offering higher salaries than those offered by local businesses, it requires tedious efforts onsite with the employees, who are expected to integrate a work ethic that was only recently imported to Romania (Heintz 2002). The migrants, who themselves had to adapt during their stay abroad to a work environment that they were not accustomed to, are particularly competent at conveying the requirements of the foreign businesses to the Romanian employees. Being familiar with work habits in Romania, they can anticipate the difficulties that could be brought about by Western-style personnel management as well as fully trained managers who had theoretically studied the subject for several years.

One young woman, for example, recounted her one year of work in a shoe-making business in the region of Milan, stressing that when this company relocated part of its production to Romania, she was first asked to participate in the prospective phase, during which she worked as an interpreter, serving as go-between with the local administration. Later, when the factory opened, she became the personnel supervisor and the link between the Italian directors and the Romanian workers. On top of the recruitment of new personnel, her role consisted of conveying the company's expectations to the new employees. Her two principal objectives at the time of our meeting were to end the numerous unexpected and unjustified employee absences, which greatly disturbed the rhythm of production, and to avoid theft of raw materials and finished products which was not so rare in state factories during communist Romania (Oprescu 2000). She attested to the difficulty of putting in place a work ethic in the context of a large factory even if it had seemed natural in Italy. At the same time, she was not surprised by these obstacles and stressed that, if the numerous Romanian migrants were able to adapt without difficulty to the Italian business spirit, it had to be possible to 'make the Romanian mentalities evolve as well'. It is indeed this role that is expected of returning migrants: that of mediator between different work environments.

Conclusion

The aim of this chapter is in no way to glorify the Western model of society; it does not aim to judge the so-termed transition process, which is inclined to transform a country deeply rooted in communism into a capitalistic society.

Its purpose was to underline the continuity within the evolution of Romanian society. I have shown that the path from one economic model to the other was supported by deeper social processes which were adapting to the evolving situation. Actually, the reform of the economic system goes with progressive changes, both in everyday life habits and in representations. The involvement of a large part of the population within the shadow economy has existed for several decades, allowing Romanian people to survive decently despite economic recession. In this sense, present survival strategies can be seen as the adaptation of the strategies developed under communism in order to resist the difficulties of those times. The transition process towards capitalism has not resolved the everyday-life difficulties, but has offered new means of skirting around them. Transnational migration, as short working stays abroad, is therefore part of the set of informal practices available to improve the life of many Romanians.

Ironically, it appears that these informal movements have contributed in some way to the formalisation of the Romanian economy encouraged by the various Romanian governments and international supports, such as the World Bank, in the period of pre-accession to the EU. Yet, whereas the subject of migration is often approached as a factor inhibiting accession to the EU[12] or otherwise as 'desertion' of the young working force at a time when the country needs all its human resources, this analysis highlights the contribution of migrants to economic and social changes occurring in Romania. It highlights the fact that the financial gains sent home, 'remittances' in the economic literature, are not the only contribution of the migrants to their country. Throughout their transnational movements, they acquire behaviour, knowledge and skills that are also reinvested in their home regions. In doing so, far from the projects of international cooperation or the programmes of cultural exchange supported by the ministries, the migrant networks promote a European standard of living which is progressively penetrating the countries that have only very recently joined the EU.

Notes

1   Data mainly come from fieldwork conducted between 1997 and 2001 in Romania, France, Spain and the UK and has been completed by occasional contacts with informants in France since then.
2   The standard of living in 2000 represented only 80 per cent of its material value in 1989 (Lhomel 2001).
3   For an average of 29.2 per cent of GDP for Central and Eastern European countries altogether and 16.7 per cent in the OECD countries in 2001.
4   This section relies on several articles from the collective publication edited by Diminescu (2003), *Visible mais peu nombreux.*
5   These statistics, published in *The Internet Jerusalem Post* on 30 October 2001, do not take account of Palestinian workers whose status is particular.
6   Aussiedler are defined by the 1953 law on refugees and displaced persons (Bundesvertriebenen- und Flüchtlingsgesetz), as German-origin minorities, from the CEE or the former USSR. They have a right to apply for German nationality.
7   In accordance with the law known as Loi Chevènement of 11 June 1998, requests for asylum from Romanian citizens are urgently processed in less than ten days and are almost systematically refused.
8   Even before the end of the visa system, the majority of Romanians travelled abroad with a legitimate tourist visa for the Schengen space. However, the interdiction to procure salaried work and the limitation of stays to a period of less than three months rendered these migrants undocumented in the countries where employed.
9   Independent migrants are those who left Romania independently in search of work or a better life, as opposed to those recruited directly by contract from Romania.
10   This remark was heard repeatedly during the interviews in Romania.

11 Several people interviewed claimed to have bribed the police in order to keep their foreign plates beyond the legal time limit.
12 The 'migratory potential' of Romania has often instigated debate in the negotiations regarding accession to the EU. See this website devoted to EU enlargement: http://ec.europa.eu/enlargement.

References

Aktar, C. & N. Ôgelman (1994), 'Recent developments in East-West migration: Turkey and the petty traders', *International Migration* 32 (2): 343-353.
Badie, B. (1995), 'Préface' in A. Colonomos (ed.), *Sociologie des réseaux transnationaux*, 15-17. Paris: L'Harmattan.
Borjas, G. (2001), 'Does immigration grease the wheels of the labor market?', *Brookings Papers on Economic Activity* 1 (69):133.
Bourdieu, P. (1985), 'The forms of capital' in Richardson (ed.), *Handbook of Theory and Research for the Sociology of Education*, 241-258. New York: Greenwood.
Colonomos, A. (ed.) (1995), *Sociologie des réseaux transnationaux*. Paris: L'Harmattan.
Diminescu, D. & R.-M. Lagrave (1999), 'Faire une saison. Pour une anthropologie des migrations roumaines en France. Le cas d'Oas', *Migrations Etudes* 91.
Diminescu, D. (ed.) (2003), *Visibles mais peu nombreux. Les circulations migratoires roumaines*. Paris: Maison des Sciences de l'Homme.
Domingues Dos Santos, M. & F. Postel-Vinay (2003), 'Migration as a source of growth: The perspective of a developing country', *Journal of Population Economics* 16: 161-175.
Drinkwater S., P. Levine, E. Lotti & J. Pearlman (2003), 'The economic impact of migration: A survey', *Discussion Papers* 0103. University of Surrey, Department of Economics, .
Duchêne, G. (1999), 'Les revenus informels en Roumanie: Estimation par enquête', *Revue d'Etudes Comparatives Est-Ouest* 30 (4): 35-64.
Duchêne, G., L.-L. Albu & B.-Y. Kim (2002), 'An attempt to estimate the size of informal economy based on household behaviour modeling', *Romanian Journal of Economic forecasting* 1: 17-24.
Durandin, C. (2000), *Roumanie: Un piège?* Saint-Claude-de-Diray: Editions Hesse, coll. Ister.
Ellman, M. & S. Laacher (2003), *Migrant workers in Israel. A contemporary form of slavery. Réseau euro-méditerranéen des droits de l'Homme (REMDH), Fédération internationale des ligues des droits de l'Homme (FIDH)* 48. Paris.
Friedberg, R. & J. Hunt (1995), 'The impact of immigrants on host country wages, employment and growth', *Journal of Economic Perspectives* 9 (2): 23-44.
Fundatia-pentru-o-Societate-Deschisa (ed.) (2006), *Living abroad on a temporary basis. The economic migration of Romanian: 1990-2006*. Bucharest. www.osf.ro/ro/publicatii.php#.
Fundatia-Soros-Romania (ed.) (2007), *Barometrul de opinie publica 1998-2007*. Bucharest. www.osf.ro/ro/publicatii.php#.
Glick-Schiller, N. & P. Levitt (2007), 'Conceptualizing simultaneity. A transnational social field perspective on society' in A. Portes & J. De Wind (ed.), *Rethinking migration. New theoretical and empirical perspectives*, 181-218. New York: Berghahn Books.
Heintz, M. (2002), *Changes in work ethics in post-socialist Romania*. PhD Thesis. Cambridge: University of Cambridge.
Kideckel, D. (1993), *The solitude of collectivism*. New York: Cornell University Press.
Lhomel, E. (2001), 'Roumanie 2000-2001. Un nouveau départ?' *Le courrier des pays de l'Est* 1016: 164-177.

Michalon, B. (2003), 'De la politique des *Aussiedler* à la circulation. Diversification des pratiques migratoires des Saxons de Transylvanie' in D. Diminescu (ed.), *Visibles mais peu nombreux. Les circulations migratoires roumaines*, 65-98. Paris: Editions de la Maison des Sciences de l'Homme.

Michalon, B. (2005), 'Dynamiques frontalières et nouvelles migrations internationales en Roumanie', *Revue d'études comparatives Est-Ouest* 36 (3): 43-69.

Mingione, E. (1991), *Fragmented societies: A sociology of economic life beyond the market paradigm*. Oxford: Blackwell.

Morokvasic, M. (1995), 'Entre l'Est et l'Ouest, des migrations pendulaires' in M. Morokvasic & H. Rudolph (ed.), *Migrants. Les nouvelles mobilités en Europe*, 119-157. Paris: L'Harmattan.

Morokvasic, M. (1999), 'La mobilité transnationale comme ressource: Le cas des migrants de l'Europe de l'Est', *Cultures et Conflits* 33-34: 105-122.

Morokvasic, M. (2004), '"Settle in Mobility": Engendering post-wall migration in Europe', *Feminist Review* 77: 7-25.

Oprescu, A. (2000), 'Les enjeux de la gestion du temps dans la Roumanie des années '80', *Annuaire de la Société d'Anthropologie Culturelle de Roumanie*: 21-50.

Pelinescu, E. (2003), 'Causes and size of informal economy in Romania', *Journal for Economic Forecasting* 1: 86-97.

Péraldi, M. (ed.) (2001), *Cabas et containers. Activités marchandes informelles et réseaux migrants transfrontaliers*. Paris: Maisonneuve et Larose, MMSH.

Piore, M. (1986), 'The shifting grounds for immigration', *The Annals of the American Academy*. 23-33.

Portes, A. (1997), *Globalization from below: The rise of transnational communities*. Princeton: Princeton University Press.

Potot, S. (2007), *Vivre à l'Est, travailler à l'Ouest. Les routes roumaines de l'Europe*. Paris: L'Harmattan.

Potot, S. (2008), 'Romanian circulation: Networks as informal transnational organisations' in C. Bonifazi, M. Okólski, J. Schoorl & P. Simon (eds.), *International Migration in Europe: New Trends, New Methods of Analysis*. IMISCOE-AUP Research Series. Amsterdam: Amsterdam University Press.

Rainer, N. (2002), 'Aspects of the informal economy in a transforming country: The case of Romania', *International Journal of Urban and Regional Research* 26 (2): 299-322.

Ratha D. (2005), 'Workers' remittances: An important and stable source of external development finance' in S. Maimbo & D. Ratha, *Remittances: Development impact and future prospects*, 19-52. Washington, D.C.: The World Bank .

Rusinovic, K. (2008), 'Transnational embeddedness: Transnational activities and networks among first and second-generation immigrant entrepreneurs', *Journal of Ethnic and Migration Studies* 34 (3): 431-452.

Sandu, D. (1999), *Spatiul social al transitiei*. Bucharest: Polirom.

Sandu, D. (2000), 'Migratia circulatorie ca strategie de viata', *Sociologie romaneasca* (2 serie noua): 5-30.

Schneider, F. G. (2002), 'The size and development of the shadow economies of 22 transition and 21 OECD countries', IZA *Discussion Paper No. 514*. University of Linz.

Stocchiero, A. (2002), *Migration flow and small and medium sized enterprise internationalisation between Romania and the Italian Veneto Region*. Rome :Centro Studi Politica Internazionale.

Tarrius, A. (1993), 'Territoires circulatoires et espaces urbains', *Annales de la Recherche Urbaine* 59-60: 50-60.

Taylor, E. J. (1999), 'The new economics of labour migration and the role of remittances in the migration process', *International Migration* 37 (1): 63-88.

Verdery, K. (1996), *What was socialism and what comes next?* Princeton: Princeton University Press.

Waldinger, R. D. (1994), 'The making of an immigrant niche', *International Migration Review* 8 (1): 3-30.

World Bank (2008), *The Migration and Remittances Factbook 2008*. Washington, D.C.: The World Bank, Migration and Remittances Team, Development Prospects Group.

13 Modernising Romanian society through temporary work abroad

Dumitru Sandu

Introduction

The consequences of migration are rarely integrated into solid theoretical constructions. The main approach in the literature seems to be focused on designing theories that explain the determinants of migration. 'Neoclassical economics', 'new economics', 'segmented labour market', 'world system', 'social capital' or 'cumulative causation' theories (Massey, Arango, Hugo, Kouaouci, Pellegrino & Taylor 1998) are all centred primarily on determinants of international migration rather than the discussion of the consequences of this phenomenon. This situation can be partly explained by the fact that it is quite difficult to build a theory of migration consequences, as consequences could be intended or unintended, manifest or latent, short-, medium- or long-term, at individual, household, community, region or national levels, at origin or at destination. The typical solution to this problem is to talk about 'migration and development' for particular countries (Escobar, Haibronner, Martin & Meza 2006) or about specific consequences of migration (Dayton-Johnson, Katseli, Maniatis, Muntz & Papademetriou 2007).

Understanding the causes of the migration process could be useful in portraying its consequences. The logic of cumulative causation in explaining migration (Massey et al. 1998: 45-50), for example, could be relevant for understanding specific chains of migration consequences. Migration culture, as a key term in the cumulative causation theory of migration, could also be highly relevant for changes that are generated by migration, but that have effects going in different directions or spheres. Changes in origin countries' local mentalities shaped by external migration experiences could be responsible for new family behaviours and new household economic patterns. Temporary migration abroad induces changes at origin that are mediated by three basic intermediary variables: remittances, network capital and changes in 'mentality'. It is quite difficult to find changes induced by migration at individual, household, community or regional levels that are not mediated by these variables. Starting from this perspective, this chapter seeks to re-construct a causal chain that explains changes in demographic beha-viour at the family and community levels in Romania, as induced by temporary emigration abroad after 1989.

Circular or temporary migration abroad from Romania is a rather re-cent phenomenon. Between 1989 and 1996, Romanians explored the world outside Romania, trying to identify appropriate niches where they could fit in and function, using their own resources and cultural abil-ities (Sandu 2006). Given the short history of this process, is it possible to identify mass consequences of temporary migration for Romanians? Some of the economic consequences are obvious: Romania is among the top ten developing countries by the total amount of remittances re-ceived in 2007 – about US$ 7 billion according to Ratha, Mohapatra, Vijayalakshmi and Xu (2007). But what about non-economic conse-quences, mediated by changes in the human, cultural and network capi-tal? Are they visible at community and regional levels?

Data, method and hypotheses

The general hypothesis of this study is that the experience of working abroad became a modernising factor for Romanian society, despite the fact that this is a new phenomenon and highly uneven at the commu-nity and regional levels. The chapter uses the case of the possible im-pact of temporary emigration experience in Romania after 2000 on fa-mily life and demographic transformations as a way to answer the ques-tions stated above. The first part of the chapter describes the types of temporary emigration experiences[1] that individuals and families have accumulated and the relationship between these experiences and social differentiation in terms of material, human, network and cultural capi-tal. These two factors are in a continuous interaction. In some cases, it is possible to infer the consequences of migration for the stock of capi-tal held by families and individuals while, in other cases, the relation-ship between migration experiences and capital stocks is so intimate that it is hard to assess the causal nature of the relationship.

The second part of the chapter explores the consequences of the mi-gration experience at the community level. This includes analysis of re-gional variations in how migration has impacted the housing market and demographic trends. Using rural community-level data, multivari-ate models are developed to compare rates of migration from, and re-turn to, each Romanian commune (in 2002) with birth, marriage and divorce rates, and the rate of construction of private houses (in the peri-od 2003-2005). Two types of hypotheses are developed: measurement hypotheses (h) and substantive hypotheses (H).

The basic hypothesis at the community level (H1) is that migration could have a delayed effect on demographic behaviour. Communes characterised by high migration prevalence rates (returned migrants plus current temporary emigrants to 1,000 people in the reference area) are expected to exhibit high divorce rates and lower birth and marriage rates only after several years, controlling for development level, socio-demographic composition of the local population, community culture and location factors (distance to the nearest city, distance to a modernised road, etc.). Community culture is correlated with the general fertility rate, calculated from the most recent census in 2002. The measurement hypothesis (h1) here states that villages (as territorial sub-divisions of communes) with high fertility rates are formed by a more traditional population, whereas those with low fertility rates have more modern populations.

Data for the individual and family levels are provided by a survey carried out in 2006 on a national representative sample.[2] The basic hypothesis at this level (H2) is that personal- and family-level effects of migration are functions of the type of migration experience. This experience could include an individual living abroad temporarily for work or non-work purposes, or living in a family where another family member lived abroad for work or non-work purposes. The intersection of these two dimensions generates four classes of migration experience: personal work experience (7 per cent), personal non-work experience (9 per cent), family work experience (14 per cent) and family non-work experience (3 per cent). The rest of the sample (68 per cent) does not have any migration experience. More than 30 per cent of the Romanians interviewed in the 2006 survey lived in households where at least one household member had lived abroad temporarily. For half of these respondents, this had been a personal experience.

A second methodological hypothesis (h2), which could help in interpreting the data, is that the four types of migration experience are associated not only with different levels of economic and human resources, as indicated by previous studies, but also with different degrees of individual emancipation or modernity (Figure 13.1). Previous surveys (2001-2004) indicate that the typical potential emigrant for temporary work abroad is young, male, with education between primary and secondary level, with previous experience of living abroad, neither rich nor poor, living in more developed communities from more developed counties from the historical region of Moldova (Sandu 2007: 37). The four types of migration experience listed above are expected to order – from higher to lower – individual modernity as a propensity to accept calculated risk for success, to value leisure time, to promote tolerance in social interaction and to use mass media as a source of information decreases.

Figure 13.1 *Relationship between emigration experience, capital resources and individual modernity*

<table>
<tr><td rowspan="2"></td><td rowspan="2"></td><td colspan="4">Economic, human and network capital resources</td></tr>
<tr><td>Low</td><td>Middle</td><td colspan="2">High</td></tr>
<tr><td rowspan="3">Individual modernity</td><td>Low</td><td></td><td></td><td colspan="2"></td></tr>
<tr><td>Middle</td><td></td><td>Family work experience</td><td colspan="2"></td></tr>
<tr><td>High</td><td></td><td>Personal work experience</td><td colspan="2">Personal non-work experience</td></tr>
</table>

Hypothesis h2 is directly supported by more recent data that shows the migration experience to be deeply rooted in personal status (Table 13.1). The respondents that worked abroad are the youngest among the four categories mentioned above. Three quarters of them are men with high school or vocational education, coming from households of medium economic status. Their network capital based on connections

Table 13.1 *Status profile function of migration experience*

	Migration experience					Total
	Personal for work reasons	*Family for work reasons*	*Personal for non-work reasons*	*Family for non-work reasons*	*Without migration experience*	
Average age	36	45	44	45	52	49
% male	73	35	44	48	47	47
% urban	53	51	77	70	51	54
Index of household goods*	6.80	6.38	8.23	8.28	5.49	6.02
Average number of years in school	11.18	9.58	12.10	11.23	9.56	9.94
Index of network capital in the country**	0.80	0.65	1.26	1.10	0.47	0.61
Index of network capital abroad***	0.57	0.41	0.46	0.30	0.14	0.24

Source: Field survey

*Index counts the available durable goods in the household – car, telephone, mobile phone, refrigerator, cable TV, colour TV, video, freezer, washing machine, automatic dishwasher, computer, internet access at home, double glazing windows. The index therefore varies from 0 to 13.

** Index counts whether useful connections were reported in health centres, judicial institutions, town hall, police, in employment services, in business and at the county level. The index therefore varies between 0 and 7.

*** Index indicates whether respondents reported having relatives or acquaintances abroad (0 = no; 1 = having *either* relatives *or* acquaintances abroad; 2 = having *both* relatives *and* acquaintances abroad).

abroad is the highest, compared to any other category in the classification. Network capital in Romania is generally high, but it is lower than for those who were abroad for non-work reasons. Those with work experience abroad come in equal part from rural and urban communities. This segment of the population has a status profile quite similar to that of people without direct migration experience, but coming from households in which another person had experience with working abroad.

Those having direct experience of living abroad for non-work reasons are older, better educated and come from households with better economic status. They are much more likely to be in urban areas than those with work experience abroad. In terms of human and material capital, they are rather similar to people from families with migration experience for non-work reasons. Considering these similarities in status profiles, one can expect that persons who have direct or indirect experience of working abroad are also similar from the point of view of migration consequences. They are expected to differ significantly from persons who had direct non-work migration experience.

The causal chain that starts from migration experience abroad at individual or family level leads to community demographic consequences by a series of first-, second- and third-order effects (see Figure 13.2). First-order effects are those involving increased financial resources, increased network capital and modern values. Many other consequences (second-order effects) in individual or family consumption, investment behaviour, choice behaviours or family life result from these first-order effects. Changes in community life are third-order effects, like those triggering modifications in housing stock, fertility, divorce rates, etc. Hypothesis H1 focuses on this type of demographic consequences of migration experience at the community level. Changes in the demographic life of the community are clearly cumulative. All these changes are selective by reference to personal/family status and to community stocks of economic, human and cultural capitals. An increase in divorce rates and decline of birth rates are not only effects 'of the diffusion of demographic modernity' (Fargues 2007: 162). Due to the fact that they are produced in the early stages of experiences of migration abroad, they are also effects of simple separation between family partners caused by working abroad and of the problems associated with the uncertainties of experiencing a new way of life in a new cultural and economic environment.

Family-level consequences

Converting experience into a 'migration ideology'

The type of migration experience generally appears to influence respondents' opinions about specific consequences of working abroad (Table

Figure 13.2   *The micro-meso level of migration consequences*

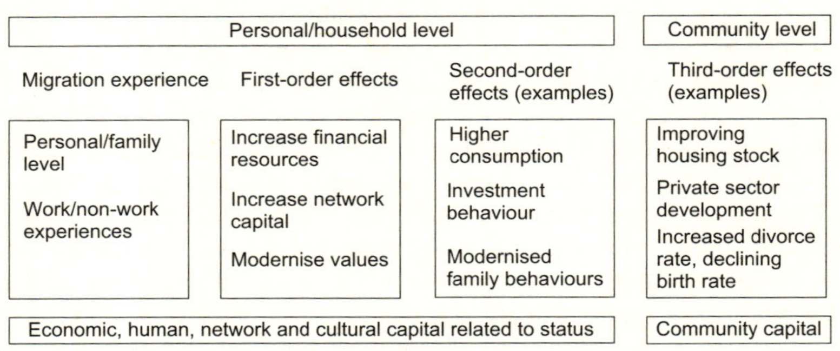

13.2). For example, more than half of the Romanian population believes that 'it is good that some people leave for work abroad'. Among those who have already worked abroad, about three quarters of respondents have a positive opinion. About 60 per cent of respondents who have worked abroad consider that after this experience, people 'think differently'. In contrast, those who had not lived abroad but were part of a family with migration experience were rather less likely to agree with this statement (45 per cent), whilst respondents who had not migrated and were not part of a family with migration experience showed the lowest level of support for this view.

A similar pattern is seen for other opinions surveyed. Half of those who had worked abroad thought that after the experience they would be likely to divorce. The same opinion was supported by only 42 per cent of those that have no migration experience. The difference could be

Table 13.2   *Opinions about working abroad*

	Migration experience					Total
	Personal, for work reasons	*Family for work reasons*	*Personal for non-work reasons*	*Family for non-work reasons*	*Without migration experience*	
'It is good to work abroad'	73	58	62	68	51	55
'It is both good and bad to work abroad'	16	19	19	18	23	21
Those that work abroad.....						
'get richer'	87	87	83	83	82	83
'get divorced more easily'	51	42	39	40	42	43
'help each other abroad'	39	46	40	35	33	36
'help those at home'	80	71	73	75	65	68
'have a different way of thinking'	60	45	56	53	32	38

Source: Field survey

interpreted as consistent with the hypothesis that working abroad favours divorce by separation and modernising experiences, although this difference is not statistically significant. In turn, experience of migration is also highly associated with the idea that whilst abroad, migrants help those who are still at home, with those who had worked abroad again showing the highest level of support for this view (80 per cent, compared to 68 per cent, the sample average).

Solidarity networks occasioned by migration are, in the social perception, more structured among family members who are in different places, abroad and at home, than among the migrants at destination. A total of 39 per cent of former economic migrants supported the view that 'migrants help each other abroad' compared to 80 per cent from the same population segment considering that 'migrants help those at home'.

The only clear exception to the rule that migration experience is related to opinions about migration concerns the view that 'those who worked abroad get richer', a statement supported by more than 80 per cent of those surveyed, irrespective of their migration experience. This shows an overwhelming consensus on the positive consequences of temporary economic emigration.

The analysis so far focuses on bivariate logic, but it is also possible to test hypotheses about the relationship between migration experience and opinions about migration using multivariate analysis – in other words, controlling for key status variables such as age, gender, education, household assets and rural versus urban residence. When such multivariate analysis is conducted, personal experience of working abroad continues to be a significant predictor of the opinion that 'migrants think differently', and the view that migrants help those still at home, compared to those with no migration experience, even after controlling for the status variables listed above. However, there is no difference between these two groups with respect to whether migration favours divorce when one controls for status variables.

Given that Romanian migration is highly regionalised (Sandu 2005; see Figure 13.3), regional variations in the pattern of migration experience might also be expected to influence opinions about migration. With this in mind, the regression models were run for each region, with opinions about migration as dependent variables and migration experience as predictors (and controlling for status variables). This analysis suggests that, whilst some regions such as Moldova and Transylvania are typical of the country as a whole, with a significant association between personal and family work experience and opinions about migration, in other regions such as Oltenia and Crisana-Maramures, it is not so much individuals who have worked abroad who have more positive attitudes about migration, but more their families.

Figure 13.3   *Temporary emigration rates by historical regions of Romania, 2002-2006*

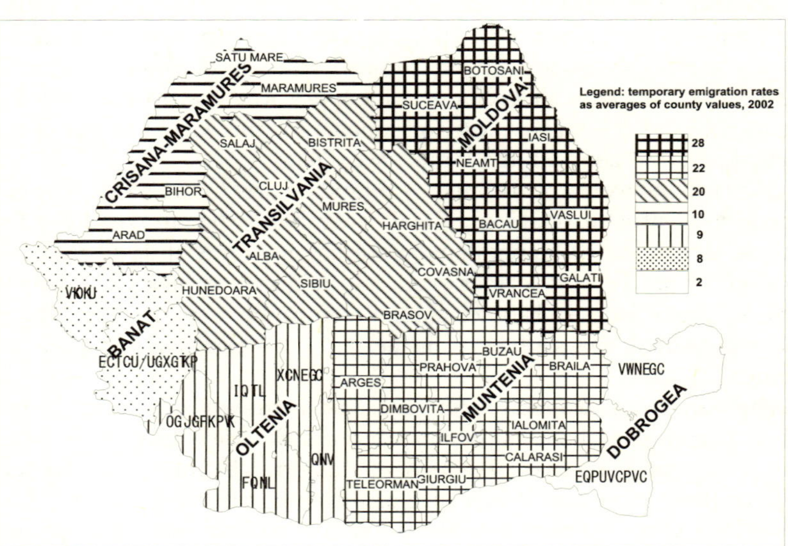

Source: Sandu (2006: 28)
Note: Regions' names are in larger block letters; county names are in smaller print.

This may reflect the fact that there were relatively few individuals in these latter regions who had personal experience of working abroad, in contrast to Moldova, the region with the highest propensity for work emigration, and Transylvania, where non-work emigration experiences are very rich, especially in counties with a large share of ethnic minorities – Covasna, Harghita, Sibiu, Brasov (Sandu 2007: 40).

The idea that working abroad brings a higher propensity for divorce is supported significantly only in the Banat region, amongst the families of former work migrants. Banat is known in Romania for a long tradition of low fertility (Trebici 1986: 104-106). It is likely that in such an environment, the population is more sensitive to factors such as migration, which could bring demographic changes. Timis, the county with the largest population in Banat, has for a long time had one of the highest divorce rates in the country (Trebici 1986: 84). In contrast, the view that work migration does not bring higher divorce rates is supported in the southern region of Muntenia, where people from families with work experience abroad systematically reject the idea that migration is a factor that increases the rate of divorce.

In addition to the opinions on migration noted above, respondents of the survey were also asked what were the 'things a person who returns home from work abroad should spend money on', with a range of choices being offered (Table 13.3). Here, the differences between population groups based on their experience of migration were minimal, with widespread agreement amongst population groups that the major items of expenditure and investment for migrants are housing, business development and meeting family needs.

Behaviour and value correlates of migration experience

Individuals think about the future on the basis of their resources, needs and values. Migration may alter any or all these factors that affect plans for the future; in turn, to the degree that changes in resources and values brought by migration are considerable, one can expect significant variations in life plans, depending on whether individuals do or do not have experience of working abroad and, also, depending on their direct or indirect experience of work, business or tourism outside the country.

The majority of former economic migrants plans to upgrade the physical structure and facilities of the current house over the next two or three years (Table 13.4), a significantly higher percentage than in the case of people without any migration abroad experience or those that lived abroad for reasons other than work. Former economic migrants are also twice as likely as those without any migration experience to have plans to build a new house, whilst they are three times more likely to plan to open a business. Both of these differences are statistically significant.

The two segments of the population with the highest propensity 'to change their lifestyles' are former economic migrants and those who did not migrate, but live in households with persons that were abroad for non-work reasons (trade, tourism, visits to relatives, etc.). An open-ended question was asked of those who planned to change their lifestyle

Table 13.3   *Responses to the question 'On what should a person returning home from work abroad spend money on?'*

Build or buy a house	32%
Develop a business	22%
Meet family needs for a better life	14%
Buy a car	5%
Invest in real estate	4%
Renovate the house	4%
Buy durable goods	3%
Assure a better future for own children	2%
Other	6%

Source: Field survey

Table 13.4   *Responses to questions about future plans 'for the next 2-3 years' (%)*

	Migration experience					Total
	Personal for work reasons	*Family for work reasons*	*Personal for non-work reasons*	*Family for non-work reasons*	*Without migration experience*	
Improve conditions in current house	56	46	43	50	37	40
Increase income by supplementary work	45	26	28	43	27	29
Get another job	35	27	14	33	21	23
Holiday abroad	35	18	51	38	13	19
Change lifestyle	27	24	16	28	14	17
Relocation to a better house	23	16	20	25	14	16
Continue studies	21	18	23	30	10	14
Build a house	23	13	17	15	11	13
Open a business	27	12	14	23	8	11
Buy land	20	10	18	8	8	10

Source: Field survey

concerning why they would do so. The majority of answers indicated a wish to 'improve their level of living'.

These differences in life plans, even if significant from the statistical point of view, could be the result of factors other than migration experience. Overall, controlling for gender, education, economic situation and residence (urban versus rural) using multivariate analysis does not cancel the significant effect of migration experience on having plans to improve migrants' housing. For example, former work migrants or persons living in households of former work migrants are more inclined to plan improvements in their current flats or houses, or to plan to build a new house, irrespective of gender, education, economic status or residence. However, adding age as a predictor changes the situation. Controlling for age differences cancels the significant impact of migration experience on plans for housing improvement, as well as on plans for changing lifestyle. The effect of migration on plans for house improvement also varies according to the regional context. The only historical region of the country where experience working abroad is associated with a higher propensity to plan for major housing improvements is Transylvania. It is here that former work emigrants have a higher propensity to make important improvements to their house, irrespective of personal characteristics (age, gender, education, goods in the household, residence).

In contrast, the intention to open a business is one of the most stable effects of having work experience abroad. This category of people is more likely to open a business, even after controlling for the personal characteristics mentioned above, age included. There are also some regional variations that characterise this relationship. It is only in the regions of Oltenia, Dobrogea and Crisana-Maramures that the experience of working abroad increases the probability of plans to open a business. In the largest regions of the country – Moldova, Muntenia and Transylvania – the link between experience of labour migration and propensity to start a business is rather poor according to the 2006 survey data used in this analysis. This regional variation is hard to explain.

Working abroad also has a significant impact on other opinions and plans that can be characterised as representing 'personal modernity'. Even after one controls for status characteristics such as education, age, gender, economic status, education or residence, those that have temporary migration experience appear more likely to take risks in order to be successful and to consider leisure time to be important in life; in turn, those who have personal non-work experience abroad are significantly more likely to consider work an important in being a successful person and to reject the idea that God is an important source of success in life.

Demographic and housing effects at community level

About one fifth of the country's communes, as basic rural administrative units, had a high rate of migration prevalence (over 30 per thousand) in 2002. These communes are mainly located in Moldova and Transylvania. At the other extreme, communes with a low rate of temporary emigration prevalence (under 10 per thousand) representing about 40 per cent out of the total communes of the country, and are located mainly in the southern regions of the country, Oltenia and Muntenia. The initial hypothesis that communes with high rates of migration will have higher rates of divorce is supported by data presented in Table 13.5. Similarly, marriage rates and rates of building new houses are also higher in regions where temporary migration is more prevalent.

However, high divorce rates may also occur in communes that are more 'modern' for reasons other than emigration – for example, because they have high levels of education or rates of marriage, low fertility rates, are closer to modernised roads and cities, or attract more in-migrants. The same may be true for birth rates, marriage rates and rates of new house building. To test this, again multivariate analysis was conducted (Table 13.6). Looking first at divorce, the analysis suggests that the effect of migration is significant even when controlling for several other important factors of community profile (age structure, education stock, location in relation to modern roads and major cities,

Table 13.5   *Demographic and housing indicators by commune*

	Rate of temporary migration prevalence in 2002*				All communes
	Very low under 1‰	*Low 2‰-10‰*	*High 10‰- 30‰*	*Very high over 30‰*	
Divorce rate 2003-2005	0.74	0.91	1.01	1.16	0.99
Marriage rate 2003-2005	11.80	14.22	15.56	17.07	15.23
Birth rate 2003-2005	9.16	10.30	11.05	11.51	10.79
New private houses 2003-2005 per 1,000 existing houses in 2003	5.93	8.68	10.12	12.24	9.87

Sources: National Institute of Statistics (NIS) data; author's own computations
Notes: Rate of temporary emigration is computed as: (number of returned emigrants in a community census in December 2001 + temporary emigrants recorded in national census March 2002) * 1,000/total population of commune in 2002.
The community census of migration is described in Sandu (2005). Averages are computed without weighting by commune population. Working with weighted data gives slightly modified figures but the same hierarchy by type of migration experience at commune level.

historical region, etc.). The aggregate data at the community level do not allow us to distinguish the effect of temporary separation within families, on the one hand, and the effects of more 'modern' attitudes, on the other. However, it is reasonable to include 'modernity' in an explanation of this phenomenon, given that we know from individual-level data that the experience of working abroad is associated with more 'modern' attitudes.

Birth rates seem to be higher in communes of high temporary emigration experience, according to the data in Table 13.5. Once one controls for several other variables as in Table 13.6, one can note that the relation has a different sense: the higher the emigration rate, the lower the birth rate, keeping under control education and age structures of the population and location factors.

The impact of temporary emigration on the marriage rate and rate of housing construction is as suggested by the bivariate data from Table 13.5. That means that, irrespective of population composition and location factors at community level, the temporary emigration has net positive effects on marriage rates and housing construction phenomena. The net positive effect of emigration on marriage rates is at odds with the H1 hypothesis that implied a negative relationship. That could be the result of the fact that the current or returned temporary migrants still have the origin community as the key reference and feel rather distant from the communities of their destination abroad.

Table 13.6 *Impact of temporary emigration on demographic and housing phenomena at rural community level (multiple regression models)*

Predictors	Dependent variables							
	Divorce rate 2003-2005**		Marriage rate 2003-2005		Birth rate 2003-2005		Private new houses in 2003-2005 per 1000 houses in 2003***	
	Coeficient	P>t	Coeficient	P>t	Coeficient	P>t		
Marriage rate 2003-2006	0.030	0.000			0.142	0.000	0.228	0.000
Education stock 2002	0.119	0.000	0.184	0.190	-2.172	0.000	4.145	0.000
In-migration rate 2003-2005	0.025	0.000	0.046	0.199	0.105	0.000	0.397	0.000
% population of 65+ years old, 2004	0.000	0.949	-0.373	0.000	-0.327	0.000	-0.281	0.000
Infant mortality rate, 2003-2005	0.000	0.950	-0.013	0.009	0.006	0.083	-0.015	0.311
Rate of temporary emigration 2002	0.001	0.000	0.011	0.000	-0.008	0.000	0.021	0.002
Population locality, 2002	-0.028	0.397	-0.057	0.807	-0.530	0.001	2.112	0.004
Geographic location (1 plain, 2 plane-hill, 3 hill 3-4 hill-mountain, 5 mountain)	0.020	0.089	0.144	0.078	-0.045	0.415	-0.802	0.002
Location close to major road*	0.103	0.001	0.212	0.337	-0.067	0.657	1.554	0.024
Distance to the nearest town/city of more than 30,000 inhabitants	-0.005	0.000	-0.008	0.273	-0.008	0.104	-0.040	0.082
Location in a southern region (Dobrogea, Muntenia, Oltenia)	0.154	0.000	1.124	0.000	-1.144	0.000	2.236	0.003
Location in Moldova region*	0.284	0.000	1.633	0.000	0.663	0.000	8.859	0.000
Location in western regions (Banat, Crisana-Maramures)*	0.069	0.087	2.009	0.000	-1.362	0.000	-3.196	0.000
Constant	-0.252	0.451	20.334	0.000	35.528	0.000	-35.475	-4.836
R2	0.140		0.28		0.440		0.18	
Number of communes for computation	2.606		2.606		2.606		2.606	

Notes on next page

*Dummy variable. Transylvania is the reference region for the dummies of regional location. Communes are the basic rural administrative units. Their number at the 2002 census was 2,686, but increased to 2,851 in 2005 (primary data sources are from the NIS; author's own computations). The significance level for regression coefficients is rather conventional as almost all communes are included in the computations. The data are not about a sample of communes but on all the statistical population of communes and the standard errors involved into computations of significance levels are related to the logic of the sampling.
**A full model included general fertility rate in 2002 as a proxy for demographic modernity of the commune. R2 increases to 0.15 and all the predictors that were significant in the restricted model continue to be in the full one. Fertility rate is a negative, significant predictor of the divorce rate, with p=0.001. Geographic location becomes a significant positive predictor in the full model.
***A full model including general fertility rate keeps the same structure of significant coefficients and R2. Fertility rate is a negative and significant predictor of housing construction for p=0.001.

Conclusions

The individual- and community-level data presented here support the initial hypothesis that migration experience abroad has a significant impact on individual- and community-level attitudes that reflect 'modernity'. The extent to which living or working abroad impacts on people's attitudes depends on the type of migration experience – whether it involved work or non-work activities, and whether it was a personal experience or the experience of a family member – and also on the regional and community context and the time period. In other words, migration abroad brings a higher level of modernity not in general, but for specific categories of people, from specific communities and regions and for certain time periods.

The modernisation of Romanian society of the 2000s as a consequence of the experience of working or living abroad can be assessed by looking at various transformations in regard to resources (influenced by remittances) and attitudes. The research emphasises modernisation effects with regard to personal lifestyle choices, but also at the community level, with regard to demographic consequences and the quality of housing. However, these modernising effects are counterbalanced by the fact that temporary migration abroad brings the costs for temporary separation from families. Each of these areas is briefly summarised below.

Values and social ideologies

Former migrant workers, irrespective of age, education, gender, economic status or residence are more inclined to base their life on risk taking, importance of work, secular motives for life success and on a higher valuation of leisure time. These are particular forms of the 'modern man syndrome' (Inkeles 1996: 572) manifested through 'openness to new experiences', favouring the time planning, the support of science and information.

Former migrants assess that working abroad is an opportunity to change one's own way of thinking in relation to work, life strategies, use of time, sociability, etc. They support such a view much more than the non-migrants.

Plans

The intention to open a business is higher for people who worked abroad, irrespective of their personal characteristics such as age, education, gender, economic status, rural-urban residence. This behaviour is a mix of higher economic resources and support for free market values, which are associated with the personal experiences of working abroad.

The analysis showed that as the experience of working abroad increases, so does the probability of having plans for more active consumer and investment behaviour, irrespective of education, gender, economic status and type of residence. However, migration experience is a differentiator with regard to consumer behaviour mainly within the same age category.

Ideologies on migration, social values and plans are differentiated significantly by type of migration experience at individual or family level, as expected, in accordance with the hypothesis H2. People who worked abroad or are part of families with non-work experience abroad are more likely to open a business or to receive income by supplementary work (Table 13.4).

Divorce

Former migrants think, to a higher degree than people without experience of working abroad, that temporary emigration is associated with a higher probability for divorce. Divorce and marriage rates are, in accordance with the hypothesis H1, significantly higher in rural communities, which have a richer experience of labour migration, irrespective of education, regional and geographic location, size of community, age structure, etc. (Table 13.6). This could be a result of new or different values, more social contacts and family separations.

Regional selectivity of migration effects

Value changes, social ideologies, plans and demographic behaviours associated with the experience of migration vary according to the regional context. Why is it that in some regions, temporary emigration has significant effects on value orientations, plans for the future or demographic or housing variables, but not in other regions? At least three types of situations could explain the variation of migration effects at the community level: the presence of a migration culture associated with high rates of temporary emigration; a longer period from the starting of the process; or a weak effect of other modernising factors at the regional level. That is the case for the Moldova region, which is poor, has very high rates of temporary emigration and a rather long experience of migration. At the other extreme is the case of Transylvania, a region that is much richer and has a much larger set of modernising opportunities.[3] Due to that configuration of factors, Transylvania is a place where temporary emigration from rural areas does not have significant effects on divorce, marriage or birth rates or the rate of new house construction. Finally, in Banat, another highly modernised region, a link is seen between migration and birth rates, but not divorce or marriage rates, or rates of new house construction. Further case study evidence would be necessary to better understand the situation in this region.

Temporary emigration is but one of the modernising factors of current time Romania acting directly at individual level. In the same series the expansion of modern mass media use could be mentioned. Access to internet is an example of how fast preconditions of cultural modernisation emerge in the country. The 2008 proportion of people aged fifteen and over who had internet access at home was around 32 per cent. This is still far from the 53 per cent average in the European Union, but the speed of the process is a considerable one if one takes the country's situation three years earlier as reference (11 per cent internet access) (Sandu, 2008).

At the structural level, the key modernising factor is the process of adjusting country institutions to the EU model. In fact, ICTs, free movement of persons and the adoption of EU institutions are acting in close connection as basic modernising factors for the post-communist Romanian society.

Notes

1   'Migration experience' in the context of this study refers to the experience of temporary emigration. Where migration is internal or permanent, this is stated explicitly.
2   Probabilistic sample of 1,400 persons, aged eighteen and over. For details on the sample see Sandu (2006a).
3   An index of community modernity was constructed as a factor score of education stock (0.83), rural to urban commuting rate in 2002 (0.85), general fertility rate in 2002 (-0.68), infant mortality rate in 2003-2005 (-0.22) and distance to the nearest city (-0.63). Figures in parenthesis indicate the loading for each variable in the component matrix from factor analysis. Based on this index, the country's regions range

from lowest to highest modernity in the following order: Moldova, Dobrogea, Oltenia, Crisana-Maramures, Muntenia, Banat, Transylvania and Bucharest-Ilfov.

References

Dayton-Johnson, J., L. Katseli, G. Maniatis, R. Muntz & D. Papademetriou (2007), *Gaining from migration: Towards a new mobility system*. Paris: OECD.

Escobar, A., K. Haibronner, P. Martin L. Meza (2006), 'Migration and development: Mexico and Turkey', *International Migration Review* 40 (3): 707-718.

Fargues, P. (2007) 'The demographic benefit of international migration: A hypothesis and its application to Middle East and North African Countries' in C. Ozden M. Schiff (eds.), *International migration, economic development & policy*, 161-182. Washington, D.C.: The World Bank & Palgrave Macmillan.

Inkeles, A. (1996), 'Making men modern: On the causes and consequences of individual change in six developing countries' in A. Inkeles & M. Sasaki (eds.), *Comparing nations and cultures: Readings in a cross-disciplinary perspective*, 571-585. Upper Saddle River: Prentice Hall.

Massey, D., J. Arango, G. Hugo, A. Kouaouci, A. Pellegrino & J.E. Taylor (1998), *Worlds in motion: Understanding international migration at the end of the millennium*. Oxford: Clarendon Press.

Ratha, D., S. Mohapatra, K.M. Vijayalakshmi & Z. Xu (2007), *Remittance trends*. http://siteresources.worldbank.org/EXTDECPROSPECTS/Resources/476882-1157133580628/BriefingNote3.pdf.

Sandu, D. (2005), 'Emerging transnational migration from Romanian villages', *Current Sociology* 53 (4): 555-582.

Sandu, D. (2006a), 'Exploring Europe by work migration: 1990-2006' in D. Sandu (ed.), *Living abroad on a temporary basis: The Romanians and the economic migration: 1990-2006*, 17-25. Bucharest: Open Society Foundation.

Sandu, D. (2007), 'Community selectivity of temporary emigration from Romania', *Romanian Journal of Population Studies* 1 (1-2): 11-45.

Sandu, D. (2008), Eurobarometer 69. Public Opinion in European Union. Spring 2008. Romania. Brussels: European Commission. http://ec.europa.eu/public_opinion/archives/eb/eb69/eb69_ro_exe.pdf.

Trebici, V. (1986), *Demografia teritorială a României [Regional Demography of Romania]*. Bucharest: Editura Academiei.

Trebici, V. (2006), *Romanian demographic yearbook*. Bucharest: National Institute of Statistics.

14 Pressure of migration on social protection systems in the enlarged EU

Krzysztof Nowaczek

Introduction[1]

Since the accession of ten new member states in 2004, the formal division between Western and Eastern European countries has diminished. However, despite clear benefits from this development, in the view of some commentators, accession has had a negative impact. One year before the enlargement, Migration Watch, a conservative London-based think-tank criticised the decision of the UK government claiming that the politicians fostered '(...) inward flows of people on a scale unknown in our history – without any apparent thought for the consequences' (Migration Watch 2003). One of the alleged consequences is a pressure of new immigrants on fragile social protection systems in Western Europe. This concern was addressed by UK Prime Minister Tony Blair in 2004, who stated that '(...) we are not against people coming here to work properly; we will not, however, allow our system to be exploited or abused' (House of Commons 2004).

For students of European integration, social policy and international migration, studying the impact of immigration on politics of redistribution in Europe might be a mutual point of departure. From a global perspective, contrary to the liberalisation of trade and capital flow, 'unblocking' free workers' circulation is lagging behind. Yet the European Union, with the guaranteed free movement of workers, has been a 'policy laboratory' where internal borders have been opened not only for goods, but also for people. For all decades of European integration, this brought about some serious socio-economic and political consequences. States have been under constant 'contradiction management' by keeping the balance between openness for migratory movements (due to labour shortages or humanitarian reasons) and closedness (caused by limited national resources and security reasons). Yet for a number of scholars, to argue whether migration poses a significant threat to the welfare state resources or if it rather provides a major support to welfare state budgets is pointless. At the current level of international migration and on the account of migration policies applied across the EU,

immigrants are not the main answer for current demographic challenges, nor do they stand at the core of the social policy-related problems. Against this background, Geddes (2003) disagrees with the
claim that migration might have a major impact on European welfare
states. Similarly, Baldwin-Edwards (2002) and Boeri and Brucker (2001)
do not identify any direct impact of migration on welfare regimes in
Europe.

In spite of this, public perception has been fuelled by less rational arguments so that policymaking has not been evidence-based but rather
anecdote-driven.[2] Summarising the concerns in the pre-enlargement
debate and referring to Borjas' research on the US case study (1997), it
might be claimed that the search for a job is not the main reason for
migration, but rather, income per se, and the welfare benefits might be
a significant source of money. Welfare magnets as such exist. It is now
debatable how important they are in terms of numbers.

The chapter is structured as follows. First, it takes stock of the studies
related to migrants' contribution to the national budget and their participation in social assistance and social security schemes.[3] It explores
the theoretical assumptions about migrants' mobility, welfare magnets
and 'organisational borders' imposed by the state. Subsequently, the
chapter focuses on the post-2004 immigration's pressure on social protection systems in the UK, Ireland and Sweden. If the thesis of 'welfare
migration' in post-enlargement Europe is to be proved correct, it should
be observed in these particular states. Finally, the chapter concludes
with some considerations on the possible changes in the scale of the
phenomenon under investigation and offers some conclusions about
the consequences of these developments for the welfare state.

Migrants' contribution to the public purse

The chapter elaborates on the case of immigrants from new member
states. It excludes from the empirical analysis the impact of third-
country nationals (see Buchel & Frick 2003; Anastassova & Paligrova
2006) but the reference to the general studies on migrants' dependence
on the welfare state and their contribution to the budget might be useful. Results of such surveys are critically dependent on the underlying
methodology and assumptions. In theory, the fiscal impact of labour
migrants on the budget largely depends on their wage, age, composition
of household and eligibility and take-up of benefits and public services.
Generally speaking, over the life cycle, natives are a net fiscal burden
while they are in compulsory education, they become net contributors
when they are employed and are a burden again when they are unemployed, retired or require extensive medical care. The pattern in the case

of migrants tends to be the same. As for the first generation, the state's budget does not fund education and newly arrived migrants might not be allowed to claim unemployment or income-related benefits for a certain preliminary period of their stay. As a consequence, it is more likely that they put less pressure on the public purse.

A cross-country comparative study on the participation of migrants in social protection systems poses serious theoretical and methodological challenges due to the variety of the types of welfare regimes, character of immigration flows and immigration policy regimes. First, the classification of welfare regimes is correlated to the scope and eligibility of social benefits and it differs across countries. For Banting (2000), this has direct consequences on migrants' incorporation. Welfare states with expansive regimes tend to have restrictive immigration control measures, but do extend benefits to migrants. On the other hand, liberal welfare regimes encourage (particularly labour) immigration, but restrict access to social benefits. However, the above typology has been criticised, especially on the account of the recent immigration policy developments and their outcomes. It has been argued that social policies' effects on migrant population have different outcomes than on citizens. In this respect, expectations regarding the migrants' access to social benefits in the countries with a given regime are not straightforward (Morissens & Sainsbury 2005). Since the research covers the case studies representing liberal (the UK and Ireland) and social-democratic (Sweden) welfare regimes (Esping-Andersen 1990), findings of this study may deepen the understanding of a relation between immigrants' dependence on social assistance programmes and the structure of the welfare state.

Second, as much as the above typology stands at the core of the problem, it is also the variety of immigration flows across time to the countries under scrutiny that should be taken into account. The level of education of migrants has a strong impact on their participation in social protection systems. In situations where low-skilled migrants prevail, it is expected that the participation of foreigners in the social protection systems will increase. Accordingly, in the 1960s, there was no evidence of immigrants relying on social benefits more heavily than natives. In the following decades, when the flow of low-skilled migrants from low-income countries intensified, economists found an increasing dependence of foreign-born population on social assistance programmes (Borjas 1999; Boeri, Hanson & McCormick 2002).

In spite of a number of studies on migrants' dependence on welfare states, the 'welfare magnet' thesis has been still an understudied subject. Both Lundborg in his survey on Scandinavian countries (1991) and Borjas on the US case (1999) found that indeed the size of the welfare system had some impact on immigration and the choice of a state of origin. To the contrary, Pedersen, Pytlikova and Smith (2004) suggested there was not enough evidence to sustain this thesis and Kaushal (2005) found that in the case of newly arrived low-skilled unmarried immigrant women, the US social assistance programmes had little effect on the choice of the target state. A generous welfare state itself might stand indeed as a 'welfare magnet', but, on the other hand, it poses some obstacles in migrants' incorporation into hosting societies. According to Bommes and Geddes (2000: 2): '(...) national welfare states can be viewed as political filters that mediate immigrants to realise their chances for social participation'. In this sense, shaping the eligibility criteria for social protection benefits has become an 'internal' method for migration management. However, as for EU citizens moving to other member states, the institutional framework built through the European Community legislation has gradually diminished these obstacles.

Welfare migration in the enlarged European Union: Consequences and solutions

For the sake of clarity of further arguments, three main principles of the European Community's social security legislation[4] should be introduced (Guild 2002). First, nationals of another member state cannot be discriminated against compared to nationals of the state. The European Court of Justice (ECJ) (1999) has already ruled against the requirement of habitual residence as a breach of the equality principle, although governments can introduce waiting periods based on contributions. Second, individuals may be affiliated to only one social security system at a time. Third, EU migrants are entitled to export their benefits to any other member state. The ECJ has interpreted these principles in a broad and favourable manner towards migrants. According to the ECJ rulings, member states could not keep their social gates closed (Ferrera 2005: 102). As Conant put it:

> (...) consistent ECJ case law has eliminated virtually every possibility to exercise discrimination based on nationality in the provision of social and tax advantages for EU nationals. (2002: 185)

In spite of the constant attempts of the European Commission and the ECJ to enhance the free movement of workers, recent reports by the European Commission on the application of European Community law show evidence of discriminatory treatment and related infringement proceedings.

Kvist's investigation (2004) built upon the assumption that western EU member states engaged in strategic interactions implying a race to the bottom in their social protection systems. The author argued that it might have been the case due to concerns about welfare migration from accessing Central and Eastern European states. Against this backdrop, three forms of mobility concerns related to enlargement were introduced. Firstly, 'social tourism' describes the migration of individuals who seek to get as many social benefits as possible with only limited contributions. Secondly, the double meaning of 'social dumping' relates to the situation in which Western companies move eastwards in order to be less constrained when it comes to wages and social standards, or migrant workers from new member states establish themselves as self-employed in EU-15 countries (on the basis of the free movement of services). The third phenomenon, 'social raid', was defined by Kvist as '(...) a surprise attack on national social security by a small or large group of people from abroad' (Kvist 2004: 306). The difference from social tourism is that in the former case, migrants do work and the work permit is actually considered as an entry ticket to welfare state benefits that are an essential contribution to the regular income. The evidence indicated by the author supports the assumptions on governmental tactic to restrain the access, eligibility and scope of social rights. Nevertheless, according to Kvist, on the basis of the developments prior to enlargement, it is impossible to claim that the EU-wide race to the bottom takes place. Different forms of restriction were merely one-time initiatives or had a temporary character.

The most critical study of free migration of citizens from accession states was Sinn and Ochel's. They argue that unrestricted intra-EU migration would lead to diminution of the welfare state (Sinn & Ochel 2003). The scholars pointed out that provisions included in the Constitutional Treaty could guarantee the constitutional right of every EU citizen to welfare migration. According to them, if 'work' is no longer a requirement before migrating, a large number of immigrants from new member states would have incentives to move to Western Europe[5] and consequently become a burden on national welfare states. Finally, this would mean that governments, trying to halt the inflow of migrants, could trigger a race to the bottom in welfare provisions. Similarly, having analysed the interaction between the welfare state and immigration policy within the old EU-15, Facchini, Razin and Willmann (2004) indicate that the 2004 enlargement and the free movement of workers might lead to an endogenous reduction in the size of the welfare state in the destination countries. This change could be the most significant in countries receiving a disproportionate share of migrants and with the most generous welfare states. In addition, Sinn and Ochel (2003) noted that east-west migration could trigger frustration about the 'too protective' welfare state. This assumption is confirmed by Alesina and Ferrara (2004) who, by application of empirical findings on the less generous US welfare state to the EU case, claimed that 'if Europeans from the middle-class come to believe that a high proportion of the poor consists of recent immigrants, this will erode their entrenched confidence in the virtues of the welfare state' (cited after Ederveen 2005: 53).

What solutions to these problems have been suggested by scholars? Bertola, Jimeno, Marimon and Pissarides (2001: 89-96) affirm that to prevent this negative trend, an EU transfer system, co-financed by the EU budget, guaranteeing a minimum welfare level to all citizens should be established. Recently, in the framework of the debate on the European Social Model, a similar idea re-emerged on the EU political agenda. In November 2006, in an interview with Prime Minister of Luxembourg, the 'Frankfurter Rundschau' Jean-Claude Juncker, made a strong plea for a 'minimum social salary throughout the EU'. However, in the opinion of politicians and scholars, this idea is not only unfeasible, but also unwise from an economic point of view. Sinn and Ochel (2003: 892-893) drew upon the 'principle of selectively delayed integration' proposed by the Ifo Institute (Sinn 2001) and the European Economic Advisory Group (2003) as an alternative to the harmonisation of replacement incomes. Following this principle, new EU immigrants would have free access to the selected provisions, yet the access to the range of other benefits would be restricted so that the social assistance payments received by migrants would be balanced to the contributions they made through taxation. This would ensure that while the rule of free movement of workers is observed, migration would be driven by genuine market signals and the abuse of the welfare state would not take place. This solution was promoted as a better and more economically rational alternative compared to the restrictions on free mobility of workers introduced by most member states following the 2004 enlargement. As a matter of fact, two countries, i.e. the UK and Ireland, followed this line of reasoning and applied provisions mirroring the 'principle of selective delayed integration'.

Migrants' dependence on welfare state: Case studies

The following sections demonstrate data on the selected countries: the UK, Ireland and Sweden. In all three countries, migrants from CEE countries have had unlimited access to labour markets. However, only in Sweden have newcomers been entitled to social benefits without any extra conditions, while the UK and Ireland introduced a requirement of a two-year long habitual residency. Each analysis commences with the pre-enlargement debate and institutional developments on the topic under scrutiny. The sections are followed by a description of the available data on the dependence of migrants from new member states on various social benefit programmes.

United Kingdom

The government's Report on Community Cohesion dramatically underlined the pressure of immigrants on local resources:

> (...) inward migration does create tensions (...) communities will perceive that newcomers are in competition for scarce resources and public services (...). The pressure on resources (...) is often intense and local services are often insufficient to meet the needs of the existing local communities, let alone newcomers. (Community Cohesion Panel 2004)

In this context, the words of Immigration Minister Tony McNulty, mirroring local sentiments, came as no surprise. Launching the Consultation on Managed Migration Routes to the UK – *Making Migration Work for Britain* – he declared that:

> (...) this country needs migration – [they] make a vital contribution to the UK economy. We need to ensure, however, that while we let in migrants with the skills and talents to benefit Britain we stop those who are trying to abuse our hospitality and place a burden on our society. (Home Office 2005)

In summer 2006, the report *Migration from Eastern Europe: Impact on public services and community cohesion* initiated a hot debate about the effects of the past and future migration flows from Eastern Europe. Most newspapers cited the most 'juicy' parts of the document stating that '(...) immigrants *from Eastern Europe* who were sleeping rough – sometimes because of the welfare ban – were becoming drunk and aggressive and filling up homeless hostels' or that 'Eastern European patients are also already 'blocking' hospital beds because they are ineligible for social care and benefits if they leave'. On top of societal and health challenges, the evidence suggested that more English teachers are required in the near future and the price of housing had risen dramatically due to the high demand. Media suggested that this might lead to 'ghettoisation' of some areas and even further social disturbance. The report was published a few months before another enlargement (January 2007) when more Bulgarians and Romanians were expected to arrive in the UK. Against this background, according to the media, the report concluded with sweet and sour predictions for the future:

(...) despite the Government's underestimation of the number of migrants, public services had generally coped (...). But the expected influx of Romanians and Bulgarians meant that this optimistic assessment may not continue to hold good in, say, a year's time.

Were such dramatic reactions justified on the basis of numerical evidence? Pre-enlargement government's estimations on a number of newcomers from A8 countries proved underestimated. This provided a very strong argument to opponents of unrestricted migration (e.g. UK Migration Watch). In the period 2005-2006, Poland, Lithuania and Slovakia were among the top five countries of origin applicants for national insurance numbers (171,000, 30,000 and 26,000, respectively). The number of National Insurance Numbers (NINos) allocated to foreigners from A8 countries increased dramatically, i.e. almost a ten-fold growth between the second quarter of 2004 and the second quarter of 2007 (see bars on Figure 14.1). While there has been an almost constant growth of issued by the UK authorities to A8 migrant workers, it is striking how few of them were allocated to 'benefit purposes' (see line on Figure 14.1). In the period between May 2004 and June 2007, 5,193 NINos for benefit purposes were issued, which accounted only for 0.7 per cent of all 681,536 NINos. Only in the first quarter of 2007, this percentage exceeded one point.

As for tax-funded, income-related benefits, the Home Office measures applications for three kinds of benefits: income support, income-based Jobseeker's Allowance and state pension credit.[6] There has been

Figure 14.1   *National Insurance Numbers allocated for employment and benefit purposes to A8 nationals, UK, May 2004 – June 2007*

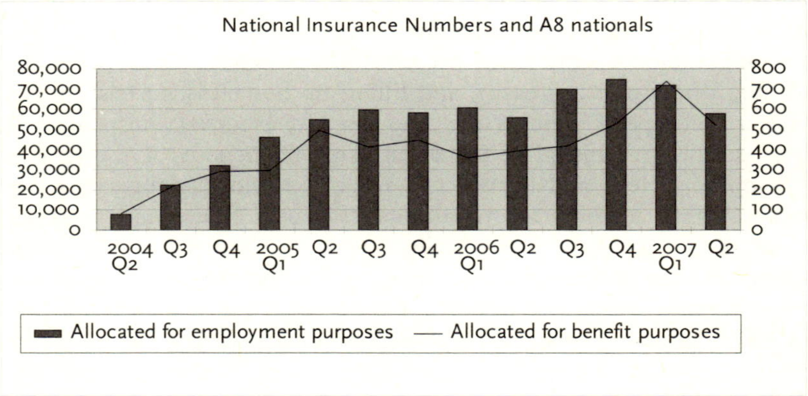

Sources: Home Office (2005: 22, 2007: 23)

a growing tendency of A8 nationals' recourses to social payments, yet the growth in absolute numbers is still minimal (Figure 14.2). In total, in the period under scrutiny (May 2004-June 2007) 3,600 applications for income-related benefits were approved. Around 1,805 applications were accepted in the first half of 2007, which accounts for almost half of all approved applications in the entire period.

A8 nationals received much more in child benefit payments. Approved applications for child benefits reached 12,000 at the beginning of 2007, which was an eight-fold increase compared to the analogical period in 2005[7] (see Figure 14.3).

Three important factors that influence migrants' pressure on the welfare state: the age of foreign nationals, the composition of their families and the length of stay, can be somewhat telling in the UK case. Immigrants from A8 countries are relatively young with over eight out of ten applicants being younger than 34. Simultaneously, between May 2004 and June 2007, only a small minority (7 per cent) of registered workers declared that they had dependents living with them in the UK at the moment of application. Amongst those who did have dependents, the average number of dependents was 1.5. In total, for each dependent, there are ten registered workers. According to the replies provided by applicants to WRS, it seems that more than half of A8 nationals do not intend to stay more than three months in the UK (Home Office 2007: 10-12).

Figure 14.2 *Applications from A8 migrants for tax-funded, income-related benefits (income support, income-based Jobseeker's Allowance and state pension credit), UK Q2 of 2004 – Q4 of 2006*

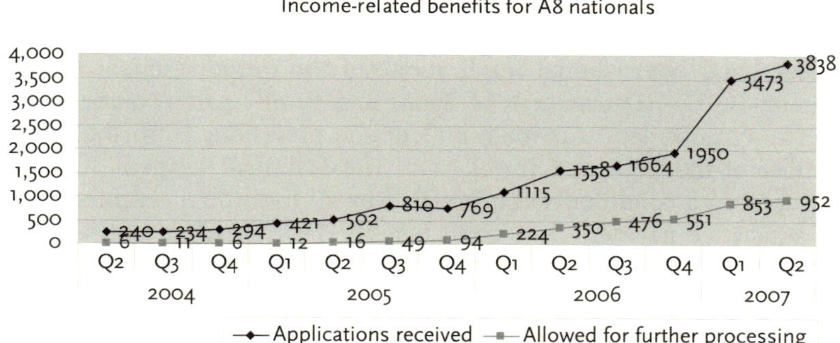

Source: Home Office (2007: 25)

Figure 14.3   *Applications for Child Benefit, UK, Q2 of 2004 – Q2 of 2007*

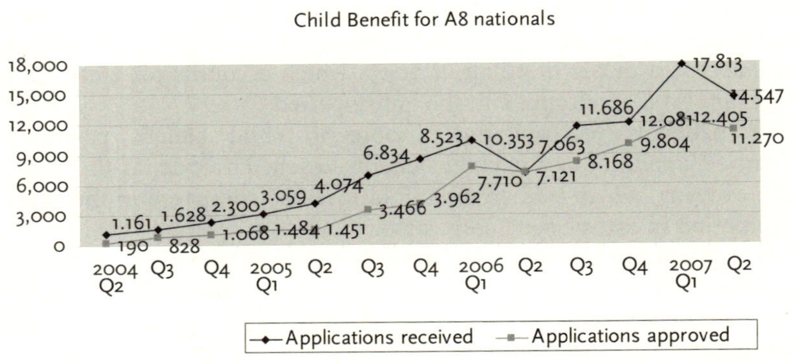

Source: Home Office (2007: 28)

Ireland

Given the very good macroeconomic indicators in Ireland, the pre-
enlargement debate in Ireland focused more on protecting the welfare
system from possible abuse rather than limiting access of new member
states' nationals to the labour market. In autumn 2003, the prime minister established an inter-departmental committee to assess the consequences of opening labour markets on Ireland's social protection system. The Department of Social and Family Affairs was one of the first
departments required to give closer consideration to the potential implications of EU migration for the provision of its services (National
Economic and Social Council 2006: 206). Several lobby groups, such
as the Immigration Control Platform and the National Platform, advo-
cated for protecting Ireland's social welfare system. Following public
pressure and international implications of the introduction of restrictions in the UK (Department of Social and Family Affairs 2004a), the
government decided to partially mirror the provisions from the fellow
member of the Common Travel Area. The Habitual Resident Test was
envisaged as a condition to be satisfied by an individual claiming a social assistance payment or a child benefit. This 'prudent and sensible
measure for the benefit of recipients and those who fund the annual social welfare budget' was introduced – as underlined by Minister for
Social and Family Affairs Mary Coughlan –, to 'ensure our social welfare system does not become over burdened'. The restriction was considered as a ring fencing the system of social protection (Department of
Social and Family Affairs 2004b).

Besides a substantial continuous period of residence (at least two years), five other criteria, officially based on the ECJ jurisprudence (European Court of Justice 1999), establish the eligibility for Habitual Residence Condition. The criteria relate to the character of stay, absence from Ireland, employment, main centre of interest in Ireland and future intentions (Department of Social and Family Affairs 2005). The introduction of HRC was a significant change in the legal regime since, until May 2004, every person legally residing in Ireland, even for a short period of time, and satisfying the conditions related to the payments was immediately upon arrival eligible for social welfare. Four months after the enlargement, Coughlan declared that:

> (...) the Habitual Residence Condition is being operated in a very careful manner to ensure that Ireland's social welfare system is no longer open to everyone who is newly arrived in Ireland, while at the same time ensuring that people whose cases are appropriate to the Irish social welfare system get access to social assistance when they need it. (Department of Social and Family Affairs 2004c)

Nevertheless, in its Letter of Formal Notice to Ireland on 22 December 2004, the European Commission challenged some rules of procedures related to access to benefits. The European Commission pointed out that the two-year requirement might be a breach to the EU Regulations 1408/71 and 1612/71. Highlighted was the fact that the new conditions were more likely to affect migrant workers than workers of Irish nationality or those already residing in Ireland before the Common Travel Area. Irish authorities were warned that these might have constituted discrimination on the grounds of nationality (Department of Social and Family Affairs 2006: 22). In particular, the European Commission pointed out that some benefits (such as child benefit or family payments) should have been available for workers from all EU countries, irrespective of the fulfilment of conditions attached to the HRC. Consequently, those considered 'workers' (or those who had previously worked and paid contributions) should become eligible for social welfare allowance regardless of the HRC. Additionally, EU workers can access child benefit even if their children are not resident in the state. With reference to the required changes, the Department of Social and Family Affairs sent a circular to community welfare officers reminding them that migrants from other EU states should be treated in the same manner that Irish workers are treated in the access to Supplementary Welfare Allowance.[8] In the internal review of the Habitual Residence Condition, the Department of Social and Family Affairs reminded the deciding officers to take into consideration the national legislation as well as the EU regulations dealing with this issue (Department of Social and Family Affairs 2006: 19). After clarifications submitted by the government and changes introduced to the domestic system, on 4 April 2006, the European Commission decided not to pursue the infringement proceeding, stating that Ireland complies fully with the European Community legislation.

From May 2004 to the end of April 2006, non-Irish citizens submitted 25,571 applications for social benefit payments. Nationals from ten new member states filed over 5,000 applications, which accounted for almost exactly 20 per cent of all applications. During this period, around 200,000 persons from A10 countries were allocated Personal Public Service Numbers. That means that the number of claimants from these states represents only 2.5 per cent of the total number of immigrants from new member states residing in Ireland. Citizens from Western Europe submitted not more than 30 per cent applications with a large majority of requests being filed by UK citizens (due to the Common Travel Area arrangements). The 'success rate' in the case of new member states' nationals' requests was around 50 per cent (Figure 14.5).

The most 'popular schemes' among foreigners were unemployment assistance and child benefit, which accounted for over 85 per cent of all applications.[9] This is not surprising since child benefit is the main income support scheme for families, while unemployment assistance is the main short-term social assistance allowance available to people of working age (Department of Social and Family Affairs 2006: 7-8).

Figure 14.5 *Total number of applications for various social assistance schemes filed by foreigners, Ireland, May 2004 – April 2006*

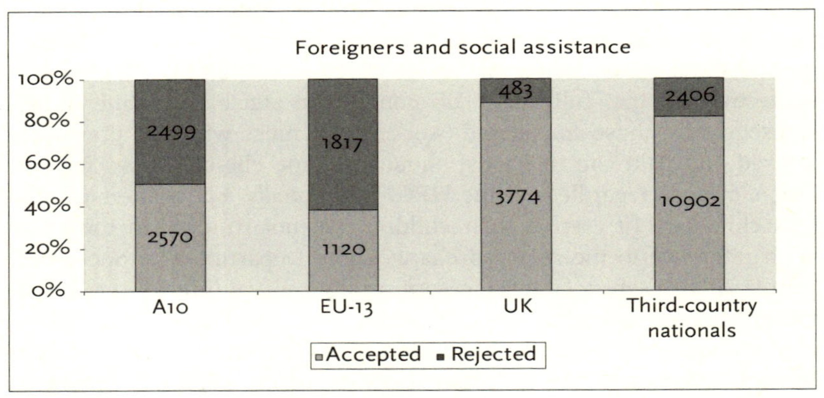

Source: Department of Social and Family Affairs (2006: 7)

Among various forms of social assistance, immigrants from new member states applied most often to unemployment assistance (around 25 per cent of applications submitted by all foreigners). Child benefit was less popular among nationals from these countries, accounting for around 15 per cent of all foreigners' applications. Over 70 per cent of all applications for child benefit were filed by third-country nationals (Figure 14.6).

Other forms of social payments are Supplementary Welfare Allowances (SWA). Basic SWA is distributed among persons with no means to meet their basic needs at a rate equivalent to other social welfare payments, such as unemployment assistance. Those entitled to Basic SWA or having an equivalent level of income are also eligible for receiving an ongoing payment in respect of house rental; its most common form is Rent Supplement. Although data available are limited only to payments made in the week ending in 30 June 2006, they give a clear picture of the recourse of foreign citizens to additional supplementary allowances (Figure 14.7). Migrants from ten new member states received more payments in total than nationals from thirteen member states from Western Europe (nearly five times more payments in the case of Basic SWA). Yet, the total number of payments distributed to the former group of migrants accounted for not more than 3.5 per cent of the entire outflow of Basic SWA and 2 per cent of Rent Supplement. This is much less than in the case of third-country

Figure 14.6   *Number of applications by scheme and nationality, Ireland, May 2004 – April 2006*

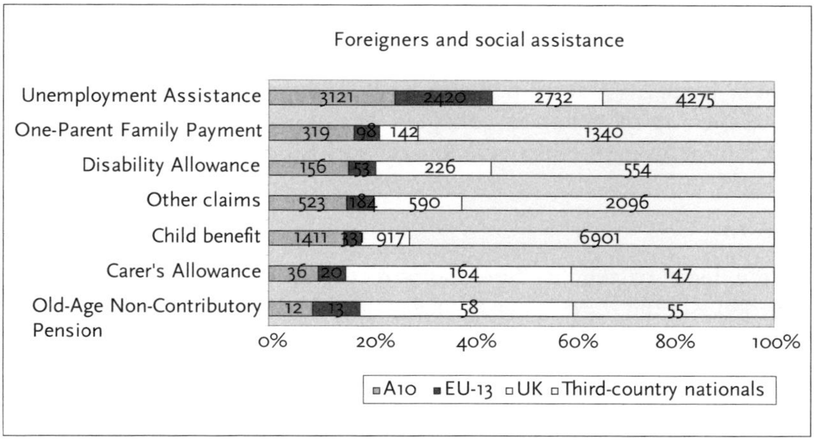

Source: Department of Social and Family Affairs (2006: 7)

Figure 14.7 *Payments of Basic Supplementary Welfare Allowance and Rent Supplement recipients made in the week ending in 30 June 2006*

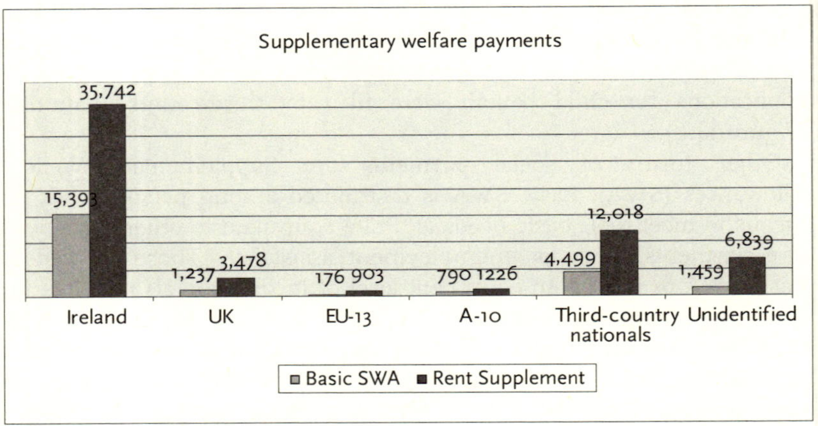

Source: Department of Social and Family Affairs (2006: 9)

nationals who received nearly 20 per cent of all Basic SWA and Rent Supplement payments.

The Irish authorities reported that more than 140 nationalities are listed for recipients of Basic SWA payment and more than 150 Rent Supplements. Besides Irish and UK citizens, migrants receiving the most Basic SWA and Rent Supplements were from Nigeria (8 per cent), Romania (around 3 per cent) and the Democratic Republic of Congo (1 per cent). Comparing to migrants from A10 countries, the top three applicants were from Lithuania, Poland and Latvia, the total number of applicants from these three countries accounted for only 2 per cent in the case of Basic SWA and 1 per cent for Rent Supplement. Payments made to this group of nationals constituted respectively 57 per cent and 50 per cent of all payments made to nationals from A10 states.

Sweden

If the logic of the 'welfare tourism' thesis is to be proved correct, Sweden should have already been flooded by immigrants from A8 countries. The 2002 government report estimated that although immigration might cause only minor disturbances in the labour market, and that it was the vulnerability of the Swedish welfare system (exposed to organised crime and unscrupulous employers) that should trigger a decision on transitional measures. In November 2003, on the basis of the findings of the government report,[10] the Swedish national television broadcast a documentary on the possible problem caused by immigrants from Central and Eastern European coming with their families, working only ten hours per week, and benefiting from the welfare provisions (SIEPS 2006: 82-83).

Before the end of 2003, the Swedish government did not consider the introduction of transitional measures. However, in November 2003, Prime Minister of Sweden Göran Persson expressed concerns about the Swedish welfare system after the enlargement and a possible abuse of the welfare system by immigrants from A8 countries (SIEPS 2006: 77). Bearing in mind the above developments, it was rather ironic that, in general, the Swedish media followed a more liberal standpoint and the great majority of articles from that period were supportive towards immigration and criticised the government's U-turn. As the analysis of the pre-enlargement poll suggested, public opinion varied depending on the specific wording of the questions asked in the surveys. In total, some anti-immigration feelings were present in Swedish society, but they were not solid enough to trigger a more radical behaviour of political parties (SIEPS 2006: 83-87).

The reports published by the Swedish Social Insurance Administration (Lönnqvist 2005, 2007), showed that the amount of payments of family benefits to EU nationals tripled between March 2004 and December 2004 and reached the level of approximately € 1.3 million. Yet throughout 2006, the monthly payments did not drop below € 1.8 million (February 2006) and reached the peak in December 2006 with nearly € 2.5 million. In 2004, out of the total amount of approximately € 8 million, 78 per cent of payments went to citizens of the other Nordic states (i.e. Denmark, Finland, Iceland and Norway) and only approximately 1 per cent of that sum (around € 108,000) was granted between May and December 2004 to migrants from the ten new member states (Figure 14.8). 2006 saw significant growth of family benefit payments to EU nationals, i.e. around € 26 million. The proportion of payments to nationals from new member states grew to 5 per cent of the entire sum and in the absolute terms it increased over eleven times to the amount of around € 1.25 million.

The Swedish reports addressed also the key concern of the Swedish public. Are our welfare benefits exported to other EU countries (and particularly new member states)? According to the Regulation 1408/71 (Council 1971), non-Swedish EU nationals working in Sweden are eligible, upon meeting certain criteria, to benefits for their family members still residing in the country of origin.[11] In 2004, out of around € 8 million paid to EU migrants, not more than € 1.5 million went to family members residing abroad. Most social benefits transferred outside Sweden were received by family members residing in Nordic countries (Finland, Denmark, Norway and Iceland), due to geographic proximity

Figure 14.8   *Allocation of family benefits to EU nationals 2004 and 2006; data for*
2004 refer to the period March – December; May – December 2004 in
the case of new member states

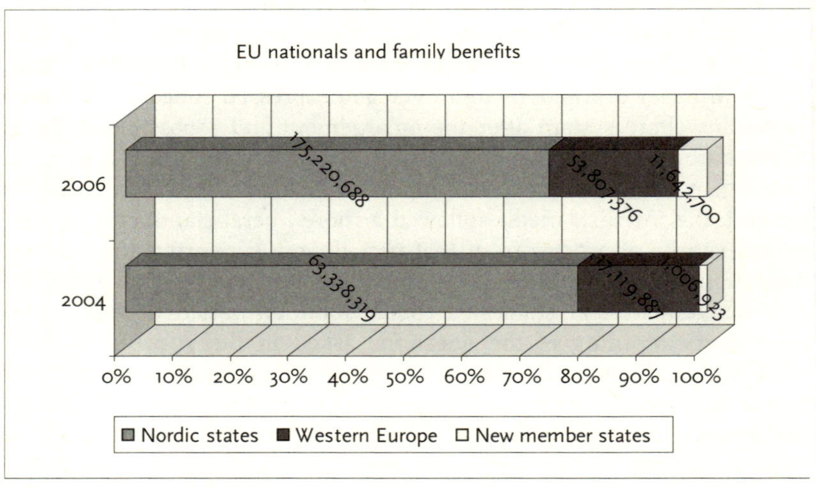

Source: Lönnqvist (2005: 14, 2007: 15)

and bilateral agreements, and some old member states (UK and the
Netherlands). Export of payments to new member states was quite insignificant. Between May and December 2004, not more than € 15,000
were sent to family members residing in the new member states.
Interestingly enough, most benefits were paid at the end of the year.
Within this group, Polish and Hungarian citizens received the highest
amount of allowances. In 2006, the entire amount of benefits transferred outside Sweden doubled to the sum of € 3.3 million. Payments
sent to new member states increased nearly six times, yet in absolute
number, around € 85,000 was still an insignificant amount
(Försäkringskassan 2005: 24, 2007: 22).

As highlighted in the Swedish Social Insurance Administration report, there is an increasing awareness of migrants regarding their social
rights under the EU legislation, also due to the government's efforts to
inform migrants about their status. The report therefore indicates that a
low percentage of migrants from new member states benefiting from
social assistance payments cannot be explained by the lack of information. The report suggests that the amount of payments will increase in
the future, but the present evidence does not suggest that the Swedish
welfare state is under threat (Försäkringskassan 2005: 8, 13). As a matter of fact, although payments of family benefits to non-Swedish

citizens increased noticeably, in absolute numbers it did not amount to worrying evidence. It is sufficient to put the 2006 amounts into the wider context to notice that only around 1 per cent of the entire spending on family benefits goes to pockets of non-Swedish EU citizens (Försäkringskassan 2007: 23).

Results and some preliminary conclusions: Implications of welfare tourism on the welfare state?

Scarce availability of relevant quantitative data on immigrants' welfare dependence was a major constraint in elaborating a genuine comparative study in this respect. Numbers provided by national administrations related to different programmes, covered different periods and different categories of immigrants. In spite of technical difficulties, some general results can be suggested. The pre-enlargement debate in the three countries was an arena for the clash of different opinions and different forces. Owing to the membership in the Common Travel Area, Ireland listened carefully to the discussion in the UK and consequently decided to follow the UK restrictions in the access to social benefits. Sweden, the most liberal in this respect, was not under very strong domestic pressure and restrained from imposing similar limitations. Sweden served as a case study to address two assumptions. Firstly, in spite of the total opening of the labour market and granting unlimited access to social assistance programmes, there was no large growth in the number of individuals from these countries before and after the enlargement. Secondly, evidence suggested that immigrants from new member states did not use the 'window of opportunity' provided by the EU legislation to export social benefits to their country of origin on a large scale.

On the other hand, a growth of applications for most social benefits was observed in the UK case and reached a peak in 2006. However, absolute numbers are still limited. Similarly, data on the Irish case provided no evidence of the public purse being under significant pressure. A number of applications were relatively small compared to those filed by UK nationals or third-country nationals. Drawing upon the 'welfare magnet' assumption, the above analysis proved Borjas' assumption (1997) wrong. For immigrants from new member states, it was not social benefits but rather work itself that was the main source of financial income; employment, rather than the possibility to receive benefits, stood at the foundation of the decision to migrate.

To understand implications of different welfare regimes for migrants' dependence on social protection programmes, one would need more data than those currently available. In future research, two working hypotheses could be tested. The first and the more obvious one would imply that, in social-democratic regimes, welfare state provisions are distributed more generously towards newcomers and, as such, play a greater factor in migrants' decision to move to the relevant country. However, to challenge this assumption it is necessary to wait for the complete abolition of barriers in free movement of workers. The second and somewhat more 'revolutionary' hypothesis could claim that in the studies on a relation between dependence on social benefits and welfare state regimes, a simple division between 'citizens' and 'immigrants' does not suffice anymore. With the rapid growth of east-west migration and hitherto unprecedented constitutionalisation of social rights at the EU level, a more persistent attempt to include in all studies a new category of recipients, i.e. intra-EU immigrants, is required. In studying immigration and welfare state, this particular category of immigrants stands somewhere in-between citizens and newcomers from third-country nationals. It is evident not only from the legal and political points of view, but also in the psychological (e.g. motivation to migrate) and social (e.g. strengthening social cohesion) contexts.

What can explain the findings provided by the three case studies in question? Demographic features (i.e. relatively young age) and family status (i.e. single and/or no children) of immigrants from new member states could be decisive why dependence on social assistance of this group of immigrants has been limited. Large numbers of immigrants considered work in another member state only as a temporary solution. In the UK case, age composition of immigrants from CEE countries has been stable throughout the last four years (around 80 per cent of registered workers were aged 18-34). While the number of dependents as a proportion of the number of registered workers still remains low, it has been steadily growing from 7 per cent in 2004, 13 per cent in 2006 and over 17.5 per cent in the first semester 2008 (it should be noted, however, that the Home Office does not verify the responses given by immigrants in WRS application on which base the number of dependents is calculated).

Several factors helped migrants apply for social benefits depending on needs. Networks of immigrants already residing in key destination cities (i.e. London, Dublin or Stockholm) provided new migrants with information about the eligibility and procedures on social assistance programmes. More details could have been found in newspapers and a number of online forums where immigrants exchanged experiences about the best paths to follow in order to access benefits. Following the transparency rules and in the framework of a campaign promoting social rights' protection, national authorities and non-governmental organisations wanted also to ensure that newcomers would be aware of the social assistance programmes. Information included on websites or leaflets was published also in the languages of immigrants and distributed even in their countries of origin.[12] Last but not least, besides being a strong advocate of uplifting the transitional periods in other member states, the European Commission has carefully observed the rules applied in the UK, Sweden and Ireland. It successfully intervened with the Irish authorities when pre-enlargement restrictions were found incoherent with the current *acquis communautaire*. This interesting development proved again that member states cannot unconditionally decide upon eligibility of EU nationals to social benefits. If this door has been closed for national authorities, is the reduction in the size of the welfare state a solution for continued flows of immigrants from new member states and the pressure on social policy expenditure?

Some preliminary ideas on this question are as follows: previous studies on immigration and redistribution proved that international migration indeed has mattered in relation to the size of the welfare state. Although all developed Western countries increased their social policy expenditures, growth was smaller in the states more open to immigration. It was mainly the pressure of the native population on mainstream political parties that might have led to a slower expansion of the welfare state in the face of growing immigration (Soroka, Banting & Johnston 2003). Owing to internal market rules and particularly the principle of the free movement of persons, member states cannot limit the inflow of EU migrants. On the other hand, their social policies are not constrained by the European Community legislation and are merely coordinated at the EU level (through the open method of coordination) and based on general standards (such as non-discrimination provisions). Is it hence the case that under the pressure of migrants, EU welfare states shrink? This question could serve as the basis of another study altogether. A quick overview of the development of the welfare state in member states suggests that it is not the case. National authorities have recently decided to allocate more financial resources to social policy-related programmes and to increase rates for social benefits' payments. In this sense, intra-EU migration has not influenced public spending on social policy. On the contrary, what has rather preoccupied policymakers was the recent trend to *enhance* social cohesion.

In all three countries under scrutiny, the amount of social benefits received by immigrants from new member states has been relatively small, but seems to be growing in scale. For the time being, EU migration has not proved to be a major challenge for welfare state systems. It might be considered problematic (especially in the public and policy discourse) in a short-term perspective. It is, however, a minor problem compared to the economies' race for increased competitiveness under the pressure of globalisation, a relatively small rate of employment and ageing societies – phenomena that are having a greater impact on the welfare state. Last but not least, intra-EU migration is perceived as a marginal challenge in comparison with the inflow of third-country nationals and the resulting implications for the European societies.

Notes

1   The author wishes to acknowledge the support of Collegio Carlo Alberto from Moncalieri (Turin), Italy, in conducting the research.
2   A survey conducted in 2001 (EUMC 2001) indicated that 52 per cent of respondents supported the statement that people from minority groups abuse the social welfare system. It was an increase of 4 per cent compared to figures from 1997.
3   As defined in Article 4 of EC Council Regulation No. 1408/71 on the application of social security schemes to employed persons and their families moving within the European Community, social security branches include sickness and maternity benefits, invalidity benefits, old-age benefits, survivors' benefits, benefits in respect of accidents at work and occupational diseases, death grants, unemployment benefits and family benefits. Naturally due to the scarcity of data and their limited relevance, not all above schemes are covered in the study.
4   For the wider coverage on the current *acquis* in this field refer to Ochel's chapter in this volume.
5   In 2001, net income in new member states was less than 30 per cent of German social assistance (Sinn & Ochel 2003: 891-892).
6   Depending on the age and family status, claimants receive £ 34,60 to £ 90,10 weekly. Weekly Jobseekers' Allowance means £ 34,60 for claimants between eighteen and 24 and £ 45,50 for persons aged 25 or over. Pension Credit guarantees everyone aged 60 and over an income of at least £ 114.05 a week for a single person, and £ 174.05 a week for an applicant with a partner. Data available at: www.dwp.gov.uk/asd/tabtool.asp.
7   For the tax year 2006-2007, the Guardian's Allowance accounts for £ 12.50 a week per child.
8   All EU workers, as long as they have a history of 'effective and genuine work' (to be decided by the Community Welfare Officer), are entitled to these allowances. Most Exceptional Needs Payments are not available to newly arrived migrants, but a different approach is employed for migrants with children at school or with the intention to stay. The Reception and Integration Agency (RIA) offers accommodation (up to three nights) to EU nationals pending their repatriation. The RIA also organises and pays for the return journey home.
9   The current rate of unemployment assistance is € 185.80 per week, with an additional € 22 for each qualified child. Monthly child benefit allowance for the first and second child is € 150; for the third and subsequent children it reaches € 185. Starting in April 2007, the rates increased by € 10. The maximum weekly rate of the Carer's Allowance is € 180 if an applicant takes care of one person and € 270 if he or she cares for two people or more.
10   Drawing upon the ECJ cases, the 2002 report stipulated that even the 'ten hour per week' employment would suffice to access social benefits. The 'ten-hour-rule' became a benchmark (at least for the Swedish public and media) and was confirmed by the European Commission in its communication on free movement of workers (Commission 2002: 5).
11   Monthly child benefit accounts for around € 100 per child. Large family supplements are also available, e.g. families with children receive an extra allowance of

approximately € 220. More detailed data available at www.forsakringskassan.se/fak-ta/andra_sprak/barnbidrag_eng/index.php.

2 According to an interview-based survey on labour migration from Poland (sample of 44 respondents), the perception of possible benefits granted by the state has been high. Almost half of respondents had some knowledge about social benefits available in Ireland and one-fourth of interviewees received a child benefit allowance. Quoted in the report, a 26-year-old 'would-be-migrant' underlined that family benefits seemed to be much higher in Ireland and '(...) moving just with children should be worth the effort' (Radiukiewicz 2006: 40).

References

Alesina, A. & E. La Ferrara (2004), 'Ethnic diversity and economic performance', *NBER Working Paper* 10313.

Anastassova, L. & T. Paligrova (2006), 'What is behind native-immigrant social income gaps?', *Luxembourg Income Study Working Paper* 432.

Baldwin-Edwards, M. (2002), *Immigration and the welfare state: A European challenge to American mythology*, paper presented at the 'Europe-Mediterranean Immigration Policy Conference', Barcelona, 30 January 2002.

Banting, K. (2000), 'Looking in three directions: Migration and the European welfare state in comparative perspective', in M. Bommes & A. Geddes (eds.), *Immigration and welfare: Challenging the borders of the welfare state*, 13-33. London: Routledge.

Bertola, G., J. F. Jimeno, R. Marimon & C. Pissarides (2001), 'EU welfare systems and labor markets: Diverse in the past, integrated in the future?', in G. Bertola, T. Boeri & N. Giuseppe (eds.), *Welfare and employment in a united Europe*, 23-122. Cambridge/London: MIT Press.

Boeri, T. & H. Brücker (2001), 'Eastern enlargement and EU-labour markets: Challenges and opportunities', *World Economics* 2 (1): 49-67.

Boeri, T., G. Hanson & B. McCormick (2002), *Immigration policy and the welfare system*. Oxford: Oxford University Press.

Bommes, M. & A. Geddes (eds.) (2000), *Immigration and welfare: Challenging the borders of the welfare state*. London: Routledge.

Borjas, G. J. (1997), 'Immigration & welfare: Solving the welfare problem will solve the welfare problem – not the immigration problem', *National Review* 6: 34-38.

Borjas, G. J. (1999), 'Immigration and welfare magnets', *Journal of Labor Economics* 17: 607-637.

Buchel, F. & J. R. Frick (2003), 'Immigrants' economic performance across Europe – does immigration policy matter?', *European Panel Analysis Group Working Paper* 42.

Commission (2002), 'Communication on Free Movement of Workers – Achieving the full benefits and potential', COM (2002) 694, 11 December 2002.

Community Cohesion Panel (2004), *The end of parallel lives?* London: The Community Cohesion Panel.

Conant, L. (2002), *Justice contained. Law and politics in the European Union.* Ithaca/London: Cornell University Press.

Council (1971), 'Regulation on the application of social security schemes to employed persons and their families moving within the Community', 1408/71, 14 June 1971.

Department of Social and Family Affairs (2004a), 'Mary Coughlan Minister for Social and Family Affairs to announce new social welfare code restrictions'. www.welfare.ie/press/pr04/index04.html.

Department of Social and Family Affairs (2004b), 'Mary Coughlan Minister for Social and Family Affairs announces restrictions on access to social welfare', www.welfare.ie/press/pr04/index04.html.

Department of Social and Family Affairs (2004c), *Missionaries, Old Age Non-Contributory Pension and Habitual Residence Condition.* www.welfare.ie/press/pr04/index04.html.

Department of Social and Family Affairs (2005), *Habitual Residence Condition.*www.welfare.ie/publications/hrc.html.

Department of Social and Family Affairs (2006), *The Operation of the Habitual Residence Condition. An internal review.* www.welfare.ie/publications/hrcreview06.pdf.

Ederveen, S. (2005), 'Destination Europe: Immigration and integration in the European Union. European Outlook 2. Annex to the State of the European Union 2005', The Hague: Bureau for Economic Policy Analysis, Social and Cultural Planning Office of the Netherlands.

Esping-Andersen, G. (1990), *The words of welfare capitalism.* New York: Polity Press.

EUMC (2001), *Attitudes Towards Minority Groups in the European Union. A Special Analysis of the Eurobarometer Year 2000 Survey.* Vienna: European Monitoring Centre on Racism and Xenophobia.

European Court of Justice (1999), *Case C-90/97 Robin Swaddling vs. Adjudication Officer.*

European Economic Advisory Group (2003), *Report on the European Economy 2003.* Munich: CESifo.

Facchini, G., A. Razin & G. Willmann (2004), 'Welfare leakage and immigration policy', *CESifo Economic Studies* 50 (4): 627-645.

Ferrera, M. (2005), *The boundaries of welfare. European integration and the new spatial politics of social protection.* Oxford: Oxford University Press.

Försäkringskassan (2005), 'Utbetalning av familjeförmåner med stöd av EG-lagstiftningen under 2004', *Försäkringskassan Analyserar* 3.

Försäkringskassan (2007), 'Utbetalning av familjeförmåner med stöd av EG-lagstiftningen under 2006', *Försäkringskassan Analyserar* 10.

Geddes, A. (2005), 'Europe's border relationships and international migration relations', *Journal of Common Market Studies* 43 (4): 787-806.

Guild, E. (2002), 'The legal framework of EU migration: Background paper', *The Working Paper of The Political Economy of Migration in an Integrating Europe* 2.

Home Office (2005) *Making migration work for Britain.* www.workingintheuk.gov.uk/working_in_the_uk/en/homepage/news/announcements/making_migration_work.html.

Home Office (2007), *Accession monitoring report, May 2004-June 2007. A joint online report by the Home Office, Department for Work and Pensions.* www.ind.homeoffice.gov.uk/aboutus/reports/accession_monitoring_report.

House of Commons (2004) *Hansard Debates, 11 February 2004.* www.publications.parliament.uk/pa/cm/cmhansrd.htm.

Juncker, J. C. (2006), *Wir brauchen in Europa ein Grundeinkommen für alle.* www.gouvernement.lu/salle_presse/Interviews/2006/11novembre/20juncker_rundschau.

Kaushal, N. (2005), 'New immigrants' location choices: Magnets without welfare', *Journal of Labor Economics* 23 (1): 59-80.

Migration Watch (2003), *Migration from new European EU members grossly understated.* www.migrationwatchuk.org/pressreleases/pressreleases.asp?dt=01-August-2003.

Morissens, A. & D. Sainsburg (2005), 'Migrants' social rights, ethnicity and welfare regimes', *Journal of Social Policy* 34 (4): 637-660.

National Economic and Social Council (2006), *Managing migration in Ireland: A social and economic analysis. A report by the International Organisation for Migration.* Dublin: National Economic and Social Council of Ireland.

Pedersen, P. J., M. Pytlikova & N. Smith (2004), 'Selection or network effects? Migration flows into 27 OECD countries, 1990-2000', IZA *Discussion Paper* 1104.

Radiukiewicz, A. (2006), *Emigracja zarobkowa Polakow do Irlandii. Report prepared for European Citizen Action Service.*
www.zbpo.org.pl/page/en/aktualnosci/raport_amp8222em.

Sinn, H. W. (2001), 'Social dumping in the transformation process?', CESifo *Working Paper* 508.

Sinn, H. W. & W. Ochel (2003), 'Social union, convergence and migration', *Journal of Common Market Studies* 41 (5): 869-896.

Soroka, S., K. Banting & R. Johnston (2003), 'Immigration and redistribution in a global era', paper presented at the annual meeting of the Canadian Political Science Association', 29 May – 1 June 2003, Dallhousie University.

15 The EU Directive on Free Movement: A challenge for the European welfare state?

Wolfgang Ochel

Introduction[1]

The European Union Directive on Free Movement (2004, herein referred to as the Directive) has extended the right of free movement to non-gainfully employed (inactive) EU citizens. At the same time, this group of persons has been given access to the welfare benefits of host countries. Moreover, the right of residence of gainfully employed EU citizens (employees and self-employed persons) has been broadened. People falling into this category already had the right to take up residence in other EU member countries. Nonetheless, permanent right of residence after a stay of five years was only granted if the applicants had sufficient resources to ensure that social assistance would not be applied for in the future. The Directive has done away with this restriction. Gainfully employed EU citizens will be granted a right to permanent residence on the sole basis of five years of uninterrupted legal residence. They will have a right to the same welfare benefits which the host country provides its own nationals.

In this chapter, I examine the extent to which these measures provoke migration to those countries with the highest levels of welfare benefits. Since the Directive was not implemented in national laws and regulations until 2006, there is no basis for formulating an answer to this question based on an ex-post analysis of migration flows. Rather, the approach pursued here is to quantify the financial incentives to migrate by comparing estimated future flows of income and costs that are relevant for the migration decision.

The analysis focuses only on financial incentives. Non-financial incentives resulting from the social sphere, language and cultural differences and from individual factors such as life expectancy, life plan and the evaluation of risk are not taken into account here, although they are important determinants of migration. So one has to be cautious drawing general conclusions from the model calculations used here.

The financial incentives are quantified for those persons who – as will be explained later – are most affected by the Directive: inactive persons (pensioners, persons unable to work, illegal migrants being officially 'inactive') and self-employed persons. In this chapter, Poland is taken as the country of origin and Germany as the host country.

The chapter focuses on the rights of EU citizens to move and reside freely within the EU, their access to the system of social assistance in Germany and the financial incentives of the different groups of inactive persons and of the self-employed to migrate.

EU citizens' right to move and reside freely in the EU

The right to free movement and residence in the EU has been considerably extended since its founding in 1957. At its inception, free movement was conceived of as an economic freedom. Workers were guaranteed freedom of movement and the self-employed were guaranteed freedom of establishment. However, those not gainfully employed had no right to establish residence outside their own country. Since the beginning of the 1990s, the right to stay in a member country other than one's own is no longer tied to participation in the economy. This was expressed clearly in the Directives on Free Movement and Residence of the early 1990s, which provided, under certain conditions, a right of residence for students, retired persons and other inactive persons. In 1993, the Maastricht Treaty explicitly provided (in Article 18) that every EU citizen, whether gainfully employed or not, has the right to move and reside freely within the territory of member states. The implementing regulations and the relevant decisions of the European Court were developed further and summarised in Directive 2004/38/EC (Hailbronner 2006).

The Directive provides for graduated regulations governing residence: no conditions are imposed on an EU citizen and his or her family members for residence in a member country other than valid identity papers for a period of up to three months. For a stay of between four to 60 months, a residence certificate is required. In order to obtain it, the EU citizen must establish his or her residence in a member state and register with the relevant authorities. At the end of five years of uninterrupted legal residence,[2] the EU citizen is entitled unconditionally to permanent residence.

Granting a residence certificate for inactive EU citizens in the period between the fourth and the sixtieth months requires that they have means of subsistence sufficient for the entire stay and that they have adequate health insurance. These requirements are designed to ensure that social assistance will not be applied for. Health insurance coverage is considered adequate when it is – in the case of Germany – equivalent to statutory health insurance. Since access to statutory health insurance in Germany is subject to restrictive conditions (Figure 15.1), as a rule, foreigners from other EU countries have to obtain health insurance from private insurers. Self-employed persons are entitled to a residence certificate, provided they exercise a gainful economic activity.

Figure 15.1   *Health insurance available for a Polish national residing in Germany*

A) Voluntary coverage in Germany's statutory health insurance
Requirements according to Art.9 of the Social Code V:
- Absolved from the insurance requirement of Polish Social Insurance (ZUS)
- During five years before being absolved, at least 24 months; or immediately before being absolved, uninterruptedly at least twelve months insured in Poland's National Health Fund (Narodowy Fundusz Zrowia – NFZ)

Additional conditions imposed by the German Federal Ministry for Labour and Social Affairs:
- Prior insurance coverage for at least one day in Germany

B) Coverage by a private provider of health insurance in Germany

C) No possibility exists to continue insurance coverage in Poland if residence is changed to Germany

Source: Compilation by CESifo

When an EU citizen registers in Germany, the registration office proceeds on the assumption that the requirements for residence are fulfilled if the person registering declares that they are. Unless there are prima facie grounds for doubt, no enquiries are instigated before issuing the certification requested. In the ensuing five years, no check on the fulfilment of the conditions for permanent residency is carried out unless the EU citizen applies for welfare benefits. In such a case the authority responsible for foreigners, after having been informed by the Social Assistance Office, can examine whether the requirements for residence continue to be fulfilled. In the case of an inactive EU citizen, the required amount of means of subsistence should not exceed the threshold defined for social assistance for nationals. At the same time, no uniform amount for means of subsistence should be fixed. On the contrary, regional differences and the personal situation of the applicant must be taken into account. Merely claiming social assistance is not sufficient grounds for expulsion; only laying a claim to excessively high benefits. What is excessive, however, is left unclear. Gainfully self-employed persons are required to exercise an independent activity. The intensity with which this activity must be exercised is also not defined by law. Yet, it is not necessary that the self-employed person be able to cover his or her living expenses from the exercise of the activity completely.

Access of EU citizens to the systems of social assistance of host countries

As long as inactive EU citizens had no right to take up residence in other member countries, they could not claim welfare benefits in those countries. The extension to them of the right of free movement has changed the situation radically. As such:
- During a stay of less than three months, inactive EU citizens are not entitled to social assistance. Parity with citizens of the host country is not provided.[3]
- During a stay lasting between four and 60 months, inactive EU citizens are, as a matter of principle, entitled to welfare benefits, although the requirement of sufficient resources and adequate health insurance coverage is designed to ensure that this entitlement remains theoretical. In case the resources are exhausted sooner than expected or when health insurance coverage is not adequate, the Social Assistance Offices grant benefits even though the conditions for residence are not fulfilled. If the host country wants to avoid this, the EU citizen's stay must be brought to an end (Sander 2005: 1016). As set out above, this involves an examination by the authority responsible for foreigners as to whether the claims to welfare were inappropriate.
- After a stay of five years, the EU citizen is entitled to the same welfare benefits as those the host country provides its own nationals.

Gainfully self-employed persons who reside legally in Germany are, from the very beginning of their stay, entitled to welfare benefits (as a rule, Unemployment Benefit II which also may supplement own income). During the first five years of their stay, however, the authority responsible for foreigners may examine whether the conditions for continued residence are still fulfilled (adequate economic activity). If conditions are not met, the residence certificate may be cancelled. At the end of the five years of legal residence, the EU citizen has a right to all welfare benefits.

Legal migration of inactive persons into welfare systems

The Directive limits the incentives to migrate in that it restricts access to welfare benefits in the host country. The migrating EU citizen must reside in the host country during a five-year waiting period before he or she can claim welfare benefits. During this waiting period, the migrant must support himself or herself out of personal resources and must pay health insurance premiums in the host country. In the case of inactive persons, income from employment is not relevant, and this means that changing residence to another EU country requires that the migrant should dispose of sufficient financial assets.

According to Borjas (1999a; 1998b), the financial migration incentives depend on the present discounted value of the net income differential, that is to say the difference of social security benefits (S), which must exceed the costs of migration (MC) plus the present discounted value of living expenses differential (LE). Non-gainfully employed persons will decide to migrate from O (land of origin) to H (host country) if the condition in (1) is fulfilled, where T is the remaining life time and r the discount rate. The living expenses include normal expenditure for subsistence plus health insurance premiums.[4]

$$(1) \quad \int_0^T e^{-rt}\{S_H(t) - S_O(t)\}\mathrm{d}t > \int_0^T e^{-rt}\{LE_H(t) - LE_O(t)\}\mathrm{d}t + MC.$$

The magnitude of the financial incentives to migrate is influenced by the characteristics of the potential migrants. Their age, gender, family status, etc., play a role in determining this magnitude (Ackers & Dwyer 2002). For practical reasons, I focus my quantifications on a small number of cases. The rationale for choosing the cases is their relevance for estimating the financial incentives to migrate under the Directive.

In addition to sufficient financial assets, migrants must be non-gainfully employed in the host country and fulfil the conditions for receiving social assistance. In Germany, they must also be at least 65 years old. At this age they receive social assistance for the elderly (Grundsicherung im Alter) even if they are able to work. This group of people includes Poles who have been active up to the age of 60 and receive a pension from the Polish pension fund at the age of 65. If they are needy, in spite of receiving a Polish pension, they are entitled to the difference between the Polish pension and the German social assistance. Having migrated to Germany, they belong to the group of amnesty-seeking international retirement migrants (Dwyer & Papadimitriou 2006).[5]

Alternatively, if they are younger they must be unable to work. Otherwise, they would qualify in Germany for Unemployment Benefit II (instead of social assistance) and would be obliged to search for a regular job, which is not covered by the Directive. We assume that our representative of this group of persons is 40 years old.

Figure 15.2 describes the migration decision of a prototype pensioner, a 60-year-old Pole who can claim old-age benefits in Poland upon reaching the age of 65. In the upper panel, assets are entered on the vertical axis and time on the horizontal axis. Assets of the amount of AB are required in order to cover living expenses in Germany during the waiting period.[6] In the case of a change of residence to Germany,

Figure 15.2   *Incentives to migrate with old-age benefit entitlement in country of origin**

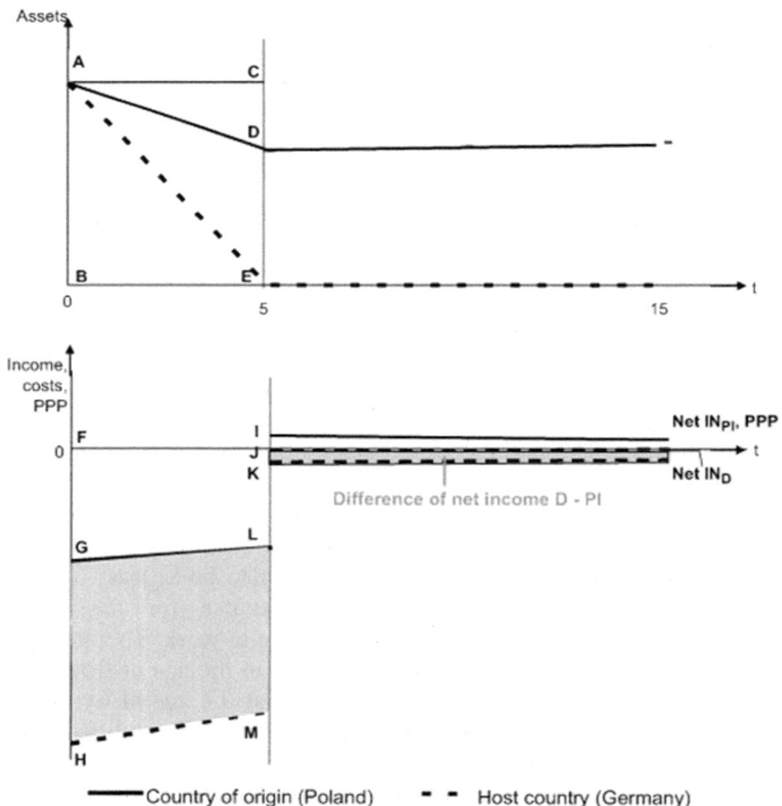

* The incomes and costs in the graph are those for a single person.
Source: CESifo

the migrant's assets will decline as shown by the curve AE. At the point in time E, they will be entirely exhausted. At the end of the five-year waiting period, the Polish migrant is a pauper fulfilling the conditions for receiving welfare benefits just sufficient to cover his or her subsistence-level consumption.

If, however, the migrant had remained in Poland, he or she would only have used up part of his or her initial assets, since the cost of living would be lower and premiums for health insurance would be less. Thus in the case of non-migration only CD of their assets would be used up; at the end of five years he or she would still own assets amounting to DE.

In the lower panel of Figure 15.2, the annual flows of income and costs that are relevant for the migration decision are shown graphically. They are converted at purchasing power parities. During the waiting period, total expenses associated with the stay in Germany amount to the area FHJM. This can be thought of as negative income. In Poland, on the other hand, the costs of living (including health insurance premiums) are lower (area FGJL). On balance, there is a difference in the expenditure for living expenses during the waiting period amounting to GHLM. After the waiting period there is no surplus of net income that compensates for this difference. The net income (Net IN: social security benefits – living expenses) in Germany is zero, whereas it is positive in Poland. Migration to Germany would not be financially attractive.

The scenarios thus far illustrated are based on calculations that are as realistic as possible. They are based on 2005 values. The decision to migrate requires that a Polish migrant has adequate monetary resources, for he or she must be able to cover his or her living expenses in Germany during the first five years out of his or her own resources. A socio-culturally defined subsistence minimum must be met at all times. In Germany, this is defined by the statutory rate for social assistance including subsidies for housing and heating costs of € 672 per month for a single person as of July 2005. Moreover, he or she needs private health insurance, with a monthly premium of € 600 for a man or € 620 for a woman. Given these hypotheses, a single person would need initial assets of € 71,876; for a couple without children, the amount required would be € 128,100 (Ochel 2007).

Apart from the possession of adequate assets, migration from Poland to Germany also depends on the expected gain in income that must be sufficient to cover the difference in living expenses as well as the direct migration costs (which are neglected in these calculations). In making this calculation, the streams of net income in Poland and Germany must be made comparable, i.e. the difference in the cost of living in the two countries must be taken into account. This has been done here by converting the stream of net income in Poland with the purchasing power parity of the euro and the zloty. Table 15.1 shows present values of net incomes. The net income streams have been discounted by a nominal interest rate of 4.5 per cent (real interest rate 3.0 per cent, inflation rate 1.5 per cent). Social assistance that could be claimed in Germany after the waiting period is compared to the old-age benefits that an average employee receives in Poland and the living expenses in the two countries. The comparison shows that starting at the age of 65, a single person in Germany can expect within the next ten years a net income that is below his or her net income in Poland by € -5,757. For a couple without children, net income in Germany exceeds the corresponding figure in Poland by € 11,973 which is not enough to compensate for the difference in living expenses during the waiting period. In both cases, changing residence from Poland to Germany is not financially attractive.

Table 15.1 *Financial incentives for changing residence from Poland to Germany for a 60-year-old non-gainfully employed person with a claim to old-age benefits at age 65 (in € , year 2005 present values)*

Expenditure during the five-year waiting period (years 1-5)		Single person	Couple, no children
(1)	Living expenses in Germany[1]	37,972	59,162
(2)	Health insurance premiums in Germany[2]	33,904	68,938
(3)	Living expenses in Poland, PPP[3]	19,900	31,008
(4)	Health insurance premiums in Poland, PPP[4]	7,478	14,951
(5)	Difference in living expenses (1 + 2 - 3 - 4)	44,499	82,141
Income starting at the age of 65 (years 6-15)			
(6)	Welfare benefits in Germany[1]	60,610	94,432
(7)	Living expenses in Germany[1]	60,610	94,432
(8)	Old-age benefits in Poland, PPP[5]	37,520	37,520
(9)	Living expenses in Poland, PPP[6]	31,763	49,493
(10)	Difference in net income (6-7)-(8-9)	-5,757	11,973

Source: CESifo

Notes:

1 The standard of living corresponds to a socio-culturally defined subsistence minimum. In Germany this is defined by the statutory rate for social assistance including subsidies for housing and heating costs as of July 2005.

2 Private health insurance: 60-year-old man: € 600; 60-year-old woman: € 620 (anonymous data supplied by financial services firm AWD).

3 The cost of living in Poland is calculated on the basis of the cost of living in Germany (subsistence minimum) adjusted by a conversion factor based on purchasing power parities. The conversion factor is 1.9081 (OECD, February 2006).

4 Rate of contribution of 11.2 per cent applied to average income of 30,000 zl and converted to EUR (EU MISSOC 2005; OECD Taxing Wages 2004-2005: 332).

5 Net old-age benefits = 0.516 x average net wages = € 2,616; € 2,616 x 1.9081 = € 4,992. (OECD, *Pensions at a Glance*, 2005 Edition: 163; OECD, *Taxing Wages 2004-2005*: 332). Contributions to health insurance have been deducted.

6 Amount is without health insurance premiums.

Different results are obtained if one assumes a 40-year-old, non-gainfully employed Polish migrant who in the foreseeable future has no expectations of old-age benefits and in case of need has only an entitlement to basic subsistence as defined in the Polish welfare system. If such a foreigner migrates to Germany, he or she has an entitlement to social assistance after five years. If he or she remains in Poland, however, he or she must exhaust his or her remaining assets amounting to DE and can claim welfare benefits only after fourteen (or fifteen) years.

The migration decision depends on the income and costs streams depicted in the lower panel of Figure 15.3. During the waiting period, negative income in the form of living costs is incurred amounting to FHJL in Germany. In Poland these costs come to FGJK. The difference

Figure 15.3　*Incentives to migrate with social assistance entitlement**

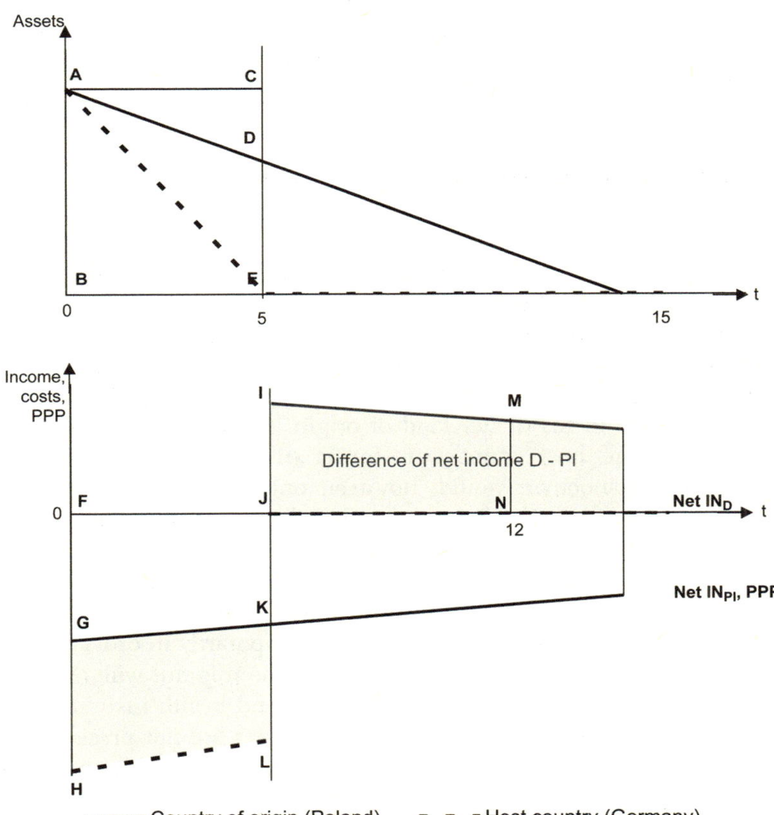

* The incomes and costs in the graph are those for a single person.
Source: CESifo

of living expenses is GHKL. Remaining assets must be liquidated to cover living costs and health insurance premiums before one can claim social assistance. The initial portfolio of assets is liquidated sooner in Germany. Starting at the end of five years, the immigrant is entitled to welfare benefits which are as high as his or her living expenses. Net income becomes zero. In Poland, the person would go on experiencing negative income. This disparity of access to welfare benefits has the consequence that migration incentives turn positive relatively early. This is the case as soon as the area IJMN exceeds the area GHKL. The difference of net income becomes greater than the difference between the living expenses incurred in Germany as compared to these expenses in Poland during the waiting period.

Calculations show that in both cases (single person and couple without children) in year 12, the present value of the differences in income exceeds the present value of the differences in living expenses. As long as the citizens considering migration expect to live beyond the age of 52 and to receive social assistance or Unemployment Benefit II in Germany, then migration from Poland to Germany would be financially attractive (Ochel 2007).

Illegal migration of 'inactive persons' into welfare systems

Up until now, the focus has been on legal migration into the welfare state. Illegal migration might be an alternative. The conditions linked to the right of permanent residence can, however, be circumvented only in part. Establishing residence in the host country and taking out health insurance are absolutely indispensable requirements. With a view to reducing the costs of living during the waiting period, an EU citizen could continue to live in his or her land of origin, whilst giving the registration office of the 'host' country pro forma an address of a relative or a friend. This manoeuvre would, however, only be practicable if travel costs are not too high. It is in any case illegal and hence involves risks.

The Directive imposes the requirement that the migrant has adequate financial assets. If the EU citizen desiring to migrate has no assets, one can imagine that relatives or friends might be willing to place the required sum at the migrant's disposal temporarily in order to show fulfilment of the requirements. Nonetheless, the migrant will, as a rule, have to cover his or her own living expenses and health insurance premiums out of his or her own resources. If assets are not present, then the only way to do this is to work in the informal sector of the economy, which – it goes without saying – is also illegal.

Figure 15.4 illustrates the migration decision. Initial assets amount to nil (not shown in the figure). During the waiting period, the EU citizen

Figure 15.4   *Incentives to migrate in the case of illegal work* in the host country*

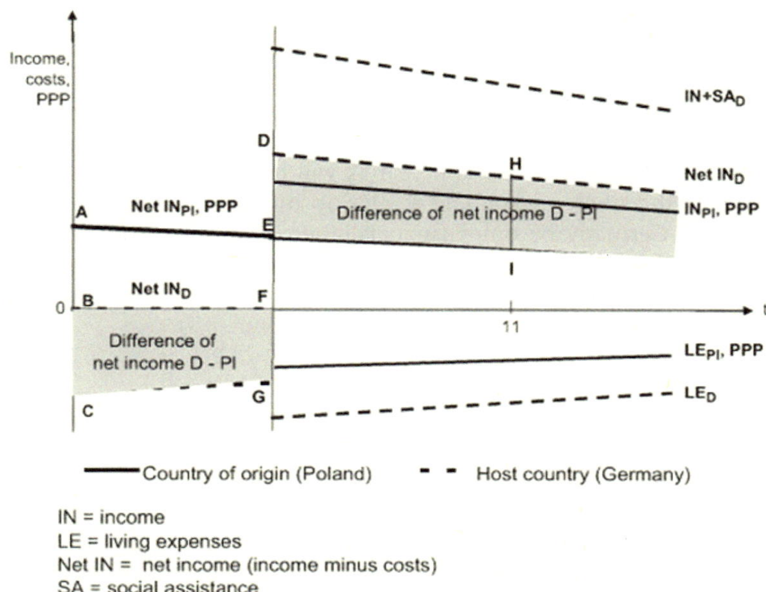

* The incomes and costs in the graph are those for a single person.
Source: CESifo.

in Germany obtains wages from work in the informal sector, which amount to living expenses and health insurance premiums so that the net income is zero. In Poland, the same person receives wages from regular employment leading to a positive net income (area ABEF). After the waiting period is expired, the migrant in Germany can expect income from social assistance and from illegal work. In Poland, he or she goes on working regularly. At the point in time at which DEHI > BCFG, migration becomes financially attractive.

In Germany, the income from illegal work must cover at least a socio-culturally defined subsistence minimum (that is to say, must at least equal social assistance, which is defined by such a standard); in addition, it must be sufficient to cover health insurance premiums. For a single person, € 55,489 is sufficient to fulfil this requirement during the waiting period. The corresponding figures for a couple without children are € 98,716. If one assumes that our immigrants would earn an average wage in Poland, then the difference in net income between Germany and Poland becomes € -25,644 for the single person and € -43,152 for the childless couple.

At the end of the waiting period, our immigrant to Germany can expect to receive social assistance or Unemployment Benefit II. Since welfare benefits minus living expenses in Germany are, on purchasing power terms, less than the net income of an average Polish employee, migration to Germany would not be financially attractive, unless the migrant goes on working in the informal sector after the waiting period is expired. In the latter case the present value of the net income received in Germany between year 6 and year 15 will be € 47,637 more than in Poland for the single person and € 88,690 more for a childless couple. Moving to Germany becomes financially attractive after ten years, not counting migration costs. However, in the cases examined here, one must bear in mind risks of not finding work in the informal sector or of being discovered in an illegal job (Ochel 2007).

Legal migration of self-employed persons into welfare systems

The Directive has broadened the right of residence of self-employed persons. Permanent right of residence after a stay of five years was, up to 2004 according to the Law of Residence of the EEC, only granted if the applicants had sufficient resources. The Directive has done away with this restriction. Self-employed EU citizens are granted a right to permanent residence on the sole basis of five years of uninterrupted legal residence and are entitled to welfare benefits.

As of 1 May 2004, the nationals and enterprises of the new member countries have the same rights of establishment in other member states as the nationals and enterprises of the old member countries. Restrictions on free movement of workers, which may be maintained for up to seven years, mean, however, that branches of enterprises from the new member states (excluding Malta and Cyprus) located in other EU countries are, except for key personnel, not allowed to employ people from their own country.

Freedom of establishment is understood as permitting the establishment of permanent economic activity in another member country. It includes the exercise of an independent economic activity as a self-employed person or the establishment and conduct of an enterprise. This independent economic activity may have the character of freelance professional work or commercial, trade or crafts activity.

With respect to a Polish citizen desiring to become a tradesman in Germany, one must distinguish between trades requiring special qualification (e.g. possession of a master craftsman's certificate) and trades for which no special proof of qualification must be presented. Since the beginning of 2004, 41 craft trades (e.g. mason, plumber, joiner, baker) have been designated as requiring certification of qualification. If the

Polish migrant has a qualification in Poland equivalent to the German master craftsman's qualification, then he or she may enrol in the register of qualified craftsmen in Germany. If the Polish migrant has no such formal qualification, he or she must have worked at least six years as a self-employed person in the trade or as responsible head of a plant or workshop in Poland before exercising the craft in Germany. This period can be shortened to three years if a three-year vocational training in the relevant craft can be documented or if the migrant has worked for at least five years as an employee in the relevant area. These periods must be certified by the competent Polish authorities. Another option for obtaining the right to exercise a craft in Germany is by passing a test (Art. 8 of the German Law Regulating the Conduct of Crafts and Trades).

For the 53 trades that may be exercised in Germany without any formal qualification, migrants need not fulfil any requirements. These trades run from tilers and parquet-layers to building cleaning contractors or photographers. The same applies for the 57 areas of activity that are classified as being similar to craft trades.

Figure 15.5 illustrates the migration decision of a 40-year-old Polish citizen who is self-employed. This person needs to have initial assets

Figure 15.5 *Incentives to migrate for a gainfully self-employed person* in the host country***

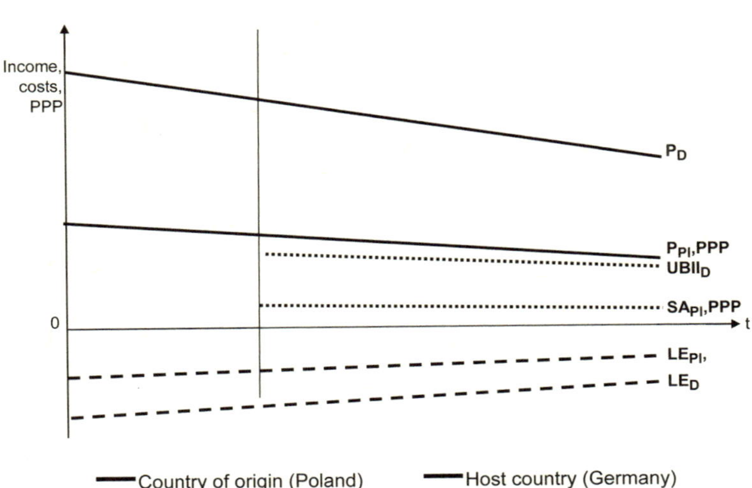

* Forty-year-old Pole
** The incomes and costs in the graph are those for a single person

Source: CESifo

sufficient to establish a business in the new location (not treated here as they may be relevant in Germany and Poland alike); no assets are required to cover living expenses and health insurance since it is assumed that the income needed to cover these will be earned in Germany. During the waiting period, the EU citizen will make a profit (P) from self-employed activity in Germany; for comparison, the profits to be expected if the same person had remained in Poland are also shown. After the waiting period has expired, the individual may wish to continue as a

Table 15.2 *Financial incentives for a Polish migrant taking up self-employment in Germany (in €, year 2005 present values)*

Net income during the waiting period (years 1-5)		Single person	Couple, no children
(1)	Income in Germany[1]	112,740	175,548
(2)	Living expenses in Germany[2]	37,972	59,162
(3)	Net income in Germany (1-2)	74,768	116,386
(4)	Income in Poland, PPP[1]	45,544	74,174
(5)	Living expenses in Poland, PPP[2]	19,900	31,022
(6)	Net income in Poland, PPP (4-5)	25,644	43,152
(7)	Difference of net income (3-6)	49,124	73,234
Income after the waiting period (years 6-15)			
For 45-year-old migrant:			
(8)	Income in Germany[1], or	179,950	278,605
(9)	Unemployment Benefit II in Germany[3]	60,610	94,432
(10)	Living expenses in Germany[2]	60,610	94,432
(11)	Income in Poland, PPP[1], or	72,695	118,393
(12)	Social assistance in Poland, PPP[4]	18,587	18,587
(13)	Living expenses in Poland, PPP[2]	31,763	49,493
For 65-year-old migrant			
(14)	Social assistance in Germany (DFM)[6]	60,610	94,432
(15)	Social assistance in Germany (LR)[7]	0	0
(16)	Living expenses in Germany[2]	60,610	94,432
(17)	Old-age benefits in Poland, PPP	37,520	37,520
(18)	Living expenses in Poland, PPP[2]	31,763	49,493

Source: CESifo

Notes:

1 Profits of self-employed (after taxes and deduction of health insurance premiums) correspond to the average net income of employees (OECD *Taxing Wages 2004-2005*).

2 See Table 15.1

3 In Germany, self-employed who become unemployed do not receive Unemployment Benefit I.

4 In Poland, the basic unemployment benefit is € 130. The actual amount paid varies according to the duration of unemployment (EU MISSOC Tables 2006).

5 In Poland, social assistance is, at most, € 108 per month and household (EU MISSOC Tables 2006).

6 Under the Directive (DFM)

7 Under the Law of Residence of the EEC (LR)

gainfully self-employed person. In the event that the business does not prosper, the individual can in case of need claim Unemployment Benefit II in Germany; in Poland the corresponding benefit would be social assistance (SA). The living expenses are shown by LE.

In Table 15.2, the income (in the form of profits) and the welfare benefit entitlements are compared. The comparison shows that a 40-year-old self-employed Polish citizen will find it attractive to set up a business in Germany; this is equally true during the waiting period and afterwards. The financial incentives to migrate emanate both from better earning prospects and from more generous welfare benefits. For a 60-year old, migration is financially attractive too. However, a single person should return to Poland at the age of 65, whereas a couple should remain in Germany.

Since April 2004, the German Association of Chamber of Crafts has collected statistics on the establishment of craft enterprises whose proprietors come from EU-12 acceding countries. On 30 June 2007, there were 25,519 such enterprises in Germany; this corresponded to 2.7 per cent of all craft enterprises in Germany (see Table 15.3). A full 97 per cent of these enterprises are crafts that are not subject to proof of qualification or are quasi-crafts. Crafts requiring qualification equivalent to

Table 15.3   *New registrations of craft enterprises since 1 May 2004 where owners are from EU-12 acceding countries (as of 30 June 2007)*

Land	Total no. of enterprises	Enterprises where owner from EU-12 (%)	Enterprises where owner from EU-12 (n)
Baden-Württemberg	128,404	1.5	1,880
Bavaria	183,056	2.9	5,383
Berlin	33,203	6.9	2,285
Brandenburg	37,789	1.5	558
Bremen	5,018	2.9	146
Hamburg	14,409	8.9	1,278
Hesse	68,094	7.5	5,091
Lower Saxony	80,110	3.4	2,691
Mecklenburg-Western Pomerania	19,442	0.5	102
North Rhine-Westphalia	176,011	1.9	3,358
Rhineland Palatinate	48,597	2.8	1,368
Saarland	11,652	0.8	92
Saxony	57,688	1.1	615
Saxony-Anhalt	29,649	0.3	78
Schleswig-Holstein	29,134	1.8	523
Thuringia	31,375	0.2	71
Federal Republic	953,631	2.7	25,519

Source: German Association of Chamber of Crafts, Establishment Registration Statistics; calculations by CESifo

that of a master craftsman are, on the other hand, scarcely represented. Craft enterprises with owners from the acceding countries are concentrated in urban centres such as Berlin, Hamburg, Frankfurt and Munich. In the Länder located near the borders to the new EU countries, there have been relatively few establishments (Hönekopp 2006).

Conclusions

Since the beginning of the 1990s, the restrictions on the freedom of movement and choice of residence of EU citizens have been progressively lifted. The Directive that went into force in 2004 laid down new and more liberal rules for movement across borders and for taking up residence in another EU country. Access to welfare benefits in host countries was made easier, although it continued to be tied to certain requirements (Sinn 2004).

The question arises as to what extent these new regulations will provoke migration within the EU from the less developed countries to the more developed countries. Since the Directive was not implemented in the member countries until 2006, it is impossible to provide an answer to this question based on an ex-post analysis. Instead, calculations have been made of the financial incentives to migrate in a number of model cases. The countries studied were Poland as the country of origin of the migrants and Germany as the host country. Since welfare benefits are more generous in Germany, migration into German welfare systems is to be expected. However, the rules and regulations in force impose a waiting period of five years, which must first be bridged. This, in turn, means that an inactive Polish citizen seeking access to Germany's welfare systems must have, at the beginning, considerable financial assets. Only few Poles are able to fulfil this requirement. Then, too, these persons must be prepared to liquidate these assets during the waiting period with a goal of later obtaining welfare benefits in Germany. This is fraught with risks for the migrant, e.g. the risk that he or she will die during the waiting period, or that there might be a subsequent modification of the rules and regulations not in the migrant's favour.

Apart from the possession of adequate assets, there should be a surplus of net income arising from migration. To the extent that after the waiting period there is an entitlement to old-age benefits in Poland, then on a purchasing power parity basis the net income in Poland will exceed the net income to be expected in Germany: there is no financial incentive to migrate from Poland to Germany in such a case. If, however, the Polish citizen is younger and not entitled to old-age benefits, he or she has to use up existing financial assets before being able to put in a claim for social assistance in Poland – and this is in all likelihood the more general case – then there is indeed a financial incentive to migrate to Germany in order to take advantage of the more generous welfare benefits there. He or she must, however, be unable to work. Otherwise, he or she would not be covered by the Directive and would not be entitled to social assistance in Germany. Not many Poles will fulfil the conditions of having sufficient financial assets and being unable to work.

If one considers persons who have no financial assets and who are capable of working, then the calculations show that migration is attractive assuming that they work in Germany in the informal sector; at the expiration of five years, they expect to also receive social assistance. This option is, however, illegal and pursuing it involves considerable risks.

For those capable of working it is more rewarding to seek employment in one of the EU countries that is open to migrants. This is demonstrated by many Polish citizens working in the UK and Ireland. There is no need for illegal migration to these countries. However, labour migration to these countries is associated with a demand for social benefits, too, which might even arise earlier than in Germany, where illegal migrants have to pass a five-year waiting period before they can claim social assistance.

Another option is to exercise an activity as a self-employed person. This is financially attractive, too. The financial incentives emanate both from better earning prospects and from more generous welfare benefits. On June 2007, there were 25,519 craft enterprises in Germany whose proprietors came from the EU-12 acceding countries. That corresponds to nearly 3 per cent of all craft enterprises in Germany.

This analysis focuses on financial incentives. However, the social sphere, language and cultural differences between the countries under consideration are also important for the decision to migrate. Then, too, individual factors such as life expectancy, life plan and the evaluation of risk influence the individual EU citizen's migration decision. All these non-financial factors have to be taken into consideration as well when future migration flows will be estimated.

A number of years will have to pass before the effects on the migration into the welfare systems of individual EU member countries arising from the Directive will be known empirically. That is why it is impossible to say at this very moment how the migration flows of inactive persons will compare to contemporary migration flows which are dominated by temporary labour migration.

But it is already possible to say that in enacting the Directive the European lawmakers have undergone a considerable risk. Access to welfare systems has not been cut off but only made difficult by imposing certain conditions. In view of the still rudimentary nature of the financial compensation framework within the EU, it is entirely possible that the freedom of movement that has been accorded will impose excessive demands on the solidarity of EU citizens in the host countries.

Notes

1 Gratefully acknowledged are comments by the participants of the IMISCOE A2 conference entitled 'EU enlargement and labour migration within the EU' that took place in Warsaw on 23-24 April 2007 and of the 63rd IIPF Congress that took place at the University of Warwick, UK, from 27-30 August 2007, as well as the support by Wolfgang Meister and Martin Werding.
2 Temporary absence of up to six months in a year does not affect the continuity of residence.
3 Nonetheless, Article 14 (1) of the Directive does not fully exclude claiming welfare benefits.
4 There are no empirical studies on the effects of different standards of welfare benefits in the EU member countries on internal migration flows. Up until now, only studies have been carried out on how the generosity of welfare systems in the EU influences the migratory decisions of immigrants from non-EU countries (willingness to migrate and choice of host country). Brücker, Epstein, McCormick, Saint-Paul, Venturini and Zimmermann (2002), who have studied migration from a large number of non-EU countries, and De Giorgi and Pellizzari (2006), who have examined migration from the Central and East European countries before they became members of the EU, come to the conclusion that there is a weak but significant connection between levels of welfare benefits and the decision to migrate. In addition to financial incentives, there are many other determinants that influence the migration decision. See e.g. Fischer, Holm, Malmberg and Straubhaar (2000).
5 Family-oriented retirement migrants, e.g. spouses who leave Poland in order to join their retired ex-worker husbands in Germany are not taken into account here because the number of regular Polish workers in Germany is small due to migration restrictions up to 2011.
6 The costs of migration are not considered.

References

Ackers, H. L. & P. Dwyer (2002), *Senior citizenship, retirement migration and welfare in the European Union*. Bristol: Policy Press.
Borjas, G. J. (1999a), 'Immigration and welfare magnets', *Journal of Labor Economics* 17 (4): 607-37.
Borjas, G. J. (1999b), 'The economic analysis of immigration' in O. Ashenfelter & D. Card (eds.), *Handbook of labor economics* 3A, 1697-1760. Amsterdam: Elsevier.
Brücker, H., G.S. Epstein, B. McCormick, G. Saint-Paul, A. Venturini & K.F. Zimmermann (2002), 'Managing migration in the European welfare state' in T. Boeri, G. Hanson & B. McCormick (eds.), *Immigration policy and the welfare state*, 1-167. Oxford: Oxford University Press.
Dwyer, P. & D. Papadimitriou (2006), 'The social security rights of older international migrants in the European Union', *Journal of ethnic and migration studies* 32 (8): 1301-19.

De Giorgi, G. & M. Pellizzari (2006), 'Welfare migration in Europe and the cost of a harmonised social assistance', IZA *Discussion Paper 2094*.

Fischer, P., E. Holm, G. Malmberg & T. Straubhaar (2000), 'Why do people stay? Insider advantages and immobility', HWWA *Discussion Paper 1/2*. Hamburg: Institute of International Economics.

Hailbronner, K. (2006), 'Union citizenship and social rights' in J.-Y. Carlier & E. Guild (eds.), *The future of free movement of persons in the EU*, 65-78. Brussels: Bruyland.

Hönekopp, E. (2006), 'Germany' in K. Tamas & R. Münz (eds.), *Labour migrants unbound? EU enlargement, transitional measures and labour market effects*, 126-148. Stockholm: Institute for Future Studies.

Ochel, W. (2007), 'The free movement of inactive union citizens in the EU: A challenge for the European welfare state?', CESifo *Working Paper 1930*.

Sander, F. (2005), 'Die Unionsbürgerschaft als Türöffner zu mitgliedstaatlichen Sozialversicherungssystemen? Überlegungen anlässlich des Trojani-Urteils des EuGH', *Deutsches Verwaltungsblatt* (DVBL): 1014-1022.

Sinn, H.-W. (2004), 'Freizügigkeitsrichtlinie: Freifahrt in den Sozialstaat', *ifo Standpunkt 53*.

Notes on contributors

Marta Anacka is a PhD candidate at the department of economic sciences and a research assistant at the Centre of Migration Research, University of Warsaw, Poland.
  mmioduszewska@gmail.com

Richard Black is a professor of human geography and head of the School of Global Studies at the University of Sussex, United Kingdom. He served as co-director of the Sussex Centre for Migration Research from 1997-2009.
  r.black@sussex.ac.uk

Venelin Boshnakov is a lecturer at the University of National and World Economy (UNWE) and a research associate at the Centre for Comparative Studies, Sofia, Bulgaria.
  venelinb@unwe.acad.bg

Krisztina Csedő completed her PhD at the department of sociology, London School of Economics and Political Science, United Kingdom. She currently works as a consultant for Towers Watson in London.
  k.csedo@alumni.lse.ac.uk

Jan de Boom is a senior researcher at the Rotterdam Institute for Social Policy Research (RISBO), Erasmus University Rotterdam, the Netherlands.
  deboom@risbo.eur.nl

Stephen Drinkwater is a senior lecturer at the Wales Institute of Social and Economic Research, Data and Methods (WISERD) in the School of Business and Economics at Swansea University, United Kingdom.
  s.j.drinkwater@swansea.ac.uk

John Eade is a professor of sociology and anthropology and executive director of the Centre for Research on Nationalism, Ethnicity and Multiculturalism (CRONEM) at the University of Surrey and Roehampton University, United Kingdom.
   j.eade@surrey.ac.uk

Godfried Engbersen is a professor of sociology at Erasmus University Rotterdam, the Netherlands.
   engbersen@fsw.eur.nl

Jon Horgen Friberg is a researcher at the Fafo Institute for Labour and Social Research, Oslo, Norway.
   jon.horgen.friberg@fafo.no

Michal P. Garapich is a research fellow at the Centre for Research on Nationalism, Ethnicity and Multiculturalism (CRONEM) at the University of Surrey and Roehampton University, United Kingdom.
   m.garapich@roehampton.ac.uk

Izabela Grabowska-Lusinska is an assistant professor and head of the research unit on social mobility of migrants at the Centre of Migration Research, University of Warsaw, and assistant professor at the Warsaw School of Social Psychology, Poland.
   igrabowska_lusinska@wp.pl

Paweł Kaczmarczyk is an assistant professor in the faculty of economic sciences at the University of Warsaw and deputy director of the Centre of Migration Research, University of Warsaw, Poland.
   p.kaczmarczyk@uw.edu.pl

Eugenia Markova is a migration research fellow at Working Lives Research Institute, London Metropolitan University, and a research associate at the Hellenic Observatory, London School of Economics and Political Science, United Kingdom.
   e.markova@londonmet.ac.uk

Vesselin Mintchev is deputy director of the Institute of Economics at the Bulgarian Academy of Sciences and chair of the board of the Centre for Comparative Studies, Sofia, Bulgaria.
   v.mintchev@iki.bas.bg

Joanna Napierała is a PhD candidate at the institute for social studies and a research assistant at the Centre of Migration Research, University of Warsaw, Poland.
  j.m.napierala@uw.edu.pl

Krzysztof Nowaczek is a research fellow at the Research Unit on European Governance (URGE) at the Collegio Carlo Alberto in Moncalieri, Italy.
  krzysztof.nowaczek@urge.it

Wolfgang Ochel is head of the department of International Institutional Comparisons of the ifo Institute for Economic Research and a fellow at the CESifo Research Network at the University of Munich, Germany.
  ochel@ifo.de

Marek Okólski is director of the Centre of Migration Research and a professor of demography and economics at the University of Warsaw and the Warsaw School of Social Psychology, Poland.
  moko@uw.edu.pl

Cristina Panţîru is a PhD candidate and an IMISCOE research officer at the Sussex Centre for Migration Research at the University of Sussex, United Kingdom.
  m.c.pantiru@sussex.ac.uk

Swanie Potot is a CNRS research fellow at the Research Unit on Migration and Society (URMIS) at the University of Nice Sophia-Antipolis, France.
  potot@unice.fr

Dumitru Sandu is a professor in the faculty of sociology and social work at the University of Bucharest, Romania.
  dsandu@dnt.ro

Erik Snel is an assistant professor at Erasmus University Rotterdam, the Netherlands.
  snel@fsw.eur.nl

Paulina Trevena is a senior research assistant at the Centre for Population Change, University of Southampton, United Kingdom, and a doctoral fellow at the Centre of Migration Research, University of Warsaw, Poland.
  p.m.trevena@soton.ac.uk

Corrado Bonifazi, Marek Okólski, Jeannette Schoorl, Patrick Simon, Eds.
*International Migration in Europe: New Trends and New Methods
of Analysis*
2008 (ISBN 978 90 5356 894 1)

Maurice Crul, Liesbeth Heering, Eds.
*The Position of the Turkish and Moroccan Second Generation in
Amsterdam and Rotterdam: The TIES Study in the Netherlands*
2008 (ISBN 978 90 8964 061 1)

Marlou Schrover, Joanne van der Leun, Leo Lucassen, Chris Quispel, Eds.
Illegal Migration and Gender in a Global and Historical Perspective
2008 (ISBN 978 90 8964 047 5)

Gianluca P. Parolin
Citizenship in the Arab World: Kin, Religion and Nation-State
2009 (ISBN 978 90 8964 045 1)

Rainer Bauböck, Bernhard Perchinig, Wiebke Sievers, Eds.
Citizenship Policies in the New Europe: Expanded and Updated Edition
2009 (ISBN 978 90 8964 108 3)

Cédric Audebert, Mohamed Kamel Doraï, Eds.
Migration in a Globalised World: New Research Issues and Prospects
2010 (ISBN 978 90 8964 157 1)

Charles Westin, José Bastos, Janine Dahinden, Pedro Góis, Eds.
Identity Processes and Dynamics in Multi-Ethnic Europe
2010 (ISBN 978 90 8964 046 8)

Rainer Bauböck, Thomas Faist, Eds.
Diaspora and Transnationalism: Concepts, Theories and Methods
2010 (ISBN 978 90 8964 238 7)

IMISCOE Reports

Rainer Bauböck, Ed.
Migration and Citizenship: Legal Status, Rights and Political Participation
2006 (ISBN 978 90 5356 888 0)

Michael Jandl, Ed.
Innovative Concepts for Alternative Migration Policies: Ten Innovative Approaches to the Challenges of Migration in the 21st Century
2007 (ISBN 978 90 5356 990 0)

Jeroen Doomernik, Michael Jandl, Eds.
Modes of Migration Regulation and Control in Europe
2008 (ISBN 978 90 5356 689 3)

Michael Jandl, Christina Hollomey, Sandra Gendera, Anna Stepien, Veronika Bilger
Migration and Irregular Work In Austria: A Case Study of the Structure and Dynamics of Irregular Foreign Employment in Europe at the Beginning of the 21st Century
2008 (ISBN 978 90 8964 053 6)

Heinz Fassmann, Ursula Reeger, Wiebke Sievers, Eds.
Statistics and Reality: Concepts and Measurements of Migration in Europe
2009 (ISBN 978 90 8964 052 9)

Karen Kraal, Judith Roosblad, John Wrench, Eds.
Equal Opportunities and Ethnic Inequality in European Labour Markets Discrimination, Gender and Policies of Diversity
2009 (ISBN 978 90 8964 126 7)

Tiziana Caponio, Maren Borkert, Eds.
The Local Dimension of Migration Policymaking
2010 (ISBN 978 90 8964 232 5)

Raivo Vetik, Jelena Helemäe, Eds.
The Russian Second Generation in Tallinn and Kohtla-Järve: The TIES Study in Estonia
2010 (ISBN 978 90 8964 250 9)

IMISCOE Dissertations

Panos Arion Hatziprokopiou
Globalisation, Migration and Socio-Economic Change in Contemporary Greece: Processes of Social Incorporation of Balkan Immigrants in Thessaloniki
2006 (ISBN 978 90 5356 873 6)

Floris Vermeulen
*The Immigrant Organising Process: Turkish Organisations in Amsterdam
and Berlin and Surinamese Organisations in Amsterdam, 1960-2000*
2006 (ISBN 978 90 5356 875 0)

Anastasia Christou
*Narratives of Place, Culture and Identity: Second-Generation
Greek-Americans Return 'Home'*
2006 (ISBN 978 90 5356 878 1)

Katja Rušinović
*Dynamic Entrepreneurship: First and Second-Generation Immigrant
Entrepreneurs in Dutch Cities*
2006 (ISBN 978 90 5356 972 6)

Ilse van Liempt
*Navigating Borders: Inside Perspectives on the Process of Human Smuggling
into the Netherlands*
2007 (ISBN 978 90 5356 930 6)

Myriam Cherti
*Paradoxes of Social Capital: A Multi-Generational Study of Moroccans
in London*
2008 (ISBN 978 90 5356 032 7)

Marc Helbling
*Practising Citizenship and Heterogeneous Nationhood: Naturalisations
in Swiss Municipalities*
2008 (ISBN 978 90 8964 034 5)

Jérôme Jamin
*L'imaginaire du complot: Discours d'extrême droite en France et
aux Etats-Unis*
2009 (ISBN 978 90 8964 048 2)

Inge Van Nieuwenhuyze
*Getting by in Europe's Urban Labour Markets: Senegambian Migrants'
Strategies for Survival, Documentation and Mobility*
2009 (ISBN 978 90 8964 050 5)

Nayla Moukarbel
*Sri Lankan Housemaids in Lebanon: A Case of 'Symbolic Violence' and
'Every Day Forms of Resistance'*
2009 (ISBN 978 90 8964 051 2)

John Davies
*'My Name Is Not Natasha': How Albanian Women in France Use
Trafficking to Overcome Social Exclusion (1998-2001)*
2009 (ISBN 978 90 5356 707 4)

Dennis Broeders
*Breaking Down Anonymity: Digital Surveillance of Irregular Migrants
in Germany and the Netherlands*
2009 (ISBN 978 90 8964 159 5)

Arjen Leerkes
Illegal Residence and Public Safety in the Netherlands
2009 (ISBN 978 90 8964 049 9)

Jennifer Leigh McGarrigle
*Understanding Processes of Ethnic Concentration and Dispersal:
South Asian Residential Preferences in Glasgow*
2009 (ISBN 978 90 5356 671 8)

João Sardinha
*Immigrant Associations, Integration and Identity: Angolan, Brazilian
and Eastern European Communities in Portugal*
2009 (ISBN 978 90 8964 036 9)

Elaine Bauer
*The Creolisation of London Kinship: Mixed African-Caribbean and White
British Extended Families, 1950-2003*
2010 (ISBN 978 90 8964 235 6)

Nahikari Irastorza
Born Entrepreneurs? Immigrant Self-Employment in Spain
2010 (ISBN 978 90 8964 243 1)

IMISCOE Textbooks

Marco Martiniello, Jan Rath, Eds.
Selected Studies in International Migration and Immigrant Incorporation
2010 (ISBN 978 90 8964 160 1)